THEODORET OF CYRUS

Theodoret of Cyrus lived during the stormy decades of the third and fourth ecumenical councils of Ephesus (431) and Chalcedon (451), when many important doctrinal questions (including the mode of interpreting Christ as God and man) were in dispute. Being the champion of the so-called Antiochene tradition and an opponent of Cyril, the mighty patriarch of Alexandria, Theodoret left behind a fascinating legacy. His biography shows that he was immersed in the highly tense dogmatic and ecclesiastical-political battles of the fifth century, whilst remaining a truly pious churchman, who had distributed his inheritance to the poor and lived a very modest life even as bishop.

The larger part of his extant writings still remains untranslated, which provides a fragmented representation of his thought and has led to his misrepresentation by ancient, medieval and some modern scholars. *Theodoret of Cyrus* offers a fresh collection of texts from all periods of his career, including two complete treatises (*On the Holy and Vivifying Trinity* and *On the Inhumanation of the Lord*) as well as representative selections from two others (*A Cure of Greek Maladies* and *A Compendium of Heretical Mythification*) so far unpublished in English, with a critical introduction concerning his life, legacy and place in the history of Christian doctrine. This book provides the reader with a more balanced picture of Theodoret's often neglected, depreciated and largely inaccessible theological legacy.

The Revd István Pásztori-Kupán is a lecturer in the history of Christian doctrine at the Hungarian Reformed Theological Institute in Kolozsvár, Transylvania (RO).

THE EARLY CHURCH FATHERS
Edited by Carol Harrison
University of Durham

The Greek and Latin Fathers of the Church are central to the creation of Christian doctrine, yet often unapproachable because of the sheer volume of their writings and the relative paucity of accessible translations. This series makes available translations of key selected texts by the major Fathers to all students of the Early Church.

CYRIL OF JERUSALEM
Edward Yarnold, S. J.

EARLY CHRISTIAN LATIN
POETS
Carolinne White

CYRIL OF ALEXANDRIA
Norman Russell

MAXIMUS THE CONFESSOR
Andrew Louth

IRENAEUS OF LYONS
Robert M. Grant

AMBROSE
Boniface Ramsey, O. P.

ORIGEN
Joseph W. Trigg

GREGORY OF NYSSA
Anthony Meredith, S. J.

JOHN CHRYSOSTOM
Wendy Mayer and Pauline Allen

JEROME
Stefan Rebenich

TERTULLIAN
Geoffrey Dunn

ATHANASIUS
Khaled Anatolios

SEVERUS OF ANTIOCH
*Pauline Allen and
C.T.R. Hayward*

GREGORY THE GREAT
John Moorhead

THEODORET OF CYRUS

István Pásztori-Kupán

Routledge
Taylor & Francis Group

LONDON AND NEW YORK

First published 2006
by Routledge
2 Park Square, Milton Park, Abingdon, Oxon OX14 4RN

Simultaneously published in the USA and Canada
by Routledge
270 Madison Ave, New York, NY 10016

Routledge is an imprint of the Taylor & Francis Group

© 2006 István Pásztori-Kupán

Typeset in Garamond by
Keystroke, Jacaranda Lodge, Wolverhampton
Printed and bound in Great Britain by
TJ International Ltd, Padstow, Cornwall

British Library Cataloguing in Publication Data
A catalogue record for this book is available from the British Library

Library of Congress Cataloging in Publication Data
A catalog record for this book has been requested

ISBN10: 0–415–30960–3 (hbk)
ISBN10: 0–415–30961–1 (pbk)

ISBN13: 9–78–0–415–30960–8 (hbk)
ISBN13: 9–78–0–415–30961–5 (pbk)

Dedicated to my wife Zita
and to our two children
Zsófia and András-Nimród
for their admirable support and patience

Anyakának, Süntöcnek és Bömböbének
sok szeretettel
Apa

CONTENTS

Preface   ix
Acknowledgements   xi
Abbreviations   xiii

PART I
Introduction   1

1   The young Theodoret   3

2   Theodoret and the Nestorian controversy   7

3   From Ephesus to Chalcedon and beyond   14

4   Theodoret's Trinitarian doctrine   28

5   Theodoret's Christology   31

6   Terminology   57

7   Theodoret's legacy   75

PART II
Texts   81

8   General introduction to the texts   83

9   *A Cure of Greek Maladies*   85

10 *On the Holy and Vivifying Trinity* and *On the Inhumanation*
    of the Lord   109
        On the Holy and Vivifying Trinity   112
        On the Inhumanation of the Lord   138

CONTENTS

11 Theodoret's *Refutation of Cyril's Twelve Anathemas*   172

12 *That Even After the Inhumanation our Lord Jesus Christ
    is One Son*   188

13 Theodoret's *Letter 16 to bishop Irenaeus*   193

14 *A Compendium of Heretical Mythification*   198

Notes   221
Bibliography   258
Index of scriptural citations   266
Index of names and subjects   269

PREFACE

On a summer afternoon in 1992 I entered an antiquarian bookshop in Pécs – at the time, I thought, merely by chance – and picked up a book containing selected works of Greek church fathers. That evening I began to read the Bishop of Cyrus for the very first time. A week later I was hunting for every other available book written by him. He simply resonated so well with what I had been brought up with.

This enthusiasm did not fade away during my undergraduate years. Being offered the possibility to study in Edinburgh in 1998, my life took a new turn. It has been an exciting but spiritually demanding time during which I had to learn to detach from my hero emotionally to be able to reflect upon his lifework with some objectivity. Whether I was successful or not in this attempt, the following work will also bear witness. Nevertheless, I do not intend to present Theodoret's life and teaching around the unsettled times of the councils of Ephesus and Chalcedon with the assumption that every ambiguous or defective point of his (or in fact anyone else's) theology and/or mode of its expression can be explained away by a skilfully chosen method of interpretation. On the contrary, I am convinced that in this sense there is no 'perfect' doctrine, even less a 'perfect' model of Christ – it simply cannot exist, for we all 'see through a mirror, dimly' (1 Cor. 13:12). Consequently, both theology in general and the model of Christ in particular have to be continually reformulated, often even within the oeuvre of one theologian. If this does not happen naturally, theology itself ceases to be the very expression of God's ever-actual message in the church, society and history. It is my belief – perhaps not without Theodoret's influence – that a so-called *l'art pour l'art* theology has no legitimacy in itself.

To a certain extent all theologians are bound to their historical period, yet even if they were not, they are doubtless confined by the inevitable analogies which they build upon and apply to their own anthropological, soteriological, pastoral and other concerns. Analogies, however, by their very nature are approximate and not absolute. Different theologians do not necessarily ask the same questions: therefore, their answers may differ accordingly.

The present volume – including the introduction and translations – is meant to be a modest contribution towards the achievement of a 'fair trial' which Theodoret deserves from modern readership. The realisation of this, however, does not simply require a nice monograph containing true sympathy towards him and his regrettable fate, with barely any understanding of the ideas of a theologian of the Word, as well as of a man of his word. It takes much more to perceive and appreciate Theodoret. One has to grasp his sole concern for the welfare of Christ's flock, his lucid rejection of 'the goal justifies the means'. There is a deep care for the future of Christianity behind each of his sentences, making them worthy to be heard. Thus, for Theodoret to be given a 'fair trial' after so many centuries is perhaps a matter of conscience for a flock like his own in Cyrus, which continuously begged him to accept any humiliation, or to stand up against them, but not to give up his see. It will only then be granted to him when the general theological opinion ceases to be based on inherited prejudices and the Christian reader is eager to accept his words – even in this unskilled English translation of a non-native speaker – with that humble respect with which his community listened to the one who truly was 'the blessed bishop of Cyrus'.

Nagyenyed, 8 January 2005
István Pásztori-Kupán
mcpasztori@yahoo.com

ACKNOWLEDGEMENTS

It seems an impossible attempt to enumerate all those who in various ways contributed to the realisation of this work. I express my heartfelt gratitude to my wife Zita and to our children Zsófia and András-Nimród for all their patience, support and loving care by which they had understanding for everything – beyond any measure that could have been expected.

I have a lot to thank my parents and grandparents (especially Nagyi) for bringing me up in the way they did. The places, people and communities which formed my life and strengthened my faith (my home village Olasztelek, the middle school in Barót, the Bethlen Gábor College in Nagyenyed, the Hungarian Reformed Theological Institute in Kolozsvár) should also be remembered with thankfulness.

My first coming to Scotland in 1998 was facilitated by the Church of Scotland. Rev. Susan Cowell, our most lovely 'Zsuzsi néni', has a special place in the heart of our entire family for so many reasons that I cannot even attempt to enumerate them, but rather ask God's richest blessing upon her life and utterly devoted ecclesiastical and human service. Isobel and Alexander Reid ought to be given special thanks for all the wonderful evenings we had the honour to spend in their home and the spiritual boost they never ceased to give me. Similar thanks are presented to Eitan and Margaret Abraham, to Bálint Joó and his wife Kim, to Stuart and Judit Blair, to Csaba Szilágyi and his family, as well as to Attila Gáll and Ábrahám Kovács for their helpful readiness in every need.

Concerning my academic formation I owe a lot to New College. My former PhD supervisor, Prof. David Wright, has won my admiration not only by his profound erudition, but for his watchful guidance which proved to be vital regarding all the aspects of this academic enterprise. His generous help was invaluable concerning the correction of my translations and the suggestions by which he sought to improve the quality of my work for which I simply cannot be grateful enough. My sister Zsuzsanna and Zoltán, her fiancé, are also due a very special recognition for their linguistic assistance. I thank Dr Paul Parvis for his clarifications concerning the Syriac sources and Dr Gary Badcock for all his encouragement and support. Prof. Larry Hurtado has been my great spiritual comforter, who also rocked the cradle of my first publications. I owe him and his family a lifelong gratitude. Together with them, the very supportive and friendly staff of New College certainly deserves a very special recognition.

The list is far from being over. I present my deepest thanks to all those persons and organisations who have enabled the continuation of my academic studies as well as the preparation of this volume: to Langham Research Scholarships and to Paul Berg, John Stott, Howard Peskett and their colleagues for all their material and invaluable spiritual assistance during emotionally stressful times; to the series editor Dr Carol Harrison for all her useful advice and great support; to the Institute of Advanced Studies in the Humanities in Edinburgh and to the Andrew W. Mellon Foundation; to the Royal Society of Edinburgh; to the Ministers' Relief Society and to Rev. Alan Lathey for his help and encouraging letters; to the Mylne Trust; to the Hope Trust; and to all those whose names I have forgotten to mention. May God's blessing be upon them and their noble endeavours.

My one year spent in Tübingen as a 'Scottish exchange student' also had its invaluable benefits. I express my deepest gratefulness towards Prof. Luise Abramowski for the privilege of being her guest and for vital information concerning some of the most crucial aspects of my research. Similarly, Prof. Jean-Noël Guinot, my former PhD examiner, and Mme Guinot are also due a very special recognition for all their invaluable assistance as well as for the two wonderful days I spent in Lyon being thrilled by the most welcoming atmosphere in the home of the Guinot family. It has truly been an honour and a profound spiritual refreshment to be around such learned, friendly and open people as Prof. L. Abramowski and M. and Mme Guinot.

At this point I would like to thank all those whom I might have forgotten. I beseech them to be convinced that this is due merely to human weakness and is certainly unintentional. I pray to God to bless all those wonderful people, mentioned or not mentioned, who have accepted to be His chosen vessels to help me reach this point for the greater glory of His name. Soli Deo gloria!

István Pásztori-Kupán

ABBREVIATIONS

ACO   Acta Conciliorum Oecumenicorum, Series I, ed. by E.
            Schwartz and J. Straub (Berlin: Walter de Gruyter, 1914–
            84); Series II, ed. sub auspiciis Academiae Scientiarum
            Bavaricae (Berlin: Walter de Gruyter, 1984ff.)
ASE   *Annali di storia dell'esegesi*
CPG   Geerard, Mauritius, ed., *Clavis Patrum Graecorum*, 5 vols
            + *Supplementum* (Leuven: Brepols-Turnhout, 1979–98)
CSCO   Corpus Scriptorum Christianorum Orientalium
CSEL   Corpus Scriptorum Ecclesiasticorum Latinorum
Curatio   Theodoret of Cyrus, *Graecarum affectionum curatio* (*A Cure of
            Greek Maladies*)
DCB   Smith, William, and Henry Wace, eds, *A Dictionary of
            Christian Biography*, 4 vols (London: John Murray, 1877–87)
DOP   *Dumbarton Oaks Papers*
Eranistes *Eranistes*, ed. by Gerard H. Ettlinger (Oxford: Clarendon
            Press, 1975)
ETL   *Ephemerides Theologicae Lovanienses*
GCS   Die griechischen christlichen Schriftsteller
HE   *Historia ecclesiastica* (*Ecclesiastical History*)
HFC   Theodoret of Cyrus, *Haereticarum fabularum compendium*
            (*A Compendium of Heretical Mythification*)
HR   Theodoret of Cyrus, *Historia religiosa* (*A History of the Monks
            of Syria*)
ITQ   *Irish Theological Quarterly*
JTS   *Journal of Theological Studies*
LXX   Septuagint (Greek Old Testament)
MSR   *Mélanges de science religieuse*
NPNF   Wace, Henry, and Philip Schaff, eds, A Select Library of
            Nicene and Post Nicene Fathers of The Christian Church,
            14 vols (Oxford: James Parker, 1886–1900)

ABBREVIATIONS

PG	Migne, Jacques Paul, ed., Patrologiae Cursus Completus, Series Graeca, 161 vols (Paris: 1857–87)
PL	Migne, Jacques Paul, ed., Patrologiae Cursus Completus, Series Latina, 221 vols (Paris: 1844–64)
RB	*Revue Biblique*
RHE	*Revue d'histoire ecclésiastique*
RSPT	*Revue des sciences philosophiques et théologiques*
RSR	*Recherches de science religieuse*
RevSR	*Revue des sciences religieuses*
SC	Sources Chrétiennes (Paris: Cerf, 1941ff)
SP	*Studia Patristica*
SPT	*Les sciences philosophiques et théologiques*
ThQ	*Theologische Quartalschrift*
TU	*Texte und Untersuchungen der Altchristlichen Literatur*
VC	*Vigiliae Christianae*
ZKTh	*Zeitschrift für Katholische Theologie*

Part I

INTRODUCTION

1

THE YOUNG THEODORET

The life and literary production of the Bishop of Cyrus have been researched in some detail by venerable scholarly authorities. Since the main purpose of this book is not the exhaustive presentation of Theodoret's biography, in Chapters 1–3 I will summarise the main events of his life, whilst referring the reader to the relevant modern scholarship.[1] A more substantial analysis of Theodoret's theology will be presented in Chapters 4–6, including his doctrine concerning the Trinity, his anthropology, soteriology and Christology, as well as the terminological background of these concepts.

The circumstances of Theodoret's conception and birth at the end of the fourth century in Antioch remind us of the biblical stories of Samson and Samuel. His mother – married at the age of 17 – had been barren and although her diseased eye was healed by the hermit Peter of Galata, according to whose admonition she embraced a more ascetic life than she had lived before,[2] it took seven more years until another holy man, Macedonius, finally promised the birth of a son. The condition put before the future parents was to dedicate the one to be born to the service of God.[3] This being accepted, the mother conceived, and after a threatened pregnancy, aided by the holy man's prayers, a son was born in the year 393.[4] His parents named him Theodoret, i.e. 'the gift of God', and together with the monks he frequently met, they instructed him to live his life as the fulfilment of this parental offering.[5] In *HR* he recalls Macedonius' words addressed to him as a child in the following manner:

> You were born, my child, with much toil: I spent many nights begging this alone of God, that your parents should earn the name they received after your birth. So live a life worthy of this toil. Before you were born, you were offered up in promise. Offerings to God are revered by all, and are not to be touched

3

by the multitude: so it is fitting that you do not admit the base impulses of the soul, but perform, speak, and desire those things alone that serve God, the giver of the laws of virtue.[6]

Theodoret lived conscientiously according to the above admonition from a very early age. In his correspondence he keeps on referring to these decisive years of his spiritual formation. For example, in his *Letter 88 to Taurus the patrician*, he wrote: 'I received the apostolic nourishment from my mother's breast and the creed laid down at Nicaea by the holy and blessed Fathers' (SC 98, 234).

Being determined to live a life dedicated to God, he acquired a substantial biblical knowledge and a close familiarity with the teachings of earlier theologians. Although the details of his education are not known to us, his works reveal a vast erudition. Apart from his mother tongue, Syriac, he mastered Greek[7] and Hebrew. His secular education was peculiarly impressive. For example, in the *Cure of Greek Maladies* alone he quotes more than one hundred pagan philosophers, poets and historians in about 340 passages.[8] Being conversant with classical literature, he always knew where a certain philosophical term or idea came from and in what manner it could be used in Christian theology. His learnedness was invaluable in the course of establishing valid dogmatic formulae, but it also caused him a lot of trouble especially because most of his opponents were nothing like as well acquainted with secular philosophy, although they used its terms all the time.

We are unaware of the details or the time of Theodoret's baptism.[9] His correspondence does not reveal anything concerning its circumstances. On the one hand, the sequence by which he presents the events in *Letter* 143 is perhaps too weak a ground to conclude that he was not baptised in infancy, but only after 'having believed': 'For thus I have been made a disciple from the beginning; thus I have believed; thus I was baptised; thus I have preached, thus I have baptised, thus I continue to teach.'[10]

On the other hand, the fact that Theodoret was a child offered to God before his conception did not automatically involve his infant baptism.[11] Up to the age of 6 he could listen to the sermons of his great fellow-townsman, John Chrysostom, who influenced by his writings not only the similarly eloquent preaching of Theodoret but also his theological evolution. By the age of 23 he had lost both of his parents and distributed his entire (although not small) heritage to the poor,[12] dedicating himself to a monastic life in Nicerte, three miles from Apamea and about seventy-five miles from Antioch.[13] There he lived between 416 and 423, until his consecration against his will – as he himself writes[14] – as bishop of Cyrus, 'a solitary town'[15] in the province of Euphratensis.

The seven years spent in the monastery before his ordination and the following seven until the outbreak of the Nestorian controversy were arguably the most peaceful ones of his life. His unwavering pastoral care bore abundant fruits on ecclesiastical and social levels. The inhabitants of the 800 parishes of his diocese were not particularly educated: this vast area had always been 'swarming with heretics'.[16] Often facing threats to his life, Theodoret brought thousands of various schismatics back into the body of the church. This was untypical for contemporary churchmen (including both Cyril and Nestorius), who rather preferred to use military force in order to obliterate physically the heresies together with the heretics.[17] Perhaps the only action for which he is reproached by some modern researchers, was the gathering and destruction of 200 copies of Tatian's *Diatessaron* in order to introduce the four gospels in their stead.[18]

From the revenues of his see he beautified the city, built an aqueduct, public bridges, baths and porticoes. He also introduced skilled crafts-men and medical personnel to look after the people. The Cyrrhestica was a fertile territory and its inhabitants were unbearably overtaxed. Apart from his impressive literary production he still found time to entreat those in charge to lessen such burdens (see e.g. *Letter 43 to Pulcheria, Letter 45 to Anatolius*). His fame as an orator competed with Chrysostom's and his sermons were also often applauded in Antioch, where he was regularly invited for preaching visits (*Letters* 83, 147). One of the best summaries of this lifelong exemplary concern for his flock is to be found in *Letter 81 to the consul Nomus*:

> Even before my conception my parents promised to devote me to God; from my swaddling-bands they devoted me according to their promise and educated me accordingly; the time before my episcopate I spent in a monastery and then was unwillingly consecrated bishop. I lived for twenty-five years in such a way that I was never summoned to trial by any one nor ever brought accusation against any. Not one of the pious clergy who were under me ever frequented a court. In so many years I never took an obol[19] or a garment from anyone. Not one belonging to my household ever received a loaf or an egg. I could not endure the thought of possessing anything save the rags I wore. From the revenues of my see I erected public porticoes; I built two large bridges; I looked after the

public baths. On finding that the city was not watered by the river running by it, I built the conduit, and supplied the dry town with water. But not to mention these matters I led eight villages of Marcionites, with their neighbourhood, into the way of truth; another full of Eunomians and another of Arians I brought to the light of divine knowledge, and, by God's grace, not a tare of heresy was left among us. All this I did not effect with impunity; many times I shed my blood; I was often stoned by them and brought to the very gates of death. But I am a fool in my boasting, yet my words are spoken of necessity, not of consent.[20]

Cyrus was a relatively desolate city and its cultural level was much lower than the learned bishop deserved. Theodoret's affection for this community was also his vulnerable point during the later development of events.

Early writings

Theodoret's pre-Ephesian literary activity is quite impressive, although not all his works written in this period have come down to us. His shorter and longer tracts and books written before the outbreak of the Nestorian controversy are the following:[21]

- *A Cure of Greek Maladies*, the last and one of the best Christian apologies, written before his accession to the see of Cyrus.[22]
- *Against the Jews* – a work no longer extant, yet it must certainly predate Ephesus, since Theodoret also mentions it at the beginning of his *Expositio rectae fidei*.[23]
- *Exposition of the Right Faith* (*Expositio rectae fidei*) – a work previously attributed to Justin Martyr, and then restored to Theodoret. It is considered an early work, written well before the Nestorian controversy.[24]
- *Questions and Responses for the Orthodox* – also attributed to Justin Martyr.
- *Against Arians and Eunomians* – no longer extant.
- *Against Macedonians* or *On the Holy Spirit* – no longer extant.
- *Against Marcionites* – no longer extant.

2

THEODORET AND THE
NESTORIAN CONTROVERSY

In 428 Theodoret's friend Nestorius became patriarch of Constantinople.[1] Cyril had already been patriarch of Alexandria since 412. The clash between the two equally passionate, and not particularly diplomatic churchmen, concerning the term *theotokos* (i.e. 'God-bearer') applied to Mary, as well as the dissensions concerning the two natures of Christ brought about a stormy debate within the Eastern church, which continued for decades after their deaths, and caused most of the unfortunate changes in Theodoret's life.

The Nestorian controversy has an extensive literature. Apart from the classical works of Hefele, Loofs, Sellers, Kelly, Scipioni, Grillmeier, Hainthaler and others, Prof. Luise Abramowski has brought to light, and continues to furnish, an impressive amount of invaluable new data on Nestorius and Antiochene theology in general, whilst Prof. Jean-Noël Guinot excels in his research concerning Theodoret. A fairly recent presentation of the events has been produced in this series by Norman Russell.[2] I shall therefore try to summarise the events leading up to Ephesus and its aftermath mainly from Theodoret's viewpoint.

His direct involvement in the debate started in 430, when John of Antioch received the letters of Pope Celestine and Cyril concerning Nestorius' condemnation by the West and by Cyril's party. The Alexandrian patriarch was very cautious in approaching the pope: he took care for all his letters addressed to Rome to be translated into Latin and did not lay too much stress upon the issue at hand, but rather made Celestine aware that Nestorius had accepted a few excommunicated Pelagians into his court.[3] The reaction was cleverly calculated: the pope took Cyril's side, the more so since John Cassian and Marius Mercator did an amazingly effective job in distorting most of the teachings of the new patriarch of Constantinople.[4]

When the aforementioned letters reached Antioch, Theodoret was also there with other bishops of the province for the ordination of

Macarius, the new bishop of Laodicea. The first action of the Bishop of Cyrus, however, was by no means condemnable, since he was the author of the often forgotten letter written in John's name to Nestorius, which in a very temperate tone attempted to persuade the patriarch not to throw the whole of Christendom into confusion for the sake of one word (i.e. *theotokos*).[5]

The issue at stake between Cyril and Nestorius was not at all simple: apart from the inherited church-political antipathy, a lot of other things were involved apart from the theological differences.[6] For example, to have Nestorius out of the way was almost a matter of survival for Cyril, since the emperor had previously appointed the patriarch of Constantinople to investigate the messy situation in Alexandria, including the sudden death of a few of Cyril's opponents, like Hypatia, the female philosopher.[7] As one of his recent editors put it, 'it will always have been unwise, and sometimes even physically dangerous, to meet Cyril as an opponent'.[8] The last thing Cyril needed was to have Nestorius as his examiner. Thus, as it could well be the case, he started a huge dispute around the term 'God-bearer', trying to prove that Nestorius was a heretic and consequently unfit to investigate his case.

The theological matter on the surface seemed to be the adequacy or inadequacy of the title as applied to the Virgin Mary. Nonetheless, both theologians saw this expression as referring to Christ. Nestorius' objection to the term was that although Christ was God and man indeed, Mary could not be titled 'God-bearer' ontologically, since the divinity of Christ would thus begin with his birth from the Virgin, which consequently makes Mary a goddess. Cyril did not mean this, of course, yet he certainly wanted to safeguard the personal unity of Christ.

An often neglected aspect of Nestorius' attitude, however, was that he did not reject the term entirely, but offered two alternatives: either Mary should be titled *theotokos* and *anthrōpotokos* (God-bearer and man-bearer) simultaneously, the former being interpreted attributively (on account of the union of manhood and Godhead within Christ) and not ontologically; or simply *Christotokos* (Christ-bearer), comprising both terms in one. Although this explanation seemed fairly reasonable, Cyril always suspected that his opponent did not truly believe in the divinity of Christ, but was a crypto-Arian. That is one of the reasons why he clung firmly to *theotokos*, rejecting either of the aforementioned alternatives.

The main divergence, however, was in the Christological model and terminology of the two theologians. Nestorius inherited the

Logos–anthrōpos (Word–man) Christology from his masters (Diodore and Theodore), which firmly held that the Word did not become merely flesh but human, thus the rational soul was very much part of the assumed human nature. Cyril also held against Apollinaris that a rational soul had been assumed, but he could not assign anything to this soul and did not grant it any soteriological significance, speaking in the manner of his Alexandrian forerunners, using a *Logos–sarx* (Word–flesh) language, which naturally irritated the Antiochenes.

Most of the terms used by the two opponents had already been applied in the theological tradition, although not unequivocally and not always in the same manner. The four main terms involved were the following:

- *ousia* (essence; in most Latin and English translations rendered as 'substantia', i.e. 'substance');
- *physis* (nature);
- *hypostasis* (hypostasis, meaning more or less a 'personal reality', although its meaning varied even within the works of the same author);
- *prosōpon* (face, countenance, person).

These terms were applied both in *theologia* (as the teaching about God's being and the Trinity was commonly labelled) and in the *oikonomia* (which mostly meant the teaching about the sense and mode of the incarnation, i.e. what we might call soteriology and Christology).[9]

The first two expressions were used to denote what was common for the three Persons of the Trinity and for the two realities which came together in Christ respectively. The second two described the individual properties of the divine Persons, whilst in Christology, *prosōpon* was the key term to indicate the oneness of the Person of Christ. The term *hypostasis*, as I shall argue in Chapter 6, was not part of the Christological vocabulary of orthodox theologians before the Nestorian controversy, having been used solely by Apollinaris of Laodicea. Thus, if in the Trinity there was one *ousia* and one *physis*, in Christ there were two *ousiai* and two *physeis*. Similarly, as in the Trinity there were three *hypostases* and three *prosōpa*, in Christ there was only one *prosōpon* (the term *hypostasis* not having been used in orthodox Christology before Cyril).

Further, the terms referring to the union of the Word with the manhood in Christ also constituted a matter of dispute. Cyril would only accede to use *henōsis* (union), whilst rejecting any other term used by the Antiochenes often bound in their works with *henōsis*, like *synapheia* (conjunction), *asynchutos henōsis* (unmingled union, the synonym of *synapheia*), *koinōnia* (community, togetherness), *enoikēsis* (indwelling), *symplokē* (combination, connection) etc.

Having been fairly uneducated in terms of secular philosophy,[10] the two main opponents did not particularly care about the ancient history or nuances of these terms and applied them rather carelessly. Whilst Nestorius used e.g. the term *prosōpon* both in the singular and plural in his description of the union, Cyril often equated *physis* with *hypostasis* and spoke repeatedly of a 'physical' as well as 'hypostatic' union, which conferred ambiguity to his formulae. Having applied the term *physis* both in the sense of 'nature' and 'person', his terminology became inconsistent. The additional problem was that whilst venerating Athanasius and trying to follow him closely, without having the necessary critical spirit that his opponents (especially Theodoret) possessed, Cyril kept on quoting Apollinarian forgeries as coming from Athanasius, making these formulae the cornerstones of his Christological interpretation. One of the most famous ones was his reiterated slogan, 'one incarnate nature of the God-Word' (*mia physis tou Theou Logou sesarkōmenē*), by which he intended to mean the one entity of the God-man Christ, the Word of God. The definition, however, came from Apollinaris, not Athanasius, a fact Cyril would not accept even though repeatedly warned about it by his opponents.[11]

Concerning Theodoret's answers to Cyril's Twelve Anathemas one may argue that it was natural for the trained critical eye of the Bishop of Cyrus to spot the terms of 'heretic flavour' in Cyril's statements and treat them accordingly. This is why Theodoret's mostly remembered act before Ephesus remains his *Refutation of Cyril's Twelve Anathemas* or *Chapters*, for which he is still criticised. When referring to this episode we should remember some often neglected circumstances. He wrote these counter-statements at John of Antioch's request and not on his own initiative (see his *Letter to John* in SC 429, 62–71). Further, Cyril's *Twelve Anathemas*, as an extreme Alexandrian disapproval of Nestorius' teaching – especially without their author's subsequent *Apology* – as E. Venables rightly observes, 'hardly escaped falling into the opposite error'.[12] The language and terminology was strongly Apollinarian,[13] and as a whole, these anathemas were far from being a peerless summary of Cyrilline orthodoxy, requiring further explanation in order to be accepted. Theodoret found a number of – mostly verbal – inconsistencies, and made several legitimate points against them. As Prof. Luise Abramowski during our personal discussions put it, these *Anathemas* were 'one of the greatest misfortunes of the history of doctrine'.

Paradoxically, without Theodoret's counter-statements, Cyril would probably have never been concerned with defending or reinterpreting his anathemas, and indeed without his own explanation the charge of 'verbal Apollinarianism' could hardly be dismissed. Thus, by his replies, Theodoret willy-nilly helped Cyril to elucidate his own position. That is why the Bishop of Cyrus could sign the *Formula of Reunion* in 434, considering that the Alexandrian patriarch no longer held the extreme position of his earlier *Anathemas*, which did not become recognised theological standards until 553.

There is another question to be raised, which is important in our attempt to describe and evaluate Theodoret's pre-Ephesian activity. Here we arrive at the double treatise *On the holy and vivifying Trinity* and *On the incarnation/inhumanation of the Lord* (hereafter: *De Trinitate* and *De incarnatione*), written shortly after the *Refutation* yet before Ephesus. In these two tracts Theodoret lays down the basic Antiochene Trinitarian, Christological, soteriological and anthropological concepts. Although representing Theodoret's positive contribution towards the formation of Chalcedonian Christology, these tracts were overshadowed by the *Refutation*, which is his negative input only, and their theological significance has often been interpreted in the light of the latter. This is due partly to the fact that *De Trinitate* and *De incarnatione* were preserved under Cyril's name and restored to Theodoret only in 1888.[14] Consequently, the important, positive contribution of our author to Christology, during the most controversial period of his life, was practically unknown to theologians for more than fourteen centuries. It is possible that if some analysts had had knowledge about them, they would not have portrayed Theodoret as an inconvertible crypto-Nestorian. Without this double treatise the pre-Ephesian Theodoret could be seen as an obstinate controversialist who did not produce anything positive to the theological question at stake, but merely rejected Cyril's Alexandrian statements.[15] Such an attitude could not be characterised as a true care for ecclesiastical unity, even less an example worthy of being followed. A close analysis of this two-part treatise, however, can show that the main charge of crypto-Nestorianism brought against Theodoret by some ancient, mediaeval and modern authors is largely unwarranted.[16] This is not only because the accusations brought against him are mostly anachronistic,[17] but also because we encounter examples where some modern analysts fail to differentiate between what is said and who is saying it.[18]

At the Council of Ephesus in 431, Theodoret, together with sixty-eight bishops (including Alexander of Hierapolis) and Count Candidian (the imperial representative) vainly protested against the opening of sessions before the arrival of John of Antioch and the papal legates.[19] Nestorius refused to appear before the incomplete, and thus illegitimately constituted, council, which was presided over by Cyril, who, as the main accuser, should certainly have been denied this role.[20] Nestorius was labelled 'the new Judas', banned and deposed by Cyril's council in his absence, without a trial. After John's arrival Theodoret joined the Antiochene 'conciliabulum' and adhered to the deposition of Cyril and Memnon, the Ephesian bishop, whose monks nearly lynched Nestorius even before the opening of the assembly. Without entering into the details, which we can find in the relevant scholarship, it can be safely concluded that the ecclesiastical gathering later known as the 'Third Ecumenical Council of Ephesus' never took place. There were two separate priestly meetings – both of them justifiable from a certain canonical viewpoint – the decisions of which were at first simultaneously validated by the emperor (since all the deposed bishops were imprisoned). Later, one of the two was given political support, the church being compelled to regard it as the sole legitimate one. Friedrich Loofs summarised most fittingly the two councils held at Ephesus: 'the Council merely acknowledged the irreconcilability of the contradictions.'[21]

Nestorius wanted to return to his monastery, but soon after Cyril got out of prison by fairly disputable means, he convinced the emperor to have Nestorius exiled, and Nestorius had to spend the last two decades of his life in utter misery, his sole comfort being Pope Leo's dogmatic letter to Flavian,[22] written in 449, which Nestorius considered his theological vindication. Nevertheless, the council's failure to accomplish the much needed unity, as well as Cyril's highly questionable method of gaining influence with the imperial court through bribery, could hardly be interpreted as a desirable outcome.[23] Theodoret's letter to Alexander of Hierapolis written in September–October 431 from Chalcedon (where both parties presented their case to the emperor after the council had failed) aptly describes the situation:

> Our desire is that both ourselves and your piety be released from this, since nothing good is to be hoped from it, inasmuch as all the judges themselves are fully satisfied with gold and contend that the nature of the Godhead and manhood is one.[24]

The gold and the other bribes, however, did their job: Cyril's party received the imperial support, the more so since the Alexandrian patriarch, who was much better trained in matters of intrigue than his rival, had won Pope Celestine over to his side well before the issuing of his *Anathemas*. The emperor clearly could not disregard this fact in making his decision. It was to be understood that Cyril's party carried the day, even if not with flying colours.

In the meantime Theodoret took part in the synods of Tarsus and Antioch, held in the same year by the Eastern party, and composed his – now lost – *Pentalogos* (the five books against Cyril and his Ephesian council), a work banned by the fifth ecumenical council of Constantinople in 553. The 'tempest of the Church', as Theodoret labelled the controversy in his famous *Letter to the Eastern monks* (written in the winter of 431–2), was far from being over.[25]

3

FROM EPHESUS TO CHALCEDON AND BEYOND

The *Formula of Reunion* and its aftermath

Although Cyril's council had declared that nothing should be added to the Nicene Creed, a common statement was needed in order to restore peace – at least formally. The famous *Formula of Reunion* between the two parties – signed by Cyril and John in 433 – had previously been drawn up by none other than Theodoret in 431. This was the *Antiochene Formula*, which the Eastern commissioners (including Theodoret) presented to the emperor after the end of both Ephesian councils in September 431.[1] This confession, which accepted the term *theotokos*, and became the basis of the *Chalcedonian Definition* in 451, could hardly be characterised as a total triumph for Alexandrian Christology, yet it built a good bridge between the two traditions:

> In accordance we confess our Lord Jesus Christ, the Only-begotten Son of God to be perfect God and perfect man [consisting] of rational soul [*psychē logikē*] and body; on the one hand begotten of the Father before the ages according to [his] Godhead, and on the other hand, the same one [born] in the last days for us and for our salvation of the Virgin Mary according to [his] manhood; the same one coessential[2] with his Father according to his Godhead and coessential with us according to his manhood. For a union of two natures [*physeis*] took place: this is why we confess one Christ, one Son, one Lord. According to this notion of unmingled union [*asynchutos henōsis*] we confess the holy Virgin [to be] God-bearer [*theotokos*], because the God-Word was made flesh [*sarkōthēnai*] and became man [*enanthrōpēsai*] and from her conception he united to himself the temple taken from her. We know that the theologians on one hand treat some of the

evangelic and apostolic words about the Lord as commonly referring to one person [*prosōpon*], whilst others they apply separately as to two natures [*epi duo physeōn*], and the God-worthy [words] they apply to the Godhead of Christ, whilst the humble ones to [his] manhood.[3]

The *Formula* contains three main terms: *ousia* and *physis* are understood as being 'two' within Christ, while *prosōpon* denotes the 'one' person. The omission of *hypostasis* (Cyril's preferred term for Christological union) is not at all accidental: it not only shows that the *Formula* was of Antiochene origin, but also that the expression *hypostasis* was not yet accepted in Christology.[4] It can be said that by agreeing to the closing part of the *Formula*, Cyril had to draw back at least a little from his firm position expressed in his fourth anathema:

If anyone takes the terms used in the Gospels and apostolic writings, whether referred to Christ by the saints, or applied to himself by himself, and allocates them to two *prosōpa* or hypostases, attributing some to a man conceived of as separate from the Word of God and some, as more appropriate to God, only to the Word of God the Father, let him be anathema.[5]

Of course, one may argue that in the anathema Cyril intended to refuse any interpretation of scriptural passages as referring to two *persons* (i.e. to the Word and to the man Jesus, as two separate subjects). In this sense he was not in contradiction with the *Formula*, inasmuch as the latter spoke of *one person* and *two natures*, but not of *two persons* as possible subjects of predication. Nevertheless, the application of certain utterances and actions as more befitting to the human *physis* (i.e. 'nature' not 'person'), and others to the divine (permitted by the *Formula*), was something the staunch defender of the *mia physis* formula would hardly have been prepared to accept, either before or at Ephesus, especially since in his third anathema he unequivocally spoke of a 'natural union'. The signing of the *Formula*, therefore, involved at least a partial compromise from both groups.

Entangled between the two Antiochene parties of John of Antioch and Alexander of Hierapolis respectively (the former achieved peace with Cyril even at the cost of accepting Nestorius' deposition, the latter remained a resolute advocate of his former patriarch), Theodoret sought for an agreement by detaching theological matters from personal antipathies. The acceptance of the *Formula* by everyone, without anathematising Nestorius, could have been the ideal solution, yet this was highly unlikely on Cyril's part, since he would not accede to withdraw his *Anathemas*. Although both parties began to regard the controversy as a matter of prestige, and apart from Theodoret's ever decreasing group virtually nobody could separate the theological debate from church-political interests, the *Formula* was signed in 433 and Theodoret adhered to it in the following year.

His differentiation between the signing of the *Formula* (with which, as its author, he fully agreed theologically) and Nestorius' condemnation, deserves some attention, since this aspect has often been neglected or oversimplified. It is perhaps true that he credited his friend with having taught the same doctrine he himself held. Nevertheless, canonically he was justified in rejecting Nestorius' deposition. He was to suffer the same maltreatment of being deposed without a trial eighteen years later. Parmentier's brilliant analysis of the Syriac version of Theodoret's *Letter 172 to the exiled Nestorius* – written in 434 after he had signed the *Formula* – and of its polemical interpolations (inserted by the Monophysite translator) is conclusive.[6] Theodoret explains here that he signed the *Formula* because he was indeed convinced of Cyril's orthodoxy, but at the same time he refuses to subscribe to the canonically unjustifiable deposition of his friend:

> Let no one therefore persuade your holiness that I have accepted the Egyptian writings [i.e. Cyril's letter to the Easterns] as orthodox, with my eyes shut, because I covet any see. For really, to speak the truth, after frequently reading and carefully examining them, I have discovered that they are free from all heretical taint, and I have hesitated to put any stress upon them, though I certainly have no love for their author, who was the originator of the disturbances which have agitated the world. For this I hope to escape punishment in the Day of Judgement, since the just Judge examines motives. But as to what has been done unjustly and illegally against your holiness, not even if one were to cut off both my hands would I ever assent,[7] God's grace helping me and supporting my infirmity. This I have stated in writing to those who require it. I have sent to your holiness my reply to what you wrote to me in order for you to know that by God's grace no time has changed me like the centipedes and chameleons who imitate by their colour the stones and leaves among which they live. I and all with me salute all the brotherhood who are with you in the Lord.[8]

Thus, the Bishop of Cyrus overcame his personal hostility towards Cyril upon realising that his opponent was not heterodox and agreed with the Alexandrian patriarch in doctrinal matters despite his friendship with Nestorius, who in his turn did not approve the *Formula*.[9] This distinction between the two (doctrinal and canon law) issues was therefore neither a betrayal of his friend nor a compromise in doctrinal matters. It rather shows Theodoret's wisdom and longing for peace, the more so since he turns towards Nestorius in two subsequent letters – only one of them extant – in order to ask for his help (!) in convincing the unyielding Alexander of Hierapolis to accept the *Formula*.[10] This was in fact a last attempt to bring the matter of accepting the *Formula* once again before Nestorius himself. Theodoret was late in adhering also because he hoped to convince his own patriarch to accept it[11] and to avoid being exiled. It did not happen so: Alexander was deposed. Theodoret, however, accepted the *Formula* rightly from a theological perspective, whilst considering the condemnation of Nestorius as being a separate issue.

Nonetheless, one widely ignored reference in Theodoret's *Letter 83 to Dioscorus* (Cyril's nephew and successor in Alexandria), written in 448, suggests that the formal adherence of the Bishop of Cyrus to the condemnation of Nestorius must have happened well before Chalcedon: 'Our own hands bear witness that we subscribed twice to the writings of John of blessed memory concerning Nestorius, yet these things are whispered about us by those who try to conceal their own unsoundness by calumniating us.'[12]

In order to settle things and be able to focus on his duties in Cyrus, Theodoret entered into friendly correspondence even with Cyril – or at least this is what he tells us in the same *Letter 83 to Dioscorus*:

> I suppose that even your holiness is well aware that also Cyril of blessed and holy memory often wrote to us and when he sent his writings against Julian to Antioch [. . .] he asked the blessed John, the bishop of Antioch to show them to the prominent teachers of the East, and in accordance with these letters, the blessed John sent us the books. We read them with admiration and wrote to Cyril of blessed memory. He wrote back to us again testifying both to our exactitude and disposition. This letter is preserved by us.[13]

It is true that no letter of Cyril to Theodoret has come down to us: nevertheless, the accuracy of the latter's report concerning their correspondence is incontestable. Theodoret wrote the above letter to

Dioscorus after Cyril's death,[14] shortly before the *Latrocinium*.[15] Taking his very delicate situation at the time into consideration, the above reference to a preserved letter from Cyril could hardly be a mere bluff. Of course, his relationship with the mighty patriarch was probably not too cordial, the more so since Cyril did not intend to reconcile with Antiochene theology, regardless of the *Formula*. The evidence can be found in Cyril's *Letter 69 to Acacius of Melitene*: 'Having studied the books of Theodore and Diodore, which they wrote, not indeed about the incarnation of the Only-begotten, but against the incarnation, I selected some chapters.'[16]

Cyril was well aware that the *Formula of Reunion* was far from being a full victory for the Alexandrian school, and, being attacked by some of his own radical followers for having signed it, he began a harsh theological campaign against Theodoret's masters: Diodore of Tarsus and Theodore of Mopsuestia. Both of them died in peace with the church. Moreover, Diodore was one of the chairmen of the Council of Constantinople in 381, having been considered by his contemporaries as the pillar of orthodoxy against Apollinarianism. Even if we regard Cyril's action, concretised in his work *Against Diodore and Theodore*, as a mere act of self-justification after the compromise he had made by signing the *Formula of Reunion*, Theodoret's reaction to defend them in his *Apology for Diodore and Theodore*[17] was legitimate. In fact, Cyril was attacking one of the key figures of the second ecumenical council, and implicitly the council itself, which, according to this reasoning, permitted 'a heretic' to be its chairman.

During these 'cold war' years between Ephesus and Chalcedon Theodoret still managed to produce valuable works, some of which are still extant:

- ten discourses *On Divine Providence*, probably delivered before a well-educated audience in Antioch;[18]
- a whole series of *Commentaries* on the *Psalms*, the *Canticle*, the *Prophets*, and the *Pauline Epistles*;[19]
- *A History of the Monks of Syria* (*Historia religiosa*);
- a *Church History* comprising the events between 325 and 428.[20]

In 438 Cyril wanted to compel all bishops to condemn Nestorian doctrine in explicit terms. John was outraged and besought Proclus of Constantinople to intervene with the emperor and reject such requests. Cyril also wrote indignantly to John upon learning that Theodoret had not expressly anathematised Nestorius when signing the *Formula*.[21]

The Monophysite controversy

The controversy was on the rise again when Cyril passed away in 444. After the death of the main leaders who had been present at the Council of Ephesus and who then signed the *Formula of Reunion* in 433,[22] their sees were taken over by bishops who were neither better theologians, nor better persons than their predecessors, save perhaps for Flavian of Constantinople.[23] The Alexandrian patriarchate was ruled for a long time by three ruthless figures in a row, who interestingly were uncle and nephew, having at least one achievement in common: to depose their colleagues in Constantinople. If Theophilus succeeded in doing this to John Chrysostom with his nephew Cyril's aid, then the latter certainly proved to be his faithful disciple in the action against Nestorius. Further, after Cyril's death, his nephew, Dioscorus, teamed up with Eutyches, the archimandrite of Constantinople and an extremist follower of Cyril's *mia physis* formula (hence the term 'Monophysitism' or 'Miaphysitism'), in order to depose Flavian of Constantinople. The Alexandrian patriarchs always coveted the see of the capital, although they despised the city, since its community lacked an apostolic foundation. The emperors, however, preferred to bring one of the Antiochenes to the capital (i.e. Chrysostom, Nestorius, Flavian). The theological differences, flavoured with personal and ecclesiastical rivalries, always bore within themselves the danger of a new clash.

The Monophysite controversy was by no means an exception. Seemingly, it all started with a slight misunderstanding between Flavian and the mighty imperial eunuch, Chrysaphius. The latter apparently used his influence to help the patriarch's election. When after the investiture he dispatched his messengers to Flavian for a reward, the bishop sent him holy bread. Chrysaphius – who expected to receive gold – was outraged. It did not take long until he and the archimandrite put in practice the timeless truth of all warfare: 'the enemy of my enemy is my friend.' If Chrysaphius could not suffer Flavian for personal reasons, Eutyches saw in him the main objector against *mia physis*. Dioscorus rapidly became the third member of this alliance.

Eutyches taught that although before the union there were two natures in Christ, after the union there was only one. Further, he is said to have claimed that despite being a perfect man, the body of Christ was of a different essence from ours. Eutyches' views – he refused to utter an orthodox confession concerning the two natures – were condemned by a local council in Constantinople in 448, presided over by Flavian. A report was forwarded to Pope Leo I, who also approved the decision in May 449 and sent his famous dogmatic letter (entitled *Tomus ad Flavianum*, commonly called 'the *Tome*') to Flavian, in which he advocated the personal unity of Christ, as well as the distinction of the natures' properties.

It became Theodoret's duty again to address the problem. Being regarded as a champion of Antiochene theology in Ephesus already – although a cloud of suspicion was hovering above him for having refuted Cyril – he could not abandon the achievements of the *Formula*, since Eutyches jeopardised even this fragile union attained at such high cost. So Theodoret wrote his work against Monophysitism in 447, entitled *Eranistes* (*The Beggar*). The whole treatise is a long discussion between *Eranistes* (or *polymorphos*, i.e. multiform) representing the Monophysite theologian who, as Theodoret suggests, has 'begged' and gathered his 'polymorph' teaching together from many old heresies, and *Orthodoxos*, who transmits the views of the author. The work consists of three dialogues bearing descriptive titles (*The immutable*, *The unconfused*, *The impassible*) and contains all the main terms later used in the *Chalcedonense*, including the idea that the two natures are indivisibly, inseparably and unconfusedly united within Christ, yet both of them retain their specific properties. A so-called 'communication of properties' would certainly have been regarded as a 'mingling of natures' in the Chalcedonian period.[24]

Deposition by the *Latrocinium*

Thus, the hardships of our author did not reach their end with the death of his mightiest opponent. Despite the fact that Theodoret quoted numerous recognised Alexandrian theologians in support of his statements, the *Eranistes* certainly did not increase the number of his Alexandrian supporters, if there were any. His reaction to Eutyches' heresy at first brought about an imperial decree confining him to his diocese, then a condemnation and deposition by the *Latrocinium* in 449 – without a trial. Under the influence of Chrysaphius, Emperor Theodosius II convoked a synod to Ephesus in 449, which was presided over by Dioscorus, who lacked both the theological and diplomatic abilities of his late uncle, whilst inheriting most of his faults. The unscrupulous Alexandrian bishop simply disregarded Pope Leo's request that the *Tomus ad Flavianum* should be read aloud and accepted as a measure of orthodoxy. Instead of doing this, those present deposed everyone who resisted Eutychian Monophysitism. So the assembly excommunicated Flavian, Theodoret, Ibas of Edessa, Domnus of

Antioch and even Pope Leo I. Flavian, however, did not live long after the disastrous gathering, since having suffered major physical injuries from the mob of monks (the mostly illiterate supporters of the Eutychian party, a band similar to Cyril's buffs in Ephesus), he passed away soon after the conclusion of the synod. Nestorius read Leo's *Tome* in his exile and praised his teaching. Being utterly indignant, Leo called the whole gathering a 'robber synod of Ephesus' (*Latrocinium Ephesinum*). The emperor's sudden death (when he fell from his horse) put a quick end to the short-lived victory of the Eutychian–Monophysite party.

The Council of Chalcedon

Pulcheria, the new empress, quickly married senator Marcian, who thus became emperor. The imperial couple approached Pope Leo with the plan of summoning a new council. The pope – fearing the repetition of the scandal – was reluctant to accept a synod gathering in the East, hoping to convene it in Italy. Nevertheless, through the emperor's insistence, he finally agreed, and a council was convoked for 1 September 451 to Nicaea of Bythinia. The conditions of the pope (who wisely refrained from attending despite the emperor's repeated requests) were the following:

- The *Tome* was to be read aloud and accepted as the measure of orthodoxy without dispute.
- The papal legates were to take part only in the sessions held in the emperor's presence and to preside over the assembly.
- Dioscorus was not to participate at the sessions of the council.

In the meantime, Theodoret, seeing the theological disaster produced by Eutyches and Dioscorus, also wrote to Pope Leo. In his *Letter* 113, after all the humiliation of being first restricted to his diocese by the imperial decree (on 30 March 449) and then condemned and deposed in his absence (in August 449), he writes:

> I lament the disturbance of the church, and long for peace. Twenty-six years have I ruled the church entrusted to me by the God of the universe, aided by your prayers. [. . .] If you bid me abide by the sentence of condemnation, I abide; and henceforth I shall trouble no man, and shall wait for the righteous tribunal of our God and Saviour. God is my witness, my lord, that I care not for honour and glory.[25]

Theodoret suffered the same treatment as Nestorius: he was charged, convicted and deposed without a trial, without any chance to defend himself. His letters written in this period bear witness to his situation:

> And those were unquestionably wrong who gave both their ears to my calumniators and would not keep one for me. Even to murderers, and to them that despoil other men's beds, an opportunity is given of defending themselves, and they do not receive sentence till they have been convicted in their own presence, or have made confession of the truth of the charges on which they are indicted. But a high priest who has held the office of bishop for 25 years after passing his previous life in a monastery, who has never troubled a tribunal, nor yet on any single occasion been prosecuted by any man, is treated as a mere plaything of calumny, without being allowed even the common privilege of grave-robbers of being questioned as to the truth of the accusations brought against them.[26]

As mentioned earlier, the death of Theodosius II (29 July 450), and the accession of Pulcheria and Marcian, created a favourable atmosphere for the orthodox party. At the emperor's request the venue was changed and the council gathered in Chalcedon instead of Nicaea, the first session being held on 8 October 451. Dioscorus was deposed on disciplinary grounds and the bishops who had been excommunicated by the *Latrocinium* were rehabilitated. Nevertheless, Theodoret's ultimate humiliation was to happen at the eighth session. The cost of his acceptance as orthodox was no less than a personal anathema against Nestorius. He stated it in the midst of such riotous, unprincipled enemies as Juvenal of Jerusalem, who had with equal readiness voted for his deposition, in his absence, two years before, and now agreed to his restoration, refusing to hear any theological statement, just the anathema against Nestorius. The pious Bishop of Cyrus made a difficult decision: he agreed to anathematise his friend, thus being able to fulfil his historical duty, that is, to save the church once again from a hardly explainable dogma, which would have needed continual correction or reinterpretation. Although some of the bishops claimed that in conformity with Cyril's Ephesian council nothing should be added to the Nicene Creed, at the emperor's firm request a *Definition* was drawn up, the text of which is constructed upon Theodoret's *Formula*:

> Therefore, following the holy Fathers we all teach with one voice that our Lord Jesus Christ is to be confessed as one and

the same [*hena kai ton auton*] Son, the same one [to be] perfect in Godhead and perfect in manhood, the same one [to be] very God and very man [consisting] of a reasonable soul and body, coessential with the Father according to Godhead and coessential with us according to manhood; [being] in all things like us, sin excepted; on the one hand begotten of the Father before the ages according to Godhead; on the other hand, in the last days for us and for our salvation the same one [to be] born of the Virgin Mary, the God-bearer [*theotokos*] according to manhood. This one and the same Christ, Son, Lord, Only-begotten is recognised in two natures [*en duo physesin*], unconfusedly [*asynchutōs*], immutably [*atreptōs*], indivisibly [*adiairetōs*], inseparably [*achōristōs*] [united], and that the difference [*diaphora*] of the natures was by no means removed through the union [*henōsis*], but rather the property [*idiotēs*] of each nature being preserved and joined together in one Person [*prosōpon*] and one hypostasis, not separated or divided into two persons [*duo prosōpa*], but one and the same Son and Only-begotten, God-Word, Lord Jesus Christ, as the prophets from the beginning [had spoken] about him, and as the Lord Jesus Christ himself had instructed us, and as the Creed of the Fathers handed down to us.[27]

The limits of the present work do not allow us to provide a close and detailed analysis of this *Definition*. Nevertheless, a few points have to be noted. The remarkable character of this confession is that it comprises the best of both traditions. Concerning the model of Christ, Alexandria followed a *Logos–sarx* (Word–flesh) Christology, whilst Antioch pursued a *Logos–anthrōpos* (Word–man) Christology. Both approaches had their advantages and disadvantages. The former upheld the union at the cost of diminishing the Saviour's human side. The latter laid emphasis upon the uniting natures with the risk of weakening the union. The *Chalcedonense*, arguably for the first time in doctrinal history, comes up with a *Logos–anthrōpotēs* (Word–manhood) picture: it lays stress upon 'the one and the same' (characteristic to Cyril), accepts the term 'God-bearer', yet states that this 'one and the same' is recognised 'in two natures' instead of 'out of two', which would have been preferred by the Eutychians. The four famous adverbs ('unconfusedly, immutably, indivisibly, inseparably') are paired: the first two remove Eutyches' exaggeration (i.e. no mixture or change is involved), whilst the second two warn against a division of the two natures (the main charge brought against Nestorius). There is a true union [*henōsis*] indeed, but not at the cost of removing the individual properties [*idiotēs*] of either nature. A 'communication of properties', therefore, taken in strict Chalcedonian terms, is not allowed. This is why, for example, the Christology of the theologians of the Ephesian–Chalcedonian period can be assessed correctly only according to the recognised theological standards of their time, i.e. the *Formula of Reunion*, the *Tome of Leo* and the *Chalcedonian Definition*. Cyril's *Twelve Anathemas*, which were not voted upon in Chalcedon, did not become properly recognised theological standards until 553. Consequently, judging any fifth-century theologian based on these is anachronistic.

Chalcedon also clarifies the terms: in Christ there are two *physeis* and *ousiai*, yet only one *prosōpon* and one *hypostasis*. Thus, by accepting Cyril's term in Christology, the *Definition* leaves no doubt concerning the fact that *hypostasis* cannot be equated with *physis* but rather with *prosōpon*, thus pursuing a subtle but clear midway between both extremes.

One might even claim that the *Chalcedonense* is a colonnaded corridor, the two extremes of which are marked by the four adverbs as one row of columns on each side, beyond which one may not go, yet within the limits of which both traditions may proceed side by side. Nonetheless, if one were to interpret Chalcedon through the fifth council of Constantinople (held in 553), this corridor is necessarily cut in two in the middle and the path of Antioch – and beyond doubt the one of Pope Leo – is forbidden, the only valid option remaining Alexandria's narrow passageway, instead of a simultaneously validated parallel course. Whatever the judgement upon the *Chalcedonense* may be, it certainly cannot be claimed that it rejects those who would use Theodoret's and Leo's manner of speech, the more so since it expressly states the preservation of the natures' unmingled properties.

A last important point ought to be raised concerning Theodoret's relationship with Leo. It is often claimed that the latter was largely unaware of the theological and church-political depths of the dispute and in his *Tome*, approved by Chalcedon, merely repeated the Western formulae without having understood the issues at stake. This seems to be a comfortable explanation as to why some passages of this letter were denounced by the Illyrian and Palestinian bishops at Chalcedon as being 'Nestorian'. This question must not be overlooked – and not merely from a church-political or canonical perspective, but also concerning our assessment of Leo's doctrinal authority.

Based on the available evidence the depiction of Leo as unacquainted with the true nature of the doctrinal issues, or as having insufficient information about other aspects of the controversy, is erroneous. He was not only aware of the questions involved and formulated his *Tome* accordingly, but knew exactly the people who were worthy of his confidence. As his correspondence bears witness, Leo could distinguish well between Juvenal's unprincipled opportunism and Theodoret's firm theological position and reliable character. For the sake of illustration I shall summarise Leo's attitude towards them before and after Chalcedon.

After Theodosius' death Leo wrote to Anatolius of Constantinople that the names of Dioscorus, Juvenal and Eustathius were not to be read aloud at the holy altar (*Letter* 80 in NPNF XII, 66). According to Leo, Dioscorus displayed his bad feeling and Juvenal his ignorance 'in the synod undeserving to be called a synod' (i.e. the *Latrocinium*). They may be accepted into communion upon anathematising Eutychian heresy in unambiguous terms. Nonetheless, Leo reserves their case 'for the maturer deliberations of the Apostolic See, that when all things have been sifted and weighed, the right conclusion may be arrived at about their real actions' (*Letter* 85 in NPNF XII, 68).

The pope wrote to Bishop Julian in 452 in similar terms warning him to be circumspect in receiving the lapsed. Despite lamenting Juvenal's injuries, he states that 'the very food he [Juvenal] had supplied them [i.e. the Monophysite party, which after Chalcedon turned against him] was turned to his own ruin' (*Letter* 109 in NPNF XII, 82). Leo was also aware of Juvenal's previous opportunistic move in Ephesus in 431 when he sided with Cyril merely in the hope of obtaining ecclesiastical presidency over Palestine, about which Cyril informed Leo (then archdeacon of Rome) in a letter.[28] Finally, in his *Letter* 139 addressed to Juvenal himself, together with saluting him for returning to orthodoxy, Leo reproaches his former conduct in quite harsh terms:

> I grieved to think you had been yourself the source of your adversities by failing in persistent opposition to the heretics: for men can but think you were not bold enough to refute those with whom when in error you professed yourself satisfied. For the condemnation of Flavian of blessed memory and the acceptance of the most unholy Eutyches what was it but the denial of our Lord Jesus Christ according to the flesh? [. . .] And therefore, because in the tithe of long-suffering, you have chosen the return to wisdom rather than persisting in folly, I rejoice that you have so sought the heavenly remedies as at last to have become a defender of the Faith which is assailed by heretics.
>
> (NPNF XII, 97)

One need only glance at Leo's *Letter* 120 addressed to Theodoret (11 June 453) in order to see just how well informed he was about the Eastern situation and how accurately he chose his partners. Apart from congratulating the Bishop of Cyrus on their joint victory at Chalcedon and his reassurance that the Apostolic See constantly holds Theodoret as being free from heresy, Leo asks for his further co-operation by the writing of periodic reports:

> We exhort you to continue your co-operation with the Apostolic See, because we have learnt that some remnants of the Eutychian and Nestorian error still linger amongst you. [. . .] We wish to be assisted in this also by your watchful care, that you hasten to inform the Apostolic See by your periodic reports what progress the Lord's teaching makes in those regions; to the end that we may assist the priests of that district in whatever way experience suggests.
>
> (NPNF XII, 89–90)[29]

It is perhaps superfluous to add that such a service was most emphatically not required from Juvenal after his swing back to the orthodox side. Leo knew exactly which source he could trust. Upon assessing his theological authority in Chalcedon, one has to concede that the *Tome* was not only the measure of orthodoxy because of its reconcilability with Cyril's writings, but in its own right as well, the more so since most of those who at Chalcedon cried out, 'Leo spoke the [teachings] of Cyril [*Leōn eipen ta Kyrillou*]'[30] had condemned the very same letter as heretical two years before. Thus, after Chalcedon, Leo chose to depend upon the assistance of those churchmen who had proven to be reliable concerning both their theological maturity and their personal commitment to the cause they were serving.

Theodoret's death and condemnation in 553

We know hardly anything about Theodoret's life after Chalcedon. He explained his subscription to the *Definition* in a letter to John of Aegea,[31] in which he identified Chalcedon's *one hypostasis* with his *one prosōpon*. This terminological usage has been assessed negatively by some modern scholars.[32] He probably composed his *Compendium of Heretical Mythification* in 452–3.[33] Even the year of his death is still a matter of dispute. Tillemont says he did not survive the year 453; Gennadius suggests 457–8; whereas according to Canivet he died before 466.[34] Honigmann argues for 466, whilst Azéma fixed 460 as being the most likely time of Theodoret's death.[35]

The Monophysite bishop Philoxenus of Mabbugh (†523) caused Theodoret's name to be removed from the diptychs at Cyrus and Sergius II restored it.[36] This is particularly interesting since, perhaps in the entire fifth century, there was no other bishop in Cyrus to whom the city could have been so grateful in any respect as to Theodoret.

The so-called fifth ecumenical council held under the Emperor Justinian in Constantinople (553), whilst condemning Theodoret in person, could not totally undo what Chalcedon had done. Thus, it condemned Theodoret's works 'written against true faith and against St. Cyril' in its Canon 13.[37] Although a learned scholar said concerning the controversy around the *Three Chapters*, that 'it filled more volumes than it was worth lines',[38] and the fifth council is well beyond the focus of this book, it ought to be borne in mind that the entire condemnation of the three Antiochene theologians was done with the hope of reconciling the Monophysite opponents of Chalcedon. Further, this action took place after the total blunder of the *Henoticon* (482), which is again an often overlooked detail. In assessing Theodoret's teaching I intend to interpret him, and his theology, not from the perspective of what was defined in a totally changed world a century after Chalcedon, but according to the theological standards of his own time.

Thus, within a century of his death, Theodoret suffered another two unfair trials (the removal of his name from the diptychs and the condemnation of some of his works in 553), caused either by prejudiced ignorance or by an honest, but inappropriately directed, good will to bring peace to the church. One of the lessons of Constantinople 553 is that in order to maintain the body of Christendom united a common goal is needed: common enemies, or scapegoats – however cunningly chosen – simply do not suffice. It is perhaps time to grant Theodoret the fair trial he has often been denied during the past one and a half millennia.

4

THEODORET'S TRINITARIAN
DOCTRINE

In this doctrinal part of the introduction, Chapters 4–6, I shall present Theodoret's theological legacy, focusing upon his Trinitarian doctrine, his Christology as well as his terminology, in relation both to his fore-runners and his contemporaries.

Theodoret inherited and developed to its best the Antiochene theological tradition of Diodore, Theodore and Chrysostom. His exegesis is primarily historical–grammatical; nevertheless, he also finds sufficient space for some allegories and typology. His Trinitarian doctrine is rooted in the inherited model of the Cappadocian Fathers: one *ousia* and *physis* – three *hypostases* and *prosōpa*.[1] Gregory Nazianzen may have had the greatest influence upon him in this respect.

In *De Trinitate* Theodoret speaks of God the Father in the short but condensed Chapter 4 (PG 75, 1152A). According to him, 'the worshippers of the Trinity' believe in *one* God. This basic Trinitarian principle can be found in an epigrammatic sentence in his *Expositio*: 'For both the Monad is perceived in the Triad, and the Triad is recognised in the Monad' (PG 6, 1220C). God the Father is without beginning, unbegotten and unborn. In the passages concerning the Son and the Holy Spirit the epithet *anarchos* (= without beginning) is also applied to the other two divine *hypostases*, thus to the entire *ousia* and *physis* of God.

Theodoret spends a considerable time emphasising the equality and co-eternity of the three divine Persons. Nevertheless, the term *agennētos* [unbegotten] remains the Father's exclusive title, thus qualifying the first Person of the uni-essential Trinity. The author is meticulous in choosing specific appellations and pointing out the particular attributes of the divine *hypostasis* he is speaking about. These titles are neither chosen nor applied distinctly, i.e. in an isolated fashion. Theodoret sees the three hypostases in their relationship with each other, and interprets their names and titles accordingly. Thus, the

Father is Father in relation to his Son, and the Son is Son in relation to his Father, etc. Yet, the Son is also Creator in his relation to humankind, because of the commonness of his *ousia* with the Father and the Holy Spirit.

Being aware of the differences between 'unbegotten' [*agennētos*] and 'unmade' [*agenētos*], Theodoret applies these titles carefully, calling the Son *gennētos* [begotten], but not *genētos* [made], whilst concerning the Holy Spirit he asserts that he 'proceeds' from the Father. The Father is an eternal Father [*aei ōn*], who did not acquire this status later. This is important to defend God's unchanging eternal nature and thus avoid any alteration [*tropē*] of the Godhead during the incarnation. Theodoret does not simply speak of God's eternity, but asserts that his *fatherhood* is eternal: 'for there was not [a moment] when he was not [a Father], but he had been Father from the very beginning.'[2] This affirmation safeguards the co-eternity and co-equality of the Son with his Father, refusing any Arian subordination. The author also suggests that all human analogies applied to God's fatherhood are limited and cannot fully describe him: 'neither had he [i.e. the Father] been a Son first, and then [became] a Father, according to the corporeal sequence.'[3]

In the above context the statement concerning God's eternal fatherhood means that he cannot be perceived through human examples or analogies. In fact, it is here that we find one of Theodoret's strongest arguments concerning God's immutability and eternity in opposition to the creation's changing nature, which is subject to time. This also seems to be what Arius defended, but he failed to realise that God did not change by becoming a Father, since his fatherhood – as opposed to the human – is not a result of some development within the divinity.

Theodoret emphasises the total equality of the three hypostases based on the same *ousia* and *physis*. The particular properties of each divine Person is carried by the *hypostasis* or *prosōpon*. Thus, because they share the same essence, the Son and Spirit are co-eternal with and equal to the Father in all respects including power, might, dominion, authority, knowledge and worship, while all three hypostases carry some peculiar attributes (*idiotēs*) which are proper to them only: the Father is 'unbegotten', the Son is 'born impassibly' as well as 'Only-begotten', whilst the Spirit 'proceeds' from the Father.[4] Theodoret extends the Nicene term *homoousios* to the Spirit also.

Our author sees the divine essence or nature in total opposition to the human. The divine *ousia* is timeless, uncreated, omnipotent, incorporeal, infinite, immutable and impassible. These characteristics will have an important role to play in Theodoret's Christology.

The relationship between the terms *prosōpon* and *hypostasis*, as well as their use by the Bishop of Cyrus from his earliest works, implies an attempt to identify them as synonyms. With the introduction of the notion of *idiotēs* (property) into his Trinitarian doctrine Theodoret stands very much in the tradition of the Cappadocians. The three hypostases retaining their properties within the one being of the harmoniously One God will have a resonance in Theodoret's understanding of the retained properties of the two natures within Christ. The heritage of Gregory Nazianzen, Basil and Gregory of Nyssa may indeed have influenced Theodoret's attitude towards *communicatio idiomatum*. The idea of the unconfused properties of the divine hypostases upheld by the three Cappadocians thus had its effect both upon the Trinitarian and Christological understanding of the Bishop of Cyrus.

5

THEODORET'S CHRISTOLOGY

We have reached the most disputed chapter of Theodoret's doctrinal legacy. From his own time until today opinions have differed concerning the acceptability of his statements from the viewpoint of Chalcedonian orthodoxy. Unfortunately, most of these disagreements are caused by Chalcedon's twofold evaluation: some analysts consider it an exclusively Cyrilline council, others speak of a hidden victory of the Antiochene school. Chalcedon, however, is a corridor rather than a tightrope-walk, where both traditions have legitimacy. Theodoret contributed positively towards the formation of this Christology, the more so since the very essence of the *Chalcedonense* is literally based on his own *Formula* of 431.

The question of divine impassibility

While discussing the reasons behind the Antiochene emphasis upon the different properties of the two natures within Christ one element must be given special attention, namely the notion of *apatheia*, i.e. (divine) impassibility. The eagerness of earlier fathers – and of Theodoret – to maintain the Word's impassible character has been addressed on several occasions by modern scholarship, frequently resulting in a negative judgement.[1] It is often proposed also that the entire idea of God's impassibility is alien to Christian doctrine, being a servile adoption of Greek philosophy by the Antiochenes.[2]

Regarding Theodoret's oeuvre in general we can clearly see that an adopted philosophical argument concerning divine impassibility is too weak a ground to motivate all his Christological concerns. One only needs to take a glance at his *Curatio* to see how effectively he differentiates between philosophical and theological arguments; moreover, how adequately he can adapt his reasoning to the reader's paradigms. The emphasis upon the full humanity of Christ as the common link between him and us occupies at least an equally important place within his theological system, as is evident for example in the Temptation-story presented in *De incarnatione*.

Further, it is not at all certain that the widespread charge concerning divine *apatheia*'s exclusively philosophical origin is entirely valid. As Chadwick has already suggested, the effect of centuries-long Christian criticism of pagan gods possessed by human passions cannot be ignored.[3] This is peculiarly valid for the author of the *Curatio*. Alongside his awareness of the issue's philosophical implications, Theodoret's understanding of God's impassibility is aimed also at preserving, as it were, God's moral integrity over and against pagan gods, who are subject to various passions.

There is another aspect of divine impassibility which has either been ignored or not investigated in detail, especially when formulated as a charge against Antiochene Christology: although it sounds almost absurd, the question relates to the proper meaning of *apatheia* itself. Those who condemn this term usually interpret it as being unsuitable for God, since it removes his ability for compassion, pity, love, etc. The chief misunderstanding here is that God's *apatheia*, as it appears in Theodoret, has nothing to do with the English word 'apathy'. If any of the ancient theologians vividly expressed God's mercy towards humankind to the extent of sending his own Son to the cross, the Bishop of Cyrus was surely one of them. His idea of divine *apatheia* does not by any means imply God's inability to partake in our sufferings, even less his lack of empathy. This is flatly contradicted e.g. by Chs 7, 8, 13, 27 [26], as well as by Ch. 24 [23] of his *De incarnatione*, where the entire motive of the *oikonomia* is God's commiseration with fallen humankind.

The meaning of *apatheia* is quite different: it targets the passions to which human beings and pagan gods are subjected, but more impor-tantly it concerns God's immutability. If God – and thus the Word of God, i.e. Christ – could be shown as being 'passionate', in the sense of being influenced by the moment and not rather being 'the same yesterday, today and forever' (Heb. 13:8), then he would unavoidably be subject to time (since changes happen in time), and would cease to be eternal and absolute. This indeed has nothing to do with his empathy towards us, since that is part of his very own eternal self and not brought about by some turn of events. His very nature is to love his creation and it does not require 'passion' to bring this feeling about. In fact, commiseration is the immutable character of his own Person, since he is merciful even when having to reprehend, and 'mixes the punishment with philanthropy' (PG 75, 1424D). God's *apatheia* therefore means that his love towards humankind never ceases, since he does not change. The term is intended to safeguard the integrity of the immutable, almighty and, by nature, merciful God.[4] Therefore, the unfortunately popular, and to some extent fashionable, modern charge against the Antiochenes concerning their refusal of Theopaschism[5] as being unbiblical, philosophical or even old-fashioned is largely based on false assumptions.

Theodoret's anthropology

To understand Theodoret's concept of Christ as being fully human and fully divine, we must define those elements which constitute a human nature for our author, as well as their theological significance.

The human body as part of human nature is the result of God's creation. Moreover, as it appears in *HFC*, the creation of the body preceded the soul: 'The most divine Moses also said that the body of Adam was formed first and then God breathed the soul [*psyche*] into him' (PG 83, 481CD). According to *De incarnatione* 2, God transformed the earth into human nature (PG 75, 1420D). This sentence stands in contrast to Ch. 8, where by the use of the same verb 'transform' (*metaballo*), the author underlines the fact that during his incarnation, the Word of God himself did not transform the divine nature into human (PG 75, 1426D).[6] Thus, he clearly distinguishes between the terminology of 'creation' and 'incarnation'. The reality of the body of Christ is an indispensable part of his true human nature, of course, without the slightest impairment to his divinity (see e.g. PG 75, 1449B).

Theodoret's Christology is simultaneously anti-Arian and anti-Apollinarian. While on the level of Trinitarian doctrine the two systems of Arius and Apollinaris are quite divergent, their model of Christ is notably similar: neither of the two theologians seems to acknowledge the presence of a rational soul within the assumed human nature, even less to find a role for this soul in salvation history. The famous sentence 'the Word was made flesh' is therefore often explained by the Bishop of Cyrus with an anti-Apollinarian emphasis, showing that Scripture often labels the whole by the part (i.e. the entire human nature by the flesh), and therefore John 1:14 has to be understood as the Word assuming the entire human nature. While the argument concerning the acceptance of a true human body by the Saviour could not meet any substantial opposition amongst the adepts of the *Logos–sarx* model, the issue of a rational soul's presence within Christ – especially the kind of participation this soul could have in actual moral choices – had long been a subject of contention between Antiochene and some Alexandrian theologians, going back to as early as Diodore of Tarsus and Apollinaris of Laodicea. As Grillmeier rightly observed, 'the soul of Christ [for Athanasius] is a physical [i.e. verbally acknowledged], but not a theological factor.'[7]

The human soul was very much a theological factor for our author, especially during his early years. It is therefore important to assess first what the human soul meant for Theodoret anthropologically in order to understand his relevant Christological concerns.

The human *psychē* is not just a life-giving source, but rather the intellectual governor of the entire human being and a substantial component of what our author calls 'human nature'. This soul is 'the imitator of the Creator', since it was for the mind's sake that the visible world was created, 'because God does not need these [things]' (PG 75, 1445CD). Thus, Christ indeed 'renewed the whole worn out [human] nature', not leaving aside the mind, which is its most valuable part: '[The mind] is the charioteer [*hēniochos*], the governor and musician of the body, by which human nature is not irrational, but full of wisdom, art and skill' (PG 75, 1448A). The term *hēniochos* is a clear allusion to the famous comparison of a human soul to a chariot with two horses and a charioteer in Plato's *Phaedrus*.[8] This image returns in the *Prologue* of *HR*, when Theodoret praises the monks for their spiritual strength by which they restrain their bodies with the charioteer mind.[9] In Theodoret's *Sixth Discourse On Divine Providence* we also read:

> For when the intellect was and is possessed of sound and perfect wisdom, the passions abate, recede, subside, and their flame is destroyed, whilst the charioteer mind drives the horses in good order. This good discipline of the passions and the soundness of the charioteer we call temperance.[10]

The charioteer soul's God-given attributes make her worthy of being saved, since even the incarnation happened for the mind's sake.[11] Moreover, sin, which in Theodoret's view is the voluntary act of the rational soul against God's explicit will or command, is a direct result of the soul being first deceived and then misleading the body:

> The entire human being was beguiled and entered totally under sin, yet the mind had accepted the deceit before the body, because the prior contribution of the mind sketches out the sin, and thus by its action [i.e. of the mind] the body gives shape to it [i.e. to sin].
>
> (PG 75, 1445C)

The emphasis upon the soul's moral responsibility is both pastoral and soteriological. With the insistence that 'human nature [. . .] drew upon itself servitude voluntarily' (PG 75, 1437B), the author prepares the soteriological ground for the restoration of the human soul's initial dignity by Christ 'accepting the sufferings of salvation voluntarily' (*De incarnatione*, title of Ch. 26).

Theodoret's anthropology is clearly bipartite. Nevertheless, he has a clear insight into the Apollinarian tripartite anthropology and does not condemn the former Bishop of Laodicea merely on the basis of misunderstanding. In Ch. 9 of *De incarnatione* he points to the common root of Arianism and Apollinarianism:

> Some of those who think the opposite of piety try to attack the doctrine of truth with apostolic words. On the one hand, Arius and Eunomius strongly maintain that the Word of God assumed a soulless [*apsychon*] man. On the other hand, Apollinaris [claims that there was] a soul [in the man] [*empsychon*], but that it was deprived of mind [*nous*] (I do not know what he meant by human soul).
>
> (PG 75, 1428A)

Our author touches here upon a crucial point: the otherwise conflicting Arian and Apollinarian systems have a common model of Christ: the *Logos–sarx* framework.[12] Thus, the common fault of Arianism and Apollinarianism lies in the assumed *apsychos anthrōpos*, i.e. 'soulless man'. Theodoret makes the necessary distinction between the two systems by admitting that Apollinaris accepted the assumption of *psychē*, but not of *nous*. Nevertheless, this does not modify the basic picture. As he says: 'I do not know what he [Apollinaris] meant by the human soul [*anthrōpeia psychē*]'. Of course he does, since he knows that the most Apollinaris could mean was 'source of life', i.e. something which by its mere presence ensures that the body is alive. He certainly did not assign any spiritual functions to the *psychē*, since the governing role belonged to the nous, the third component of Apollinaris' anthropology which the heresiarch denied to Christ. Theodoret considers the soul as being a *psychē logikē*, i.e. both a life-giving and governing mind, and this latter function of the rational soul is what he is concerned with. His works show that he has understood the Apollinarian tripartite anthropology and that he finds it faulty. This is demonstrated by his recurrent formula: 'He [Christ] took a besouled [*empsychon*] and rational [*logikēn*] flesh' (PG 75, 1433A–B).

For Apollinaris the *sarx* and the life-giving *psychē* form human nature. The *nous*, when added to these two, brings about a human person in his system, which he cannot allow to be assumed in order to safeguard the personal unity of the incarnate Word. This is where the famous Apollinarian formula (which Cyril attributed erroneously to Athanasius) of 'one nature, one hypostasis, one inner operation ["inworking"], one person' of the incarnate Word emerges from.[13] In Theodoret's bipartite anthropology the full human nature involves two elements, which in the Apollinarian structure means three. The Bishop of Cyrus knew that his anthropology was biblical as opposed to that of Apollinaris, since he wrote in *Letter* 146 at the beginning of 451:

> Apollinaris asserted indeed that he [the Word] assumed a soul
> with the body, yet not the reasonable one, but the soul which
> is called vivifying or animal. For, he says, the Godhead fulfilled
> the function of the mind. Hence, he learned [about] the
> distinction of soul and of mind from the outsider [i.e. secular]
> philosophers. The divine Scripture says that man consists of
> soul and body. For it says [quoting Gen. 2:7]. And the Lord
> in the holy Gospels said to his apostles [quoting Matt. 10:28].
>
> (SC 111, 182)

It is evident that the biblical verse 'man became a living soul/being' means for our author that man also became a rational being. Indeed, for Theodoret, who argues from a biblical perspective, the human body and rational soul together form a complete human essence or nature. He does not share Apollinaris' concern that this union would constitute a human person already. If the Bible does not distinguish between soul and mind, the theologian is not allowed to do so either. Thus, the main motive behind Theodoret's emphasis upon the assumption of a rational soul is not merely his eagerness to maintain the Word's divine impassibility but to validate Scripture's teaching about the human being exegetically.

Apart from anthropological reasons, the clear soteriological and forensic argument concerning the assumption of a rational soul by Christ is that the same nature has to pay the price for the one that trespassed. The whole analysis of the temptation of Christ, which is the soteriological heartland of the young Theodoret, is based on this idea.[14]

Thus, the assumption of a rational soul is a sine qua non of Theodoret's Christology. The Saviour has to be made equal *in all* to us, sin excepted. His birth, baptism, temptation, passion, death and even the resurrection are presented in the light of this consideration. Further, it is a widely shared scholarly opinion that the Antiochenes had laid strong emphasis upon the unimpaired properties of the two natures within Christ. Theodoret inherited this from Diodore and Theodore. So, in his Christology one can expect and find a consistent emphasis upon the 'retained properties'. The fundamental point here is that the union of the manhood with the Word involves an utterly unique relationship between a created and an uncreated reality.

Theodoret's explanation concerning 'the form of God' and 'the form of the servant' (based on Phil. 2:5–7) in his anti-Arian and anti-Apollinarian polemic is also noteworthy, since he knew that the crossing point of Apollinaris' and Arius' theology was that while Arius united the lessened Godhead with the diminished manhood, Apollinaris united the full Godhead with the diminished manhood, thus both of them impaired at least one of the two Pauline 'forms'.[15] Theodoret's occasional practice, to render the Saviour's human nature in concrete terms (a practice which gradually disappears from his works after Ephesus), could partly be interpreted as a reaction to this incomplete human model of Christ. The preservation of both natures' properties involves his insistence that before, during and after the incarnation neither nature was subject to change. Notably, he raises this point both against Arius and Apollinaris: 'Apollinaris, together with Arius and Eunomius can learn again, that the unchangeable God-Word was not changed into the nature of the flesh, but by assuming our essence, he achieved our salvation' (PG 75, 1432A).

The language of these passages often depends on the author's viewpoint. When regarding the Person of Christ and his work, he sees the union (looking, as it were, at the whole picture from outside), whereas when entering the details and the internal 'hows' of one particular issue involving the participation of both natures on different levels (e.g. ontological or attributive), he is more likely to spot the natures' specific properties. While no alteration of the Word is admitted, the assumed human nature undergoes a positive change after resurrection. Theodoret puts the following words into the mouth of the resurrected Ruler Christ:

> In this way, he says, the nature assumed from you has obtained resurrection by the indwelling of and union with the Godhead, having put off the corruptible together with the passions, entered into incorruptibility and immortality. In the same way you also shall be released from the burden of the slavery

of death, and having cast off corruption together with the
passions, you shall put on impassibility.

(PG 75, 1468D)

I shall return to the expressions 'indwelling' and 'union' in Chapter 6.
Nevertheless, the change of the human nature is quite interesting: it
entered into incorruptibility and immortality to prefigure our glorious
redemption. Christ donates to his redeemed people something that,
since the expulsion from Eden, was characteristic of the Godhead only,
placing humankind back in its pre-fallen condition. This is not at all
alien from the Athanasian idea of God becoming human to make us
divine. While the Word's immutability has to be upheld, the change
of our nature after redemption is required in order for us to enter God's
kingdom. Thus, the divine quality of being exempt from passions,
which is the primary meaning of *apatheia* for Theodoret, is passed onto
the human nature – this is perhaps one of the very few occasions when
Theodoret can be said to profess a kind of *communicatio idiomatum*. The
admonition at the end of Ch. 36 [34] of *De incarnatione* refers again to
this received quality: 'We shall be taught [to perceive] perfection, when
we shall not be harmed by false pretension, nor fall into boasting, but
shall live free from passions.'[16]

The other sign of an attempt to ascribe the actions of the manhood
to the Word, on account of the union, is to be found in Theodoret's
usage of the term 'appropriation' (*oikeiōsis*) as it appears for example at
the beginning of Chapter 32 [30] of *De incarnatione*:

> Thus the God-Word appropriates [*oikeioutai*] the wretched-
> ness of the form of the servant and [although] being God, he
> wants to be called man. And as he shared [*metelabe*] in the
> humility of the man, in the same fashion he confers on him
> exaltation.

Communicatio idiomatum or *communicatio onomaton?*

On the whole, the Bishop of Cyrus can hardly be shown to admit a
clear *communicatio idiomatum* between the two natures of Christ. The one
I have mentioned above refers to the manhood receiving impassibility
after redemption and is thus not directly related to this idea, which
is usually applied to the actions of Christ before his resurrection.
Similarly, the use of *oikeiōsis* is not frequent enough to be invoked
as conclusive evidence supporting this claim. Clayton did not find

any indication of *communicatio idiomatum* in Theodoret's oeuvre and recognises this as a main defect of his Christology. His argument is that the Bishop of Cyrus merely taught a *communicatio onomaton*, i.e. a communication of names and titles which were applied to the common *prosōpon* or 'outward countenance' of Christ instead of a real union.[17] This is what we also find in the above example, where Theodoret connects the idea of 'appropriation' with that of 'naming', as he says, '[the Word] being God, wants to be *called* man'. Before addressing the issue of 'naming' in Theodoret's oeuvre it is important to determine the validity of the idea concerning the 'communication of properties' or *communicatio idiomatum* in Theodoret's own time.

In assessing Theodoret's Christological ideas – or in fact anyone else's – two aspects ought to be considered: first, to understand him within his own tradition; further, to measure him against the recognised theological standards of his own time. The former is important to assess whether he remained faithful to the legacy he inherited, or to what extent he broke away from it. The latter is necessary to avoid making anachronistic charges.

Concerning Theodoret's relation to his own theological heritage we can say that he is very much inside the tradition which professed the unmingled preservation of the properties of both natures. For example, in his explanation of John 2:19, Amphilochius of Iconium had already taught that 'in him [i.e. in Christ] the unconfused properties of the different natures are preserved'.[18] To comply with the second point we need to investigate the valid standards which would give us an idea concerning the generally accepted contemporary attitude towards *communicatio idiomatum*. The most obvious one is the *Chalcedonense* itself, which apart from the famous four adverbs already quoted, clearly asserts: 'The difference [*diaphora*] of the natures was by no means removed through the union [*henōsis*], but rather the property [*idiotēs*] of each nature was preserved' (ACO II, 1, 2, p. 129, lines 31–3).[19] Although the grammatical structure and the recurring 'One and the same' in the *Chalcedonense* may indicate the use of an early form of 'communication of properties', this is rather the safeguarding of the unity of the Person (which neither side disputed) and not a starting point for claiming the validity of *communicatio idiomatum* – as we have it e.g. in John of Damascus and Thomas Aquinas – as a recognised standard in 451. What the *Chalcedonense* primarily claims is that 'the One and the same' is the subject of all actions, but without the slightest impairment to the properties of either nature. The words 'by no means' [*oudamou*] and 'rather' [*mallon*] in the above passage – together with the four adverbs – clearly express this emphasis. Thus, the union does not remove the differences of the natures at all (or 'by no means') but *rather* the property of each is preserved. The other universally acknowledged contemporary source – validated by the same council – is Leo's *Tome*, in the third part of which we find the following:

> Accordingly *while the properties of each nature and substance were preserved*,[20] and both met in one Person, lowliness was assumed by majesty, weakness by power, mortality by eternity. [. . .] The same one, who, remaining in the form of God, made man, was made man in the form of a servant. For *each of the natures retains its property without defect*; and as the form of God does not take away the form of the servant, so the form of the servant does not impair the form of God.
>
> (ACO II, 2, 1, p. 27 – my italics)

The limits of the present work do not permit a deeper investigation of the matter, yet the evidence is unambiguous. In the first half of the fifth century and even in 451 both Theodoret's theological heritage and the ecumenically accepted standards of faith pronounced themselves clearly against any idea which later became known as *communicatio idiomatum*.[21] Further, apart from the impressive elaboration of this doctrine by John of Damascus and by Thomas Aquinas, no ecumenical or regional church council has ever included this teaching among the elements of *fides recta* (i.e. 'the right faith'). Thus, it is fair to say that a charge brought against any theologian of the Ephesian–Chalcedonian period concerning their failure to apply this doctrine in their Christology is anachronistic. The profession of such teaching in those years would most certainly have raised the suspicion of a mingling or confusing of the natures.[22] Later theological development did indeed accept *communicatio idiomatum* (although its application differs quite notably even in the sixteenth century),[23] but the reading back of its sophisticated arguments into this early period is unacceptable.

As to the charge that Theodoret professes a *communicatio onomaton*, i.e. a communication of names and appellations (*onoma* = name), we can say that the 'name' and 'naming' are certainly not of secondary importance to our author. A name is not a mere epithet: it is ontologically proper to its bearer and thus becomes a theological statement whenever it is applied, especially if the appellation derives from Scripture. As Theodoret often puts it, the name usually 'teaches' us something. It would perhaps be useful to review a few representative occurrences of 'naming' from *De Trinitate* with a little paraphrase:

Ch. 4 (concerning God the Father): 'Neither had he [i.e. the Father] been a Son first, and then [became] a Father, according to the corporeal sequence, but since ever he is – yet he is eternally – Father he both is and is called' (PG 75, 1152A). – If he is called so, he is Father indeed.

Ch. 6: '[the apostles] nowhere called [in Scripture] the honourable Child of God a creature' (PG 75, 1153B). – If they did not call him a creature, he is not a creature.

Ch. 11: 'That is why [Scripture] uses these names [of Father and Son] so that from them we would learn the sameness [of their possessors' nature]' (PG 75, 1161C). – The names themselves teach us the sameness.

Ch. 24: 'If those who received the grace of the Spirit in a greater or smaller measure are indeed called temples of God, from this appellation we shall conclude that [the Holy Spirit] is akin [to the Father and the Son]' (PG 75, 1181D). – This is one of the most eloquent examples showing the extent of the ontological relevance of biblical appellations.

These examples already give an impression of Theodoret's biblical rationale: if Scripture uses a specific name to denote a person, this ought to be taken as being appropriate in an ontological sense also. 'Naming' is present throughout Theodoret's oeuvre, and not only concerning Jesus Christ. The variety of verbs used to express 'naming' is noteworthy: *apokaleō* (= to call, invoke), *didaskō* (= to teach), *kaleō* (= to call), *legō* (= to say, assert), *onomazō* (= to name), *prosagoreuō* (= to label), *chrematizō* (= to title). In Ch. 20 of *De incarnatione* we read:

> If the child of the Virgin received this appellation [i.e. Emmanuel], it is clear that he was God and man simultaneously, being one and having taken on the other, perfect in each respect. By the [expression] 'with us' the perfection of the man is shown, because each of us possesses the human nature perfectly. Yet by 'God', with the addition of the article, the Son's Godhead is acknowledged.
>
> (PG 75, 1453C)

Thus, the biblical appellation 'Emmanuel' is an ontological proof in itself that Jesus Christ is truly human and divine, perfect in both respects. As Theodoret argues, Paul proclaims the unity of the *prosōpon*, 'that is why he names Jesus Christ both man and God'.[24] In fact, the very juxtaposition of *theotokos* and *anthrōpotokos* in the last chapter of *De incarnatione*, from which Theodoret will withdraw soon after Ephesus, does not express anything other than this simultaneous recognition of the double coessentiality of the same Christ:

> Therefore [. . .] nobody should be lame [in faith] about the *oikonomia*, but should confess the Christ born of Mary as God and man, perfect in both respects. That is why the holy Virgin is labelled both God-bearer and man-bearer by the teachers of piety,[25] the latter because she bore [someone] similar to her by nature, the former, inasmuch as the form of the servant has the form of God united [to it].

> (PG 75, 1477A)

This arguably justifiable juxtaposition was indeed not germane to Theodoret's thinking. After signing the *Formula of Reunion* (which did not contain *anthrōpotokos* in its original form of September 431 either) and realising the extent to which it was discredited because of being attached to Nestorius' name, the Bishop of Cyrus simply does not use it at all, defending this abandonment of it in his *Letter 16 to Irenaeus*. Cyril refused to compromise, excluding any orthodox interpretation of this conjunction.[26]

The manner of understanding the biblical titles of Christ as ontologically proper to him from a primarily eschatological viewpoint can be observed concerning the names 'Jesus' and 'Christ':

> Truly the names 'Jesus' and 'Christ' are significant of the *oikonomia*. Yet the *oikonomia* happened neither before the creation, nor immediately after the creation, but in the last days. Therefore the name 'Christ' indicates not only the assumed one, but also the assuming Word together with the assumed (for it is significant for both God and the man). Paul attributes the creation and arrangement of all also to the visible [i.e. to human nature], because of the union with that which was hidden [i.e. the Godhead]. That is why elsewhere he calls the Christ 'God above all' also, saying 'and of them [i.e. the patriarchs], according to the flesh, is Christ, who is God above all' (Rom. 9:5). Not because the descendant of David is God by himself and God above all, but because he was the temple [*naos*] of God who is over all, having the divinity united and conjoined with himself.

> (PG 75, 1472AB)

Apart from the *naos* (temple), a typically Antiochene technical term denoting the assumed human nature, we can observe how, in Theodoret's mind, our view of the *oikonomia* has an undeniable eschatological dimension which primarily enables us to comprehend the appellations applied to the Person of Christ in an ontological sense. The fact that the name 'Christ' indicates both the assuming and the assumed nature raises the question of whether the author interprets it merely as being an ornamental epithet, i.e. as a title of the common *prosōpon* to which everything can be ascribed as to a more or less third entity (*tertium quid*). The above text helps us to clarify two relevant points: first, that whatever name or title is given to the incarnate Christ, it becomes proper to him ontologically based on the authority of Scripture. Christ is not a *tertium quid*, since Paul attributes the creation also to 'the visible' manhood and not only to the 'hidden' Godhead. The second observation is that for the sake of preserving the unconfused union, the author distinguishes between the application of biblical titles and the natures' properties respectively. It may be said that the names are valid ontologically, whereas the properties are ascribed to the natures attributively, i.e. on the account of the union. Therefore there is a *communicatio onomaton* indeed, but this derives from the biblical narrative and is applied with ontological authority within the eschatological standpoint. The *communicatio idiomatum* is missing, yet that – at least for our author and for the recognised theological standards of his time – would mean the acceptance of a degree of confusion between the natures. This is why Christ is indeed God above all according to Paul's words, yet not because his humanity as the seed of David is divine by itself. The above passage is meant chiefly to exclude such mingling – as a result, it carries the risk of being open to subsequent negative interpretation.

The fact that the manhood in the above text is called 'man' draws attention to a peculiar way in which Theodoret conceives the incarnation. The humanity is sometimes addressed in concrete terms in Theodoret's early works, especially in *De incarnatione*, but exclusively so after its union with the Word. The reason for this can again be found in the title 'Christ', which indicates both natures and returns in Ch. 34 [32]: 'For the one conjoined with the other is named Christ, whereas the bare form of the servant unclothed of the Godhead was never called so by the teachers of piety' (PG 75, 1472D). Apart from the obvious Arian danger of calling Christ a mere man Theodoret here tries to avoid another idea, namely that the humanity might be regarded as being worthy in itself of the name 'Christ'. If the name 'Christ' is denied to the bare form of the servant, it is because the human nature does not deserve this appellation by itself ontologically. Thus, the relevance of ontological 'naming' is expressed again. The humanity is raised to a 'personal' status only after its union with the Word and is addressed in concrete terms accordingly (i.e. exclusively after the union), although the mature Theodoret will gradually abandon this practice also. The suspicion that the names 'Jesus' and 'Christ' are mere titles of the shared outward *prosōpon* or countenance (thus denoting a *tertium quid* resulting from the union of God and man) is contradicted by Theodoret's *Letter 147 to John the oeconomus* written in early 451:

> Our Lord Jesus Christ is not a different person [*prosōpon*] from the Son who completes the Trinity. For the same one before the ages was Only-begotten Son and God-Word, and after the resurrection he was called Jesus and Christ, receiving the names from the facts. Jesus means Saviour: 'you shall call his name Jesus for he shall save his people from their sins' (Matt. 1:21). He is also named Christ as being anointed with the All-holy Spirit according to the humanity, and called our high priest, apostle, prophet and king [. . .] Let nobody then senselessly suppose that the Christ is any other than the Only-begotten Son.
>
> (SC 111, 206–7)

This is perhaps one of the clearest explanations of Theodoret's onto-logical *communicatio onomaton*. The Word is called 'Jesus' and 'Christ' after the incarnation, being anointed according to the humanity by the Spirit and taking on his triple office for our sake: high priest, apostle and prophet, as well as king. The use of the name 'Christ' by Theodoret may sound suspicious, yet our author firmly states that 'the Christ is none other than the Only-begotten Son of God' (SC 111, 202). Of course, his Christological standard remains as it were a *finitum non capax infiniti* (= the finite cannot contain the infinite). His consistency can be seen at the beginning of Ch. 25 [24] of *De incarnatione* also:

> Thus was the Ruler Christ born [. . .] (for after the birth it would not be correct to call him only God-Word or man unclothed of Godhead, but Christ, which indicates both the assuming and the assumed natures).
>
> (PG 75, 1461B)

The main reason for applying the biblical titles to Jesus Christ, therefore, is to keep the integrity of both natures within the union. The eschatological–ontological communication of names may not have been the ultimate solution to the problem, yet it was the farthest an Antiochene theologian could go towards a real union in Christ in the fifth century. Since the communication of properties was not a valid standard in Theodoret's heritage and time, it was not a viable option for him either. Whether this resulted in too loose a connection between the two natures or not is the next subject of our investigation.

The subject of predication

This section is dedicated to a brief presentation of one representative passage of *De incarnatione*, where the author arguably introduces 'a second subject' of predication within the Person of Christ, or at least ascribes important words and deeds within salvation history to the manhood. This is one of the most controversial aspects of Theodoret's early Christology, the more so since his generally constant attitude seems to have undergone a change in its mode of expression after Ephesus. It relates, particularly, to the concrete designations for the human nature which fade out during the years of theological maturation. Nevertheless, since these concrete appellations play an important role in the soteriology and Christology of the young Theodoret, I shall try to give them an equitable place within the analysis.[27]

It is important to note that whilst we have some standards to measure Christological orthodoxy, we do not possess any concerning soteriological orthodoxy. A different soteriological scheme, however, leads to different questions and answers, shaping one's Christology accordingly. For example the two assertions: 'only God can save fallen humankind' and 'the same nature has to show obedience and undergo the punishment which trespassed' are equally acceptable, yet if both were taken as valid soteriological starting points they would almost certainly result in Christological differences.[28]

We must now turn to the conclusion of the Temptation-story in *De incarnatione*. The Pauline analogy of the first and second Adam is crucial for Theodoret's interpretation of Christ's suffering, temptation and obedience. As he argues, the Word 'permits hunger to occur', and Christ 'hides' his divinity upon hearing Satan speak, moments which confirm the Word's presence (Ch. 13). Nevertheless, it is important from the viewpoint of God's justice that humanity must once again be given the same chance as in Eden to say freely 'no' to the devil. This is undoubtedly a very subtle, and peculiarly Antiochene point, emerging from the synoptic narrative itself. This was the case for Theodoret's masters as well. As Anastos observes:

> Theodore [of Mopsuestia] wished to emphasise the perfect humanity of Christ. He was careful to insist that Christ was without blemish, but he deemed it essential for the salvation of mankind that Christ should have been free to choose evil and to sin had he wished to do so.[29]

This is exactly the point to which Alexandria would not go: Christ cannot even be supposed to have had the possibility to choose otherwise than he did. This is Theodoret's way of understanding it too – and it is why he underlines so diligently Christ's complete sinlessness – but he wants to avoid another difficulty, namely that Christ did not play a divine game upon earth, that he had a truly free, sinless human will and that his temptation and sufferings were completely real and human, otherwise the whole salvation of humankind is in jeopardy, since God cannot be tempted. This is in fact the argument of the devil's shockingly dramatic discourse in Chapter 16 [15] of *De incarnatione*:

> Because if the God-Word replaced the mind in that which was assumed, even the devil could find some justified excuses, and reasonably might say: 'Ruler and Creator of the universe, I did not begin the fight against you, because I know your dignity, I am aware of [your] might, and recognise [your] dominion. I acknowledge my servitude even suffering from apostasy [i.e. despite being an apostate]. I yield victory even to the angels and to all the heavenly hosts, [although] once I, the miserable one, was also one of them. Nevertheless, I started the fight against this one, whom you formed out of clay, created after your image, honoured with reason, made the citizen of paradise and presented [as] the ruler of earth and sea. This one I have defeated by using deceit, not force. Until today I am still the one who defeats [him], prostrates [him] and sends [him] to death. Bring this one to the arena and command him to fight with me, be the spectator and judge of the combat yourself! Even be his trainer if you want, teach him to fight, show him the grips of victory [*or* the holds of success], anoint him as you wish, just do not fight with the wrestler [i.e. on his side]. I am not so audacious and mindless as to attempt fighting against you, the Creator.' The devil

could have justly said this to the Saviour Christ, if he were not
man [indeed], but [only] God, fighting in place of man.

(PG 75, 1444)

This is one of the most famous and most disputed passages of
Theodoret's oeuvre, which has inspired a longstanding suspicion
concerning its author's orthodoxy, starting from his own day until
recent scholarship. It was quoted and criticised by Marius Mercator.
Jean Garnier included it in his edition of Theodoret (see PG 84,
81C–84B), whilst considering the author a Nestorian. Two renowned
modern scholars, H. M. Diepen and Jean Daniélou, have crossed swords
over this selfsame passage. Paul Parvis and Paul B. Clayton[30] commented on it in their doctoral theses. Thus, before proceeding with its
analysis, I shall try to summarise at least the main lines represented by
modern scholarship.

Diepen seems to follow Mercator's and Garnier's judgement, severely
condemning Theodoret for his 'two-subject Christology' and for dissolving Christ's hypostatic union. Clayton shares this opinion and does
not see any evolution within Theodoret's Christology until the end of
his life, and depicts him as an inconvertible crypto-Nestorian. Marcel
Richard, Jean Daniélou, Marijan Mandac and Günter Koch represent
the view that Theodoret's exposé can be interpreted in an orthodox
manner, despite its dramatic internal tensions. Koch emphasises the
one subject, whilst admitting the prominence of the human nature.[31]
In opposition to Diepen, Jean Daniélou argues that both Theodoret and
Cyril were orthodox, yet both of them used certain formulae which
later appeared to be insufficient.[32]

It is almost impossible to reconcile the various views. Thus, instead
of reiterating scholarly arguments, I would prefer to admit that on
certain issues one has to accept disagreement and still assess individual
contribution positively. The approaches of Diepen and Daniélou are
still relevant in their descriptions of the fundamental differences
between the two positions. Daniélou defends Theodoret's orthodoxy
precisely on the basis of this rather difficult paragraph, and shows how
it can be interpreted in an orthodox sense.

Let us return to this passage in order to define the subject to whom
all actions of Christ are ascribed, i.e. the subject of predication. The text
is obviously aimed at the Arian–Apollinarian model, yet another aspect
must be observed: the soteriological starting point is decisive, i.e.
the 'why' precedes the 'how'. The same nature which disobeyed God's
command has to show obedience. As the devil says, he defeated God's
creature and not God himself – by deceit and not by force. In the battle

he wants to face human resistance and not divine might. For some theologians it may not be a question of theodicy for God to deceive Satan – it is for Theodoret, who diligently evinces that God treated even sin with righteousness, removing its power (literally: 'throwing it out of power') only after proving its injustice.[33] What the devil offers God here is nothing else than a bargain: he is ready to accept God's power over everything if God were to acknowledge his [i.e. Satan's] unchallenged rule over fallen humankind. Of course, this would mean the handing over of God's most precious creation to the devil. This is by no means possible for the Creator who loves his creation. Nevertheless, he also loves his justice. In order not to play off God's love for humankind (which would dictate a divine crushing of the devil)[34] against his impeccable justice (which demands the just punishment of the disobedient human nature), Theodoret sees no other way than to bring the manhood of Christ – referred to here in concrete terms as 'the wrestler' – into the battlefield to terminate the dominion of the Evil One over the whole of fallen mankind. The Word's impassibility is not the primary concern in this case.

Thus, God – who is righteous even towards Satan – accepts the challenge. The obedience is shown by the manhood of Christ, permitted by the Word to feel hunger and to be tempted. Theodoret's ominous sentence – 'just do not fight with the wrestler' – is thus the very cornerstone of this argument in his attempt to find an equitable balance between God's justice, his almighty power and his ineffable philanthropy. Does this result in a necessary division of the one subject of predication within his Christological model? If the manhood were abandoned by the Word for the time of the fight, yes. But as far as Theodoret's soteriology is concerned, in his mind there is a substantial difference between the Word 'not fighting' together with the wrestler and 'abandoning' human nature altogether. The Word has clearly not abandoned the assumed perfect human nature, since the union is indivisible, but has rather permitted the rational soul to make a choice, in the name of, and for the redemption of, all mankind, so the devil may learn that his rule over the human race has ended. In fact, the choice was the same as if it were taken by the divine Word, showing that the perfect human nature – as God's restored image – can be in accordance with God's will.

The answer to the above question, however, may still depend on whether one considers 'the Saviour Christ' in the quoted passage as the single subject of predication, to whom the work of deliverance is ultimately ascribed on account of a real union (the properties of each nature being preserved), or whether one regards the title 'the Saviour

Christ' as a mere epithet for the commonly shared *prosōpon* or 'outward countenance' of both natures. Bearing in mind the ontological importance of 'naming' outlined above, it is my understanding that our author may be credited with the first option. Nevertheless, I also admit that the opposite view has its own quite justified Christological arguments, although they are based on a similarly valid but different soteriological premise. The concluding passage shows our author's main concern:

> If there was no human mind [*nous anthrōpinos*] in him, God replacing the mind and taking over the work of the mind, then God hungered with the body, God thirsted, suffered, slept, grieved, was afraid and endured all the other human torments also. Yet if God had fought and won, then I have been deprived of victory, [because] God fulfilled all right-eousness, since the God-Word would not have received it [i.e. the mind], as the followers of the claptrap of Apollinaris are upholding, on the grounds that it was impossible to fulfil the laws of righteousness with a human mind.
>
> (PG 75, 1444C)

It is interesting that here the issue of divine impassibility (often imputed to Theodoret) has far less weight than God's justice. The ultimate question is 'my participation' in the victory of Christ. Since for Theodoret the common link between Christ and us is his human nature, his victory over the devil can be ascribed to us only if it had been carried out by his human obedience. Thus, the triumph of Christ's manhood over Satan is simultaneously ascribed to the Word on account of the union without confusion, and to us on account of the same (human) nature. I think this is the most plausible explanation of Theodoret's theological arguments, yet it does not necessarily mean that all the obscure or defective points of his system can or should be explained away.

In relation to the concrete terms which Theodoret occasionally applies to the assumed man or manhood in his early works, we ought to remember that this practice was by no means an exclusively Antiochene peculiarity. As M. Richard has shown, even the Monophysite bishop Severus of Antioch, who harshly condemned Theodoret's Christology, had to admit that concrete designations for the human nature of Christ were not merely tolerated but also applied by venerable theologians like Athanasius, Basil and even Cyril until after the Council of Ephesus.[35] Most of the concrete designations for the assumed perfect

49

manhood are biblical terms turned into technical ones, like 'the form of the servant', 'the temple', 'the seed of David' etc.[36]

The union of worship – the 'cultic *prosōpon*'

Theodoret defends a real union (*henōsis*) without any confusion or diminishing of either nature. The restored title of Ch. 22 [21] of *De incarnatione*[37] contains three important expressions: 'distinction' [*diakrisis*], as opposed to 'division' or separation, 'union' [*henōsis*], as opposed to 'confusion' and 'person' [*prosōpon*] as opposed to 'persons' [*prosōpa*]. The title 'Demonstrating the distinction of natures and the unity of the Person from the Epistle to the Hebrews' is meant to serve this purpose. As our author writes, 'It can be seen more clearly from the Epistle to the Hebrews, that the divine nature and the human are different one from another according to their operations, but are united in the person and indicate the one Son' (PG 75, 1456A). The dissimilarity between 'different' and 'united' underlies this idea of unmingled union: although the operations are different, the 'being together', i.e. 'the union' is real, since it happens on the level of the one *prosōpon*. The author repeatedly uses 'one Son' to contradict a virtual union. While expressing his views on this *henōsis*, Theodoret comes to assert the single worship of the one Son:

> But how can God, denominated with the article [i.e. *ho Theos*], whose throne stands forever and ever, be anointed by God? How could he receive a kingdom by ordination, when he [already] owns the kingdom by nature? [. . .] So then again we shall understand, that whose throne is for ever and ever is God, the eternal one, whereas the latter being later anointed for his hatred towards sin and his love for righteousness is that which was taken on from us [i.e. the manhood],[38] which is of David and of Abraham, which has fellows and exceeds them by anointment, possessing in itself all the gifts of the All-holy Spirit. Let us worship the one Son in either nature.
>
> (PG 75, 1456CD)

The last sentences of the passage are not easily translated into English in order to reflect Theodoret's formulation accurately. The author speaks of the manhood assumed from David and Abraham as 'what', granting it the title of 'person', i.e. of 'who', only from the moment of its union with the Word. The pre-existence of a separate human person as opposed to the person of the Word *preceding* the union does not possess any support within the entire oeuvre of the Bishop of Cyrus, although Theodoret refers to the assumed manhood in concrete terms *after* the union has been effected. As he himself will assert in Ch. 34 [32] of the same work, 'We both recognise the nature of the God-Word and acknowledge the essence of the form of the servant; nevertheless, we worship either nature as one Son' (PG 75, 1472D).

The duality of persons is in both cases refuted by the unity of worship. This is what, during our private consultations, Prof. L. Abramowski came to label as the Antiochene 'liturgical' or 'cultic' *prosōpon*, or even 'the one worship of the one *prosōpon*', emphasising that the confession of a true personal union is valid if supported by a union of worship, since the liturgical act is one of the most fundamental and least changing features of any ecclesiastical tradition. To this we may add that in both aforementioned cases Theodoret speaks of a worship belonging to both natures as to 'the one Son', admitting, as it were, the Word's prevalence within the one veneration. Theodoret is in substantial agreement with Cyril's eighth anathema, despite his counter-statement (which is rather concerned to speak of the same one while preserving the properties of each nature).[39] Moreover, Theodoret already recognised the Son, i.e. the divine Word and the Son of Man as being 'one and the same' [*heis kai ho autos*] after the union, without division [*chōrismos*] in his early years, as he himself wrote in Ch. 12 of the *Expositio*.[40]

The importance of Theodoret's 'union of worship' of the one *prosōpon* cannot be ignored, the more so since the idea is present in four of his replies to Cyril's anathemas. The first three occurrences are noteworthy because they appear before the reply to the eighth anathema, which is the only one related specifically to the question of worship.[41] While interpreting Cyril's 'hypostatic union' in *Anathema* 2, Theodoret concludes:

> Therefore, the union according to hypostasis, which in my opinion is put before us instead of mixture, is superfluous. It is sufficient to talk about the union, which both shows the properties of the natures and teaches us to worship the one Christ.
>
> (ACO I, 1, 6, p. 115)

The emphasis upon this 'union of worship' due to the one Christ is not an empty or negligible formula, but rather the counterpart of the equal worship given to the three *hypostases* of the Trinity.[42] As Theodoret asserts at the end of Ch. 8 of *De Trinitate*, 'the Word [. . .] receives the same worship with the Father from the believers' (PG 75, 1157B).[43] This is Theodoret's way of showing that the Word 'is eternally with the Father' (PG 75, 1157B).[44] The union of worship expressing the unity within the Triad is articulated by a recurring use of the formula 'we, the worshippers of the Triad' in Chs 4 and 15 of *De Trinitate*.[45]

Similarly, the worship offered to Christ is not merely a liturgical, but also a Christological, issue. This is why Theodoret emphasises the 'union of worship' against that which he thinks involved a mixture in Cyril's fifth anathema. The Son is the Person and the manhood is the object: 'Therefore, whilst we apply the phrase "partaking" [*koinōnia*] we worship both him who took and that which was taken as one Son, nevertheless, we acknowledge the distinction [*diaphora*] of the natures' (ACO I, 1, 6, p. 126). This single worship of the one Son in both natures is one of the most decisive factors in Theodoret's mind to determine who is teaching 'two Sons'. The idea reappears in his other works and correspondence. In his little apology entitled *That even after the inhumanation our Lord Jesus Christ is one Son*, written in 448,[46] the entire defence of his orthodoxy is axed upon the recurrent idea of the union of worship combined with the perfection of natures, as well as with the ontological naming analysed above:

> Therefore we worship one Son, but we behold in him each nature in its perfection, both that which took, and that which was taken; both the one from God and the [other] from David. That is why he is named both Son of the living God and Son of David, each nature attracting its suitable appellation.
>
> (PG 83, 1436AB)

It is superfluous to repeat the issues already discussed. Nevertheless, a very representative occurrence in the same tract ought to be observed, since there the author connects his concept of Christological union with specific acts of worship:

> The slanderers who assert that we venerate two sons [are refuted by] the flagrant testimony of the facts. Since for all those who come to the all-holy Baptism we teach the faith laid forth at Nicaea. And when we celebrate the mystery of rebirth we baptise those who believe into the name of the Father, and of the Son, and of the Holy Spirit, pronouncing each name by itself. And when we perform divine service

regularly in the churches it is our custom to glorify the Father
and the Son and the Holy Spirit: not sons, but Son. If then we
proclaim two sons, which [of the two] is glorified by us and
which one remains without honour? For we have not quite
reached such a level of insanity as to assert two sons, yet not
to honour one of them with any respect. From this, therefore,
the slander becomes clear, since we worship one Only-
begotten Son, the God-Word made man.

(PG 83, 1437AB)[47]

Thus, the issue at stake for the Bishop of Cyrus concerning a true
confession of the one Christ as the single subject of ultimate attri-
butions is unambiguous single worship. He invokes this argument
repeatedly in his correspondence,[48] and in his commentaries,[49] often
bound together with the idea of the reality of both natures and the
communicatio onomaton we have presented above. This reasoning also
appears in the second dialogue of the *Eranistes*, when, upon being
reproached by the Beggar that he divides the Only-begotten Son into
two persons, Orthodoxos replies: 'On the one hand I both know [*oida*]
and worship [*proskynō*] one Son of God, the Lord Jesus Christ; on the
other hand, I have been taught the difference [*diaphora*] between
Godhead and manhood' (*Eranistes*, 135; NPNF III, 193).

The evidence gathered here at some length is conclusive. In Theodoret's understanding one's Christological orthodoxy is measurable
by the question 'whom do you worship?' Although the difference of
the natures cannot be ignored, this does not impair the unmingled
union [*asynchutos henōsis*] within the one *prosōpon*, who is One and the
same Son, the Word and Ruler Christ, and who should be worshipped
with a single veneration.

Interestingly, this approach was not an exclusive peculiarity of the
Bishop of Cyrus in the Ephesian–Chalcedonian period, but was used
by other theologians too, including Athanasius, who uses a recurrent
Alexandrian expression concerning the single worship 'of the Word
together with his own flesh',[50] and even Apollinaris, whose two famous
works, *On the incarnation of the God-Word* and *The detailed confession of
faith* (both held, and repeatedly quoted, by Cyril as coming from
Athanasius) lay strong emphasis upon the 'one worship' belonging to
the one Christ.[51] It appears that this issue was not of secondary importance for Alexandrian theologians, although Apollinaris introduces
a 'natural union' deriving from this union of worship, which the other
party – and the whole church indeed – did not approve, while still
clinging to the one veneration.

The aforementioned second work of Apollinaris is arguably one of the main sources of the eighth Cyrilline anathema and constitutes the very charge Theodoret continued to fight against. While recognising the difference [*to diaphoron*] between the natures (which Apollinaris did not admit of course, hence that is why he was heterodox), he simultaneously refused any *diaphoron* in the worship. We shall return to the Alexandrian party contemporary to Theodoret, yet before that let us take a glance at his own tradition. The idea of a single worship is very much present for example in Theodore of Mopsuestia's *Confession*,[52] and in John Chrysostom's treatise *On the Holy Trinity* (PG 48, 1096A). It is therefore fair to assume that in both traditions the single worship of the one Son incarnate was by no means of secondary importance regarding the Christological personal union.

Further, Theodoret's contemporaries, like Paul, Bishop of Emesa (in his homily uttered in Alexandria in Cyril's presence) also used this liturgical argument.[53] Cyril himself is one of its most vigorous defenders, the idea reappearing in his *Epistola dogmatica to Nestorius* and in his eighth anathema, notably bound in both cases to the union of the person:

> So we shall confess one Christ and Lord, yet not as worshipping a man together with [*symproskynountes*] the Word, in order to avoid any appearance of division by using the word 'together with' [*syn*]. But we worship him as one and the same [. . .] as one according to the union, together with his own flesh.[54]

Thus, a duality of subjects is refuted by the denial of a divided worship or a 'common worship'. We shall reflect upon Cyril's overall suspicion concerning the preposition '*syn*'[55] in Chapter 6. Nevertheless, it ought to be observed how much weight he lays upon the one worship as the proof of a true confession of the unity in Christ in his eighth anathema.[56]

As shown by the evidence, although he did not share Cyril's worries concerning the preposition '*syn*', Theodoret emphasised the 'one worship' as *proskynēsis* (= worship) rather than *symproskynēsis* (i.e. 'worshipping along with' or 'co-worshipping') as rejected by Cyril in Anathema 8. In his short reply to Cyril's statement Theodoret asserts that 'the doxology which we bring forth to the Ruler Christ is one', explaining that this does not remove the natures' properties, which in their turn do not impair the union.

Without lengthening the discussion any further,[57] I would like to refer to one of the most interesting examples concerning the avowal of a single worship bound together with the confession of both natures. This is the case of Basil of Seleucia, who according to the Acts of Chalcedon, asserted: 'I worship our one Lord Jesus Christ, the Only-begotten Son of God, the God-Word [who] after the incarnation [sarkōsis] and the inhumanation [enanthrōpēsis] is known in two natures [en duo physesin]' (ACO II, 1, 1, pp. 92–3). According to the minutes of the council a huge uproar followed this sentence from the side of the Egyptian and Eastern bishops, who repeatedly protested against 'the separation of the indivisible'. Although Basil defended the union, he did not shrink from speaking of the natures' properties and said: 'Anathema to the one who separates, anathema to the one who divides the natures after the union; yet anathema also to the one who does not recognise the properties of the natures' (ACO II, 1, 1, p. 93).

It was an almost impossible situation, since the Egyptians labelled the 'two natures' formula as Nestorian. I cannot follow the story further, since that would divert us from our theme, nevertheless, the fact that Basil's assertion, quoted above, ultimately became the key phrase of the Chalcedonense is taken positively by modern scholarship. According to Sellers, the famous 'in two natures' of the Definition may well have had its origin in Basil's earlier comment on the Formula of Reunion: 'We worship our one Lord Jesus Christ known in two natures [en duo physesin]' (ACO II, I, 1, p. 117).

André de Halleux, who is the author of probably the best analytic article so far on the Chalcedonense, also reaches the same substantial conclusion concerning the source of 'la formule basilienne'.[58] Basil had asserted this at the home synod in Constantinople in November 448; he was forced to retract it at the Latrocinium, only to revert to this statement again in Chalcedon.[59]

If one were to compare the above with Theodoret's assertion in De incarnatione, 21, the resemblance is obvious, especially concerning the union of worship: 'let us worship the one Son in both natures' (PG 75, 1456D). In fact he restated this in a similar fashion at Chalcedon, which, together with the anathema upon those teaching 'two sons' and the confession of worshipping the one Son also met the approval of the Eastern bishops. According to the minutes, 'Theodoret, the most reverent bishop said, "anathema to the one who asserts two sons; for we worship one Son, our Only-begotten Lord Jesus Christ"' (ACO II, 1, 1, p. 111).[60]

The alternative to this position was earlier asserted by Bishop Logginos and Presbyter John respectively in the following manner:

> After the inhumanation the one Godhead of the Only-begotten Son of God and our Saviour Jesus Christ is worshipped out of two natures [*ek duo physeōn*].
>
> (so Logginos in ACO II, 1, 1, p. 120)

> After the inhumanation of the God-Word, that is after the birth of our Lord Jesus Christ, one nature [*mia physis*] is to be worshipped as the nature of the incarnate God made man.
>
> (so John in ACO II, 1, 1, p. 124; cf. pp. 159 and 161)[61]

One ought to observe the manner of reference to 'worship' within these statements to see how important this liturgical point became in the Christological debates during and after the Nestorian controversy. If we compare these with Basil's recantation[62] at the *Latrocinium*, it becomes obvious that concerning the worship belonging to the one Son of God incarnate the issue at stake was whether this also determined the number of natures to be confessed after the union. As far as the testimony of the *Chalcedonense* goes, it was decided that the 'one worship' [*mia proskynesis*] – which remained totally unchallenged through the entire period – is not bound to the 'one nature' [*mia physis*] formula (as it appears in Apollinaris' and indeed in Cyril's writings), but belongs to the One Person (*prosōpon* and *hypostasis*) of Christ, recognised 'in two natures' after the union. On the basis of the available evidence we can conclude that Theodoret's early works (e.g. *De incarnatione*), as well as his later position expressed in his letters, commentaries and other writings were in substantial agreement with this ecumenical conclusion.

6

TERMINOLOGY

To provide an overall view of Theodoret's way of using various expressions, in this chapter I summarise the most important terminological issues. We begin with the four basic expressions concerning the notions of 'essence', 'nature' and 'person' (*ousia*, *physis*, *hypostasis* and *prosōpon*), then continue with the terms defining the union (*henōsis*, *synapheia*, *koinōnia*, *enoikēsis*), referring also to those that Theodoret considered inappropriate for the union (*synchusis* = mingling, *tropē* = change, *chrasis* = mixture, *metabolē* = alteration), as well as to the image of soul and body describing the *oikonomia*.

'Essence', 'nature' and 'person'

The terms *ousia* and *physis* are practically synonyms in Theodoret's Trinitarian and Christological vocabulary. The author uses both terms in his works in relation to the incarnation, yet the overall occurrence of *physis* is notably higher than that of *ousia*, which suggests Theodoret's intention to provide a solid ground for his 'two natures' Christology.[1] Although the meaning of the two terms in relation to each other is virtually the same,[2] their Trinitarian function is the opposite of the Christological. They represent the common essence and nature of the Triad, yet they carry the specific attributes of the uniting Godhead and manhood respectively within Christ. Nonetheless, they are also used consistently in both contexts, since they denote the divine nature/essence both in *theologia* and *oikonomia*.

The most problematic term: hypostasis

Without lengthening the discussion concerning the fairly evident meaning of *ousia* and *physis*, I proceed to the analysis of their relationship with probably the trickiest term of the period, i.e. *hypostasis*.

Concerning its doctrinal history I refer the reader to the excellent
scholarship of J. H. Newman, Marcel Richard and G. L. Prestige.[3] The
expression in itself is a correlative substantive of *hyphistēmi*, i.e. 'to
stand', 'set' or 'place under'. As Prestige argues,

> Broadly speaking, it may be said that the purport of the term
> is derived in one group of usages from the middle voice of the
> verb *hyphistēmi*, and in another from the active voice. Thus it
> may mean either that which underlies, or that which gives
> support.
>
> (*God in Patristic Thought*, 163)

In classical Greek, in the material sense it means 'foundation',
'sediment', 'groundwork' or even substantial nature. It also means
'substance', 'reality', something 'underlying' a specific phenomenon
or essence. In the New Testament it occurs three times in the sense of
'confidence' (2 Cor. 9:4, 11:17; Heb. 3:14), once in the sense of 'reality'
or 'assurance' (Heb. 11:1) and only once with a meaning the church
more or less began to assign to it (Heb. 1:3). Its application in theology is therefore caused largely by Heb. 1:3 and at first it becomes the
synonym of *ousia* in Epiphanius and his contemporary anti-Arian
theologians. As opposed to *ousia*, in which the emphasis is upon the
single object disclosed by means of internal analysis, *hypostasis* draws
attention to the externally concrete independence, i.e. the relation to
other objects. The primary theological sense of the word was also
subject to continuous development.

The phrase '*hypostasis* of *ousia*' (Heb. 11:1) – according to Prestige –
may be translated as 'substantial objectivity'. *Hypostasis* soon gathered
the sense of 'genuineness', or 'reality', i.e. positive, 'concrete and distinct
existence, first of all in the abstract, and later [. . .] in the particular
individual'.[4] Its use becomes more and more common by the time of
the Cappadocians, meaning largely 'objective individual existence'.
Hypostasis gradually gains the meaning of 'individual' in Clement,
Origen, Athanasius and Basil.[5] As Prestige concludes,

> Instances could be multiplied, but those which have been
> quoted are sufficient to show what the word hypostasis really
> means when it comes to be applied to the prosopa of the triad.
> It implies that the three presentations possess a concrete and
> independent objectivity, in confutation both of the Sabellian
> type of heresy, which regarded them all merely as different
> names, and of the unitarian type of heresy, which regarded the

second and third of them as abstract qualities possessed by the first or impersonal influences exerted by His volition.[6]

Before entering the Eastern debate concerning the interpretation of *hypostasis*, another linguistic issue, namely its Latin translation, has to be discussed. In this volume I have chosen to translate *homoousios* with 'coessential', instead of 'consubstantial', partly because *ousia* is the equivalent of *essentia* (= essence) and not of *substantia*. One of my main concerns was that while addressing Theodoret's terminology, I could not ignore the fact that, etymologically, the Latin *substantia* (*sub-stantia*) was much closer to the Greek *hypostasis* (*hypo-stasis*) than to *ousia*. It is beyond doubt that the Western usage of *consubstantialis* made it the equivalent of Nicaea's *homoousios*. The translation of *ousia* with *substantia* already occurred after Nicaea in Latin theology. For example, in his *De fide ad Gratianum* (CSEL 78, I, 19, p. 128) Ambrose uses *substantia* purely in this sense.[7]

Further, the application and usage of *substantia* to denote *ousia* in the early Western church is legitimate as far as Nicaea is concerned, since the Nicene Creed (more exactly the anathema following it) did not distinguish between *ousia* and *hypostasis*. This was probably a reaction to Arius' distinction between the three *hypostases* to express a difference between the *ousia* of the Father and the Son. Thus, the usage of *consubstantialis* to translate *homoousios* – at least until the distinctions introduced by the Cappadocians – is fully Nicene and orthodox. Nevertheless, in the fifth century the Western practice of translating only *ousia* with *substantia* was not unanimous, thus causing occasional problems.[8]

Socrates Scholasticus provides useful information concerning the debates around *ousia* and *hypostasis*. According to him the two terms were allowed in the absence of more fitting ones in order to exclude Sabellianism. He also mentions that the Greek philosophers provided various definitions of *ousia*, yet they did not notice *hypostasis*, concluding that although the ancient ones rarely mentioned this term, the more modern thinkers have frequently used it instead of *ousia*.[9]

While the philosophical meaning of *hypostasis* is more or less inconclusive as to what extent it could denote a concrete individual reality or a universal essence,[10] its ecclesiastical application is even more complicated. The term enters Trinitarian doctrine first – a long time before being accepted in Christology. The arguably Origenian picture of 'one *ousia* – three *hypostases*' in the Trinity is challenged by Arius, who operated with three *hypostases* in order to attack the doctrine of the Son's *homoousia* with the Father. This is partly why the anathema at the end of the Nicene Creed did not distinguish between the two terms.[11] The same is valid for the subsequent *Creed of Sardica* (347), which states that 'the *hypostasis*, which the heretics call *ousia* of the Father, the Son and the Holy Spirit is one'.[12] The Roman Council held under Damasus in 371 asserts that the three Persons are of the same *hypostasis* and *ousia*.[13] The Council of Alexandria in 362 led by Athanasius and Eusebius of Vercelli decided to leave both the sense and use of the term open, thus to enable the different schools to speak either of one *hypostasis* or of three.[14] Rowan Williams observes the following:

> Both Arius himself and the later critics of Nicaea insist on the catholic and scriptural nature of their language, and see themselves as guardians of centrally important formulae – God is the sole *anarchos* [unbegun], He begets the Son 'not in appearance but in truth', there is a triad of distinct *hypostases*, and so forth. But Arius was suspect in the eyes of the Lucianists and their neo-Arian successors because of his logical development of the traditional language in a direction that threatened the reality and integrity of God's revelation in the Son; hence the attempts in the credal statements of conservative synods in the 350s to bracket the whole Nicene discussion by refusing to allow *ousia*-terms of any kind into professions of faith.[15]

Further, if the above picture were not already puzzling, we have to acknowledge that the use of the two terms may not be consistent even within the oeuvre of individual theologians. Athanasius, for example, tried to apply *hypostasis* both against the Arians (thus equating it with *ousia*) and for the three divine Persons. In his *Epistula ad Afros episcopos* he wrote: 'The *hypostasis* is *ousia*, and represents nothing else than that which exists' (PG 26, 1036B). Nonetheless, the same author in another work speaks of three *hypostases* and of one *ousia*.[16]

It could be claimed that Origen's heritage was developed on the one hand by Arius in the sense of Trinitarian subordination, yet on the other hand by Athanasius in the direction of coessentiality. The meaning of *hypostasis* varied accordingly. We should emphasise again: this happened strictly within the limits of Trinitarian doctrine. No Christological application of *hypostasis* is to be found in the Nicene and Neo-Nicene fathers.

The unique journey of *hypostasis* in Christian theology, however, was far from being over. Without its gauntlet-run in Trinitarian doctrine being entirely finished, the expression received a second blow from the zealous Bishop of Laodicea. Apollinaris was the first, and remained the only, theologian before Cyril of Alexandria who applied the term in Christology. According to the research of Marcel Richard, only Apollinaris (and Theodore of Mopsuestia, as Richard thought in 1945) could be shown to have used *hypostasis* in Christology before Cyril. Apollinaris uses the term 'one *hypostasis*' three times in his *De fide et incarnatione*:

> One *prosōpon*, one *hypostasis*, whole man, whole God.[17] [. . .] The Jews, having crucified the body, crucified God and there is no division between the Word and his flesh [. . .] but he rather is one *physis*, one *hypostasis*, one operation [*energeia*], one *prosōpon*.[18] [. . .] Although he was named Son of Man, yet he showed divine power as God and through the blood of his *hypostasis* he saved the whole creation.[19]

Here we have first-hand evidence concerning the provenance of 'one *hypostasis*' in Cyril's Christology. Marcel Richard attempted to prove that no other ancient writer used the term in Christology before Cyril – save for Theodore.[20] He argued that of the two surviving versions of a Syriac fragment of Theodore (Brit. Lib. add. 12156 and 14669 respectively) the latter was the genuine one, containing 'one *hypostasis*' instead of 'one *prosōpon*'.[21] As a result, this is the way the two fragments are listed in the 1974 edition of CPG (No. 3856). Luise Abramowski, however, corrected this conclusion. According to the decisive evidence furnished by her in 1995 the former fragment (in BL 12156), containing 'one *prosōpon*', is the authentic one, thus their order in CPG ought to be inverted.[22]

Prof. Abramowski's correction bears an enormous significance upon my subsequent argument concerning the validity of one *hypostasis* in Christology around Ephesus, since according to this very recent evidence, the only theologian who had indeed used *hypostasis* in Christology before Cyril was Apollinaris. Apart from the correction concerning Theodore, the conclusion of Richard, after having analysed a whole series of pseudepigraphic texts, remains fully authoritative:

> This florilegium of pseudepigraphic texts could undoubtedly be prolonged, yet without any major profit. The present one shows already sufficiently the impossibility in which the theologians of the sixth and seventh century found themselves in [their attempt] to justify by a historical tradition the introduction of the term *hypostasis* into the *Definition of Chalcedon*.[23]

Thus, the famous Apollinarian formula *one physis, one hypostasis, one operation, one prosōpon* of the incarnate Word did not have any other ecclesiastical authority behind it apart from the Laodicean heresiarch. Although Cyril held the phrase as coming from his venerated master Athanasius, whom he sought to follow in every respect, the term was indeed alien to orthodox Christology during the entire fourth century. In Latin theology for example, the term 'one nature' was expressly banned in 400 by the thirteenth anathema of the first Council of Toledo: 'Whoever says or believes the divinity and the flesh to be one nature in Christ, let him be anathema.'[24]

We have arrived at Theodoret and the issue of *hypostasis* within the Christological debates of his time. What we have known only since 1995 (thanks to Prof. Abramowski) – and Cyril did not know at the time – Theodoret already knew at the outbreak of the Nestorian controversy: the term *one hypostasis* as referring to the incarnation and specifically denoting the union 'according to hypostasis' in Christ, as it appears in Cyril's *Twelve Anathemas*, was most emphatically *not* used by any of the orthodox fathers, who reserved this term exclusively for the properties of the divine Persons.[25] One may even be entitled to reformulate one of the basic scholarly assumptions concerning the authoritativeness of hypostatic union before 431. It was not part of the tradition, yet Cyril's recurrent emphatic references to his pseudo-Athanasian sources almost 'created a history', as it were, for this phrase – and perhaps not only in the minds of some fifth-century theologians. This largely unchallenged assumption has filtered through the centuries into modern scholarship, becoming part of our doctrinal subconscious. That is why the findings of M. Richard and L. Abramowski are so important. I cannot rewrite this chapter of doctrinal history in the present volume; nevertheless, I find it indispensable to make a clear distinction between what can be considered as genuine *tradition* as opposed to subsequent general *assumption*.

It is this perspective from which one should assess Theodoret's reaction, who, upon encountering *hypostasis* in Cyril's anathemas, wrote:

> Having been persuaded by the divine teachings of the apostles, on the one hand we confess one Christ and we name the same one both God and man on account of the union. On the other hand, though, we are entirely ignorant [*pantapasin agnooumen*] of the union according to the hypostasis as being alien and foreign to the divine Scriptures and to the Fathers who have interpreted them.
>
> (ACO I, 1, 6, p. 114)[26]

The profound accuracy of the above statement concerning 'the union according to the hypostasis' as being totally alien to the former teachers of the church was hardly ever taken into serious consideration. Nevertheless, since the publication of the articles referred to above, by M. Richard and L. Abramowski, one simply cannot ignore the fact that the Bishop of Cyrus was wholly justified in stating the above in his refutation. In his *Letter to the Eastern monks* composed shortly after Ephesus, he repeats this charge concerning Cyril's verbal Apollinarianism:

> In his second and third chapters [. . .] he [Cyril] introduces the union according to hypostasis, and a meeting according to a natural union, and by these notions he teaches that some mixture and confusion took place of the divine nature and of the form of the servant. This is the fetus of Apollinaris' heretic innovation.
>
> (SC 429, 100)

Cyril's orthodoxy – as well as the Chalcedonian validity of *hypostatic union* – is not in question within this presentation. Nonetheless, two important observations have to be made. First, the only occasion where Theodoret could be claimed to admit two *hypostases* in Christ in his entire theological career is his answer to the third Cyrilline anathema.[27] He never challenges the expression again. Further, in the context of scholarly evidence, he was justified in saying that the term was alien to the fathers' vocabulary of the *oikonomia*, being prima facie 'the fetus of Apollinaris' heretic innovation'. Thus, without denying the theological virtue of Cyril's positive application of *hypostasis* and his subsequent contribution due to which the term became accepted by Chalcedon two decades later, one ought to see that both the moment and the manner in which *hypostasis* re-entered the theology of the incarnation[28] after more than four decades of absence,[29] were more than suspicious – and not merely for Antiochene theologians. It *was* an innovation – just as Theodoret reproached Cyril in the above letter – although it proved to be a positive one.

Theodoret's reaction was not motivated by ignorance but rather by a common concern about any compromised term in any period of doctrinal history. To give only one example: the expression 'man-bearer' connected inseparably with 'God-bearer' could have become an orthodox statement as a legitimate confession of the true humanity and divinity of Christ[30] – if it had not been bound to the ill-fated name of Nestorius. Similarly, the phrase 'union according to the hypostasis' as referring to Christ – despite the indisputable virtue conferred later on it by Cyril – cannot indeed be claimed to have had any sort of authority, but rather a bad reputation, in the context of *oikonomia* at the outbreak of the Nestorian controversy. Consequently, Theodoret could not be expected to embrace an expression used by the most ferocious opponent of his two teachers – an opponent condemned by the first canon of Constantinople 381 (which was presided over for a while by Diodore himself) and regarded by the whole church as having died in his heresy – and accept it as the very criterion of Christological orthodoxy. It necessarily took some years of theological evolution – including Cyril's indispensable subsequent clarifications – until the content of the expression could be regarded and accepted as orthodox. The Bishop of Cyrus cannot be blamed for not having made it his key term of Christological union, unless one intended to argue from the perspective of the 'assumption', which I have distinguished above from the 'tradition'. Evidently, such a charge is again anachronistic. Moreover, apart from Theodoret's remarkable reluctance to attack the Cyrilline formula ever again after 431, it ought to be observed that one of the very obstacles in the way of his acceptance was Cyril's rather unfortunate and often ambiguous equation between *hypostasis* and *physis*, subsequently corrected by Chalcedon.[31]

Theodoret does not find a place for *hypostasis* in his pre-Ephesian Christology, although after Chalcedon he manifests a tendency to identify it with *prosōpon*.[32] Before drawing final conclusions we need to assess an important occurrence and explanation of the term in the *Eranistes*.[33] After the agreed acceptance of the one *ousia* of the Trinity and Orthodoxos' interpolated question (i.e. whether one has to reckon *hypostasis* to signify anything other than *ousia*, or to take it as another name for *ousia*), the Beggar asks the following:

> Eranistes: Is there any difference between *ousia* and *hypostasis*? Orthodoxos: In secular philosophy there is not, for *ousia* signifies that which is [*to on*], and *hypostasis* that which subsists. But according to the teaching of the Fathers there is the same difference between *ousia* and *hypostasis* as between the common and the particular, or the race and the special or individual.
>
> (*Eranistes*, 64)[34]

The above answer of Orthodoxos shows on one hand Theodoret's familiarity with philosophical literature, i.e. with 'the wisdom outside' Christendom. His judgement is generally consonant with Socrates,[35] the other contemporary church historian: for the philosophers *ousia* signifies that which is or exists [*to on*], while *hypostasis* represents that which 'gives support' or 'subsists' [*to hyphestos*].[36] Further, our author is aware of the Neo-Nicene refinements of the Cappadocians, since he writes that according to the teaching of the fathers the difference between *ousia* and *hypostasis* is the same as between *to koinon* (that which is common) and *to idion* (that which is particular) or *to genos* (the race, genus) as opposed to *to eidos* (that which is seen, the species) and *to atomon* (the indivisible, the individual). This explains his reluctance to accept *hypostasis* in Christology, since – as it appears in Cyril – the term may be equated with *physis*,[37] yet this latter expression is the synonym of *ousia* for Theodoret (as we have seen above), which in its turn is different from *hypostasis*[38] 'according to the teaching of the fathers'. *Mutatis mutandis*, in Theodoret's understanding, *hypostasis* – if accepted – can be introduced in Christology only as a synonym for *prosōpon* but not for *physis*, which is what he finds at first sight in Cyril's anathemas.

Finally, in evaluating our author's general terminology, including his use of *hypostasis*, we have to consider also that the only valid theological standard of the 430s (and indeed the terminological milestone between Ephesus and Chalcedon), i.e. the *Formula of Reunion*, does not contain the term. It states the double *homoousia* of Christ (i.e. with God the Father and with us), it affirms the unmingled union of two *physeis*, confesses the one *prosōpon*, sanctions the use of *naos* (temple) in the same manner Theodoret did in *De incarnatione*, yet it does not even mention *hypostasis*. The first ecumenically accepted Christological use of the expression is validated by the *Chalcedonense* in 451, in an environment which leaves little doubt about the fact that in reference to the incarnation it should be taken as a synonym for *prosōpon* rather than for *ousia* or *physis*, as we have already quoted it above.[39]

Prosōpon: 'person' or 'outward countenance'?

We have arrived at the term *prosōpon*, used by our author to denote the One Person of Christ. Prestige shows that *prosōpon* originally meant 'face', but adds: 'It is sometimes expressly opposed to the sense of "mask", as when Clement (*Paed.* 3. 2, II. 2) inveighs against those women who by painting their countenances made their *prosōpa* into *prosōpeia*.'[40]

The term was introduced both into Trinitarian and Christological doctrine with the meaning of 'person' although not in a fully equivalent sense of our present understanding of the English word. After the Sabellian challenge it becomes sharply contrasted with *prosōpeion*, thus to denote that the *prosōpa* are not merely the outward countenances of the one and the same 'Son–Father' [*Hyiopatēr*], who in the manner of a Greek actor changes his masks. Its accepted presence in Christology precedes by many decades – if not centuries – the introduction of *hypostasis*, and as Prestige concludes, 'there does not seem to be any evidence whatever for the view that the term prosopon was ever discredited in orthodox circles at any period of theological development'.[41]

Montalverne argued that Theodoret's Christological use of *prosōpon* did not derive from his Trinitarian doctrine, but rather from his Antiochene Christological heritage.[42] Mandac disproves this conclusion, showing that Theodoret applies *prosōpon* in his *Curatio* when commenting on Gen. 1:26–7. He discerns the *prosōpa* of the Trinity again in the same work.[43] The term occurs three times in *De Trinitate* in the sense of 'person'. On two occasions it distinguishes the Son from the Father and once it shows the divinity of the Holy Spirit.[44] It comes up in the *Expositio*,[45] bound with the term *hypostasis*, customary to Theodoret's Trinitarian language. The Neo-Nicene distinction between *ousia* and *hypostasis* is thus present in the theological thinking of both the young and mature Theodoret.

Concerning the Christological meaning of *prosōpon* for Theodoret there is one passage commonly cited from his *Commentary on Ezekiel* (11:22–3) based on which it has been claimed that for him the term retained its notion of 'countenance'.[46] Speaking of the Saviour's ascension from the Mount of Olives, Theodoret writes: 'Therefore, and at that time naturally appearing [*phaneis*] in human shape [*schēma*], he also showed [*deixas*] the two natures [as] one *prosōpon*' (PG 81, 901CD). The suggestion that 'appearing' and 'showed' represent a remnant of the meaning concerning the outward appearance as 'shown' or 'manifested' by Christ, rather than 'proving' to be the *prosōpon* himself, can be answered by other passages from Theodoret's commentaries. In the same *Commentary on Ezekiel* we read: 'I, the Lord, he says, have spoken. For it is sufficient to show [*deixai*] the truth of the manifestation [*dēlōsis*] of the *prosōpon*' (PG 81, 868BC).

If *deixai* in the above passage were to be taken as mere 'showing' or 'displaying' rather than 'making manifest' in the sense of 'confirming', then the whole rationale would lose its emphasis upon 'the truth of the manifestation of the *prosōpon*'. To this we might add the frequent references to 'the Ruler Christ' on account of whom, or referring to the Person of whom [*ek prosōpou autou*], Isaiah, Ezekiel, David and others were speaking in the same manner as they spoke in the Person [*ek prosōpou*] or on account of the Father.[47] Further, commenting on Isa. 45:14 Theodoret writes:

The Jews saw the two *prosōpa* proclaimed in one: 'For God is in you and you [are] God and there is no God beside you'. These [words] refute both the madness of Arius and Eunomius: if there is none beside him, how can he be God who is God in himself? [. . .] [John 14:10, John 10:30] [. . .] Therefore the prophetic speech refuted both the Jews who circumscribed the divinity into one *prosōpon* as well as Arius and Eunomius, who attempted to introduce a different nature [*physis*] of the Godhead.

(SC 315, 32)

Thus, if the *prosōpon* of 'the Lord', to whom the assertions in John's gospel are attributed, is only an outward countenance, the entire argument against the Jews, who 'limit the divinity to a single *prosōpon*' (i.e. of Yahweh), is invalidated. The identification of the second *prosōpon* of the Trinity with the one of Christ is evident in many passages of Theodoret's commentaries. One last quotation from his commentary on Isa. 45:23 is noteworthy, especially because here the author uses a version of Rom. 14:10, which contains 'of Christ' [*Christou*] instead of 'of God' [*Theou*]. Theodoret asserts that what Isaiah had said about the *prosōpon* of the Father, Paul attributed to the *prosōpon* of the Son, who is 'Christ' in the version used by Theodoret (consequently, equated with the *prosōpon* of the Son): 'What the prophet here said as of the *prosōpon* of the Father, the divine apostle attached to the *prosōpon* of the Son, speaking in this manner, "for we shall all stand before the judgement seat of Christ"' (SC 315, 40; cf. ibid., note 1).

Finally, both the verb 'show' [*deiknymi*] and 'appear' [*phainō*] in the quoted passage from the *Commentary on Ezekiel* appear in *Expositio* with the clear meaning of 'being manifested' or 'proven', rather than 'appearing' as referring to the *prosōpa*.[48]

Therefore, Theodoret's concept of *prosōpon* as it appears in his doctrinal treatises and commentaries is indeed far from being a mere *prosōpeion* and thus is a valid equivalent of the Latin *persona*. There is no substantial evidence in his writings to prove the contrary. That is why it is a fitting term for Christological union in *De incarnatione*, where the One Son is not merely 'shown up' but 'manifested': 'It can be seen more clearly from the Epistle to the Hebrews, that the divine nature and the human are different one from another according to their operations, but are united in the *prosōpon* and indicate [*hypodeiknysas*] the one Son' (PG 75, 1456A). It is therefore this one *prosōpon* of the one Son, i.e. of Christ, in whom the natures are united without confusion: 'For he does not show [*epideiknysi*] us any other *prosōpon*, but the

Only-begotten himself surrounded by [or wrapped in] our nature' (SC 111, 198).

The author repeatedly refuses the charge of teaching two *prosōpa* (PG 75, 1472C), yet he maintains the two *physeis* within the one *prosōpon*. This is again in contrast to Apollinaris, who wrote, 'neither two *prosōpa*, nor two *physeis*'.[49] Let us now analyse the terms describing this 'prosōpic' union in Christ.

Terms describing the union

Since *De Trinitate* and *De incarnatione* were primarily targeted by Theodoret's critics in their attempt to evince his 'crypto-Nestorianism', it may be useful to begin with some statistics concerning the occurrence of terms in these tracts describing the union in Christ.

The most frequent technical term for 'assuming' is [*syn*][*ana*]*lambanō* (to assume) and its derivatives (occurring for more than fifty times throughout both tracts). The other is *synaptō* (to conjoin). Both represent an action always ascribed to the Word. The expressions *synapheia*, *synēpse*, *synēphthai* and *synapsas* occur eight times in *De incarnatione*. The term is mostly bound with *henōsis* (PG 75, 1457A, 1469D, 1473A, 1473B). Its verbal forms always refer to 'the God-Word', who 'conjoins' the human nature (or the temple) with himself (PG 75, 1460D, 1468C) as opposed to a transmutation (*metabalōn*) of the divine nature into human (PG 75, 1425D). On one occasion *synaphtheisan* refers to the human soul of Christ rejoined with his flesh after the resurrection (PG 75, 1453A) and it is also used – together with *henōsthai* (to unite), *oikein* (to dwell) and *energein* (to work inside) – to describe the soul–body relationship (PG 75, 1473A). This term shall be discussed together with *henōsis*.

Another frequent occurrence is *oikonomia* (four times in *De Trinitate*, sixteen times in *De incarnatione*), which is often the replacement for *enanthrōpēsis*, i.e. 'inhumanation' (occurring once in *De Trinitate* and three times in *De incarnatione*). As mentioned already, it is a technical term to denote something we would call Christology and soteriology, but does not need further discussion. The emphasis upon Christ being 'one' [*heis*] (i.e. the One Son, One Christ, one *prosōpon*) appears ten times in *De incarnatione* either as the author's own statement or in biblical quotations introduced by explanatory passages concerning the 'oneness' or the 'union'.[50] It is noteworthy that one of Theodore's favourite expressions, *symplokē* (connection), does not appear at all in either tract – in fact, it never had a Christological function in Theodoret's entire career.

The verb *syneimi* (to be together) and its passive participle *synēmmenos* appears five times in *De Trinitate* describing the Son being together with the Father, and only three times in *De incarnatione* in a Christological sense: once preceded by *henōsis* (PG 75, 1472B), once bound with the word 'inseparably' [*achōristōs*] (PG 75, 1469B) and once concerning the union in the *prosōpon* (PG 75, 1456A). Due to its notably few occurrences and its being an obvious synonym for *henōsis*, a detailed discussion of the expression is not necessary. The terms *koinon* (common) and *koinōnia* (togetherness) occur ten times in *De Trinitate*, but never in a Christological sense; similarly, they appear twelve times in *De incarnatione* but only once in the sense of Christological union and even then in an enumeration preceded by *henōsis* and *synapheia* (PG 75, 1473B). Thus, *koinōnia* does not qualify as a major technical term either.

The term *enoikēsis* (indwelling) appears three times in *De Trinitate*, but not in a Christological sense,[51] yet it describes the union eight times in *De incarnatione*: four times bound with *henōsis*,[52] and four on its own.[53] This expression deserves some attention, not because of the number of its occurrences, but due its interpolation in the eleventh anathema of Cyril, who sensed in it a danger of Adoptionism. *Enoikēsis* was widely used not only to describe the 'indwelling' of the Holy Spirit in believers (see 1 Cor. 3:16–17) but as referring to Christ as well. Interestingly, this latter practice was not discredited even after the challenge of Paul of Samosata. To mention only a few of the most reputed theologians: Amphilochius of Iconium, Athanasius and John Chrysostom use this kind of language in their works.[54]

For Theodoret *enoikēsis* describes the Word's 'indwelling' within the assumed temple. It functions normally as a qualifying term for *henōsis* – with which it is often coupled – and is used in order to uphold a union together as well as maintaining the natures' properties. It plays an occasional role in the author's clarifying statements concerning the manner of attribution. Based on its usage within Theodoret's oeuvre as a whole, any idea of Adoptionism or 'two sons' is excluded. The author employs the term in much the same manner as it was used by earlier fathers.

The most frequent term is *henōsis* together with its derivatives, which is the author's key expression for Christological union. It occurs fifteen times in *De incarnatione*: eight times by itself[55] and seven times bound with one of the other expressions, often preceding them.[56] It is analysed below together with *synapheia*.

Henōsis and synapheia: synonyms or contradictory terms?

In order to avoid repetitions and to represent the author's thought more faithfully, we will discuss the two crucial terms (*henōsis* and *synapheia*) together. While *henōsis* is generally accepted as being Theodoret's crucial term for Christological union,[57] *synapheia* was regarded with suspicion after the outbreak of the Nestorian controversy.

Cyril's express refusal of *synapheia* in his third anathema[58] shows that he cannot interpret it otherwise than of a loose connection 'according to rank' [*kata tēn axian*] or 'honour' between two separate hypostases, excluding any real union. The term's best and most exhaustive analysis was furnished by Luise Abramowski in her excellent study '*Synapheia* und *asynchutos henōsis* als Bezeichnung für trinitarische und christologische Einheit'. Starting from the earliest philosophical foundations, through an impressive list of patristic arguments, the author shows conclusively how *synapheia* (or *synaphē*) was a valid synonym for *asynchutos henōsis*, i.e. 'unmingled union', not only in Christology but in Trinitarian doctrine from Tertullian's time through to Basil, Gregory Nazianzen, Ambrose, Augustine, Novatian and others.[59] Due to lack of space I cannot expose the full rationale of this thoroughgoing study. As the German scholar argues, 'in the Trinitarian doctrine the term *synaptō* etc. serves to denote the oneness, whilst *synaptō* and *henoō* were used as synonyms'.[60]

Cyril's reluctance to accept 'unmingled union' as the valid meaning of *synapheia*[61] is to a large extent answered by his eighth anathema, where he expresses his general concern about the preposition *syn*. It appears that any word containing this particle was suspected by him as a tendency towards separation when referred to the Person of Christ. As he wrote in his eighth anathema, 'the addition of the expression "along with" [*syn*] will always necessarily imply this interpretation'.[62] As Cyril cannot be proven to have been familiar with the philosophical background of *synapheia*, which was often used by the Antiochenes,[63] he seems to manifest a preconceived negative judgement about any term beginning with *syn*, since this preposition, to his mind, cannot introduce or describe anything which is truly one, but only something composite, the elements of which are merely in a loose connection with each other. According to Abramowski's compelling evidence this was not the case at all with *synapheia*, in the sense in which earlier fathers, and indeed Theodoret, used it; nevertheless, their usage of the term was based on a philosophical tradition virtually unknown to the Alexandrian patriarch.[64]

The above means that for our present investigation concerning Theodoret's use of *synapheia* as describing an unmingled union, Cyril's authority cannot be held as decisive. His third anathema cast a shadow of doubt upon a legitimate term used for more than two centuries with a meaning he would not grant it. Therefore, without spending time on this unfortunate terminological bias, I present a few patristic examples and Theodoret's understanding of *synapheia*.

Basil, who uses the term quite frequently both in his Trinitarian doctrine and in Christology, writes: 'the God-carrying flesh, he says, is sanctified by its conjunction [*synapheia*] with God.'[65] The use of *synapheia* to express the unmingled union between Father and Son, as well as between the humanity and divinity of Christ, is commonplace enough in Gregory of Nyssa's *Contra Eunomium*. It also appears in his *De perfectione Christiana ad Olympium monachum*.[66] Apart from the Trinitarian application in his anti-Arian polemic, Athanasius often uses the term in a Christological sense, showing that it does not denote a separation.[67]

Finally, based on the observation of Sellers,[68] we find even Apollinaris using *synapheia* and *symplokē* (!) in Christology. Although his chief concern was the closest possible Christological union, Apollinaris himself confesses 'the conjunction [*synapheia*] [of the Word] to the body'.[69] Nevertheless, as perhaps opposed to Cyril, Apollinaris was indeed well versed in secular philosophy.

The term *synapheia* was therefore a valid term for both Trinitarian and Christological unity. It had been the equivalent of 'unmingled union' for quite some time before the Ephesian–Chalcedonian period. It is this concept of *asynchutos henōsis* which Theodoret defends in his *Letter to the Eastern monks*. The phrase is used precisely for the sake of terminological clarity: 'Therefore we confess our Lord Jesus Christ [to be] very God and very man, not dividing the one in two *prosōpa*, but we believe that two natures united unconfusedly [*asynchutōs*]' (SC 429, 110).[70] This 'unmingled union' is the key term in the *Formula of Reunion* drawn up by the Bishop of Cyrus five months before the above letter. The Virgin is named 'God-bearer' according to this very notion of *asynchutos henōsis* inherited through the centuries from earlier theologians.[71] A very plausible reason why its valid synonym *synapheia* did not appear in the *Formula* is precisely Cyril's misunderstanding as we have seen above.[72] Theodoret's irenical purpose is remarkable especially because upon seeing that the other party was unaware of the term's traditional meaning, he did not strive to impose it but rather used an equivalent which represented the same for all.

Nonetheless, it would be a mistake to consider that this termi-nological concession is a result of Theodoret's having been persuaded of the 'ambiguous meaning' of *synapheia* – since he does not abandon the term entirely[73] – yet during and after the Nestorian controversy he applies it very sparingly and with qualifications. His main term for 'union' remains *henōsis* throughout his career, testifying his openness to terminological reconciliation. This aspect of Theodoret's peaceful theological character (in the same fashion as his doctrinal 'armistice' concerning the Christological application of *hypostasis* after 431) is noteworthy – and perhaps not merely from the viewpoint of a positive terminological evolution.

Rejection of misleading terms and the 'image' of the oikonomia

Having assessed the traditional meaning of *synapheia*, which qualifies the *henōsis* in Christ, we will now briefly examine those terms which are unsuited to describe this union. Theodoret enumerates them e.g. in *De incarnatione* 34 [32]:

> Pious [teaching] is to speak not about mixture [*krasis*], but about unity/union [*henōsis*] in Christ. Therefore we neither confound the natures, nor teach a mixture of Creator and creature, nor do we introduce the [concept of] confusion [*synchusis*] by means of the word 'mixture', but we both recognise the nature of the God-Word and acknowledge the essence of the form of the servant. [. . .] Those who speak about 'mixture', together with mixture introduce confusion, and with confusion change [*tropē*][74] is involved. Once change has appeared, God would neither remain in his own nature, nor man in his own. For that necessitates each [of them] leaving the limits of their essence, and God would neither be recognised as God, nor man as man anymore. This cannot be accepted, even for the structure of the human being, by an accurate thinker. We do not say that the soul is mixed with the body, but rather that she is united [*hēnōsthai*] and conjoined [*synēphthai*] [with it], dwells [*oikein*] and works inside [it] [*energein*]. Nobody would say that the soul is mortal or the body immortal without being entirely in foolish error. So while we distinguish each [nature], we acknowledge one living being composed [*synkeimenon*] out of these. We name each nature with separate names: the former 'soul', the latter 'body', yet the living being composed out of both we call by a different name, for we label that 'man'. Therefore, taking this also as an image of the oikonomia, let us avoid that blasphemy

TERMINOLOGY

[i.e. the confusion of natures], and abandoning 'mixture', let us apply consistently the terms of 'union' [*henōsis*], 'conjunction' [*synapheia*] and 'togetherness' [*koinōnia*], teaching the distinction of nature, and the unity of the person [*prosōpon*].

(PG 75, 1472D–1473A)

So Theodoret refuses already in 431 all the expressions condemned by Chalcedon two decades later (e.g. *krasis*, *synchusis* and *tropē*). The rejection of these as unsuited for the incarnation is an important step towards the evolving Chalcedonian terminology. The term *krasis* and its synonyms, occasionally used for Christological union, were replaced by *henōsis* and *synapheia* as early as the end of the fourth century – to a great extent because of the Apollinarian danger.

In order to understand better Theodoret's emphasis upon the terms 'mixture', 'confusion' and their like as being unsuited or 'blasphemous' within Christology, let us focus on the 'image of the oikonomia' as presented here through the relationship between the human soul and body. This has a peculiar connection with Theodoret's earlier theological ideas, since in the *Expositio* 11 he already argued that in some ways the human soul–body image is suitable to describe the incarnation and in some ways it is not (PG 6, 1225B–1228C). It is adequate insofar as we speak about the union of two different natures (i.e. of body and soul) within one human being in the same fashion as the incarnate Son of God has two natures. Nevertheless, as Theodoret explains further, the human being is not two natures, but out of two (PG 6, 1225C). Thus, consisting out of the conjunction [*synapheia*] of soul and body, the human being is a third entity (PG 6, 1228B).

This is the aspect of the soul–body image which does not describe the incarnation faithfully, since – as our author argues – Christ is not a third entity (a *tertium quid*) out of the divinity and humanity, but He is rather both, i.e. two natures and not one (PG 6, 1228B). While the human soul suffers [*sympaschei*] the torments of the body, the divinity of Christ cannot be said to undergo the manhood's passions (cf. PG 6, 1228C) without involving a suffering *qua Logos* for our author, since, as we have seen, the properties of each nature are preserved in the One Christ, otherwise they would cease to be two natures – at least for Theodoret.

In the above passage from *De incarnatione* the Bishop of Cyrus does not discuss this aspect, yet his emphatic rejections of mixture, confusion, change and their synonyms like *metabolē* (alteration) can be understood better in the light of his *Expositio*. Nevertheless, in comparison to the quoted passage from the earlier *Expositio*, a passage

73

which arguably exposes Theodoret's weakness to emphasise the oneness of Christ, the text of *De incarnatione* 34 [32] with its final emphasis upon the union ('teaching a distinction of nature, and the unity of the person') already demonstrates a step forward in the course of his theological evolution, since he accepts here a peculiarly Alexandrian model of conceiving Christological union and makes it his own. His *Letter* 146 *to the monks of Constantinople*, composed in the first half of 451, shows more clearly this subsequent acceptance of the anthropological analogy:

> But this bragging is unnecessary, for these men [. . .] do not even dare to assert that they have ever heard us say anything of the kind; but they affirm that I preach two sons because I confess the two natures of our Ruler Christ. And they do not want to perceive that every human being has both an immortal soul and a mortal body; yet no one has been found so far to call Paul two Pauls because he has both soul and body, [any more] than Peter two Peters or Abraham or Adam. Everyone recognises the difference [*to diaphoron*] of the natures, and does not call the one [Paul] two Pauls. In the very same fashion, when calling our Lord Jesus Christ the Only-begotten Son of God, the God-Word made man, both Son of God and Son of Man, as we have been taught by the divine Scripture, we do not assert two sons, yet we do confess the properties of the Godhead and manhood. Those, however, who deny the nature assumed from us are annoyed upon hearing these arguments.
>
> (SC 111, 178–80)

It is obvious how Theodoret's thinking evolved since the writing of the *Expositio*. There is hardly any *communicatio idiomatum* in this Christological union, nevertheless, its being a 'union' is not merely a verbal fact – arguably even from an Alexandrian viewpoint. Perhaps it is not an overstatement if we conclude that this aspect also strengthens the validity of the judgement concerning the generally irenical character of Theodoret's oeuvre, who both terminologically and also in his use of analogies, began to build bridges between Alexandria and Antioch upon the foundations of a common theological heritage, for a prospective reconciliation in Chalcedon, a reconciliation which at the time of the composition of most of his works seemed far from achievable.

7

THEODORET'S LEGACY

Theodoret's theological thinking was deeply rooted in the tradition of ideas both within and outside the Antiochene school of thought. His doctrine on the Trinity represents the adoption and further elaboration of the Neo-Nicene refinements of the Cappadocian fathers. His Christology presents us with a 'two natures – One Person' model within which both elements (i.e. the natures and the Person) are important and should not be played off against each other. It is an inherited rather than invented model of Christ, based on a vivid soteriology permeated by an authentic pastoral concern, sharply focused upon God's justice and mercy shown to us by the fully divine and human Saviour's life, teaching and sacrifice. The ascription of his deeds to us for our justification is carried out attributively, through his human nature, which is the same as ours, sin excepted. He does not only save us from damnation, but also strengthens our belief that, since he defeated sin, Satan and death through his manhood, they no longer rule over us. Our duty, then, is to live our life accordingly, following 'the trodden path of the pious'.

Holy Scripture testifies that our Saviour is very God and very man, and the only proper way for us to understand and fully acknowledge him, according to Theodoret, is to receive both the biblical teaching and the fathers' doctrine concerning his unique Person, who is at once Creator and creature, who suffers as man, but is beyond passions and can deliver us from these as God. In his assumed full humanity, in the destroyed and resurrected temple, we may thus contemplate the archetype of our redemption through the work of salvation achieved on our behalf by the One who was the second Adam indeed, yet dwelt among us as the Only-begotten of the Father. His utterances and works are therefore both human and divine, whilst some would seem more human than divine or vice versa. Although one may interpret his divine manifestations as pertaining to his divinity whilst those uttered and performed in the state of humiliation could be reckoned as appropriate for the assumed temple, it is the One Son who is contemplated and worshipped in both these natures. Within the unharmed integrity of his complete Person the two natures retained their properties while he dwelt upon earth (the Word appropriating the sufferings and the wretchedness of the manhood), yet after resurrection the human nature received divine glory, impassibility and incorruptibility, thus to prefigure our own glorification as a result of this achievement.

There is no worship of a separate human being over against the Only-begotten, but of the One Son in both natures as he manifested himself to humankind. Being the Only-begotten Son of God, he made us his mercifully adopted children, who have the same human nature he assumed, a nature which was perfect and was inseparably, unchangeably and unconfusedly united with the 'indwelling' divinity. One is entitled to call him by different names, as Scripture does, yet not as two persons or *prosōpa*, but only as referring to the natures, since some of these names are ontologically more befitting to one nature than the other (i.e. the Son of Man to the manhood; the Son of God to the Word). Nevertheless, all these names are proper to him, the Son made man, who is the *prosōpon* of the inseparable union.

Further, there are names which are suitable to denote both his Godhead and manhood simultaneously. The name 'Jesus Christ' should be given prevalence, since this is the name by which Scripture chiefly made him known to us as the Only-begotten of the Father and the Firstborn among many brethren. This is the name to which his church justly clings.

Concerning the Christological terminology which Theodoret presents us with throughout the stormy decades between the third and fourth ecumenical councils, without trying to make him a Chalcedonian before Chalcedon, it can be admitted that in addition to the 'two natures – One Person' model, several key terms are anticipated in his oeuvre with virtually the same meanings as they received in 451. Nonetheless, these expressions neither appear as an innovation, thus constituting his laudably original contribution, nor are they motivated by sheer philosophical limitations. They are the distilled expression of a centuries-long doctrinal tradition deriving from the very meaning of the unmingled and indivisible union of Father, Son and Spirit on the one hand, and from a union without confusion in the incarnate Word, i.e. from a *henōsis* qualified by *synapheia*, on the other. Consequently, Theodoret is far from original in introducing as it were seemingly new 'philosophical' and thus 'alien' ideas into Christian doctrine, such as God's philosophical impassibility or the Stoic doctrine of being. On the contrary, he is rather faithful to an undeniably vast ecclesiastical tradition, which already incorporated such ideas, yet on primarily biblical grounds aided by expressions borrowed from secular philosophy. Theodoret's 'originality' – if it could be claimed at all – resides perhaps within his remarkable consistency, by which he harmonised this tradition terminologically in a time when a whole range of old orthodox terms were seriously questioned, facing the danger of elimination, whilst others with a 'heretical flavour' began to replace them, whilst becoming filled with new meanings. In this attempt he may be easily shown to have failed in proclaiming a *hypostatic* union or a genuine *communicatio idiomatum* in Christ, nevertheless, it has to be said that such concepts in his time *were* the innovation – *not* the tradition. They ultimately proved to be useful and their validity is not under question in this book. Nonetheless, to say the least, one of Theodoret's most valuable contributions to theological development is his consistency in the usage and correction of terms. He was one of the very few figures in the history of doctrine with an impressively wide-ranging knowledge of previous traditions from Asia Minor to Rome or Syria. This is why his most difficult, but indispensable, work of terminological clarification in the midst of a highly heated controversy, caused him so much adversity, an adversity which he carried with admirable honour.

Being a church historian and a philosophically trained apologist, he always knew what he was talking about and from where a particular expression came. He was reluctant to dismiss old orthodox terms – especially those attached to an ecclesiastical authority (i.e. a synod's decree) – yet corrected those which were proven to be unsuited for the purpose some earlier fathers occasionally tried to use them for. Without his contribution, our present Christological vocabulary would be considerably poorer. Without his oft-blamed 'stubbornness' to defend some very old phrases, filling them with new meanings, they could easily have disappeared in the turmoil of the fifth century, leaving us with a much more simplified picture of how our fathers once spoke and thus how one may speak of our Lord incarnate. His repeated admonition concerning the scriptural and patristic boundaries of our own theological capabilities faces us with the very challenge that although perhaps what we say about these issues ought to be said and may be right, we cannot forget that only the Word of God is perfect – and not our time-bound theological ideas:

> Let us remain within the limits we inherited, not modifying the boundaries fixed by our Fathers. Let us be content with the

teaching provided by the Spirit. We should not want to surpass Paul's knowledge [*gnōsis*], who said that both his knowledge and prophecy were imperfect and he saw the truth in a mirror dimly (1 Cor. 13:12). [. . .] At present let us stay within the teaching of the Fathers, in order that by seeking for more we do not fall [even] from the less, as our forefather Adam suffered: for he desired to become God and lost even [the state] of being the image of God.[1]

During the decades following the Council of Chalcedon a series of divergent interpretations arose concerning its doctrinal meaning. Without entering the details of the so-called 'Neo-Chalcedonian' disputes and the *Three Chapters* controversy, we may assert that the fifth ecumenical council of 553 changed the entire way of thinking about the *Chalcedonense*. This council, in the attempt to save what it deemed to be worthy of saving from Chalcedon, unavoidably cut its doctrinal corridor in two, accepting only the Alexandrian–Cyrilline interpretation as legitimate. It raised Cyril's *Twelve Anathemas* to the level of a universal theological standard and interpreted all doctrinal issues accordingly. This necessarily involved the condemnation of all those who either did not fully agree with Cyrilline orthodoxy or were unacceptable to the Monophysite party, the group which Justinian intended to win back. This reunion was not achieved and in the same fashion as the *Henoticon* (482), it displeased everybody. The schism deepened not only between the Eastern Monophysite and Dyophysite groups themselves, but also between Constantinople and Rome.

During these unsettled years, which then became unsettled centuries with temporary reconciliations and long-lasting tensions, the evaluation of Chalcedon remained essentially twofold, although the model of Christ as being 'One and the same' was universally accepted. One of the very interesting later developments was constituted by the sixth council in 680–1, conducted in a more relaxed spirit in comparison to the previous ones. Here – based on the teachings of Maximus the Confessor – it was established that there are not only two natures but also two wills and two 'operating forces' [*energeiai*] in the one Person of Christ. This again points back to the long forgotten orthodox Antiochene emphasis upon the 'unmingled union' of the two natures.

It is indeed quite difficult to reconcile the statements of the fifth council with those of the sixth, since the latter seems to have returned to a certain interpretation of Chalcedon which the former had already banned. In order to do justice to both theological traditions and to resist Monotheletism and Monoenergism effectively, one inevitably needs to look at Chalcedon through the pathway which was blocked off by the fathers gathered in 553 in Constantinople. The dramatic presence of the 'two wills' in Christ in Theodoret's treatment of the Temptation-story, his emphases upon the will of the manhood and that of the Godhead in Gethsemane, and all the related biblical passages, are far too obvious to be ignored in connection with the Monothelite controversy. One might even say that the virtue of his Christological approach could have proven extremely useful later in time (i.e. during the sixth ecumenical council in 680–1), had it not been forbidden by a previous synodal decision (i.e. by the fifth council in 553).

Although this Theodoretian reading of Chalcedon and understanding of the Person of Christ did not gain any major theological support in the East – save perhaps in Cyril Lukaris' *Catechism*, which was banned by the Eastern church quite soon after its publication in the seventeenth century – the legacy of Theodoret and of orthodox Antiochene theology surfaces in later mediaeval and sixteenth-century Western theology.[2] Without introducing a new subject at the end of the analysis, I would like to quote Karl Barth's assessment of these similarities to illustrate how far in history these two (not conflicting but rather complementary) parallel traditions have influenced and shaped the doctrinal thinking of later theologians. In the volume of his *magnum opus* dedicated to my theological home, the Hungarian Reformed Theological Institute in Kolozsvár, Barth writes:

> We are dealing with testimonies to one reality, which, though contrary to one another, do not dispute or negate each other. That must be remembered when we are compelled to adopt a position towards the antitheses which repeat the same variety in Church history, namely between the Christologies of Alexandria and of Antioch, of Luther and of Calvin. It is in the succession of the Johannine type that we have obviously to see Eutyches' and later Luther's interpretation of Christ, in the succession of the Synoptic type that of Nestorius and of Calvin.[3]

According to Barth, the Christological understanding of the two ancient schools derives from the tradition of John and of the Synoptic Gospels respectively. This, of course, does not mean a harsh distinction at all, implying as it were that both schools may have used only one of the two available alternatives, since this is not true for any representative of either.

The final conclusion of this investigation therefore is that, although between the parallel Christologies of the orthodox Alexandria and of the orthodox Antioch (together with their late appearances in the Middle Ages, the sixteenth century or even in our era) there are undeniable differences, nevertheless, these are differences of emphasis rather than of substance. If, for the sake of orthodoxy there had to be a choice between Theodoret and Nestorius, between Theodoret and Eutyches, between Cyril and Nestorius or between Cyril and Eutyches, there need not be a choice between Cyril and Theodoret, unless we want to lose something truly valuable in terms of Christian teaching. Unity in this sense does not necessarily mean uniformity, although most of the fathers gathered in Constantinople in 553 probably held the contrary opinion, when upon failing to find a common goal they sought and found a common enemy in the representatives of the equally ancient parallel tradition. This choice did not effect the desired union: on the contrary, it continued the division. Consequently, one may consider it unfortunate, not only from a doctrinal but also from an ecumenical perspective that, as a result of the narrow-minded decision of the fifth ecumenical council, one ancient method of Christian teaching about Jesus Christ is still surrounded by suspicion, and that this attitude clearly impairs our commonly assumed and accepted Chalcedonian heritage.

Part II

TEXTS

8

GENERAL INTRODUCTION
TO THE TEXTS

Due to the late, but partial, condemnation of Theodoret in 553, a considerable number of his literary productions have come down to us. Thus, in the course of selecting the texts for this volume I have tried to serve a variety of purposes. First, I wanted to represent Theodoret's oeuvre faithfully in a chronological sense, thus I have included complete works or selections, both from those written in his youth and during the Nestorian and Eutychian controversies, as well as those written in his last years, after Chalcedon. Further, there was the need to give at least an impression of the remarkable spectrum of genres which constitute his legacy, since our author composed apologetical, exegetical, dogmatic, polemical, historical, and heresiological works as well as sermons, whilst his correspondence (from which I frequently quoted in Part I) is an important source for those interested in the ecclesiastical life and teaching of the fifth century.

However, a third criterion required serious consideration: since there are only a few translations available in English (or, in some cases no translations at all into any modern language, whether English, German or French), I have tried to offer the modern readership some representative texts, which are often quoted by scholars, but which were so far inaccessible to those unfamiliar with Greek. I have also kept an eye towards other, currently emerging translations of Theodoret in English: among them, the series of *Commentaries* provided by Robert C. Hill as well as the new translation of the *Eranistes* by its former critical editor, Gerard H. Ettlinger (for further details, see the Bibliography).

As a result, I have decided to include two complete works so far unpublished in any modern language (*De Trinitate* and *De incarnatione*), the first chapter of the *Curatio*, a representative selection from the *HFC* (neither yet published in English) as well as the *Refutation of Cyril's Anathemas*. A short letter and a little doctrinal tract complete this selection. My profound indebtedness to Prof. David F. Wright for his tireless work in checking my translations must be restated. The remaining inadequacies, inappropriate use of terms and any other shortcomings are my responsibility: therefore, I appeal to the reader's kind understanding for my having ventured to translate from fifth-century Greek into a language which is not my own.

As I have already commented, due to its multiple meanings, in many cases I have not translated the Greek term *oikonomia* with 'dispensation', but have instead often transliterated it. The plural is rendered as *oikonomiai* (see e.g. the chapter *About Marcellus* in *HFC*). In a similar fashion, *hypostasis* is also transliterated, while I translate *prosōpon* as 'person'. In order to make a clear distinction between 'becoming flesh' and 'becoming human', I have translated *sarkōsis* as 'incarnation' and *enanthrōpēsis* as 'inhumanation', although in the text of the Introduction in Part I I have made occasional use of 'incarnation', in the sense of 'becoming human'. Since I have translated *ousia* as 'essence', the term *homoousios* is rendered as 'coessential' (instead of 'consubstantial'), for the reasons already mentioned. The Greek term *nous* is translated as 'mind', although the expression in Theodoret's usage has a much wider meaning. As it appears in e.g. Chapter 18 [17] of *De incarnatione*, *nous* can mean a rational or even personal soul. The practice of translating *nous* as 'mind' (although sometimes 'intellect' would seem more fitting), and *psychē* as 'soul' (occasionally 'life', when needed), ventures to help the reader in identifying what the original text contains.

The expression *Despotēs*, a Christological title preferred by the Antiochenes, is translated 'Ruler', thus to distinguish it from *Kyrios*, which I render as 'Lord', while the less frequent term, *Prytanis*, is translated as 'Sovereign'. These designations do not bear substantially different meanings for Theodoret. In order to represent the author's thought faithfully, whenever he speaks of a 'what' (expressed e.g. by a neuter pronoun), I have always translated it as 'that which . . . ' (e.g. the manhood 'that which was assumed'). Similarly, when he means 'who' (e.g. by a masculine pronoun), I have rendered it as 'the one (who) . . . ' (e.g. 'the one born of the Father'). The additions and interpolations are in square brackets; Scriptural references in round ones; important Greek terms are put in square brackets and italicised. For further or specific details the reader is referred to the introductions preceding each text.

9

A CURE OF GREEK MALADIES

Introduction

Theodoret's apologetical work *A Cure of Greek Maladies* (*Hellēnikōn therapeutikē pathēmatōn*), or *Graecarum affectionum curatio*, is one of the best Christian answers to pagan philosophy, yet surprisingly one of his most neglected writings. Although he quotes more than one hundred secular writers and both his eloquence and argumentation are second to none, apart from Gaisford's commendable critical edition[1] there were no major scholarly attempts to bring this remarkable Christian apology to an English-speaking readership. In fact the only full-length translation in a modern language (French) is that of Pierre Canivet, who published the latest critical edition for *Sources Chrétiennes*.[2]

The limits of the present volume permit us to provide only a translation of the *Preface* and of the first discourse entitled *On the faith*. The author himself offers a short summary of all twelve discourses in the *Preface*. Theodoret's mode of presenting his arguments differs from his other works (e.g. there are hardly any biblical references in the first discourse in comparison to the numerous quotations from various ancient writers), but this was the only effective way to present a valid Christian answer to Greek philosophy: one has to accept a different way of thinking, a different set of arguments and authoritative texts which are held in high respect by the non-Christian community. A valid answer could and should only be given by making full use of this vast literature, which was so well known to our author. It is beyond doubt that Theodoret learned a lot from Clement of Alexandria's *Stromata* as well as from Eusebius of Caesarea's *Praeparatio evangelica*, nevertheless, the entire manner by which he captures the reader's attention is remarkable.

Concerning the date of composition, modern scholars express somewhat varying opinions. Since the author refers to it in *Letter* 113, the work must have been written before 449. Further, if the allusion in the *Expositio* to his books written 'against Jews and Greeks' (PG 6, 1208A) is indeed a reference to the *Curatio*, then it must predate 431. A few scholars argue for 437 as the latest time of production.[3] Nevertheless, Canivet's introduction[4] provides conclusive proof that we should accept the *Curatio* as one of Theodoret's first works, most likely written before his consecration as bishop in Cyrus.

The present translation is based on Canivet's critical text. The subtitles – which do not appear in the Greek original, yet are very helpful for the reader in keeping abreast of the argumentation – are also borrowed from this edition. In order to keep the length of this volume's bibliography within reasonable limits, I have not included the complete bibliographical entries of all ancient writers like Plato, Porphyry, Aristotle and others, but have merely given the relevant references in a note, wherever a quotation or allusion occurs in Theodoret's text. I have also tried to introduce notes very sparingly, so for further details or lengthier observations I refer the reader to Canivet's edition. I hope that the translation of this first discourse of Theodoret's *Curatio* may trigger the production of a full English text, so that one day we might also begin to refer to this work as the *Cure* or the *Therapy* of Theodoret.

TEXT: *A CURE OF GREEK MALADIES*
(Selections: SC 57, 100–36)

Preface

The purpose of the author

I have often come across convinced adepts of Greek mythology who mock our faith under the pretext that we do not say anything else to those whom we instruct in divine things, but merely command them to believe. They accuse the apostles of ignorance, labelling them barbarians, because they do not have the subtlety of eloquence; and they say that the cult of martyrs is ridiculous, considering it completely absurd for the living to seek assistance from the dead. They have added some other similar objections which this book will present.

As for me, I shall explain to them what is necessary to dissolve their accusations; nevertheless, I thought that it would be unholy and impious to disregard their victims, i.e. the simple people, and not to write to refute the vanity of their allegations.

I have divided my treatise into twelve discourses and given a plain character to my style, because I assume that this is useful for teaching. Besides, using both the testimonies of Plato and of other philosophers, my style should not completely diverge from, but possess some likeness to theirs.

The structure of the work

The first discourse constitutes the defence concerning our faith and the apostles' lack of education, bringing forth arguments from Greek philosophers.

The second takes into account opinions concerning the principle[5] of the universe by the most famous wise men in Greece and by those who received the title of philosophers among them. Then it sets in parallel the true theology of Moses, the most ancient of all philosophers, and refutes their false accounts, while demonstrating the radiant truth of his teaching.

The third on the one hand teaches what was mythologised by the Greeks about the gods they call 'secondary', and on the other hand what the divine Scripture teaches us concerning bodiless yet created natures, thus to show again by comparison the praiseworthiness of our [pious] observances, and to expose the ugliness and stench of their foul myths.

The fourth has matter [*hylē*] and the world as its subject and shows that our cosmogony is more befitting than Plato's and the others'.

The fifth undertakes the debate concerning the nature of man, exhibiting both Greek and Christian opinions and teaching the measure of difference between light and darkness.

The sixth place was allocated to the discussion concerning providence. The account of God and of those made by God has to be followed by this chapter, which refutes the atheism of Diagoras, the blasphemy of Epicurus, the small-minded thoughts of Aristotle concerning providence, and which commends the doctrines about providence of Plato, of Plotinus and of all who are of the same mind as these. By means of arguments taken from nature, it also demonstrates that providence is observed in the creation and manifested in every work of God.

Since the uselessness of sacrifices has to be shown as well, it is the content of the seventh chapter, which condemns Greek sacrifices by philosophers' texts and demonstrates the infantile character of Jewish legislation by the prophetic ones.

The accusation against those who honour the victorious martyrs and, of course, their defence, is contained in the eighth chapter. By means of the testimonies of philosophers, historians and even poets, it shows that the Greeks performed not only libations but also sacrifices in honour of their dead, some of whom they called gods, others demi-gods or heroes, and most of whom spent their lives in debauchery.

I thought that it would also be proper to confront the most famous lawgivers of Greece with our own – I mean the fishermen, the cobbler[6] and the tax collectors – and to show again the difference by comparison just how those laws [i.e. of the Greeks] have been consigned with their authors to the darkness of oblivion, yet those of the fishermen are flourishing not only among the Greeks and Romans, but also among the Scythians, the Sarmates, the Persians and other barbarians. The ninth chapter contains this examination.

The tenth chapter on the one hand teaches what kinds of things the divine oracles predict, and how they are fitted to God and adapted to the good dispositions of the people, and on the other hand, what the Pythian, the Dodonian[7] and the other false seers of the Greeks foretold, who were observed to be lying, foretelling nothing of the future, yet prophesying in such a manner that no decent man would agree to propose.

Since those who are ignorant of what we and they [the Greeks] teach respectively about the end {of the world} and of the judgement should be informed, this is the teaching that the eleventh chapter proposes to those who wish to encounter it.

I also demonstrate the difference in the practice of virtue, because I see Greek society boasting exceedingly about its ancient philosophers and people endeavouring to praise their lifestyle and their words. Therefore the twelfth chapter will show how their lives are unworthy not only of philosophers, but also of commended slaves, yet [the life] of the apostles and their followers is higher than human nature and similar to [the life] of those freed of their bodies who inhabit heaven.

The title

The title of this book is *A Cure of Greek Maladies*, or *Knowledge of Evangelical Truth {apart} from Greek Philosophy*.[8] For my part, I have undertaken this labour for the sake of curing the ill and doing a service to the healthy. As to those who encounter the fruits of others' labours [i.e. books written by others], I beseech them that if all the writing is well done, to sing hymns to the giver and to repay their labours with prayers; yet if there are some defects, not to condemn the whole work at once because of them, but to preserve the profit of what is well spoken.

I. On the faith

If there is a medical treatment for the body, there is one also for the soul, and it is also evident that each of them are subject to many sufferings, involuntary for the former, yet, in general, voluntary for the latter. God knew this well, since he is clearly all-wise and creator of souls, bodies and of the universe, and assigned suitable remedies for each nature. Moreover, he instituted doctors, some of whom he trained to be skilled in the body, others in the soul, and commanded them to fight and defeat the illnesses.

Those who do not feel well physically are annoyed because of the disease and desire to be cured. They submit to doctors not only when they offer mild remedies, but also when they cut, cauterise, prescribe a diet or offer them cups filled with bitter and unpleasant [potions]. Once these distressing treatments bear the fruit of health, they pay the fees to those who have thus cured them. While in receipt of treatment, they are not interested in the preparation of medicines, for it is indeed the recovery they yearn after without investigating its method.

But those who have contracted the leprosy of disbelief are not only ignorant of the grave illness, but also suppose they enjoy the best of fortune. And if someone specialised in treating these [illnesses] wished to offer an effective remedy for the affliction, they turn away immediately like frenetics, casting off the cure they are offered and fleeing healing as a sickness. Thus it is necessary for specialists to bear with these difficult persons, to endure their insults, even if they punch with their fist or kick. For clearly it is in this way that the foolish are offending. The doctors are not impatient in these situations, but they bind the [patient], they wash the head forcibly and conceive all kinds of procedures to cast out the malady and to restore the former harmony of its members to the whole [body].

This is what we also have to do and we have to give such affected persons [all] the attention possible. Since even if there are very few enslaved to an affliction, like some dense sediment which cannot pass through the holes of the filter because of its thickness, nevertheless, one should not forsake them or neglect their being destroyed by the torment. One has to seek for all means to scatter the fog which envelops them and to show up the radiance of intellectual light. No diligent cultivator cuts numerous thistles and tolerates them when few, but if he finds two or even one, he would pull it up by the roots and weed the field clean. Certainly, much more ought we to act, because the law of our husbandry prescribes not cutting down, but rather transforming the thistles. Let us go to it, then, and as with thistles, let us apply the farmer's hoe and with the mattock of the word [*logos*] let us dilate the furrows of their ears, so that no obstacle placed in its course would hinder the flow of irrigation; moreover, let us wash them like the sick and supply delivering and healing medicines.

The conceit of the educated and the contempt of the Scriptures

Before everything else, let us heal the affliction of conceit. It is evident that some who are acquainted with the writings of poets and orators or have even tasted Plato's eloquence, despise the divine oracles as totally lacking the ornaments of fine style, and disdain being taught by fishermen the truth concerning the One Who Is (cf. Exod. 3:14). When they pick the fruits of every craft, they are not interested in the language of the craftsmen: they do not demand that the cobblers should come from Attica, nor the blacksmiths, the architects, the painters, the constructors of boats or the pilots – but even if these were to be Scythians or Sarmatians, Iberians or Egyptians, they joyfully have the benefit of their skill, demanding only a careful job, and are not in the least annoyed about the difference of nationalities. When listening to a cithara player, they expect only the harmony of sounds without being at all interested in knowing whether he is Greek or barbarian. Thus, it is only the teaching of the truth they refuse to receive in all simplicity, but they consider themselves dishonoured if a barbarian instructs them in this language; and this conceit can be found among people who have not even reached the summit of Greek philosophy, but, so to speak, have lightly tasted a few morsels with their lips and who have begged[9] from here and there some petty ideas.

The Greeks in the school of the barbarians

Nevertheless, the most illustrious of Greek philosophers whose memory nowadays is still retained by distinguished spirits, Pherecydes of Syros, Pythagoras of Samos, Thales of Miletus, Solon of Athens, and above all the renowned Plato, son of Ariston and pupil of Socrates, who overshadowed all with his eloquence, did not hesitate to travel all over Egypt, Thebes, Sicily and Italy for the sake of finding the truth at a time when these peoples, far from being ruled by a single empire, had institutions and laws that varied from city to city: some, for example, adhered to democracy, others to oligarchy; some were under tyranny, others under a constitutional monarchy. Nevertheless, none of these obstacles hindered them from running to barbarian people to learn from them things they assumed them to know better than they themselves. Hence, it is said that in Egypt they were taught concerning the living God not only by the Egyptians, but also by the Hebrews. This is what Plutarch of Boeotia teaches, that even Porphyry teaches, who raged against the truth, or Numenius the Pythagorean and many others.[10] They say that Pythagoras underwent circumcision having learned of it from the Egyptians;[11] the Egyptians, however, received this law from the Hebrews. The patriarch Abraham had received from the God of the universe the commandment of circumcision and his people preserved it; they dwelt in Egypt for a long time and the Egyptians imitated the Hebrews. The fact that the circumcision of the newborn was not an old custom in Egypt is sufficiently attested by Pharaoh's daughter: having found Moses abandoned by the bank of the river, she saw at once his circumcision, recognised his race and called the newborn baby a child of the Hebrews.[12]

Consequently, those who had been so well educated were so passionate about the love of knowledge, that disregarding both wars and the widest seas, they went to the school of the barbarians and from everywhere they gathered what they deemed necessary. Socrates, son of Sophroniscus, the best of philosophers, did not reckon it unworthy of philosophy to learn something useful even from women; he did not blush to call himself the student of Diotima, and he constantly attended on Aspasia also.

As for our opponents, most do not even know what the anger of Achilles is, from which the high-quality instruction for young people customarily begins. Others have borrowed some trifles from poets and orators, but do not even know the names of the philosophers, except of two or three of the most renowned: and they call the Holy Scripture barbaric considering it shameful to learn the truth from it. The sickness of their arrogance is generated by ignorance. If they had read the histories of Greece, they would undoubtedly know that the Greeks were taught the most advanced sciences and the majority of arts by barbarians. They say that geometry and astronomy were discovered first by the Egyptians; astrology and the calculation of horoscopes are said to be inventions of the Chaldaeans; the Arabians and the Phrygians were the first who contrived the craft of augury; the trumpet is the work of Tyrrenians and the flute of the Phrygians, according to the teaching of the tragedies and afterwards of the histories. According to the Greeks the alphabet is a Phoenician invention, and Cadmos introduced it first into Greece; they say that medicine originates from the Egyptian Apis and that later on Asclepius developed its technique; they relate that the first ship was constructed in Libya. The initiations of the Dionysia, the Panathenea, and surely of the Thesmophoria and Eleusis were introduced to Athens by Orpheus, a man from Odryse, who, on arriving in Egypt, transformed the secret rites of Isis and Osiris into those of Demeter and Dionysus, as Plutarch from Chaeronea in Boeotia as well as Diodore of Sicily teach,[13] and as the orator Demosthenes remembers and says that Orpheus showed them the most sacred rites.[14] The [mysteries] of Rhea or Cybele or Brimo – name her as you wish – for you have an abundance of names attached to non-existent beings![15] – in any case the Greeks imported her celebrations and the initiations in them from Phrygia into Greece: the above-mentioned authors testify to this explicitly.

Yet if the arts, sciences, rites of demons and rudiments of knowledge were taught by the barbarians to the Greeks, who were proud of their teachers, how come that you, who are not even capable of understanding their works, refuse to learn the truth from men who received God-given wisdom? And if you refuse to pay attention to them because they were not born in Greece, then do not call Thales wise, nor Pythagoras and his teacher Pherecydes [to be] philosophers. For Pherecydes was from Syros[16] and not an Athenian, neither Spartan, nor Corinthian. Moreover, Aristoxenus, Aristarchus and Theopompus say that Pythagoras was a Tyrrenian, whilst Neanthes calls him a Tyrian [i.e. from Tyre]. Some say that Thales was from Miletus, but Leander and Herodotus label him a Phoenician; further, even Aristotle was a Stagyrite,[17] Diogenes [came] from Sinope and Alcmeon, son of Peirithos, from Croton, who is said to have been the first to write a book about nature. Empedocles was from Agrigentum, a Sicilian town.

If you assert, then, that these men were both born and brought up outside Greece, yet still practised the Greek language, admit first that wise men were born in other nations also. You surely admire both Zamolxis the Thracian and Anacharsis the Scythian for their wisdom, and the Brahmans have a great reputation in your country: yet these [are] Indians indeed, not Greeks!

Philosophy and literary culture

Next you are convicted on another ground, of wrongly putting eloquence ahead of the truth, for you too surely admit that Socrates, son of Sophroniscus, was the best of Greek philosophers; nevertheless, he was born of a stonecutting father, moreover, he practised the paternal craft for a long time. Many writers asserted this, among others even

Porphyry, who wrote in the third book of his *History of Philosophy*, as follows:

> Let us tell about Socrates what other [writers] considered worthy of remembrance. On the one hand we consider for a moment what learned men related in many ways in order to praise or to criticise him, yet on the other hand, we leave uninvestigated whether he practised with his father the craft of stonecutting or if his father did it all by himself, because this did not diminish his wisdom at all if he exercised it only for a short time. But if he was a sculptor indeed, so much the better: for the skill is a pure one and irreproachable.[18]

The following [passages] contain the same opinion, for he presents some [authors] who report that Socrates practised the art of stone-engraving. He could have been a stone-engraver when he was young, and later, enamoured of poetry and eloquence, become educated. But not even this can be said, for Porphyry asserted entirely the contrary, as follows:

> He was not ungifted, but to speak frankly, he was completely uneducated. He was almost entirely ignorant even of the alphabet, making himself ridiculous when he had to read or write because he stuttered like children.[19]

Plato also makes him speak in this way in his *Apology*:

> By Jove, men of Athens, you will not hear elegant discourses, adorned like theirs, with expressions and terms, but things said at random, with words that will come to me.[20]

And a little later he adds this again:

> Now I make this request of you, a fair one, as it appears to me, to disregard the manner of my speech (for perhaps it may be worse or better), and to examine this one thing and give your mind to it: whether what I say is just.[21]

And yet, he who spoke the language of the ignorant and uneducated, merited not only greater respect than all others, but more even than Plato who triumphed over all Greeks through his eloquence. And this even Ariston himself would not deny. How could he, since he ascribed and adapted all his published *Dialogues* to Socrates, preparing them to be deemed the products of his mind?

The true philosopher according to Plato

Moreover, even Plato himself, who eclipsed all humankind and not only the Greeks, but even the Athenians themselves, by the fluency of his language and the beauty of his expressions, recommends attention not to refinement of speech but rather to the harmony of arguments. Listen to him saying this explicitly in the *Politics*, 'If you guard against being obsessed with language, you will appear richer in thoughtfulness as you grow older.'[22]

Listen to what he says in the fifth book of the *Republic* also,

So all these and other students of similar pursuits and prac-
titioners of minor arts – are we to call them philosophers?
By no means, I say, but they are similar to them. – Yet the true
ones, he resumes, who are they, according to you? – Those
who love to contemplate the truth, I answered. For it is neither
in geometry which is based upon postulates and hypotheses
that philosophy consists, nor in music that is conjectural, nor
in astronomy which is stuffed with approximate and fluid
considerations about nature, but through knowledge of the
good itself and through truth.[23]

You have heard the philosopher, gentlemen, describing the experts in music, geometry and other such arts not as 'philosophers', but 'similar to philosophers', while naming genuine teachers of the truth 'philosophers'. In the third book of *Laws* he also says,

Then let it be thus established and declared that those of the
citizens who are ignorant of these things cannot be entrusted
with any authority and that they have to be blamed for their
ignorance, be they expert in calculation and thoroughly versed
in all techniques which conduce to the elevation of the soul.[24]
The people who possess the opposite [qualities], are to be
called wise men, even if according to the proverb, 'they know
neither how to read nor to swim', and authority should be
entrusted to them as to sensible people.[25]

How could one disapprove more truthfully and wisely the ignorance and self-conceit which presently prevail? For obviously the head of the philosophers does not define wisdom by the study of letters, but by knowledge of the truth. He calls 'wise' those who have acquired this, even if they are ignorant of the most elementary things. But he debars and expels those who have had a comprehensive education but do not possess the knowledge of truth and of justice, and does not entrust leadership to them.

Moreover, in the *Theaetetus*, he attacks the stargazers in these terms,

> My dear Theodore, as soon as Thales looked up to study the stars, he fell into a pit; an elegant and witty Thracian hand-maid is said to have made fun of him as so eager to know the things in the sky that what was behind him and at his feet escaped his notice.[26]

And again, in the same dialogue,

> A rustic who is uneducated through want of free time, by such necessity becomes nothing less than a shepherd, surrounded by a wall like a sheepfold in the mountain. Yet when he hears that someone owns more than ten thousand acres of land or more and also gains possession of a wonderful domain, to him, accustomed as he is to think of the universe, this seems very little.[27]

He also adds this to the above,

> For knowledge of this is indeed true virtue, and ignorance [of it] is indeed palpable wickedness; and all the other kinds of apparent cleverness and wisdom become oppressive in civic life and government, and ignoble in the arts and crafts.[28]

This is what they, who were versed in all literary genres, knew perfectly well that the truth is more honourable than phrases and words and that ignorance of such refinement does not damage it at all.

Antiquity of the Hebrews

So why is it, my friends, that you do not want to learn the meaning of the apostolic teaching, yet the only thing you object to is its barbaric expression, whilst hearing from your own philosophers that the Greeks were led astray from the truth and that instead the barbarians have found it? Even that Porphyry, who undertook a ferocious war against us, expresses himself in [his work] *On the Philosophy of the Oracles* in this manner,

> For the road to the gods is barricaded by iron, [it is] raw and difficult. The barbarians found many of its pathways, yet the Greeks were led astray. Those who were already in possession have corrupted it. Hence, God testified to the Egyptians, Phoenicians, Chaldaeans, Lydians and to the Hebrews that they have found it.[29]

If the bitterest of all our enemies blames the Greeks for having been enslaved by error, yet attests that the Hebrews, Phoenicians, Egyptians and Chaldaeans [have] the truth according to Apollo's oracle, why in the world do you not credit the philosopher and why do you not accept the oracle of Delphi's tripod, why do you not listen to the prophets of the Hebrews and to the apostles? For even the Pythian [Apollo] called these 'the discoverers of truth'. If he linked them [i.e. the Hebrews] with both the Egyptians and the Chaldaeans, as well as with the Phoenicians, it should be known that the Phoenicians who had a common border with them, being their neighbours, learned the truth from them, if they learned it at all. Surely, the Egyptians had the most benefit from their contact with them, for the Hebrews dwelt in Egypt for a long time. The Chaldaeans gained the greatest advantage from them, for they lived with them after deporting them to Babylon as prisoners of war. It was from the miracles of the furnace and the lions' den, which happened there, that they realised that the Hebrews were worthy of teaching them the truth. Further, Cyrus, son of Cambyses, having Daniel as his personal friend, took part in the lessons of piety: and when he subdued the Lydians and brought them under subjection, he surely communicated to [these] subjects what he had learned from him [i.e. from Daniel].

Relativity of the philosophical systems

So even the Pythian [Apollo] testified concerning the truth [given] to the Hebrews and Porphyry also mentioned his oracle: this is sufficiently proven. Nevertheless, he [Porphyry] still blames the Greek philosophers for their total ignorance. Listen to how he expresses himself in his letter to Boethos *On the soul*; among many other things he also says this, 'which one of the statements of philosophy is indisputable?'[30] He writes in such wise to Anebo the Egyptian as well,

Let me begin my friendship towards you from the gods, the good demons and the philosophical doctrines akin to these: these issues were also most abundantly treated by the Greek philosophers, but it is said that their starting point was more conjecture than faith.[31]

And again a little further,

There is a lot of word-dispute among us, inasmuch as we portray the good from human reasoning; but for those who attempt to unite with the better, this opportunity is always present for investigation.[32]

Divergences between the philosophers

Thus, if the doctrines of the philosophers are contestable (for reasoning is a human invention) and there is a lot of contention and word-dispute among them without armistice, yet if Porphyry attested that it was to other people to be together and in communion with God, why do you, my friend, hang upon human and disputable words and do not accept the teachings of God's friends?

Conclusion of the argumentation

If you refuse to accept [the teachings of God's friends] on the pretext that they are barbarians, you risk contradicting yourselves. For you are also persuaded by Pythagoras, who according to some was a Tyrrenian, according to others, a Tyrian; you follow the Stagyrite [Aristotle] as a teacher; you admire the Sinopian [Diogenes the Cynic] and the others whose homeland is not Greek but barbarian. We have also shown that even Solon and Plato were taught mostly by barbarians. We hear even the Egyptian priest addressing Solon (quoted in Plato's *Timaeus* also), 'Solon, Solon, you Greeks are always children: there is no old man in Greece, for you do not have a science grizzled by time.'[33]

Now if the knowledge of the Greeks is fairly recent, yet the oldest and most antique [teaching] of the Hebrews contains the truth that blossoms with time, it evidently has to be preferred and judged as superior to new and disputable [systems], which are instead false and not persuasively constructed. Nor is the coarseness of the language sufficient to excuse your refusal, for we have shown that Socrates, the coryphaeus of the philosophers, was not initiated in Greek education, and that Plato preferred the truth before all technical knowledge or fluency of tongue.

The notion of faith and the reception of God's word

Now if it is the term 'faith' itself that you are attacking (for I have heard you saying also that we do not bring forth any proof of our doctrines, but merely direct our disciples to believe), you utterly and openly malign our teaching, because we indeed connect the testimony of the facts themselves to our words. Yet again, according to the proverb, you are wounded by your own feathers! In fact even the famous Pythagoras, son of Mnesarchus, student of Pherecydes and founder of the Italian school, gave as a rule to his students to keep silence for five years and to listen only to him in order to accept what they were told without dispute and contestation; thus, to believe and not to be inquisitive, as though in doubt. Indeed, even his successors, to anyone demanding demonstration of what had been said, customarily replied, 'He said it!', thus both assuming themselves and demanding others, to hold the word of Pythagoras stronger than any demonstration. If both speakers and listeners deemed the doctrines and instructions of Pythagoras sufficient for belief, who is then so foolish or rather quite moonstruck to doubt the God of the universe in his teaching, and neither to believe his words nor to impart to the God of the universe as much veneration as was accorded to Pythagoras by those who were recipients of his teaching? How is it not pitiful, my dear friends, that whilst Plato recommends to believe undoubtingly even in poets, you rage against us, since it is evident that we exhort [you] to believe in God the teacher? Or were these not the words of Plato,

> Concerning the other demons, it is beyond ourselves to say and to know their origin. One has to believe those who have spoken before [us], being descendants of the gods, as they claimed, and bound to know their own ancestors very well! Therefore it is impossible to disbelieve the children of gods, although they speak without plausible or coercive demonstrations; yet as they declare they are speaking of their own family matters, we must follow the custom and believe them.[34]

Plato said this concerning the poets in the *Timaeus*; he also prescribed belief in Homer, in Hesiod and in the other mythologising poets, and he was not afraid to say that they spoke without rational or rigorous demonstrations, elsewhere even ridiculing what they said, as we shall expound clearly in another passage. If Plato recommends believing the inventors of such claptrap, and the makers of the most infamous fables, without demanding from them the least demonstration, how much more religious and just it is to believe in the inspired apostles and prophets, who do not say anything shameful, neither mythical, nor improbable, but all they teach is worthy of God, all-holy and salvific!

The philosophers demand the faith from their disciples

Moreover, those who followed the opinions of the philosophers, letting themselves be guided by faith, cleaved to different [philosophers]: it is quite easy to give an account of their doctrinal divergences through a close examination.

Whilst some affirmed that the soul was immortal, others [said] that it was mortal, and again others defined it like a sort of mixture, claiming that one part of it was mortal, another immortal. As for visible things, they are not created for some, created for others, and some say that they are constituted of earth, others of matter, and again others of atoms. For some the universe has a soul, for others it is soulless. Nevertheless, despite speaking differently, each of the groups had some who believed what they said. Moreover, neither set of followers would admit that this or that [doctrine] were true if a certain faith did not persuade them to accept what was said. This is why even Plato's Socrates in *Gorgias*, after talking a lot about those condemned in Hades, added [this] concerning the people there declared to be righteous, 'This, oh Callicles, is what I have heard and believe to be true.'[35] And yet, [he said this] about things that are neither evident nor visible, but remain hidden for most people, being acknowledged [only] by a few. Nonetheless, he said that he believed it was true, and neither did he furnish any demonstration of his faith, nor did his audience demand it. Moreover, in the first book of *Laws* Plato founded the discourse about the faith and spoke in this manner,

> If the [body] of your laws was sufficiently established, one of the best laws should not allow any of the youth to inquire what was good or not good among them, but require all [of them] to concur with one voice and mouth that all was well.[36]

In this passage Plato does not even permit too much research, but [he wants] the legislation to be accepted with faith, without scrutinising whether it is good or not. The Sicilian poet Theognis also advocates the nourishing of the faith[37] and says, 'The man of faith,[38] Cyrnos, is worth his weight in gold and silver in [times of] grievous dissension.'[39]

If he says that in discord the faithful person is worth more than gold and silver, to what could one compare the person who believes unambiguously in the divine oracles? Nonetheless, I simply think that what Heraclitus of Ephesus said suits you contradictors equally well: 'When they listen without intelligence, they resemble the deaf; the saying testifies that "they are absent while present".'[40]

In accordance with the Ephesian [philosopher], Empedocles of Agrigentum also speaks in this manner, 'It is very much the [custom] of the wicked to disbelieve rulers. Look what our Muse invites us to believe.'[41]

Unbelievers belong to the evil ones according to the Agrigentian. Moreover, the same ones are unintelligent and resemble the deaf according to Heraclitus.

The object of the faith

Furthermore, even Parmenides of Elea, the pupil of Xenophanes of Colophon, evidently recommends attaining intellectual realities by faith. He says, 'contemplate it, despite its absence; it is surely present to your mind.'[42]

This means that intellectual things are approachable only through the mind; yet without faith the mind [ho nous] cannot see any intelligible things.[43] Solon also alluded to this: 'It is most difficult to know the hidden measure of judgement, for it alone surely comprises the limits of all things.'[44]

If it is most difficult to know, then it is absolutely impossible to speak [about it]. Even Empedocles says about invisible things, 'It is not [possible] to approach and reach them with our eyes or take them into our hands; for human beings persuasion is the greatest road which descends into the mind [eis phrena].'[45]

Antisthenes, the pupil of Socrates, then a leader of the sect of Cynics, exclaims about the God of the universe, 'He is not knowable from an image, unseen for the eye; he resembles nothing; this is why nobody can learn of him fully from an image.'[46]

Thus, faith is necessary for those who want to contemplate intellectual things, precisely because one cannot find an image corresponding to them. Xenophon of Athens, the Socratic [philosopher], son of Gryllus, also wrote in accordance with these other philosophers, for he says, 'The one who certainly moves everything yet [remains] immovable is someone both great and powerful, this is clear; nevertheless, the sort of form he has is unclear.'[47]

Undoubtedly, faith is needed for those straining to learn unclear things. One may listen also to what Bacchylides says in his *Paeas*, 'it is not easy at all to find the gates of ineffable words.'[48] Therefore, we need the eyes of the mind to perceive intelligible things, and just as we require the eyes of the body in order to observe visible things, we surely must resort to faith to attain initiation[49] into the divine things. Since the eye is clearly in the body, in the same fashion faith is in the mind [*dianoia*]. Moreover, just as the eye needs light to show forth visible things, similarly the mind [*ho nous*] clearly needs faith to show forth divine things and to keep watch over their constant splendour.[50]

Consequences of disbelief

As for those who do not want to contemplate intelligible things, listen how Plato attacks them,

> Observe carefully, he says, and keep alert lest any of the uninitiated hears [us]: for these [people] there exists nothing except what they can hold tight with their hands; action, origins,[51] and anything that is not visible, they do not accept as belonging to existence [*en ousias merei*].[52]

You also belong to this company – but do not be annoyed by this reproach – for you hold onto visible things only, adore handmade statues, but do not accept any teaching about the nature of the invisible. Perhaps it was for people of this disposition that the comical poet Epicharmus adapted this iambic verse: 'Human nature – a nurtured belly!'[53]

Nevertheless, it is the property of the sound-minded neither to be the slaves of preconception,[54] nor to be tied to ancestral customs [usages], but to seek what is true and to gather what is useful from everywhere. Is this not precisely what Socrates also said to Crito, 'For me, not only at present, but always I am like this: of all that is mine, I have no confidence in anything save reason, for it appears to me on reflection the most reliable.'[55]

Through this he shows that it was by using his reason that he sought to pursue his interest and that he had no law subjecting him to preconception. Thus he persuades Alcibiades to learn by first removing the conceit of knowing. Indeed at first he convinced him of his ignorance; then, to Alcibiades' question, 'But you do not suppose that I could find [. . .]?', he replied, 'Certainly, if you searched for it.' When Alcibiades uttered, 'So you think that I would not search?', he answered by saying, 'Indeed I reckon you will, on condition that you do not have the pretension of knowing.'[56] Thus, the beginning of knowledge [*gnōsis*] is the knowledge of [our] ignorance.

The purifying faith

Now in addition to this, one also needs to drive out evil lessons from the soul, and thus to receive divine ones. This is again what Plato taught, saying, 'It is not permitted for the impure to touch what is pure.'[57] This is also what Orpheus says, 'I shall address myself to those to whom it is permitted: close the gates, you profane!'[58] Euripides echoes this when he cries out, 'uninitiated mortals have to ignore ineffable [mysteries]!'[59]

Indeed, how could someone propose divine teachings to the uninitiated? Yet how could one be initiated if the doctrines brought forth by the teachers are not strengthened in him through faith? How could one believe if at first he has not eliminated from his thought what had been wickedly inserted there? Hence the truth of that tragic word spoken by Euripides in the *Phoenicians*: 'The unjust word, [being] the disease in itself, needs wise physicians.'[60]

Nonetheless, God assists [*synergei* = works together with] those who desire to be cured, as the same tragic poet says, 'God also helps the one in distress.'[61] Thus, faith is of the greatest use, since according to Epicharmus (I mean the Pythagorean): 'It is the mind [*nous*] that sees, the mind that hears: the rest are blind and deaf.'[62] Now again Heraclitus recommends being guided by faith, in these terms: 'If you do not hope, you will not find what you did not hope for, for it is unsearchable and inaccessible.'[63] And again: 'Gold-seekers dig up much earth and find very little!'[64] If those [people] endure so much suffering and even risks for a little gold dust, who could be so indifferent towards divine things as to flee from the teaching of truth which offers infinitely greater advantages?

Faith and reason

Therefore, my friends, nobody should speak against faith, since it is evident that even Aristotle called faith the criterion of science [*critērion epistēmēs*];[65] Epicurus even labelled it the preconception of the mind [*prolēpsis dianoias*].[66] Preconception, which acquires knowledge [*gnōsis*], becomes comprehension. According to our concept, faith is a voluntary assent [*ekousios synkatathesis*] of the soul, or a contemplation [*theōria*] of the obscure things, or a stance concerning what exists and a direct grasp of the invisible [world], commensurate with [its] nature, or an unambiguous disposition [*diathesis anamphibolos*] fixed in the souls of its {i.e. faith's} possessors. Faith surely needs knowledge just as knowledge [*gnōsis*] needs faith, for neither faith can exist without knowledge, nor knowledge apart from faith. Still, faith precedes knowledge and knowledge follows faith; impulse[67] fastens on knowledge and it is followed by action [*praxis*]. One has to believe first and then learn; once knowing, be eager; and having become eager, act. For even the alphabet cannot be learned if one does not believe the schoolmaster what one should call the first letter, then the second and so on. It is evident that if one were at once to contradict [the teacher] saying that the first [letter] should not be called 'alpha', but be given a different name, one would not learn the truth but inevitably would go astray and accept falsehood as truth. But if one believes the teacher and accepts the lessons according to his rules, faith will be very swiftly followed by knowledge. Thus it is advantageous to believe the geometer when he teaches that a point is something absolutely indivisible, and a line is a length lacking width. Nevertheless, no one could ever rationally demonstrate this, because if one removes width from a line, the length will surely disappear with it. Still, the geometer commands [us] to think like this, and the one who desires to study these geometric forms submits oneself and believes readily. Pupils believe astronomers in the same fashion: they give the number of the stars, calculate the distances which separate them from each other, and estimate how many thousand stades[68] separate the visible sky from the earth. And what divergences there are in their measures! Some speak of four million seven hundred thousand stades, others of less, others of many more. Despite this, students submit themselves to their teachers and believe the things they say.

Again, there is also a lot of dispute among them concerning the sun. Anaximander and Anaximenes affirmed it to be twenty-seven times bigger than the earth; for Anaxagoras it was bigger than the Peloponnese and for Heraclitus of Ephesus it was one foot [in diameter]! Who would [not] rightly deride such disagreement? For their divergences were not about some insignificant dimension, but rather such an infinite one that words cannot even convey it. For who would make a complete circuit of the earth with a measure, then multiply the length by twenty-seven, do the calculation and express it in terms of the measure of the human foot? Despite all this, there are some who follow one line, others another; in believing some accept one statement, others another. Therefore, why on earth do you let pass such an utterly irrational faith, and accuse ours only, which, free from such myths and nonsense, receives divine and intelligible things intelligently?

Some analogies of the faith

Besides what has been said let us observe this also: every person who wishes to learn a certain profession goes to a school of a specialist capable of teaching him and cherishes the lessons presented by him. The cobbler shows how one should hold the knife and cut through leather, and surely also how to sew it and shape it to the last. [The apprentice] believes what he is told and does not contradict his master. Whilst the latter possesses knowledge of what is being done, the former is content with faith, yet little by little, through faith he acquires knowledge. This is also the way indeed the shipwright instructs the one eager to learn how to hold the plumbline, how to handle the saw, how to use the axe, the gimlet and the borer. The apprentice learns each of these things, executing what is commanded, making himself a law from the words of his master and believing for sure that, through him [the teacher], he will master the craft. In the same way the physician does not only teach his science, but also cures the sick. He it is who knows the theory of medicine, while the one fighting against the disease does not, yet he surely believes he will be delivered of the sickness through medical science. Yet again only professional helmsmen know [how] to steer the ship straight; the sailors are confident that thanks to them they will land on the desired coasts.

You see now, my dear friends, that faith is a certain common property of everyone: both of those who long to learn any art, and of navigators, and cultivators, and those who turn to physicians. Knowledge, on the contrary, does not belong to all, but only to specialists. Thus, for example, when we want to know if gold has been tested and refined, we do not take it to the touchstone ourselves, but ask the specialist to examine it; he then, using either the stone or fire, will show whether it is base or pure. In the same way, when we buy precious stones, we do not rely on ourselves to assess them, but those whom time and experience have made experts. If someone wants to buy a silk dress embroidered and interweaved with gold, he relies on the reputation of those skilled in weaving to estimate its price. Finally, someone who wants to learn the weight of certain gold or silver objects or coins, brings them to a specialist in weighing, who shows him the weight and he believes his information without dispute.

Faith and knowledge of mysteries

Therefore, science does not belong to all, but to those who, by means of teaching, time and experience, have acquired it. Faith, on the contrary, belongs to all who are eager to learn something. Moreover, faith is certainly the basis and foundation of science. Even your philosophers defined faith to be the 'voluntary assent' of the soul and science as an unchangeable state [brought about] by reason. It [would be] out of place and exceedingly absurd that while teachers possess the science and pupils have the faith in all professions, only in the case of the instruction in divinity the order should be reversed, demanding science before faith – because for invisible things we need the eyes of faith. This is why the divine apostle also cries out so explicitly, 'For whoever would approach God must believe that he exists and that he rewards those who seek him' (Heb. 11:6). This is also why we bring forth the teaching of faith before everything else to those who approach us and desire to learn the divinity; and once they have been consecrated and initiated, we show them the hidden meaning of the mysteries. Neither among you does everyone know what the hierophant[69] says; the masses watch the sacred performance and those who are called priests accomplish the ritual ceremonies, yet the hierophant is the only one who knows the meaning of the words and he makes them known [only] to those he deems fit. Some of the initiated know that Priapus was the son of Dionysus and Aphrodite; but why is he called their son? And being so small, why is a member enormous in erection attributed to him? It is the hierophant of these disgusting mysteries who knows, and whoever has come across their accursed books. They name pleasure Aphrodite, drunkenness they label Dionysus, and the product of both they call Priapus, because when pleasure unites with drunkenness, it produces the erection of the genital members. Again, in the same manner the comic poets call the male member the phallus of Dionysus and the feast of the phallus is called phallagogy by the Greeks; and all those taking part in the orgy worship and kiss it, yet they do not know why. The one called hierophant knows of Osiris and Typhon: how the parts of Osiris' body were cut into pieces by Typhon and dispersed to all directions, and how Isis, sister of Osiris reassembled them carefully without succeeding in finding the phallus, and therefore made an image of it, commanding it to be worshipped by all. Having learned these Egyptian orgies, Orpheus of Odryse transferred them into Greece and organised the feast of the Dionysia.

In consequence, if the meaning of these repugnant and disgusting orgies is unknown to all save those who are called hierophants, it is plain madness to aspire to the knowledge of the all-holy and divine mysteries before faith [i.e. before believing]. Perhaps you are neither persuaded by Pindar the lyricist who clearly forbids 'to open the ancient word to all'.[70] Plato gives the very same advice, for he says,

Take care, lest these [doctrines] ever fall into [the hands of] uneducated people, because, in my opinion, it is almost impossible for most of them not [to treat] them when heard as quite ridiculous, while for the well-bred souls there is nothing more admirable and more inspired. Yet often repeated, always heard, and over many years these [doctrines] are hardly purified like gold, at great effort.[71]

You have also heard in the previous pages what Orpheus says, 'I shall address myself to those to whom it is permitted: close the gates, you profane!'[72] Thus, let faith lead and knowledge will follow. The Lord who is believed in grants knowledge to those who believe unsophisticatedly and purely, and knowledge adding to faith brings the science of truth to perfection. Hence, the one who possesses it is happy and thrice happy. This is what Plato also expresses in his *Laws*, for he says: 'The one who wants to be blessed and happy needs to share in the truth from the very beginning in order to live truly for the longest time.'[73]

Heaven and the abodes of angels have been prepared for those who have participated in the truth and lived worthily of it. But the one who lacks it and is unqualified and uninitiated into the all-holy and divine mysteries, shall be deprived of these benefits and handed over to eternal torture. In the *Phaedo*, Plato also reverts to this idea once again; he brings the words of those who have granted them the initiation, 'Whosoever arrives at Hades without having been consecrated and initiated, will wallow in the [sea of] mud; yet the one who arrives there purified and initiated will live with the gods.'[74]

The Greek philosophers and the Revelation

Obey therefore, friends, your philosophers who in advance initiate you and teach our [doctrines]. They simply resemble those of the song-birds which imitate the human voice while being ignorant of the words' meaning. In the very same manner also these [philosophers], when discoursing about divine realities, did not recognise the truth of what they said. I believe that to some extent they may be excused, for they had the benefit neither of the torches carried by the prophets, nor of the guiding light of the apostles, having as guide only nature, whose letters, carved by God, the error of impiety had long ago defaced. Still, the Creator renewed some of these, not permitting them to be completely faded, displaying through the creation his own forethought for humankind. This is what the divine apostle made plain in his discourse in Lystra, where, among other things, he said this:

> In past generations he [God] allowed all the nations to follow
> their own ways; yet he has not left himself without a witness
> in doing good – giving you rains from heaven and fruitful
> seasons, and filling your hearts with food and joy.
>
> (Acts 14:16–17)

The race of Abraham both received the divine law and benefited of the prophets' grace. As for other peoples, through their nature and the creation the Sovereign of the universe guided them towards the true religion. For example, the great Benefactor sends rain principally on cultivated land for the provision of humankind, yet in surplus and munificence it rains also in the deserts and mountains (and thus the arable land produces cultivated crops and unfarmed land produces wild ones; we also sometimes see fig trees growing both on tombs and walls). Similarly, the gift of the knowledge he had given especially to the godly [people], but also to those who are not such, nor like rain on deserts and thickets. Hence there often grow even some edible fruits resembling those of cultivated land, nevertheless, they obviously lacked the prophetic husbandry: some acridity and bitterness is mixed in them. Those who know how to distinguish harvest what is worth picking and send the rest away; in the same fashion as those who look after rose gardens discard the thorns and gather the blooms. Clearly, this is the native method of the bees also, who sit not only on sweet but also on bitter flowers: they draw the sweetness from them, turning away from the bitterness, and from various qualities like bitterness, acridity, dryness and sourness, they prepare for man the sweetest honey.

The method of the apologist

We also imitate them, preparing sweet honey from your bitter fields for your benefit. Just as those who cure the body prepare beneficial medicines from venomous beasts, even vipers, throwing away some pieces, boiling others, and by these driving out many sicknesses, so we also, having the works of your poets, historians and philosophers in our hands, leave aside what is harmful, while preparing other ingredients with the science of teaching, present you with an antidote-treatment. And those whom you consider as our adversaries, these we shall demonstrate that they defend our doctrines and show them to be the teachers of the faith.

Thus, with God's help, we shall also supply you with the continuation of our teaching. Now that you are taught how necessary faith is, cherish the Pythagorean silence and listen quietly to our presentation, accepting our account with faith, for in this manner you will surely be able rapidly to learn the truth.

10

ON THE HOLY AND VIVIFYING TRINITY AND ON THE INHUMANATION OF THE LORD

Introduction

These two treatises, *On the Holy and Vivifying Trinity* and *On the Inhumanation of the Lord*, written before the council of Ephesus,[1] survived under the name of Cyril of Alexandria in a Vatican manuscript (Vat. gr. 841). Cardinal Angelo Mai discovered and published them in the nineteenth century under the name of Theodoret's one-time opponent, and they were reprinted in Migne's PG in this way.[2] In 1888 Albert Ehrhard proved that they were in fact composed by Theodoret.[3] Further textual discoveries were published by Eduard Schwartz, Joseph Lebon, Robert Devreesse and Marcel Richard.[4] A modern critical edition of both treatises is being prepared by Prof. Jean-Noël Guinot for Sources Chrétiennes.[5] Nevertheless, since an adequate presentation of textual history and related issues is not yet at hand for an English readership, a few summarising remarks would be appropriate.

The two tracts were written before the council of Ephesus as a summary of Antiochene Trinitarian and Christological thinking, or as Theodoret and other fathers labelled it, of *theologia* and *oikonomia*. Theodoret himself mentions these tracts twice in his correspondence:

- in his letter written in the first half of 432 to the people of Constantinople;[6]
- in his letter to Pope Leo written after the *Latrocinium* in 449.[7]

Marius Mercator, in his anti-Nestorian work (written between 428 and 432, during the author's stay in Constantinople), gives three quotations from *De incarnatione* under Theodoret's name.[8] These fragments were published in the seventeenth century by the Jesuit scholar Jean Garnier.[9]

Other than Mercator, several authors quoted from or referred to these tracts (principally to the second one). As Lebon showed,[10] in his *Contra impium Grammaticum* written around 520, the Monophysite bishop Severus of Antioch quotes both from *De Trinitate* and *De incarnatione*, works which he credits to Theodoret. In fact he is the only theologian who cites *De Trinitate* under the name of its real author.[11]

Severus is an important source concerning the clarification of some textual differences (such as the correct form of the title of Ch. 22 [21] of *De incarnatione*), based on which Lebon suspected that a pseudepigraphy had been purposefully created by a neo-Chalcedonian theologian.[12] Later, having access to the original text of Vat. gr. 841, Prof. Guinot dismissed the theory of a deliberate text alteration and of a sixth-century pseudepigraphy.[13] Further, Severus' references to *De incarnatione* have enabled scholars to locate two unnoticed chapter titles within the text.[14] Interestingly, despite Severus' harsh criticism against this work, the council which condemned the famous *Three Chapters* in 553 did not mention Theodoret's *De Trinitate* and *De incarnatione*.[15]

In 1080 Nicetas of Heracleia wrote his *Catena of Luke*. His quotations from *De incarnatione* are the last ones known to us to appear under the name of its original author. His excerpts from the second treatise have enabled me to make textual corrections and additions which are noted in the translation.[16]

The earliest, and in fact (apart from Vat. gr. 841 itself) the only, testimony which ascribes the two treatises to Cyril dates from the twelfth century. A Byzantine theologian, Euthymius Zigabenus, in his *Panoplia Dogmatica* quoted several chapters from *De incarnatione*, ascribing the work expressly to Cyril. Nevertheless, one ought not to forget that this ascription comes from 'a compiler' and from a time when, in the East, the critical approach towards the genuineness of a work was largely absent; thus one may not give this ascription any text-critical authority.[17] Further, it has recently been discovered that Euthymius quotes not only from the second, but also from the first tract (again, under Cyril's name), and is thus the only theologian (apart from a single sentence preserved by Severus) who cites from Theodoret's *De Trinitate*.[18] The quotations preserved by Euthymius are also taken into consideration and applied whenever necessary in the following translation.

From the history of these tracts, it is clear that after having been criticised in 520 by Severus, quoted for the last time under the name of the real author by Nicetas in 1080, cited by Euthymius in the twelfth century, and finally copied into Vat. gr. 841 (a codex coming from the fourteenth or fifteenth century) – they were very soon forgotten.[19] There was no complete edition of the two tracts preceding their discovery and publication by Angelo Mai. Nevertheless, some excerpts of the second work, edited by mediaeval and early modern scholars, deserve a brief presentation.

Jean Garnier's posthumous edition of Theodoret's works was published in 1684 as a fifth volume to Jacques Sirmond's four volumes containing the oeuvre of the Bishop of Cyrus.[20] Garnier, being one of the most thoroughgoing researchers of his time, listed both tracts among the lost ones of Theodoret.[21]

The posthumous volume of Garnier has another interesting feature. On the one hand it states that the work in question is lost (on p. 256); on the other hand in the same volume several fragments of *De incarnatione* are published under the title *Theodorētou pentalogion {peri} enanthrōpēseōs* on pp. 40–50.[22] Thus, the same volume contains excerpts of a work whilst declaring it to be lost!

The Dominican father François Combefis published some passages from Theodoret's *De incarnatione*, under the name of Theodoret, in a Latin translation.[23] Another scholar, Andrea Gallandi, re-edited the two Latin fragments found by Combefis.[24] These excerpts published on the basis of Nicetas' *Catena* by Garnier, Combefis and Gallandi are thus the only ones known to have been edited before Angelo Mai's discovery of Vat. gr. 841.

Cardinal A. Mai was thus the first modern scholar to discover and print the two treatises under Cyril's name.[25] He was obviously thrilled by this discovery and convinced about the work's genuineness. In his footnotes, commenting on the second treatise, Mai derides the Monophysites' groundless claim, in which they ventured to quote Cyril in their own favour.[26]

In the year 1859, Jacques-Paul Migne reprinted both works, based on Mai's *Nova Patrum Bibliotheca*, in PG 75 – including all the comments and notes of the former editor – but unfortunately he separated the two tracts from each other. Thus, *De Trinitate* ended up amongst Cyril's Trinitarian treatises (PG 75, 1147–90), whereas *De incarnatione* was reprinted in the context of Cyril's Christological works (PG 75, 1419–78). Migne's edition has a peculiarity common with Garnier's: quite long identical texts are edited both under Cyril's, and then under Theodoret's, name.[27]

We have mentioned the theological importance of these two tracts in Part I. They contain those Trinitarian, soteriological and Christological ideas with which the Bishop of Cyrus arrived at Ephesus, one of the most important milestones in his life and in doctrinal history.

The present translation is based on the PG edition, nevertheless, having consulted the relevant manuscripts, I have put all the additions or textual variants from other sources in *italics*, adding an explanatory note concerning their provenance.

TEXT: *ON THE HOLY AND VIVIFYING TRINITY* (PG 75, 1147–90)

Foreword

Every writing requires time and tranquillity, together with a mind free of worries.[28] It is necessary for all those enlightened by the name of our Saviour Jesus Christ, and being the glorified sheep of the Shepherd who laid down His life for us, to hear the voice of the Shepherd, and grazing in the pasture shown by Him, to remain within the boundaries and rules of evangelic faith, adoring the pure teaching of the apostles. Yet, many [heretics] were moved by arrogance, craving for hollow fame and being ignorant of themselves, esteeming the conceptions of their own erroneous minds above the divinely inspired teaching, left the straight path that leads to the city in the highest[29] and stepped onto death-bringing passages with many splits.[30] And since all have been deluded likewise, not because of having pursued the same deceitful road similarly [to the heresiarchs], but by following the treachery of their reasoning in various ways:[31] I consider appropriate for those who follow the regal path trodden by the pious [i.e. the ortho- dox], to commiserate with the misguided, uncover the fraud, reveal the [true] piety and direct the adherents, keeping away from the deviations of each [heretic] side until they reach the royal city.[32]

1. God highly estimates the salvation of humankind

This is why the Saviour of the universe also sent the holy chorus of the apostles into the world: – to enlighten those, who were nurtured in the darkness of ignorance, by the rays of God's knowledge; to gather the dispersed and to pasture those sheep exposed to wolves with care; that by the art of the Spirit to change the wild olive-tree into a cultivated one;[33] by the Word of teaching to 'fish out' those sunk into the depth of impiety. Since the dearest [thing] for the Creator of all people is the salvation of humankind, the law of nature being to help our neighbours in need of assistance, we also invest the talents given to us by the Lord of knowledge with the bankers, not to be condemned together with the slothful servant (cf. Matt. 25:26–7). We present the teaching of divine doctrines as a reminder for the well versed, and as instruction for the uninitiated.

2. What is the characteristic of church doctrine

The word of evangelical faith should be proclaimed both simply and didactically, neither in a controversial, nor in an argumentative fashion, but rather as befitting the church of God: tersely, without ostentation; instructively, not in a long-winded manner; lacking finesse, yet abundant in theology. [It should] not be inquisitive about the inaccessible, or inspect the unintelligible, nor circumscribing the incomprehensible with reason and words, [even less] change the greatest knowledge [i.e. true piety] into skilful methods [i.e. theological speculation], nor requiring the demonstration whilst omitting faith. The pattern of divine teaching [i.e. of orthodoxy] is this: by following the fishermen and tracking the cobbler [i.e. the apostle Paul], being led by the tax collector, enlightened by the prophetic lamp, and illuminated by the sun of the gospel, [one should] not mingle anything [into the biblical teaching] from his/her own reasoning, but assemble all the teaching of the All-holy Spirit.

3. Concerning how this teaching will be [addressed] to the pious

In our other writings we have already refuted the heretical blasphemies, taking each of them separately, and by stripping off the veil of deceit we revealed their naked impiety.[34] This time, however, with God's help we shall expound for those nurtured in faith the God-given doctrines of the church, without overburdening the readers with lengthy speeches or corrupting accuracy with laconic talk. Instead, we have chosen a midway between both extremes, thus to avoid tiring the listeners with lengthiness and to present clearly the teaching of the divine science [*theognōsia*]. I shall start then from the beginning, turning to the fountainhead of all benefactions.

4. What kind of opinion should one have concerning God the Father

We, the suitors, worshippers as well as great-voiced and great-minded heralds[35] of the Trinity, believe in one God [and] Father, unbegun and unbegotten, [who is an] eternally existent Father, [who] did not become [Father] herein after [i.e. after a certain event]. For there was not [a moment] when he was not [a Father], but he had been Father from the very beginning. He was neither a Son first, and then [became] a Father, according to the corporeal sequence, but since ever he is – yet he is eternally – Father he both is and is called.[36]

5. How one should think about the Son

We believe in one Son, [who is] co-eternal with his Begetter, whose existence had no beginning, but he is eternally; moreover, he is [eternal] together with the Father. Thus, since ever the Father exists – yet he is eternally Father – [so also] the Son [is] from him. Therefore, they exist inseparably from each other according to their names as well as to their realities. For if the Son is not eternal, but there was when he was not,[37] then neither can the Father be eternal, because he bears the name [Father] only since [the moment] he [the Father] has begotten. But if God the Father is eternal (since it would be a blasphemy indeed to subordinate to time the existent One [who himself is] the creator of time, and according to time intervals to pronounce [as] second [*deuteros*] the begetting which is timeless and beyond time), then the Son is also eternal, since he was born ineffably of the Father, being eternal together with the Father, and perceived together with him.

6. The Scriptures teach the Son [as] co-eternal with the Father

'In the beginning, [Scripture] says, was the Word, and the Word was with God, and the Word was God. This was in the beginning with God' (John 1:1–2). Thus, [he] who existed in the beginning [already], when was he not? For [John] did not say, that he *came into existence* [*egeneto*] in the beginning, but that he *was* [*ēn*] in the beginning. If for example we were eager to surmount the [expression] 'was' with our reasoning, we would be unable [to move] beyond the inception. Everything is subsequent [in comparison] to the One existent in the beginning, both time [*chronos*] and aeon [*aiōn*] or anything temporal, which one could conceive [within each] period. If the Son had not been together with God the Father eternally, but came into existence later, then it is necessary to place a certain [period of] time or aeon between the Father and the Son. This being granted though, the creature is found to precede the Creator [i.e. the Son]. Since 'all things were made by the Son; and without Him not *one* thing was made' (John 1:3), says the evangelist. Yet, *one* of all [that was created] is the aeon or time![38]

The blessed Paul speaks thus, 'in these last days he has spoken to us by [his] Son, whom he had appointed heir of all things, by whom also he created the ages' (Heb. 1:1–2). If the ages are the creation of the Son, they do not precede their Creator. But since the ages did not [yet] exist, it is evident that time – which is made up and measured by days and nights – [did not exist] either. The rising and setting of light generates the days and nights – yet the light was made after the heaven, the earth and the air. The God-Word created all these and those within them by [his] word, according to the good will of the Father.

So among the times, aeons and all other things created by the Word, there is not one [creature] between the Father and the Son, but God is eternally Father, and the Son is eternally with the Father. That is why the evangelist exclaims: 'In the beginning was the Word.' Paul the apostle also says: 'Who is the brightness of His glory, and the express image of his person [*charactēr tēs hypostaseōs*]' (Heb. 1:3). And elsewhere: 'Who, being in the form of God, did not regard it as robbery to be equal with God' (Philem. 2:6). So neither does the former [i.e. John] omit the [verb] 'was', nor the latter [i.e. Paul] the expressions 'is' and 'being',[39] since both are proclaiming the eternally existent One. That is why, a little later, the evangelist says, 'he was life, and the life was the light of humankind' (John 1:4). And anew, 'the true light that enlightens every man was coming into the world' (John 1:9). Again: 'the Only-begotten Son, who is in the bosom of the Father' (John 1:18). [John] says in the Epistle also, 'That which was from the beginning' (1 John 1:1). Thus had the divine Spirit instructed those who from the beginning were eyewitnesses and servants of the Word (cf. Luke 1:2) in the theology concerning the Only-begotten Word of God. That is why they did not count the Creator with the creation; they did not rank the Maker among the creatures; [and for this reason] they nowhere called the honourable Child of God a creature. They never conjoined the [expression] 'became' with the Godhead, but [John] indeed [says], 'In the beginning was the Word' and not 'in the beginning the Word *came into existence*'. Paul says, 'Who *is* the brightness of His glory, and the express image of his person', and not '[who] *became* brightness and express image'. And again, 'Who *being* in the form of God' and not '[who] *became* the form of God', but rather 'who *has* [*ever*] been in the form of God'. And [he says] elsewhere: 'Who is the image of the invisible God' (Col. 1:15). He does not say, 'Who became the image of the invisible God', but rather 'who is [the image himself]'.

7. Demonstration from the Old [Testament] that the Son is eternal

Thus the [expressions] 'was', 'being', 'existent' and 'is' are everywhere connected with theology [*theologia*]. When he spoke to the great Moses, God entitled himself, 'I am who I am' (Exod. 3:14). And again: 'Say this to the children of Israel: I AM has sent me to you.' That these are the Son's words even the champions of blasphemy themselves testify, claiming that the Father is incomprehensible and labelling the Son a mediator between the Father and the creation, assuming that he [the Son] had appeared and spoken to the patriarchs and to the prophets. Yet the God-Word himself clearly teaches us through the prophet Jeremiah, saying:

> In those days and in that time I will make a new covenant with the house of Israel and with the house of Judah: not according to the covenant that I made with their fathers in the days when I took them by the hand to bring them out of Egypt.
>
> (Jer. 31:31)

So let us investigate who gave the new covenant. Is it not clear for all that the Ruler Christ is its author? He himself exclaims in the holy Gospels:

> It was said to those of old: you shall not kill. But I say to you: every one who is angry with his brother without cause is worthy of judgement. It was told to those of old: you shall not swear falsely. But I say to you: do not swear at all.
>
> (cf. Matt. 5:21–33)

He issued his other [statements] similarly: 'it was said so . . . , but I order it in this way. I do not transgress the existing law, but rather I improve the legislation, while teaching the mode of keeping [it].'[40] Therefore, the Ruler Christ gave us the new covenant. Further, the one who made this [new covenant] possible, had given the old one also to Israel after the release from Egypt. The giver of the old covenant and the deliverer from Egyptian slavery was undoubtedly the [same] one who had sent Moses to Pharaoh. He himself said, 'Say this to the children of Israel: I AM has sent me to you.' The prophet also makes this clear elsewhere, saying:

This is our God! No other can be compared to him! He found
the whole way to knowledge and gave it to his servant Jacob,[41]
and to Israel, whom he loved. Afterward he appeared on earth
and lived with humankind.

(Baruch 3:36–8)

Therefore, starting from the end, let us investigate the meaning of the
prophecy. Who then is the one who appeared on earth and lived among
the people? I assume it is clear for all those endowed with reason [*nous*]
that it is the God-Word, who assumed our nature, who did not regard
it as robbery to be equal with God, but emptied himself and took on
the form of a servant. So he gave the way of knowledge to his servant
Jacob and to Israel, his beloved one, he declared the old law in the
desert through Moses. The author of that law, before giving it, during
his conversation with Moses, declared, 'Say this to the children of Israel:
I AM has sent me to you.' Wherefore the prophet exclaimed: 'This is
our God! No other can be compared to him!' – testifying not his
insignificance, but his incomparable [greatness].

Observe how the prophetic message is similar to the evangelical
teachings! Moses proclaims 'the [eternally] existent one' [*ho ōn*]. The
God-Word affirms the 'I AM' [*ho ōn*][42] even more emphatically about
himself. Paul also uses the [term] 'existent' frequently, but adds to it
the [expression] 'being' [*hyparchōn*], which means the same as 'existent'.
He asserts 'is' [*estin*] also, which – according to its meaning – is
equivalent with the others. Similarly, John the theologian[43] also inserts
the word 'existent' in several places of his gospel. He adorns even the
prologue with these expressions, since he proclaims not once, or twice,
or thrice, but rather many times the [One, who] 'was'.

8. Different [things] are suitable to the God-Word and to the assumed nature

While the heralds of truth are teaching these [facts], who [could be]
so recklessly audacious or conceited to assert 'was not' against 'was'?
Or, despite the terms 'existent' and 'being', [who could] label a [mere]
creature the One who was born timelessly and impassibly of the Father,
and dwells in his bosom? Since who 'is' was not created, and who 'exists'
was not made. Those entrusted with the mysteries of divine knowledge
use [such expressions as] 'was made', 'assumed' and their like not theol-
ogising [i.e. speaking of God's divinity], but rather to proclaim the
oikonomia [i.e. referring to the incarnation].[44] The blessed John was
the first to announce that 'the Word was made flesh' after he had already

117

said that 'in the beginning was the Word'. After having applied the term 'was' repeatedly to the Godhead, upon turning to the oikonomia of the inhumanation [i.e. to the question/dispensation of the incarnation], he necessarily adds the expression 'became'. That which the God-Word took from us was not eternal from the beginning, but came into being and was assumed by the God-Word towards the end of the ages. The blessed Paul does the same, saying, 'being in the form of God', and adding, 'he did not regard it as robbery to be equal with God'. He adduces: 'he emptied himself and took on the form of a servant.' He [Paul] attaches the verb 'took on' to 'the form of the servant', while coupling the phrase 'the form of God' to [the expression] '[ever] was'. Consequently, the pre-existent, or rather ever existent, form of God took on the form of the servant. So the Word of God is neither a creation, nor a creature, nor of the non-existent [things],[45] but the one begotten of the Father who is eternally with the Father and together with the Father receives worship from the kind-hearted [believers].

9. On the begetting from the Father

Upon hearing the word 'begetting', nobody should think about the sufferings of our birth, weaning, flow [of blood], labours,[46] or anything similar to these, since these are the passions of bodies. God, however, is incorporeal, impassible, changeless and immutable and will eternally remain so. If someone were to argue that painless birth does not exist, [he] should also receive the argument from the [biblical] passages on the creation: since if there [i.e. at human birth] there is cutting and flow of blood, in the same fashion the creatures are closely accompanied by worries, toil, sweat, instruments [*organa*] and the pre-existent matter, by failures [*apotuchiai*][47] and other things akin to these. If the mere will is sufficient for God to create everything, and by his will he immediately brought the non-existent into being, the adversary should also admit that God's begetting was free from all sufferings. And since he did not create as humans do, in the same fashion he did not beget in the same way either.

10. What is the meaning of the Lord's titles?

For these reasons the Word is also named Son, being born without torment, like the word which emerges impassibly from the mind. He is also called Son as the one proceeding of the Father by begetting. He is also labelled 'God', as partaker of the Father's [divine] nature, and also 'the unchangeable image' of the begetting God.

Now concerning the God-Word one should believe that he is Only-begotten, born as One of the One in a unique way; he is the reflection of [God's] glory, representing the Father in himself and being always together with his Begetter, like the brightness with the light. He is the express image of [God's] person [*hypostasis*], to be confessed not as a mere [divine] operation [*energeia*], but rather a living person [*hypostasis*], fully portraying his Begetter in himself. The [title] 'Firstborn', however, is not the name of the divine nature, but of the oikonomia. How would it be possible for the God-Word to be Only-begotten and Firstborn also? The two names are contradictory: the 'Only-begotten' denotes the sole descendant, whereas 'Firstborn' indicates the one born before others, thus preceding them with [his] birth. The God-Word does not have a brother, since he is Only-begotten. But how could the Firstborn be the one who alone was born of the Father? Therefore it is evident, that the name 'Firstborn' belongs to the oikonomia.

If anyone were in doubt, he should learn from Paul, who exclaims: 'For those, whom he foreknew, he also predestined to be conformed to the image of his Son, that he might be the Firstborn among many brethren' (Rom. 8:29). Yet, according to nature, whose brothers are the believers? Not of the God-Word, but of the manhood of the same nature, since they are also fashioned akin to it [*symmorphoi*]. Elsewhere he also says: 'Who will change our vile body to be fashioned like [*symmorphon*] his glorious body' (Philem. 3:21). He is then also Firstborn, having many brethren, about whom he [David] says in the Psalms, 'I shall declare your name unto my brethren' (Ps. 22:22).[48] We do not say that the Only-begotten is different from the Firstborn, but that he is the same [person], although not for the same [reason]. He is named Only-begotten according to his initial [i.e. divine] birth, and called Firstborn, as the first one who relieved the pains of the life-giving [human] birth. That is why he is also named Firstborn from the dead (Col. 1:18, Rev. 1:5), as the first risen and the one who opens the gates of death. He is also the Firstborn of the whole creation (Col. 1:15), who, being born first in the new creation, renewed it by his birth. About this [new creation] the blessed Paul says, 'if any one is in Christ, he is a new creation: old things are passed away, behold, all things have become new' (2 Cor. 5:17).

If those who are fond of strife, and esteem contention higher than persuasion, were to say about the God-Word [himself] that he is 'the Firstborn of every creature' – we laugh at their ignorance. Let us agree, then, to demonstrate in this way also the truth which is abundantly with us. He is the 'Firstborn' [*prōtotokos*], but he is not labelled 'the first creature' [*prōtoktistos*] of all creation. So it is evident that he was indeed begotten before all creation, and nothing precedes the Son, but he had always been together with the Father and existed before the whole creation. The entire nature of creatures is thus subsequent, if it owes its existence to Him. In consequence, nothing remains [to support] the blasphemers.

11. Nobody knows the Son, but the Father, and nobody knows the Father, but the Son

In order to demonstrate the equality of the Father and the Son, let us move onto the Lord's teaching itself: 'No one knows the Son, he says, but the Father; neither knows anyone the Father, except the Son, and anyone to whom the Son wishes to reveal Him' (Matt. 11:27). What can be more evident than these words? He says:

> The knowledge [*gnōsis*] is equal to us, for I know the Father and am known through Him; the Father also knows me, he being also known through me. The whole creation, however, is excluded from our knowledge. For how could it be possible, that whosoever does not share our nature would be partaker of our knowledge? Yet some [people] do get a small share of that insight, because I reveal to those whom I want to the knowledge concerning the Father as in a mirror, dimly.
>
> (cf. 1 Cor. 13:12)

We have learned this from the Ruler's teaching: what place do the [notions of] smaller and greater have?[49] What kind of creature [*ktisma*] knows the Creator in the way the Creator [*ktistēs*] knows him? What sort of created thing/being [*poiēma*] could become equal to its Maker [*poiētēs*]? Or do we not know how the divine Scripture speaks about the creation? Let us remember then the prophet's words:

> Of old had you, oh Lord, laid the foundation of the earth: and the heavens are the work of your hands. They will perish, but you will remain; and all of them will wax old like a garment. You will change them as a clothing and they will be changed. But you are the same, and your years will have no end.
>
> (Ps. 102:25–7; LXX: Ps. 101:26–8)

And again: 'Who makes the winds His messengers and His ministers a flaming fire.'[50] This is the difference between creature and Creator.

So there is equality and by no means creature and Creator, but rather Father and Son. That is why [Scripture] uses these names so that from them we would learn the sameness [of their possessors]. He says: 'no one knows the Son, but the Father; neither knows anyone the Father, except the Son.' The saying 'no one' denotes the creation. The exclusion of the creation points to the one remaining above the creatures, being naturally united [*physikōs synēmmenon*] with his Begetter: 'No one knows the Son, but the Father; neither knows anyone the Father, except the Son, and any one to whom the Son wishes to reveal him.'

The enemies of the truth will say: 'How should one read the divine Scripture? Clinging to the letter or searching for the meaning?' On the one hand, if they were to assert the second [option], then they will have to learn from what they say and if they were to do this with their own statements, they could also investigate the true meaning of things. On the other hand, if they were to say that the letter is sufficient for accurate teaching, then let me refute their reasoning from the things set forth. For the Son is found inaccessible, yet the Father accessible; the former [is found] inconceivable, whereas the Father [is found] visible. When the Lord Christ said about Himself that 'no one knows the Son, but the Father', he did not add: 'and any one to whom the Father wishes to reveal Him'. He rather continued: 'neither knows anyone the Father, except the Son', whilst adding immediately: 'and any one to whom the Son wishes to reveal Him.' He not only made the Father comprehensible, but he also subordinated this comprehension to his own power. If those, who usually do this [i.e. commit blasphemy], wanted to hurt the Son impiously even ten thousand times, we do not tolerate the acceptance of a blasphemous statement concerning God the Father. We believe that the God of the universe is invisible and inconceivable. For how could the imperceptible be the Son of the perceptible? So we assert that the Father and the Son are similarly unintelligible, inaccessible and imperceptible, but we believe that through the Father and the Son the knowledge is revealed for the vision of the mind and for the sight of faith: 'no one knows the Son, but the Father; neither knows anyone the Father, except the Son.' Elsewhere he says, 'as the Father knows me, even so I know the Father' (John 10:15). No more and no less, but as I know [Him], so I am known.

12. The power of the Father and of the Son is equal

Those whose knowledge is equal have equal power also. And those who have equal power obviously have one essence [*ousia*] as well. Concerning the equality of the Father's and the Son's power the Saviour himself taught us again, saying:

> Those of my sheep hear my voice, and I know them, and they follow me, and I give them eternal life; and they shall never perish, neither shall any one pluck them out of my hand. My Father, who gave them to me, is greater than all; and no one is able to pluck them out of my Father's hand. I and the Father are one.
>
> (John 10:27–30)

Observe, how he does not merely affirm 'I and the Father are one', foreseeing the heretical malice, thus to prevent them from applying this affirmation [merely] to the intention and will [of the Father and Son], but rather he establishes first the equality of power [between the Father and the Son], and then turns to the next [matter]. He says:

> I give eternal life to the sheep, which follow me, so that none of them shall ever perish. For who is so strong as to be able to snatch my flock out of my hand? Inasmuch as it is not feasible for any one to overcome the right hand of the Father, who is greater than all, in the same fashion it is impossible to snatch any of my protected ones, since 'I and the Father are one'.

Where, then, are the [notions of] greater and smaller? If it is impossible for anyone to snatch [anything] from either the Son's or the Father's hand, then there is no place for 'the greater' [between them]. Since the Father is greater than all and nobody can snatch anything out of his hand, it follows also that the Son is greater than all, because in the same fashion nobody can pluck out anything from his hand either. That is why he continues, 'I and the Father are one.' If we follow the letter [of the text] again, we shall see that the Son is mentioned first. For he says, 'I and the Father' and not 'the Father and I'. Thus he shows the two persons [*prosōpon duada*] and proclaims the sameness of nature. With the statement 'I and the Father' he indicated the number of hypostases, and with the addition 'we are one' he evinced the invariability of the [same] power.[51] Therefore those who have equal knowledge, power and will, obviously have one nature [*physis*] also, no matter how impudently the blasphemers might object [to it].

13. The equality of the Father and the Son is to be learned from various [Scriptural] texts

The Father having the same power [with the Son][52] can be learned from elsewhere: 'My Father is working still, he says, and I work' (John 5:17). And here: 'As the Father raises the dead and quickens them, even so the Son gives life to whom he will' (John 5:21). He said [he gave life] 'to whom he will' and not to whom he was ordered to; to whom he wants and not to those to whom he was appointed to. Both the servitude and the supremacy is [the Son's] very own. Again elsewhere:

> If I am not doing the works of my Father, then do not believe me. But if I do them, though you do not wish to believe me, believe the works: and you will know that the Father is in me and I am in Him.
>
> (John 10:37–8)

Observe again the equality of the Father and the Son from this also, for he says, 'the Father is in me and I am in Him.' This [relationship] is impossible between superior and inferior [parties]. I say this: the God of the universe does not merely contain in himself both the visible and the invisible creation, but he rather holds it in his hand, as [Scripture] says, 'In his hand are the deep places of the earth' (Ps. 95:4; LXX: Ps. 94:4). And again, 'He owns the circle of the earth, and the inhabitants thereof are as grasshoppers' (Isa. 40:22). Elsewhere: 'Who has measured the waters in the hollow of his hand, and the heaven with the span, and the whole earth by bundle?' (Isa. 40:12). The Creator of the universe holds the whole creation in his hand, as I said; the creation is unable to contain him. Therefore it is impossible for unequal parties to contain each other reciprocally. If this is true – as it verily is – yet the Son contains the Father in the same manner as the Father [contains] the Son, then it is clear that the statement concerning the inequality [of the Father and the Son] is rejected, and the equality of Father and Son is acknowledged.

14. Proving that the Father and the Son deserve equal worship

The Ruler Christ himself teaches this again to us elsewhere, saying, 'I am the door. No one comes to the Father, but by me' (John 10:9 and John 14:6). And somewhere else: 'No one comes to my Son, unless my heavenly Father draws him' (cf. John 6:44). We are taught from this that as the Son draws the saved to the Father, in the same fashion the Father also [brings them] to the Son. Where is then the heretics' worship suitable for the servant? Where is the service befitting the creature? Where does [Scripture] show the inequality between the Father's supremacy and the Son's servitude? Since we heard just now how the Son leads those longing for salvation to the Father, and that the Father does the same also by drawing those nurtured in faith to the Son.

15. The nature of the Father and Son is one

We learn from this that the Father and the Son deserve equal worship.[53] This is also taught elsewhere, when the Lord himself speaks to the Jewish listeners. After explaining many things, he finally turns to say:

> Though I bear witness of myself, yet my testimony is true: for I am not alone, but I and the Father who sent me. It is also written in your law, that the testimony of two people is true. I am one bearing witness of myself, and the Father who sent me bears witness of me. Then the Jews said to Him: 'where is your Father?' – Jesus answered them, 'you neither know me, nor my Father: if you had known me, you would have known my Father also.'
>
> (John 8:14–19)

Oh, how immense is the madness of the heretics! What a sheer frenzy the heirs of Arius' and Eunomius' blasphemy suffer from! Apart from insanity, there is much lofty impudence to be observed in them. They endlessly mention the sending [of the Son] and claim that the sender is more honourable than the one being sent. How ignorant are they of the Scriptures! They do not even consider that – in respect of [human] nature – Jacob, being sent by Isaac to Mesopotamia, because of this [task] was not at all inferior to the one who sent him. Similarly, Jacob also sent Joseph to find his brothers, but nobody ever claimed that Joseph did not share his father's [human] nature, just because he willingly accepted the assignment from his father.

Nevertheless, they claim that even if, according to the rules of nature, the above senders are not superior to their messengers, in respect of paternal dignity they nevertheless retain the primary honour. 'Oh, you senseless', I would tell them, 'but we can find [such examples], when those of lower rank send those of higher standing, and by this we do not disrobe at all those being sent of their own dignity.' For Jonathan was sent by David: the son of the king by the fugitive; the one who ruled together with his father by the one who would not dare to show up even among the order of servants. Therefore – since one is the sender and the other the messenger – according to your definition[54] the messenger is not a king, and the sender is not a fugitive anymore. On the contrary: the dignity of his messenger is transferred to the sender David, whereas the hardships of the messenger are shifted to his emissary, Jonathan. But nothing like this happened.

But why should one enumerate human [examples]? We find [situations where] God is sent and man is the sender. The one who wrestled with him, told Jacob:

'Let me go, for the day breaks.' Jacob said to him, 'I will not let you go until you bless me' (Gen. 32:26).[55] What could the wise experts of faith have to say against this? From the Ruler's words we perceive [this] in a different manner, because the sending Father himself is together with the Son being sent: 'for I am not alone', he says, 'but I and the Father who sent me' (John 8:16). And further: 'My Father has not left me alone' (John 8:29). Elsewhere: 'My Father who dwells in me, he does the works' (John 14:10). So if the sender is in him and with him, where is the inferiority of the one being sent? From where, and to which place, was sent the One who fills all? The word 'sending' suggests a change of location. Yet if the Father and the Son fill all, then neither did the Father send the Son to those whom he apparently was away from, nor did the Son go from one specific place to another. Thus nothing remains, but that the sending [of the Son] is to be taken as referring to the assumed manhood.

It is time to turn to the explanation of the Ruler's words. 'It is written in your law' he says, 'that the testimony of two people is true' (John 8:17). He then adds: 'I am one bearing witness of myself, and the Father who sent me bears witness of me' (John 8:18). So looking at the image [of Christ], let us recognise the archetype. 'The testimony of two people is true', he says. Everybody agrees that the [human] nature of two people is evidently one. Accordingly, the Father and the Son have one essence, which is recognised and confessed through the [same] image [*mia eikōn*]. While previously [we spoke about] two human beings, in a similar fashion here [we speak about] God and God, [about] Father and Son, and by the names themselves they already show the sameness of their nature.[56] For neither does the true God differ in nature from the true God, nor is the Son [of] different [nature][57] from him, being the Son of God. Upon hearing these things, the Jews asked him: 'Where is your Father?' Jesus replied, 'you neither know me, nor my Father: if you had known me, you would have known my Father also' (John 8:19).

Observe again, how the coessentiality [of the Father and Son] is thus manifested! For he says: 'If you had known me, you would have known my Father also.' Something of one essence is not recognised through another of different essence. Things of dissimilar or alien nature do not represent each other. Yet those sharing the same nature can be recognised through each other. The nature of the whole humankind becomes visible through one human being, and the whole genus of sheep through a single sheep respectively. But [one] cannot [perceive] lions through sheep, nor sheep through lions, nor angels through human beings, nor human beings through angels; for each creature is expressive of his/her own nature. Therefore, if the Only-begotten Word is God's creation and was made of non-existent [things][58] and of some different nature [than that of the Father], how can he exhibit the Father trustworthily in himself? If the Father is known through the Son, and he who knows the Son knows the Father, then let all blasphemous tongues be bridled, and cleave to the roof of their mouth, according to [the words of] the prophet (Ps. 137:6; LXX: Ps. 136:6). We, the worshippers of the Trinity, hereby receive the accurate knowledge of coessentiality, maintaining that the Father cannot be recognised in the Son in any other fashion, unless he shared the same essence, and we adore our Saviour, awaiting the fruit of our supplication, the giver of which is the Father himself according to the Lord's word: 'if any one serves me', he says, 'my Father will honour him' (John 12:26). John, the admirable theologian says: 'whoever believes in the Son has eternal life; whoever disobeys the Son will not see life, but must endure God's wrath' (John 3:36).

16. The Lord taught in various places that his essence and the Father's is one

In order to demonstrate the coessentiality by other testimonies, let us listen to the Lord himself, who exclaims and says, not only to the apostles but to the Jews as well:

Whoever believes in me, believes not in me, but in him who sent me. And whoever sees me sees him who sent me. I have come as light into the world, so that everyone who believes in me should not remain in the darkness.

(John 12:44–6)

So if someone looking at the Son [sees the Father and] believes in the Father, where are the [notions of] greater and smaller? In that which is inferior the superior thing is diminished, and is not recognised. So, if the Father is greater, how can he be contemplated in the Son? Yet if the Father is observable in the Son, then he is evidently recognised [in the Son] as in his [i.e. the Father's] equal. Their mutual equality is thus evident. A little later, the Lord himself again addresses the disciples:

> I am the way, the truth and the life: no one comes to the Father, except through me. If you know me, you will know my Father also: from now on you do know him, and have seen him. Philip said to him, 'Lord, show us your Father, and it suffices us.' Jesus said to him, 'have I been with you all this time, and you still do not know me, Philip? Whoever has seen me has seen the Father. How can you say then, "Show us the Father?" Do you not believe that I am in the Father, and the Father is in me? The words that I say I do not speak on my own: but the Father, who dwells in me, he does the works. Believe me that I am in the Father and the Father is in me: but if you do not, then believe me because of the works themselves'.
>
> (John 14:6–11)

What can be clearer than these words? What can be more evident than this teaching? And yet, it seems, the veil of the Jews (cf. 2 Cor. 3:13–16) darkened the minds of the heretics: that is why they do not want to see what is brighter than the sun, being covered by the fog of ignorance they have voluntarily chosen. We, however, should listen to the Lord, who says: 'If you had known me, you would have known my Father also: henceforth you know Him, and have seen Him.' He says this to Thomas who asked him, 'We do not know where you are going, how could we know the way?' (John 14:5) – and teaches him and the rest of the apostles, that the one who believes in him, contemplates him with the eyes of wisdom, and has become the contemplator of the Father also, that is, of the Father made known through him [i.e. the Son]. Philip did not understand this and asked him, saying: 'Show us your Father and it suffices us.' But he was not praised, as he desired to see 'the greater one' in the manner of the heretics. He was reprehended instead for not observing the Father in the Son. 'Have I been with you all this time', he says, 'and you still do not know me, Philip?' But Philip craved to see the Father, not him. Why was he reprehended then as if he had not recognised the Son? [Jesus] throws light upon the cause of the admonition in the following part [of his answer]: 'whoever has seen me', he says, 'has seen the Father. How can you say then, "show us the Father?"' For I am different, he says, [from the Father], regarding personhood [*kata to prosōpon*], but not according to nature [*ou kata tēn physin*]. I bear the Father wholly within myself, since I am the unaltered seal of my Begetter, the express image of his person [*hypostasis*], [in a word] the natural image [*eikōn physikē*] coexisting with my Begetter. So if you want to see him, [just] look at me, and you will see [us] both, yet not with the eyes of the body, but with the eyes of faith. With the eyes of faith, however, you [will see] to such an extent that you will recognise the operations, but neither the nature nor the essence: for this perception surpasses every mind. That is why he continues:

> Do you not believe that I am in the Father, and the Father is in me? The words that I say I do not speak on my own: but the Father, who dwells in me, he does the works. Believe me that I am in the Father and the Father is in me: but if you do not, then believe me because of the works themselves.

Thus if these [works] are ascribed to the Father, and the Father remains in him as well as he in the Father; and if he who sees and knows him, sees and knows the Father, then it is evident for all having common sense, that the Father and the Son have one nature, and the Son is in possession of everything which belongs to the Father. For he did not represent the Father in himself differently [i.e. in an altered fashion], but possessed everything like the Father, except fatherhood itself, which is the Father's own attribute, just as sonship belongs to the Son.

17. A different demonstration of the Son's equality with the Father

This equality is also taught elsewhere, as follows: 'Jesus said: Now is the Son of man glorified, and God is glorified in him. God will also glorify him in himself, and glorify him at once' (John 13:31–2). And again: 'Father, the hour has come; glorify your Son that your Son also may glorify you' (John 17:1). O, measureless heretic folly! They claim that the one who glorifies is greater than the glorified. On the one hand the Father glorifies, on the other hand the Son is glorified: therefore, [in their opinion] the Father is greater than the Son. So if not only the Son is glorified, but he also glorifies [the Father] who glorified him [before], then what kind of place is retained for the [notions of] greater and smaller? From the preceding statements it would follow that the superiority is passed onto the one who glorifies. In this manner the Son is found to be of lower rank when being glorified, but superior once he is glorifying [the Father]. To claim this, however, would be utmost madness and frenzy, since here we are taught not about the superior and the inferior, but rather the equality of Father and Son. We have heard, that as the Father glorifies the Son, he is also glorified by the Son; and as the Son is glorified by the Father, he also glorifies the Father. The one who was glorified did not receive what he did not possess [before], but what he [had always] possessed. [The Lord] teaches this in the same place, saying: 'Now, oh Father, glorify me in your own presence with the glory which I had with you before the world existed' (John 17:5). Thus if he had had this glory before the world was made, how could he ask to receive something, which he always had?

18. The dominion[59] of the Father and of the Son is one

[The Lord], after having shown that not only is he glorified, but he glorifies [the Father] as well, continues: 'I have manifested your name to the people' (John 17:6). A little later, he covers the mouths of the heretics, saying: 'All mine are yours and yours are mine' (John 17:10). He neither divides the common dominion; nor does he want to show some [things] *as belonging to Him* while other important things [belong] to the Father.[60] But since those uttering every blasphemous word against the Only-begotten claim that he [merely] accepts, and the Father is the one who gives, [the Lord] demonstrates that he possesses the same dominion with the Father over everything. 'All mine are yours and yours are mine', he says, teaching not the division of the dominion, but the commonness of the dominion.[61]

Nevertheless, I have overstretched the discourse about faith, and have surpassed the brevity promised in the introduction. I wanted to show from the evangelic teaching the dignity of the Only-begotten, and have thus elaborated at more length than promised, although I tried to be concise in the commentaries. Therefore, whilst directing the pious to the evangelic and prophetic books themselves – since these are full of the theology of the Son – I shall now turn to the next question.

19. On the Holy Spirit

As I have said, we believe in God the Father who is without beginning, and in God the Son who is by nature co-eternal with Him, who was begotten by the Father, and is eternally together with the Father, according to the word of the Gospel: 'In the beginning was the Word.' We also believe in the righteous, the guiding, the good and the counselling Holy Spirit, who proceeds from God;[62] he was not begotten, because there is one Only-begotten; nor was he created, since nowhere in Holy Scripture do we find him being enumerated along with the creatures, but rather ranked together with the Father and the Son. We have heard that he[63] comes from the Father, yet we do not inquire about the mode of his procession, but rather acquiesce in the limits the theologians and blessed men have fixed for us.

20. The Spirit is of equal rank with the Father and the Son

We are taught by our Saviour, Jesus Christ himself, that the Holy Spirit completes the Trinity: 'Go therefore', he says, 'and make disciples of all nations, baptising them into the name[64] of the Father, and of the Son, and of the Holy Spirit' (Matt. 28:19). Being confessed together with the Father and the Son, [the Spirit] is superior to all creation. That is why the blessed Paul perseveres in proclaiming the Spirit together with the Father and the Son, saying: 'The grace of the Lord Jesus Christ, and the love of God the Father, and the fellowship of the Holy Spirit be with you all' (2 Cor. 13:13).

21. Explanation of the dominion of the Holy Spirit

And again [we read]: 'Now there are varieties of gifts, but the same Spirit; and there are varieties of services, but the same Lord; and there are varieties of activities, but it is the same God who works all in all' (1 Cor. 12:4–6). Proclaiming the power of the Spirit, [Paul] exclaimed: 'But all these are effected by one and the selfsame Spirit, who divides his gifts to every believer individually, according to his steadfast will' (cf. 1 Cor. 12:11). Through him we receive forgiveness of our sins; by him we become partakers of freedom and benefit from the gift of sonship. Paul says: 'we did not receive the spirit of slavery to fall back into fear, but we have received the Spirit of sonship, whereby we cry: Abba, Father!' (Rom. 8:15). And elsewhere: 'For the law of the Spirit of life has set me free from the law of sin and death' (Rom. 8:2). And somewhere else: 'Now the Lord is the Spirit: and where the Spirit of the Lord is, there is freedom' (2 Cor. 3:17). If someone sets others free, he is not a slave. Otherwise how could he give to his fellow slaves what he himself does not have, or cannot be a partaker of, yet what he would certainly want to attain, but is unable to? Yet, if he transmits freedom to believers and sets slaves free, it is evident that he does not serve, but rules: and as a ruler, he grants freedom to those he wills. That is why the blessed Paul also says that 'all these are effected by one and the selfsame Spirit, who apportions to each one individually as he wills.' The prophet in the Old [Testament] enunciating his power for the same reason, exclaimed: 'The Lord and his Spirit has sent me' (Isa. 48:16). Even God himself reprehended the Jews, saying: 'they achieve a purpose, but not through me; and they make a covenant, but not by my Spirit' (Isa. 30:1). He demonstrates that the Holy Spirit is a partaker of the dominion. And elsewhere: 'that is why I am with you and my Spirit remains in the midst of you' (cf. Hag. 2:4–5).

22. The Counsellor is [also] Creator

Job also confesses the Spirit as being Creator and Ruler, but neither a servant, nor a creature. 'The divine Spirit created me, and the inspiration of the Almighty taught me' he says (cf. Job 32:8). If [the Spirit] created human nature, then he has the same essence as the Father and the Son. When creating the human being, God said: 'Let us create man in our image, after our likeness' (Gen. 1:26).[65] Those having one [i.e. the same] image, evidently have one essence also.

23. The Holy Spirit is of God

That the Holy Spirit is of the divine nature, God himself teaches us through the prophet Joel, saying: 'In those last days I shall pour out my Spirit upon all flesh' (Joel 2:28). The Ruler Christ teaches us also, when addressing the disciples: 'When they hand you over, do not worry about how you are to speak or what you are to say; for it is not you who speak, but the Spirit of your Father who speaks in you' (Matt. 10:19–20). And Paul again: 'But you are not in the flesh, but in the Spirit, if the Spirit of God truly dwells in you' (Rom. 8:9). A little later: 'For those being led by the Spirit of God, are sons of God' (Rom. 8:14). And elsewhere:

> These things God has revealed to us through his Spirit: for the Spirit searches everything, even the depths of God. For what

human being knows what is [truly] human except the human spirit that is within? So also no one knows what is truly God's except the Spirit who is of God.

(1 Cor. 2:10–11)

From these texts it is evident that the Holy Spirit is neither of different kind, nor of a different essence, but is of the divine nature. That is why he also perceives the depths of God and knows what is truly God's, just as our soul [is aware of] her own issues. And if anyone would consider this search [of the Spirit] as ignorance, he shall find it in reference to the Father also: 'For he who searches the heart', he says, 'knows what is the mind of the Spirit' (Rom. 8:27). Thus if the God of the universe does not investigate because of being ignorant, but rather knows everything clearly before its coming into being, and if the Holy Spirit of God does not search God's depths as a result of ignorance; how could one harmonise the ignorance with the fact, that as the spirit of the human being knows the things [happening] within the person, in the same fashion nobody knows the things of God, except the Spirit of God? The search is antithetic to knowledge. The soul, however, does not search for the things concerning her, but rather knows them exactly. Thus, the Holy Spirit knows God fully. And as nobody knows the Father except the Son, and nobody [knows the Son] but the Father, in the same fashion, [as Scripture] says, nobody knows the things of God except the Spirit of God. From what is said we are taught the similarity of the nature [of the Father, Son and Holy Spirit].

Since those suffering from all impudence – I mean the disciples of the blasphemy of Arius and Eunomius – assert that God himself is the Spirit of God, the blessed Paul necessarily shows the personhood [prosōpon] of the Spirit. He says:

We have received not the spirit of the world, but the Spirit which is of God: that we might perceive the gifts freely given to us by God. Which things also we speak, not taught by human wisdom, but taught by the Holy Spirit; comparing spiritual things with spiritual. The natural man does not receive the things of the Spirit of God: for they are foolishness to him: and he cannot understand them, because they are spiritually discerned. For who has known the mind of the Lord, so that he may instruct Him? Hence, we have the mind of Christ.

(1 Cor. 2:12–16)

[Paul] therefore, with the statement 'we have received not the spirit of the world, but the Spirit, which is of God' teaches, not that the Holy Spirit is of the same origin as the world, but that he is partaker of the divine nature. In addition, he also teaches [us] by speaking, not of God the Father, but of the Holy Spirit, the grace of whom believers receive. That is why he says that the Spirit is of God, teaching that he receives his existence from the Father, shares his nature, though *neither by creation nor by begetting*,[66] but in a manner that is known only to the Son-knowing [Father], the Father-knowing [Son] and to [the Holy Spirit] who knows both the Father and the Son. We have learned that [the Spirit] is of God, but we have not been instructed about the mode [of his procession]. We are satisfied with the measure of knowledge we were bestowed with, and do not investigate the incomprehensible things ignorantly.

24. The great apostle knows the Spirit as being God

Paul teaches us again that the Holy Spirit is God, saying, 'you are washed, sanctified, and justified in the name of our Lord Jesus Christ and in the Spirit of our God' (1 Cor. 6:11). On whose account are we called temples of God, receiving the grace of the Spirit through baptism, if the Holy Spirit is not God? Yet the same apostle teaches that believers are called temples of the Spirit, saying, 'don't you know that your body is the temple of the Holy Spirit within you, which you have from God, and you are not your own? For you were bought with a price' (1 Cor. 6:19–20). The temple proclaims the indwelling God. That is why Paul said earlier: 'Don't you know that you are the temple of God and that the Spirit of God dwells in you? If any one destroys God's temple, God will destroy him: for God's temple is holy, which temple you are' (1 Cor. 3:16–17). So, if believers receive the grace of the *Spirit* through baptism, and we – being honoured by this gift – are called the temple of *God*, it follows that the Holy Spirit is God indeed. *That is why the indwelling of God is effected in the receiving temples*;[67] yet, if those who benefit from the grace of the Spirit are the temples of God and are *called* so, it is clear, that the Holy Spirit is of the divine nature and is coessential [*homoousion*] both with the Father and the Son. If [the Spirit] were a creature of a different essence, it would be unjust to call God's temples those who received his gifts. Yet, if those who received the grace of the Spirit in a greater or smaller measure are indeed called temples of God, from this appellation we will conclude that [the Holy Spirit] is akin [to the Father and the Son]. The foremost apostle also teaches this in the book of the Acts, when repudiating the theft of Ananias.

25. The divinely inspired Peter also agrees [with Paul] regarding the Spirit,

For he says: 'Ananias, why has Satan deceived your heart to lie to the Holy Spirit and to keep back part of the land's price for yourself?' And a little later: 'You have not lied to men, but to God' (Acts 5:3–4). Therefore, since Ananias thought he could keep it secret from the apostles – as from [ordinary] men – that he had withheld from the price of the property what he wanted, the head of the apostles teaches him that those having the grace of the Spirit clearly know everything that happens in secret. He says: 'you did not lie to us, but to the Holy Spirit. Therefore, do not think that you deceived men, for it is God to whom you lied. You did not lie to men, but to God. You did not betray us, he says, but you have betrayed the Holy Spirit, who is very God, having his existence from God, and sharing His nature.' The same thing is made clear by Luke later in the Acts, when he says, that the Holy Spirit thus spoke to the brethren serving the Lord and fasting in Antioch:

26. A wider demonstration that the Holy Spirit is God

'Separate for me Paul and Barnabas for the work to which I have called them' (Acts 13:2). Later [Luke] tells, how they went down to Seleucia being sent by the Holy Spirit, and describes how they travelled through Cyprus, Lycia, Lycaonia, Pamphylia and Bithynia, preaching the Gospel. Luke then continues:

> And from there, Barnabas and Paul sailed back to Antioch, where they had been commended to the grace of God for the work that they had completed. And when they arrived, they called the church together, and related all that God had done with them.
>
> (Acts 14:26–7)

At the beginning, [Luke] mentions the Spirit, who chose Paul and Barnabas for the work to which he called them. He uses the name [Spirit] after their departure; and he applies the appellation 'God' twice. First he says that they sailed to Antioch where they had been commended to the grace of God for the work that they had completed.

Secondly, that they called the church together, and related all that God had done with them. And of course, the Holy Spirit was the one who performed the miracles, bestowed wisdom and understanding upon them, he strengthened the preachers and inspired them with the word of teaching. That is why Paul also said:

> For to one is given by the Spirit the word of wisdom; to another the word of knowledge according to the same Spirit; to another faith by the same Spirit; to another the gifts of healing by the same Spirit (1 Cor. 12:8–9); and so on.

So while teaching that the Holy Spirit does not continue giving these gifts like a servant, but rather bestows them on whom he wills, like a Ruler, [Paul] continues: 'All these are effected by the one and the selfsame Spirit, who apportions to each one individually as he wills.' Thus, if the *Holy Spirit* accomplished these things through the apostles according to His will, yet Paul and Barnabas told the congregation gathered around them that *it was God* who had done all [these things] with them, then the Holy Spirit is God indeed, according to the words of the apostles.

The same thing also happened in Jerusalem, according to the most divinely inspired Luke, who says: 'Then all the multitude kept silence, and listened to Barnabas and Paul, as they related what signs and wonders God had done through them among the Gentiles' (Acts 15:12). Thus, the Holy Spirit is God indeed, since he himself miraculously performed the wonders and signs. That is why the Lord also says in the Gospel, 'But if I cast out demons by the Spirit of God, then the kingdom of God has indeed come upon you' (Matt. 12:28). In Acts, Luke again says about Paul, that he 'chose Silas, and departed, being commended by the brethren unto the grace of God' (Acts 15:40). Here [Luke] calls the Holy Spirit 'God', who, through the brethren in Antioch, selected [Paul] for the work to which he had appointed him. The blessed Paul says again in his Epistle to the Corinthians: 'those whom God has ordered in the Church: some as prophets and apostles, while some as pastors, teachers and evangelists, for the perfecting of the saints.'[68] In Miletus, gathering together the brethren and remembering the grace received [from God], he says: 'Take heed therefore to yourselves, and to all the flock, in which the Holy Spirit has made you overseers, to pasture the Church of the Lord, which he had gained with His own blood' (Acts 20:28).[69]

Observe again, how here also [Paul] calls the Holy Spirit God.[70] Since there [i.e. in Eph. 4:11–12] he mentioned the pastors, teachers and evangelists as being ordained by God. Here he speaks of the Holy Spirit: 'in which the Holy Spirit has made you overseers, to pasture the Church'. He teaches that the Holy Spirit is God, and that it is the same to say 'God' or 'Spirit' because of the commonness of the nature. The Son and the Spirit participate in the things effected by God the Father, whereas God the Father simultaneously gives His consent [*syneudokei*] to those accomplished by the Son and the Spirit.

Again, the blessed Paul proclaims elsewhere that the Holy Spirit is God, saying: 'But if all prophesy, an unbeliever or outsider who enters is reproved by all and called to account by all; after the secrets of his heart are disclosed, that person will worship God by falling on his face, declaring that God is really among you' (1 Cor. 14:24–5). The gift of prophecy belongs to the Spirit and through the revelation of the Spirit the secrets of the heart are manifested. Nevertheless, it is God's attribute to know the mind of human beings, thus it necessarily follows that the one convicted by the prophecy will worship God humbly, declaring that God is in you indeed, whereas [you] actually have the gift of the Spirit. Yet if God was in them because they benefited from the gift of the Spirit, it follows that the Holy Spirit is God and of God indeed.

27. The Holy Spirit [is] of God in an uncreated fashion, thus he is also called eternal

The most inspired Peter says in his Catholic letters: 'If you are reproached for the name of Christ, you are blessed: for the Spirit of glory, of power and of God rests upon you' (1 Peter 4:14). The blessed John also says in his Epistle: 'Hereby we know that we remain in him and he in us, because he has given us of his own Spirit' (1 John 4:13). The one proclaimed to be of God is not a creature, but of the divine essence. That is why the blessed Paul calls him eternal and existent without beginning: 'If the blood of bulls and of goats and the ashes of a heifer sprinkling the unclean, sanctifies to perfection, how much more shall the blood of Christ, who offered himself through the Holy Spirit?' (Heb. 9:13–14).[71] Thus, if the Holy Spirit is eternal and God is eternal also, the conclusion is evident. Nevertheless, we leave to the laborious to gather all the testimonies about the Holy Spirit, which proclaim him as God and Lord and rank him together with the Father and the Son: as for us, we move on to the conclusion of our present teaching.

28. The summary of faith

Therefore, we believe the nature and the essence of the Trinity to be one perceived in three characteristics,[72] the power is undivided, the kingdom without partition; [there is] one Godhead and one lordship. The unity [*monas*] is also shown in the sameness of the essence, whereas the Trinity [*trias*][73] is perceptible not in the bare names, but in the hypostases.[74] For we do not call the One 'three-named' according to the contraction and mixture of Sabellius, Photinus and Marcellus. We do not [say], that [there are] three [persons] of different kind and distinct essence, unequal and dissimilar, one superior to the other, measurable and definable by [human] mind and tongue, according to the impious meddling of Arius, who separated and estranged [the Persons of the Trinity] from each other. Rather we speak of three hypostases, but one nature of the Trinity, [a nature which is] incorporeal, unchangeable, immutable, endless, immortal, infinite, incorruptible, indescribable, boundless, invisible, indistinguishable, ineffable, inexpressible, incomprehensible, imperceptible, inconceivable, self-existent, spiritual light, the fountainhead of benefits, the thesaurus of wisdom, Creator of the universe and provider of all, the Wisdom steering the ship of creation. This faith we preserve, since this we were taught by the theologians. To those who argue on the basis of [human] reasoning, we shall say: that is your share, your heritage according to your fate; our share however, is the Lord, and following Him we shall not forsake the right way, for we have the divine Scripture as [our] teacher. That is why we rightly exclaim: 'Your law is a lamp unto my feet, and a light unto my paths' (Ps. 119:105).[75] Being illuminated by this light let us recognise the footprints of the foregoing fathers and let us follow them until we all reach the resurrection of the dead in Christ Jesus the Lord, to whom shall be glory forever. Amen.

TEXT: *ON THE INHUMANATION OF THE LORD*
(PG 75, 1419–78)

1. The remembrance of the divine oikonomia is useful for the listeners

We have completed the treatise on the doctrine of the Holy Trinity, which is, in my opinion, appropriate for the congregation of the pious and those who accept the evangelical teachings. At present our aim is not to contradict the impious, but to expound the faith for the disciples of the apostles, because the greatness of divine benefits sets afire the aspiration of those who love God. Their ardour thus becomes even more enthusiastic towards him. I therefore necessarily commence this work, by connecting theology with oikonomia,[76] and showing how greatly the Creator looked after our kind, because the fountainheads of divine gifts never cease to pour their benefits upon the people.

2. Enumeration of God's deeds {which served} for the benefit of man from the beginning

Ever since the Creator made [this] entirely harmonious world, he filled our nature with all kinds of benefits. First he created the one who did not exist, dignifying him by creation, and transformed the earth into human nature as he willed, gave beauty and soul[77] to the formless clay, bright eyes, pure serenity, smooth brow, gentle tongue and blood vessels connecting all the members of the body, carrying sufficient fluid for the flesh and supplying both nerves and skin, a strong bone skeleton containing the precious marrow, and everything else which is seen in the human being. In addition, he gave [man] a governing and guiding mind filled with wisdom, infused with all knowledge and skill; he made the clay-figure rational, created the statue of dust in his own image, and gifted that which was ruling, autocratic and creative with the spiritual and immortal soul. Then he ordained him ruler over the animals, quadrupeds, reptiles, aquatic and amphibious [creatures], and over the birds of the air. Before all this, he extended heaven above [him] like a gracious portico, placing in it the meadow of the stars, which is both beneficial and magnificent. He ordered the sun to rise and go down, to create days and nights and measure time by its motion; [he ordered] the moon to wax and wane, to enchant with its perpetual transformation as well as to indicate the yearly cycle. He expanded the Earth below, gave it a colourful ornamentation, dividing it into valleys, fields, and pastures. He raised mountains up high and deepened canyons, displayed plateaus and plains, caused springs to rise in the midst and give way to unfailing rivers, and [created] all that beautifies the earth and sea.

3. Why did [he] name the human being Adam?

Thus creating the first human being and honouring him with his image,[78] as well as bestowing plentiful gifts on him, God gave man the name of his nature, since he called him Adam, which in Hebrew means 'earth'. This was also one of the [signs] of his care towards the human being. So many good things were to come [to man] to delight [him], and he became the governor and king of so many creatures. So that he might not become over-confident because of the richness of the gifts [he was given], and being conceited by the peak of masterhood not to disdain the Creator, and because of his [possible] revolt not to receive the greatest punishment (like that first apostate who fell like lightning from heaven[79] because of his imposture), the wise Sovereign of the universe necessarily prevented the haughtiness of his arrogance by calling him Adam, so that by remembering his origin from the appellation and considering the provenance of his nature, as well as beholding his ancestry, i.e. the dust before his eyes, he would recognise himself, and worship the One, who bestowed on him dignity and magnificence. After the creation, this was God's first providential act towards man. Thus he carried on guiding and healing him, as well as teaching him [moral] excellence from the beginning as Father, Healer and Teacher.

4. Why did [God] create the woman from [Adam's] rib?

Thus having formed and named him, [God] immediately created for him a helper, a fellow-worker, a life-companion. He [God] did not take the origin of her fashioning merely from the earth, as in the case of Adam, but he took one of his ribs and using this as a groundwork and foundation he created the feminine nature: not because of lack of material, for his will alone was sufficient for the creation of the universe, but because he wanted to place the bond of concord into the [human] nature. He prepared a garden also, ornamented it with all sorts of plants and granted it to man as home. As an exercise of virtue, he gave him neither a wearisome, nor a perspiring commandment, but one which is quite easy for the sound-minded.

5. Why did he give him a law?

God allowed the enjoyment of all the plants, but he forbade the savouring of one. He did not do this arbitrarily, but for [man] to recognise his Creator and bear the law of the Maker as a yoke, thus to learn that as he rules over those on earth, he in turn is ruled by the Maker. He commands but is also commanded; he governs, but is also governed; he leads, but is also led. Otherwise, the giving of law is also suitable for the rational [creatures], because lawless existence is proper only to the irrational. The Creator gave him a law concerning food, because at that time the issuing of other laws would have been senseless. What else could he forbid? 'Do not kill'? But there was nobody to be killed. Or 'do not commit adultery'? Even if he wanted to, he would not have been able to, since there was no other woman. Or 'do not steal'? The [property] of whom? – since everything belonged to him. The world was very harmonious at that time, not only for the first [couple], but also for their newborn children as well.

6. Concerning Adam's exile[80]

After he accepted the deceit by the devil's envy and the woman's voracity, (because the enemy of our nature had deceived first the weaker, and through her, the gullible one, he assaulted Adam), he [Adam] was immediately driven out of paradise. He was sent out to the earth of the same origin [as himself] jointly inheriting perspiration, weariness, and exhaustion and was handed over to toil in the field, to bear suffering and the other hardships of life. Since he did not accept that untroubled and painless life [in paradise] indulgently, he is bound together with misfortune, so that by striving he could be released from the illness, which followed the good times. By [human] death, however, the lawgiver [God] cuts even the path of sin, showing his philanthropy with the penalty itself. Since the legislator [God] conjoined death with trespass [i.e. for disobedience to be punished by death], and the transgressor [i.e. man] entered under that penalty, [God] dispensed [*oikonomei*] for the punishment to become the deliverance. For death dissolves this living thing and on the one hand ceases the action of wickedness; on the other hand, it saves [man] from [further] anguish, liberates him from sweat, drives away pain and sorrow, and brings the body's sufferings to an end. The Judge mixed the punishment with such philanthropy!

7. Presentation of humankind's ingratitude and God's care

But even after all this, the ungrateful human race did not understand [the use of the punishment], but repaid its Benefactor with even greater insensitivity. It immediately ventured to commit fratricide, [to accept] envy, mendacity, impetuosity, lewdness, injustice, mutual homicide, robbing each other's possessions, and to all evil generated by sin. But even so, the Creator did not repudiate the [human] nature he fashioned. He accomplished [his purpose] wisely and variously by healing, rebuking, demanding, guiding [people] towards [their] duties, advising, threatening and carrying his threat out, punishing the wicked and crowning the good. He acclaimed one and reformed another; he saved one in the ark together with his folk to preserve the spark of [human] nature,[81] flooded the earth, and with water destroyed those who committed sin. He multiplied the human race again, and performed general healing with particular admonitions. He destroyed impious cities with fire falling from heaven, and saved from reprisal the one who lived among, but did not share, the impiety of the inhabitants. He provided plenteous years, granted rain at an appropriate time, ineffably multiplied the seeds sown by the people, commanded the trees to bear fruits abundantly, disciplined with hunger those for whom the prosperity was not beneficial, sent illness upon them and removed it again, struck the life-giving crops with hailstones, covered the sun by a cloud of locusts, ruining the crops, then favoured [people] again and chased the hardships away. He did not abandon those who loved piety, but rather appeared and talked to them in a friendly manner, foreshowing the future through them.

8. The inhumanation of God is pure philanthropy

But since these and other numberless, uncountable benefits of the divine dispensation [*oikonomia*] availed for only a few people, while the rest of them remained incurable, the great and ineffable mystery of the oikonomia finally happens. The Word of God himself, the author of all creation, the immeasurable, the indescribable and immutable, the fountainhead of life, the light of light, the living image of the Father, the brightness of his glory and the express image of his Person (Heb. 1:3), assumes human nature and recreates his own image which was corrupted by sin. He renews its statue aged by the rust [or poison] of evil[82] and shows it even more beautiful than the first,[83] but not by forming it of earth, like before, but by accepting it himself. He does not change the divine nature into human, but conjoins [*synapsas*] the divine with the human. Remaining what he was, he took on what he was not. The blessed Paul also teaches this *plainly*[84] to us, when he exclaims:

> Let this mind be in you, which was also in Christ Jesus, who, being in the form of God, thought it not robbery to be equal with God, but rather emptied himself, and took the form of a servant.
>
> (Phil. 2:5–7)

From this it is clear that the form of God, remaining what it was, took the form of the servant. He calls 'form' not only the appearance of the human being, but the entire human nature. Just as the form of God signifies the essence [*ousia*] of God, since the divine is formless and shapeless – and nobody would say, unless insane, that the bodiless, the *simple*[85] and the non-composed has form and is divided into members – in the same manner the form of the servant does not only indicate this visible [thing], but the whole essence of the human being.

9. Reprehension of the heretics' impiety

Some of those who think the opposite of piety try to attack the doctrine of truth with apostolic words. On the one hand, Arius and Eunomius strongly maintain that the Word of God assumed a soulless [*apsychon*] man. On the other hand, Apollinaris [claims that there was] a soul [in the man] [*empsychon*], but that it was deprived of mind [*nous*] (I do not know what he meant by human soul). Marcion and Mani, as well as the rest of that impious band, frankly deny the whole mystery of the oikonomia. Even the ineffable conception and childbearing of the holy Virgin they consider as being myth and forgery. They declare that the Godhead was concealed in a phantasm-body,[86] and in this manner was manifested as man among men.

That is why it is necessary to reveal the clear meaning[87] of the apostolic words for the pious. He says, 'being in the form of God, he thought it not robbery to be equal with God, but emptied himself, and took the form of a servant, and was made in the likeness of men, and was found in the fashion of a man' (Phil. 2:6–7). Each of the afore-mentioned heretics establishes his audacious and false doctrine based on the appropriation of this [biblical verse]. Arius, Eunomius and Apollinaris and their followers declare that the 'form of a servant', 'fashion' and 'likeness of man' signify the visible [part] of our nature.

Those of the even more detestable sect[88] conceive the 'fashion' and 'likeness' as being some shadow, image and phantasm similar to the [human] body.

10. Explanation of [the words]: 'who, being in the form of God'

We shall immediately refute the folly of both [heterodoxies]. As we have shown, [Scripture] calls the essence of the servant 'form'; well, if the form of God indicates the essence of God, it is clear that the form of the servant signifies the essence of the servant. Yet, the apostle applied the [words] 'he was made in the likeness of men, and was found in the fashion of a man' not as names of nature, but rather of operation. Although the Ruler Christ owns our nature, yet he did not receive our wickedness, but he [remained] totally free *from sin*,[89] as the prophet exclaims, 'he had done no lawlessness, neither was any deceit in his mouth' (Isa. 53:9). John, the dweller of the desert testifies together with him [i.e. Isaiah], saying 'Behold the Lamb, who takes away the sin of the world' (John 1:29). The blessed Paul necessarily declared the one who was free from the sinful deeds of humankind as being in the likeness of men and being found in the fashion of a man. That is why he said elsewhere also:

> What the law could not do, in that it was weak through the flesh, God sending his own Son in the likeness of sinful flesh, and for sin, condemned sin in the flesh; that the righteousness of the law might be fulfilled in us, who walk not according to the flesh, but according to the Spirit.
>
> (Rom. 8:3–4)

Observe how by these [words] [Paul] disperses the obscurity of those [heretics]. 'God', he says, 'sent his own Son in the likeness of sinful flesh.' He did not simply say 'in the likeness of flesh', dissolving the blasphemy of the impious doctrines (for the grace of the Spirit foresees everything), but 'in the likeness of sinful flesh', for us to learn that he added 'likeness' because our Saviour is free from all sin. He became man according to nature, but not according to sin, that is why in the likeness of sinful flesh he condemned sin in the flesh. He assumed human nature, but did not accept the yoke of sin, which ruled among the people, but rather put away all its dominion, and showed that in human nature it is possible to overcome the arrows of sin.

Thus he condemned sin in the flesh, proving its feebleness, ending its tyranny, and teaching people how to defeat it. That is why the blessed Paul adds: 'that the righteousness of the law might be fulfilled in us, who walk not according to the flesh of the law,[90] but according to the Spirit' (Rom. 8:4). Weren't we made righteous by the condemnation of sin in the flesh?[91] Our Saviour, being in the likeness of sinful flesh, condemned sin in the flesh. He assumed human nature, but he did not accept sin, which dominated it from long ago. This is how the holy Paul, in a few words, dissolved the whole crowd of heretics, refuting the insanity of Arius and Eunomius, in the beginning of the words quoted before:

> Let this mind be in you, which was also in Christ Jesus, who, being in the form of God, thought it not robbery to be equal with God, but emptied himself, and took the form of a servant.

Neither does he say that 'he was made [*genomenos*] in the form of God', but that 'he was [*hyparchōn*] in the form of God'. Nor does he say, that [Christ] thought it no robbery to be equal with himself or equal with angels or equal with the creation, but he rather says [that he thought it not robbery to be] equal with God the Father, with his Begetter, the unbegun, the unbegotten, the infinite, the Ruler of all.

Arius and Eunomius here receive the powerful refutation of their own impiety. The blaspheming Sabellius, Marcellus and Photinus – who deny the three hypostases and confuse the properties of the Godhead – are also confuted here. For according to the hypostasis the one being in the form of God is different from the other in whose form he is. Again, the one who thought it no robbery to be equal with God is different from the other with whom he is equal [i.e. with God the Father]; nevertheless, he did not snatch the equality for himself. Furthermore, by these words themselves even the impiety of the false-named Paul [i.e. Paul of Samosata] receives its well-earned shame, who on the one hand denied the begetting of the Saviour before the ages, and on the other hand, according to Jewish thinking, confessed only the [birth] from the Virgin. The divine Paul teaches that the Word of God is the One who takes on, and human nature is that which was taken; that the form of God is the pre-existent, and the form of the servant is that which was assumed by the form of God in the fullness of times. Apollinaris, together with Arius and Eunomius can learn again, that the unchangeable God-Word was not changed into the nature of flesh, but by assuming our essence, he achieved our salvation. We have shown by what we said before that human essence is labelled 'form of a servant'. If the form of God [is] the essence of God (for the divine is formless, unshaped, absolute [*or* single], non-composed and without scheme), then the form of a servant also could reasonably be perceived plainly as the essence of a servant. The essence of a servant, that is of the human being, does not only mean the visible body for the sound-minded, but the whole human nature. Moreover, the champions of impiety, and the chief authors of blasphemy against true belief, who even call themselves Christians, but who exceed even the erroneous polytheism of the idolatrists (I mean Marcion, Mani, and all those initiated in, and disciples of, their pestilent chair [*kathedra*]) can recognise their own madness by these same words. Those who do not accept the birth of the Lord according to the flesh and his inhumanation [should] listen to the teaching of the most divine Paul, that the form of God took on the form of the servant. But the form of the servant was neither some phantasm, *nor an image/idol*,[92] nor a shadow, nor some ethereal illusion, nor is it called any other such thing, but the nature of the servant.

If they would object to us with the following words, [namely, that Christ] 'was made in the likeness of men, and was found in the fashion of a man', and from the Letter to the Romans with 'in the likeness of sinful flesh', then let us refute their senselessness first. Because if the phrase 'in the likeness of men, and was found in the fashion of a man' designates some human phantasm, yet the form of a servant [indicates] the human nature, then the apostle is contradictory. But if the apostle's words are not contradictory, then we should learn that the form of a servant denotes the essence of the servant, and the words '[he] was made in the likeness of men, and was found in the fashion of a man' we shall understand as follows: our Lord Jesus Christ, [although] possessing our nature, was not in all respects equal to us: he was born of a woman also, but not like us, since he came forth from a virgin womb. On the one hand, he was a perfect human being, like us; on the other hand, though, he was greater than us because of the indwelling [*enoikēsis*] and of the union [*henōsis*] of the Word of God. He had an ensouled[93] and rational flesh like us, yet – apart from us – he did not experience the actions of sin, but in the body assaulted by sin he abolished the tyranny of sin. This is why 'he was made in the likeness of men, and being found in the fashion of a man, he humiliated himself and became obedient unto death, even the death of the cross' (Phil. 2:8). The word 'humiliation' itself shows the assuming of the humble [i.e. inferior] nature. Besides, when talking about [Christ] being in the form of God, Paul adds: '[he] was made in the likeness of men, and was found in the fashion of a man', thus teaching, that the bodiless

Word of God appeared as man, assuming human nature. That is why he adds 'as a man', for us not to conceive that some change of the invisible God had taken place, but to believe that he assumed a living flesh with a rational [soul], being God he was made in the likeness of men, and was found in the fashion of a man. The great protagonist of piety, I mean the blessed Paul, in this way dissolved the various and differing utterances of the heretics. The Word[94] conducted us here, disproving the madness of the heretics, making clear the teaching of truth for those nurtured in piety. It is time then, to return to where we departed from.

11. For what reason did the God-Word assume human nature?

So the Creator, who pitied our nature for being threatened by the Evil One, and being exposed to the bitter arrows of sin was sent over to death, [comes to] defend his image and overwhelm the enemies. He shattered the opponents neither by using the Godhead's naked power, nor his royal might, nor by bringing angel soldiers and archangels into battle, nor by arming [himself] with lightning and thunder against the antagonists, nor by appearing on earth amidst the Cherubim to judge and condemn our adversaries, but became a subject, one of the endangered, hiding the magnificence of Godhead within the poverty of manhood. He anointed the visible man for the battle and crowned the winner. Beginning from his childhood he educated him for virtue, led him to the apogee of righteousness, preserved him unconquered and free from the arrows of sin. Similarly, however, he permitted him to come under death in order to prove the injustice of sin and destroy the power of death.

If death is the punishment for those who came under sin, it was obviously right for this [man], being totally free from it, to have the benefit of life and not [receive] death. Therefore, the injustice of sin was proven, which being conquered, sentenced to death its conqueror, and brought for him the same judgement which it usually applied to the defeated. While sin sent to death [only] its subordinates, it could do so justly; but after casting under the same condemnation the innocent and blameless one, the one deserving a crown and acclamation, it is necessarily deprived of power as being unjust.[95] The blessed Paul teaching this, said:

For what the law could not do, in that it was weak through the flesh, God sending his own Son in the likeness of sinful

flesh, and for sin, condemned sin in the flesh; that the righteousness of the law might be fulfilled in us, who walk not
according to the flesh, but according to the Spirit.

(Rom. 8:3–4)

What he says is the following: the aim of the law, he affirms, was to
justify the nature of humankind. It was not able to do this, not because
of its own weakness, but because of the indolence of [its] hearers, who,
being inclined towards the pleasures of the flesh, ran away from the
toilsome [fulfilling] of the law, and adhered to bodily delights. That
is why, he says, the God of the universe sent his own Son in the likeness
of sinful flesh – that is human nature but free from sin – and because
of sin he condemned sin in the flesh, proving its injustice, because it
cast the innocent and the one free from [any] iniquity under the condemnation of sinners. He did this not to justify the man he assumed,
but – as he says – so that the righteousness of the law might be fulfilled
in us, who walk not according to the flesh, but according to the Spirit.
The benefaction of our Saviour extends to the whole nature of humankind: as with our forefather Adam, we both share the curse and have
all arrived under the [power] of death like him; in the same way we also
appropriate the victory of the Saviour Christ, will partake of his glory
and share the joy of [his] kingdom. The blessed Paul is a witness of this,
too, who, reminding [us] about the old [things] and the new, also
shows that the righteousness of our Saviour means the deliverance from
the former [state of condemnation].

12. As we share in Adam's death, so in the life of the Lord also

'For if the many died through the one man's trespass', he says, 'much
more surely have the grace of God and the free gift in the grace of the
one man, Jesus Christ, abounded for the many' (Rom. 5:15). And a
little later:

Therefore as by the offence of one, condemnation came upon
all men, even so by the righteousness of one [came] the
justification of life. For as by one man's disobedience many
were made sinners, so by the obedience of one shall many be
made righteous.

(Rom. 5:18–19)

In the Letter to the Corinthians he teaches even more clearly, saying:
'For as in Adam all die, even so in Christ will all be made alive' (1 Cor.

15:22). From these texts it is evident that our victory is the victory of our Saviour, since the fall of our forefather also became our common fall. As we are partakers of his common defeat, in the same way should we enjoy the benefits with the one who was taken from and crowned for us. That is why the holy apostle also said:

> For whom he did foreknow, he also did predestine to be conformed to the image of his Son, that he might be the firstborn among many brethren. Moreover, whom he did foreordain, them he also called: and whom he called them he also justified: and whom he justified them he also glorified.
>
> (Rom. 8:29–30)

Elsewhere Paul says: 'And if children, then heirs; heirs of God, and joint-heirs with Christ; if, in fact, we suffer with him so that we may also be glorified with him' (Rom. 8:17). And again: 'If we suffer, we shall also reign with him' (2 Tim. 2:12). So – for the sake of our entire nature – the God-Word of God assumed our first-fruits {i.e. the human nature of Christ}[96] that by leading it through all virtues to challenge the adversary [Satan] to fight against it, and to show that his athlete [Christ] is invincible; to crown this one [Christ] and to declare the other one [Satan] defeated, to encourage and strengthen everybody against him. That is why in the holy Gospels, on the one hand he says: 'I saw Satan as lightning fall from heaven' (Luke 10:18); and on the other hand: 'unless one should enter the house of the strong man and bind the strong man, how will he spoil his goods?' (Matt. 12:29). The human nature he calls the house of the strong man, which fled to him, having promised to do all his orders, and drawn upon itself servitude voluntarily. Somewhere else: 'have no fear', he says, 'I have overcome the world' (John 16:33). And elsewhere: 'Now is the judgement of this world: now shall the prince of this world be cast out. And I, if I will be lifted up from the earth, will draw all [people] to myself' (John 12:31–2). And going further, he says this even more clearly.

13. The oikonomia of the Saviour is a common benefit for all mankind

'About judgement, because the prince of this world was [already] judged' (John 16:11), and further: 'for the prince of this world comes, and has no [power] over me' (John 14:30), because he is discharged from any accusation, not having any of the devil's seeds in him. This is why he *also condemned him*,[97] ceased his tyranny and cast him out, bruised him under the feet of his former slaves, whom he exhorts, saying: 'Behold, I give unto you power to tread on serpents and scorpions, and over all the power of the Enemy' (Luke 10:19). In order to see his struggle with the devil let us proceed to the narrative of the Gospels. After baptism, Jesus was taken by the Spirit into the wilderness to be tempted by the devil. Yet not the God-Word, but the temple taken on by the God-Word from the seed of David, was taken [there]. The Holy Spirit did not bring the God-Word to battle against the devil, but the temple formed in the Virgin for the God-Word. *He fasts, but not exceeding the measure of nature*;[98] [Jesus] spent forty days and the same number of nights without eating. He did not want to exceed the ancient measure of fasting, so that the opponent would not run away from the struggle against him, lest recognising the one who was hidden, he should flee the battle against the visible [thing]. That is why after the aforementioned number of days passed, he shows the suffering of the human nature, and allows hunger to occur, thus giving the grip [or opportunity] for [the tempter] by hunger.[99] Otherwise [Satan] would not have dared to approach him, because he had seen so many divine things concerning him. At his birth angels formed a choir around him, a rising star led the magi, the leaders of their phalanx to worship him, and [the devil] saw him pursuing complete righteousness from his childhood, detesting evil, abhorring wickedness. This was also foretold about him by the prophet: 'before he shall know good and evil, he will not obey malice, because he will choose good' (cf. Isa. 7:16).[100] John exclaimed also: 'Behold the Lamb of God, who takes away the sin of the world' (John 1:29). The Father testified from above: 'This is my beloved Son, in whom I am well pleased' (Matt. 3:17). The grace of the Spirit came upon him. The devil was astounded by these and other similar things, and did not dare to approach the champion of our nature. Yet as he discovered the occurrence of hunger, saw him needing human food, and [observed that] he could not endure more than the old men, he came closer to him, thinking that he had found the greatest grip [or opportunity], believing that he would win easily.

14. How did the Ruler Christ defeat the devil?

In battle, when somebody wants to shoot [another] fully covered in armour, he looks at the whole [person] thoroughly, examines him from a distance, seeking for the uncovered part, to fling the dart there and wound the adversary. In the same manner, the devil, seeing Christ fully armoured with complete righteousness, and in search of the ideal spot to launch [his] spear at, as soon as he noticed[101] the appearance of hunger, he daringly approached him, as if he had found what he was looking for, observing in him the weakness of the forefather. He [Satan] had also deprived him [Adam] of his untroubled life by food and harnessed him into the yoke of swelter, humiliation, and death. Therefore, he came near and said: 'If you are the Son of God, say that these stones[102] should become bread' (Matt. 4:3). He would not have done that if the Saviour did not accept the suffering of hunger. One might learn this clearly from later [events]. When [Satan] was defeated in battle and learned from experience that he [Jesus] was the one foretold by all the prophets, he could not bear even his close look, but immediately ran away [from him], shouting: 'What do you want with us, [oh] Son of God? Why did you come before time to torture us?' (Matt. 8:29). And: 'I know who you are: [you are] the Son of God.[103] I beseech you, not to torture me' (cf. Mark 1:24; Luke 4:34). He [Satan] was so afraid, and confessed [Jesus] as judge! Before the temptation, however, he did not speak in this manner, but he drew near [to Jesus] confidently, saying: '*If you are the Son of God*,[104] say that these stones should become bread. I heard the voice coming from above', he says, 'which called you like this,[105] but I do not believe it until taught by experience. Convince me by facts that you are indeed what you are called! If I learn this, I shall run away and flee. I shall withdraw myself from battle against you, because I know what a difference there is between me and you. Show then the miracle, and *by the wonder teach {me} who is the author of the miracle*:[106] say that these stones should become bread.'

Upon hearing *these words of the Evil One, the Lord*[107] conceals [his] Godhead and speaks from his human nature: 'Man does not live on bread alone, he says, but by every word coming from the mouth of God' (Matt. 4:4). I can nourish myself without bread, he says, because not only bread sustains the life of people, but rather the word of God is sufficient to maintain the entire human nature. So did the people of Israel nurture itself, gathering manna for forty years, and benefiting from catching birds, provided by God's will. Elijah was fed by ravens, and Elisha nourished his disciples with herbs of the field. But why should I enumerate the old things? John, who recently baptised in the Jordan, spent all his life in the wilderness, eating locusts and feeding [himself] with the fruit of wild bees. So it is not unbelievable that we can also be nourished by God with unknown food and do not need bread.

The devil heard this and on one hand he felt pain at being *once*[108] defeated, but he did not abandon victory, because he heard that [his opponent] was man. *For, as he says, 'man does not live on bread alone'.*[109] That is why he brought forth temptation for the second and even for

the third time. First he said: 'If you are the Son of God, throw yourself
down from above!' (Matt. 4:6) – *plotting against him by empty fame.*[110]
Then he presented him with the kingdoms of the world, and promised
to give them over to [Jesus], if he should receive worship from him
beforehand. Yet as [Jesus] reminded him again of the old law, saying,
'it is written: worship the Lord your God, and serve him only' (Matt.
4:10) and explained that he would not offer divine praise [i.e. the praise
belonging to God] to anyone else, and reminded him of other words
and teachings of God, which forbid tempting the God of the universe,
[Satan] ran away, being unable to bear the shame of defeat, being afraid,
trembling and waiting for the abolishing of his tyranny. After having
emptied all his darts and having brought forth all tricks of his deceit,
he found the athlete unwounded and invincible. He went to him as
he had to Adam [before], but he did not find whom he expected.[111]
Angels, who saw the battle from afar, now came to the victor, serving
him like suitors,[112] surrounding him, praising the athlete, crowning
and proclaiming him, celebrating the liberation of human fellow-
servants, being delighted to see the adversary's defeat.

15. If [Christ] did not assume a [human] mind, the victory against the devil would mean nothing for us. Against Apollinaris

These [facts] refute Apollinaris' thoughtless talk, who said that the
Word of God dwelt in the place of mind in the assumed flesh. If the
assumed nature did not possess a human mind, then it is God who
fought against the devil, and God is crowned in victory. Yet if God is
the winner, I gained nothing from the victory, as not having contributed to it with anything. I have been deprived even of the joy
concerning it, like one who is bragging with someone else's trophies.
The devil, however, would boast, swagger, haughtily gloat and disdain,
like one who fought with God and was defeated by God. Since for him
even being overwhelmed by God [is] a great [achievement].

16 [15]. If the God-Word replaced the mind in that which was assumed, even the devil could find some justified excuses,[113]

and might reasonably say:

> Ruler and Creator of the universe, I did not begin the fight
> against you, because I know your dignity, I am aware of your

might, and recognise your dominion. I acknowledge my servitude even being an apostate.[114] I yield victory even to the angels and to all the heavenly hosts, [although] I, the miserable one, was once also one of them. Nevertheless, I started the fight against this one, whom you formed out of clay, created after your image, honoured with reason, made the citizen of paradise and presented [as] the ruler of both earth and sea. *This one I have defeated by using deceit, not force.*[115] Until today I am still the one who defeats him, prostrates him and sends him to death. Bring this one to the arena and command him to fight with me, be the spectator and judge of the combat yourself! Even be his trainer if you want, teach him to fight, show him the grips of victory [*or* the holds of success], anoint him as you wish, just do not fight with the wrestler [i.e. on his side]. I am not so audacious and mindless as to attempt to fight against you, the Creator.

The devil could have justly said this to the Saviour Christ, if he were not man [indeed], but [only] God, fighting in place of man. If there was no human mind in him,[116] God replacing the mind and taking over the work of the mind, then God hungered with the body, God thirsted, suffered, *slept, grieved, was afraid*[117] and endured all the other human torments also. Yet if God had fought and won, then I have been deprived of victory, [because] God fulfilled all righteousness, since the God-Word would not have received it [i.e. the mind], as the followers of Apollinaris' claptrap are upholding, on the grounds that it was impossible to fulfil the laws of righteousness with a human mind.

17 [16]. Sinners have an excuse, if the Word-God did not assume the mind because of its weakness

When saying this, first of all they are attributing a considerable feebleness[118] to God himself, if, as they claim, he could not justify the man together with the presence of the human mind. Secondly, they open the door of excuses for all sinners and transgressors of godly laws. Then these can fairly say to the God of the universe:

We did not commit, [oh] Ruler, anything unforgivable or deserving punishment, because the governing mind received [from you] is weak and is unable to keep your laws. Even the patriarchs, the prophets, the communities of people loved by God before and after the law, married or unmarried, rich or

poor testify that they could not fulfil your commandments
because of this, even though they were helped by your All-
holy Spirit. But why should one say more? You yourself, oh
Ruler, when you arrived in flesh, on the one hand assumed
our flesh, on the other hand you rejected and did not accede
to take on the mind, which hinders the gain of virtue and
easily accepts the deceit of sin. *You* replaced the mind [in] the
flesh, and in *this* manner you fulfilled righteousness. In *this*
way you defeated sin. Since you are God, you do with your will
what you want, you change reality with a nod. But we possess
a human mind, which you did not want to assume. Thus
we are necessarily fallen under sin, being unable to follow your
footsteps. [Anyway], what is a human mind compared to
God's power, to God's wisdom? [What is it compared to your]
light, [to your] righteousness and life, and all the other
operations of your being [*ousia*], which emerge like rays and
brightness out of your nature [*physis*]?

Those who chose to serve sin could justly say this, *if the God-Word really
assumed a man without a human mind.*[119]

18 [17]. Establishing that the assumption of human mind was appropriate

Let us leave their prating for now, and return to the proposed subject,
showing that the oikonomia of our Saviour was necessary. The entire
human being was beguiled and entered totally under sin, yet the mind
had accepted the deceit before the body, because the prior contribution of the mind sketches out the sin, and thus by its action [i.e. of the
mind] the body gives shape to it [i.e. to sin]. That is why the Ruler
Christ, wishing to raise fallen nature, reaches his hand out for the
whole, and uplifts both the fallen flesh, I say, and the mind made after
the image of the Creator. [The mind] is invisible and unseen, unreach-
able and incomprehensible, not knowing even itself; and above all this:
it is boundless. If we really look at the visualising power of its thoughts,
its being honoured with guiding power and authority, decorated with
arts and sciences, [we see that] it is a kind of small and new demiurge,
or, to speak more truly, the imitator of the Creator. [It is] a king of the
visible creation, or an image of the king, who collects tributes from the
earth, sea and air, from the sun, moon and stars, from the sky and
clouds, from sheep and cattle and from other domestic animals. [The
mind] is rather the beneficiary of all their fruits, since the visible

[things] were created for its [i.e. the mind's] sake, because God does not need these [created things].

Therefore [the Saviour] did not disdain the one so precious, which needs healing [i.e. the mind]. He did not assume the [flesh] submitted to destruction, to illness, to ageing and death by neglecting the rational and immortal [mind] created after his image precisely when, as they say, this part [of human nature] went to the bad. On the contrary, he renewed the whole worn out [human] nature. Or did he fully renew [only] this [part] [i.e. the flesh], while forsaking the aged and wretched [mind]? Yet this [latter one] was the more valuable, honoured with immortality, adorned with reason, belonging to the order of the intelligible. How inappropriate [it would have been for him] to assume, take on and install on the right hand side of majesty the body of clay and dust, [which is] bound to passions, while rejecting the invisible and immortal mind and not conferring the same honour to it as for the body. [For the mind] directs the living [creature/person], being made in the image of God, and honoured with incorruptibility. [It is] the charioteer,[120] the governor and musician of the body, by which human nature is not irrational, but full of wisdom, art and skill. Because of it [i.e. the mind] the body became [part of] the rational creation. Because of it were the laws and prophecies given; the wrestling, the struggles, the victories, the commendations and crowns [happened] for its sake; and by the mind even the body, as partaker of the struggle, receives its prize in the contest, the kingdom of heaven. Even the coming of our Saviour happened for the sake [of the mind], thus is the mystery of the oikonomia being accomplished: for he did not receive the salvific sufferings for [creatures] without soul or mind, nor for irrational cattle or soulless stones, but for people possessing immortal souls within [themselves]!

19 [18]. Solving the counter-arguments of the heretics

Apollinaris, who had more respect for idle talk than for the truth, and placed his own prating above the pious teachings, said that the God-Word assumed the flesh and used it like a veil. There was no need for mind, because he [i.e. the God-Word himself] took the place of the mind for the body.

'But, my dear fellow' – could someone tell him – 'the God-Word would not need the body either, for he was not in want! He could have accomplished our salvation [simply] by his mere command!' But he wanted us to be partakers in [his] success: *that is why* he took on the nature that had sinned and made it right by his own sufferings, released it from under the bitter tyranny of sin, of the devil and of death. He honoured it [i.e. the human nature] with a heavenly throne, and by that which was assumed he gave freedom to the whole [human] race.

The wisest [Apollinaris], however, not realising anything of these [facts], assumes that John the evangelist, the high-voiced herald of theology confirms his own senselessness. For 'the Word, he says, was made flesh and dwelt among us' (John 1:14). Yet he undoubtedly knows that the divine Scripture often labels the whole with the [name of one] element; for instance it denominates the entire human being with the soul [only], or designates the complete living [creature] with the flesh. For it says, 'all the souls, which came into Egypt with Jacob, were seventy-five' (cf. Gen. 46:26–7; Exod. 1:1–5; Deut. 10:22; Acts 7:14). It is evident that the sons and descendants of Jacob were not bodiless, merely that the historiographer designated the whole by the part. And again: 'the soul that sins, has to die' (Ezek. 18:4). Nobody knows of such a soul that committed sin without body. And anew: 'My Spirit shall not [always] remain in these people, for they are flesh' (Gen. 6:3). The prophet elsewhere says: 'all flesh is dust,[121] and all human glory as the flower of the field' (Isa. 40:6). The blessed David also says, 'it is remembered that they are flesh, going and not returning wind [or spirit].'[122] It is certainly clear for everyone, that those whom he denounces, and for whom he makes laws and whose nature he refers to, were not soulless.

Nevertheless, *you may find* not only the condemned, but also the most greatly praised *to be called 'flesh'*.[123] The blessed Paul also testifies to this in [his Epistle] to the Galatians, saying,

> When it pleased God, who chose me from my mother's womb, and called me by his grace, to reveal his Son in me; imme-diately I did not confer with flesh and blood, but[124] I went to those who were apostles before me.
>
> (cf. Gal. 1:15–17)

If the meaning of 'flesh' is not reduced to fleshly and mortal, but [extended] to the whole human nature, it is clear that the statement 'the Word was made flesh' does not signify only the visible [part] of the living [creature], but the entire human being. Neither does [John] say that the divine essence was somehow turned into flesh, but proclaims that the human nature was assumed by the God-Word. Thus, the [affirmation] 'Christ redeemed us from the curse of the law, being made a curse for us' (Gal. 3:13) does not suggest that the foun-tainhead of [all] good was changed into a curse, but [expresses] what happened through him: the salvation from sin, i.e. from the curse. Also the [assertion] 'he, who knew no sin, became sin for us' (cf. 2 Cor. 5:21) does not mean the alteration of righteousness – for the divine is unchangeable and unalterable, as he exclaims through the prophet: 'I am, and I change not' (cf. Mal. 3:6) – but [it refers to] the taking up of our sins. 'Behold the Lamb of God', he says, 'behold the one who takes away the sin of the world' (John 1:29). In the same fashion [as above], 'the Word was made flesh' does not assert the alteration of the Godhead, but the assumption of the human nature. The evangelist proclaims God's unspeakable philanthropy, when he teaches that the One who was in the beginning was God also, and was with God, and was never non-existent; [the one], who made everything, brought the non-existent into being, [who was] life [itself], the true light, assumed the corruptible nature, and made the human suffering his own, when he accomplished the salvation of humankind. And because [John] wanted to present even better the greatness of his benefaction, he did not mention the immortal soul, but [spoke about] the passible, mortal and corruptible body, which had been made of clay. Thus, with the component he indicated the entire nature, as [is] confirmed by the continuation: 'for the Word, he says, was made flesh, and dwelt among us'.

The temple is different from the [one, who] in the sense of nature dwells [in it]. That is why he also told the Jews: 'Destroy this temple, and in three days I will raise it up' (John 2:19). The temple's destruction is the soul's detachment from the body, since death is the division of the soul from the body. Therefore, the separation of the soul causes the destruction of the temple. So if the Jews destroyed the temple, giving it to crucifixion and death – the destruction of the temple [meaning] the separation of the conjoined things [i.e. of soul and body] – and the God-Word redeemed this destroyed [temple], then I think it is evident to the reasonable, that the God-Word did not assume a soulless and irrational [body], but a perfect man.[125] If the God-Word had replaced the immortal soul in the assumed body, he would have said to the Jews: 'Destroy me, and in three days I shall rise again.' Yet, he teaches here both the mortality of the temple then and the power of the indwelling Godhead. 'Destroy this temple', he says, 'and in three days I will raise it up.' He did not say, 'you shall destroy me', but '[you shall destroy] the temple I have assumed.' And it was destroyed, [in order] to enjoy an [even] greater resurrection: in order that the mortal nature might be laid aside; in order to take off corruptibility and put on incorruptibility; in order to dissolve the might of death, [and] to be the [very] first among those fallen asleep; in order that by relieving the labour-pains of corruption[126] to appear as the firstborn from the dead (Col. 1:18), and by his own resurrection to proclaim the gospel of resurrection of all humankind.

20 [19]. Demonstrating that the God-Word assumed a rational soul[127]

The foremost of the apostles testifies that these things are so, when he says in the Acts that his soul will not be left in hell, neither shall his flesh know decay (Acts 2:27). So then the destruction of the temple is a separation of soul and body, and again, resurrection is the returning [of the soul] into her own flesh. Therefore, if every human being had two souls, as the leaders of heresy are saying, one vivifying and the other rational, and flesh were inconceivable without vivifying soul (for, he says, this is named body and not flesh), yet Peter said, that not the body of the Lord, but the flesh of the Lord shall not see destruction (1 Pet. 3:18) and his soul will not be forsaken in hell, it is evident that the corrupted flesh possessed the vivifying soul (or I do not know how they call it), because without her, as they say, it [the flesh] could not be named flesh. Yet even the immortal and rational [soul], which is entrusted to govern the living [creature], was not forsaken in hell, but returned to her own flesh; and in vain do they babble, labelling the temple of the God-Word soulless or irrational. We shall follow Peter, who preached that neither did the flesh receive corruption, nor was the soul forsaken in hell, but she returned and was conjoined with her own body. We also believe the Lord himself, who said: 'My soul is deeply grieved, even to death' (Matt. 26:38). The rational [soul] in us accepts the sensation of sorrow, but if the God-Word replaced the mind and accepted the passions of the mind, then [the God-Word] himself grieved, was afraid, ignorant, agonised, and was strengthened by angelic aid. So if the heirs of Apollinaris' idle talking proclaim these things, they should be ranked together with Arius and Eunomius among the enemies of Christ. For it is right, that those [who teach] the same blasphemy should belong to one group.[128] We, however, should listen to the Lord who said: 'I have power to lay down my soul, and I have power to take it again. Nobody takes it away from me' (John 10:18). From these words we can learn that different is the one who lays down [the soul], and different is what is laid down. On the one hand, God is he who lays down and takes on; on the other hand, the soul is that which is laid down and taken on; and God is the One having the power, whereas the soul is subjected to that power.

157

21 [20]. The prophets affirm the assumption of the perfect nature

Isaiah the prophet concurs with the above [when he] affirms, exclaiming: 'Behold, the virgin shall conceive in her womb, and bear a son, and they will call his name Emmanuel' (Isa. 7:14), which, according to the teaching of the Gospels, is interpreted as: 'God with us'. Yet 'God with us' means 'God with humankind'. Therefore, if the child of the Virgin received this appellation, it is clear that he was God and man simultaneously, being one and having taken on the other, perfect in each respect. By the [expression] 'with us' the perfection of the man is shown, because each of us possesses the human nature perfectly. Yet by 'God', with the addition of the article, the Godhead of the Son is acknowledged. The blessed Paul also teaches this, saying: 'In him dwells all the fullness of the Godhead bodily' (Col. 2:9). Luke, the divinely inspired evangelist distinctly shows us the human mind of the Saviour Christ: 'For the child, he says, grew, and waxed strong in spirit, filled with wisdom: and the grace of God was upon him' (Luke 2:40). And a bit later: 'Jesus increased in stature and in wisdom, and in grace in front of God and men' (Luke 2:52). Nonetheless, 'increased in wisdom' cannot be stated about the wise God, who is not in want [of anything], is eternally perfect, and accepts neither increase nor decrease, but about the human mind, which develops along with age, needs teaching, receives arts and sciences, and gradually perceives the human and divine [realities].

22 [21]. Demonstrating the distinction of natures and the unity of the Person[129] from the Epistle to the Hebrews

It can be seen more clearly from the Epistle to the Hebrews, that the divine nature and the human are different one from another according to their operations, but are united in the person [prosōpon] and indicate the one Son. This teaching is already contained in the letter's prologue, isn't it? The divine Paul says: 'Who is the brightness of his glory, and the express image of his person, upholding all things by the word of his power' (Heb. 1:3). Showing him also as timeless and [existent] before ages (because, he says, even the ages were created by him), Paul adds: 'he sat down at the right hand of the Majesty on high, having become as much superior to angels as the name he has inherited is more excellent than theirs' (Heb. 1:3–4). 'To become' is contrary to 'to be', because he who is the brightness of the glory and the express image of

[God's] Person, did not *become* better than the angels, but *is* better than them, far more than that: [he is] their Creator and Ruler also. But if 'is' is opposite to 'became', then under the former we shall understand the eternal One, and under the latter that which was assumed from us [i.e. the human nature] and became superior to the angels by its union with the one, who assumed it. Again, a little later, he says to the Son:

> Your throne, O God, is for ever and ever: a sceptre of righteousness is the sceptre of your kingdom. You loved righteousness, and hated lawlessness; therefore God, your God, has anointed you with the oil of gladness above your fellows.
>
> (Heb. 1:8–9)

But how can God, denominated with the article [i.e. 'the God'], whose throne stands forever and ever, be anointed by God? How could he receive a kingdom by ordination, when he [already] owns the kingdom by nature? For he says, 'your throne, oh God, is for ever and ever'. *Being* king is of course contrary to being *anointed* as king because of loving righteousness and hating lawlessness. Such kingship is the reward of [hard] labour. So then again we shall understand that whose throne is for ever and ever is God, the eternal one, whereas the latter being later anointed for his hatred towards sin and his love for righteousness, is that which was taken on from us, which is of David and of Abraham, which has fellows and exceeds them by the anointment [of the Spirit], possessing in itself all the gifts of the All-holy Spirit. Let us worship, then, the one Son in either nature.

Again the blessed Paul invokes David to testify saying: 'Oh Lord, what is man, that you are mindful of him? Or the son of man, that you watch over him? You made him a little lower than the angels; you crowned him with glory and honour' (Heb. 2:6–7). He adds: 'But we see Jesus, who was made a little lower than the angels for the suffering of death, crowned with glory and honour; that he by God's grace should taste death for everyone' (Heb. 2:9). This [verse] demonstrates best of all the perfection of the assumed man. For he says: 'What is man that you are mindful of him?' *he does not say 'what is flesh that you are mindful of it' or 'what is the body that you are mindful of it'*,[130] but rather 'what is man', similarly including the entire nature. On the one hand he names the indwelling God-Word 'Lord', who, remembering his own image manifested ineffable philanthropy; on the other hand, he names the temple assumed from us 'man', which he visited by his arrival, conjoined with himself, and by the union he accomplished [the work of] salvation. Explaining this, [Paul] said: 'But we see Jesus, who was made a little lower than the angels for the suffering of death.' It was not the immortal God-Word that died, but the mortal nature. That is why he was made just a little lower than the angels, because they are immortal, but this one [i.e. the human nature] is mortal. The God-Word is not lower than the angels, but the Ruler of angels: 'For in him were all things created, either visible or invisible, whether they be thrones, or dominions, or principalities, or powers, or angels or forces: all were created by him and for him' (Col. 1:16). And much later on he says:

> Who in the days of his flesh offered up prayers and suppli-
> cations with strong crying and tears unto him who was able
> to save him from death, and was heard for his godly fear.
> Although he was a Son, he learned obedience from what he
> suffered, and being made perfect he became the source of
> eternal salvation for all those who obey him.
>
> (Heb. 5:7–9).

Who was it then who prayed, offering up pleas and supplications with strong crying and tears? Who lived in reverence [in order] to persuade thus the One he implored? Who learned obedience from what he suffered, accepting the test as teacher, not having known this [i.e. obedience] before being tested? Who received perfection gradually? Not the God-Word, the perfect, the one who had known all [things] before their genesis, but [who] does not learn by experiencing; who is venerated by all, but adulates none; who wipes away all tears from every face, but is not constrained by suffering to weep. Who is impassible and immortal, yet has no fear of death, and does not beseech with crying to be delivered from death.[131] These then are the properties [*idia*] of the assumed manhood, which feared death and persisted in praying, the indwelling Godhead making room for the fear in order that through the sufferings the nature of that which was assumed might be demonstrated. And again: 'For verily he did not espouse angels, but he embraced the seed of Abraham. Therefore he had to be made like [his] brethren in all respects, in order to gain reconciliation for the sins of the people' (Heb. 2:16–17). Inasmuch as he himself suffered being tempted, he is able to help those in temptation. And a bit later: 'For we have not a high priest unable to sympathise with our infirmities, but one who in every respect has been tempted like [we are], yet without sin' (Heb. 4:15). So the seed of Abraham is different from the One who assumed it. The blessed Paul knows the Saviour

Christ as the seed of Abraham according to the flesh, for he says, 'he did not say: "and to your seeds" as to many, but as to one: "and to your seed", who is Christ' (Gal. 3:16). Yet to be tempted like [us], but without sin, is not a property of the God-Word, but of the assumed seed.

23 [22]. Jesus Christ is named both God-Word and man[132]

In this way the most divine Paul proclaims through the whole letter [to the Hebrews] both the properties of the natures and the unity of the person. That is why he names Jesus Christ both man and God: 'The Lord Jesus Christ is one', he says, 'through whom [are] all things' (1 Cor. 8:6). And again, writing to Timothy, he says: 'There is one Mediator between God and humankind, the man Christ Jesus' (1 Tim. 2:5). Also in the Letter to the Hebrews itself: 'Jesus Christ is the same yesterday and today and forever' (Heb. 13:8). If they wish, anybody can find numberless other testimonies in the Holy Scriptures proclaiming the perfect human being and refuting the folly of the heretics. But at present we do not have spare time to enumerate these. Therefore, passing this work onto the laborious [people], we proceed with the following argumentation.

24 [23]. On the ineffable birth from the Virgin

Thus the Creator, commiserating with his own threatened image [i.e. human nature] exposed to death, bent down the heavens and descended, not [in the sense of] changing place or going elsewhere, for he fills all things and is, rather, infinite and boundless, holding everything in his hand as the prophet says: 'Who has measured the waters with his hand, and meted out heaven with the span, and the whole world with [his] palm?' (Isa. 40:12). David says again: 'For in his hands are the margins of the earth' (Ps. 95:4).[133] Even God himself [says] through the prophet: 'The heaven is my throne and the earth is the footstool of my feet' (Isa. 66:1). Therefore, let us understand the descending [of God] as condescending: so he bent down the heavens, descended and chose the virgin womb of a holy maiden nurtured in piety. He announced the birth by angelic voice, elucidating beforehand the mode of conception, and dispelling virginal fear by explanation. He moved in and prepared himself a temple, formed the intact and pure tent;[134] and because the first man[135] served sin, he arrived without a father, having only the earth as [his] mother: 'God', he says, 'took the dust of the ground and formed man' (Gen. 2:7). This is why the blessed Paul also says: 'The first man is of the earth, earthy; the second man is the Lord from heaven' (1 Cor. 15:47). It was for this reason that the Only-begotten Word of God took the origin of his fashioning only from the Virgin, and in this manner created his untouched[136] temple, and uniting it with himself, came forth of the Virgin. He did not loosen the Virgin's girdle by his conception, and did not break it by his birth, but rather preserved it undefiled and unblemished, performing this great and inexpressible miracle. It is truly great and incomprehensible,[137] and surpasses the power of reason: to see a bunch of grapes rising from the earth without a vine-twig; wheat growing without seed; a garment being woven without thread and weaving hands. Bread is baked, yet not by milling, handwork and fire, but unspeakably made of virginal flour, and covers the world. Above all these: a Virgin breastfeeds her own infant, offering him the fountainhead of milk; *and she becomes mother whilst cautiously preserving her virginity*,[138] becomes mother who did not take the law of marriage on herself; becomes mother who does not know how to become a mother; becomes mother who did not become a wife first. Yet she shows in her virginity the growth of her womb and carries its fruit around in her arms; fulfils her maternal duties whilst preserving her virginity. *And on one hand the mother is called virgin, on the other hand the virgin is labelled mother*,[139] because she conjoins both the opposite names, as well as states.

25 {24}. Brief narration of Christ's activity after his birth

Thus was the Ruler Christ born, *paradoxically of the holy Virgin*[140] (for after the birth it would not be correct to call him either God-Word only, or man unclothed of Godhead, but Christ, which indicates both the assuming and the assumed natures). He received our passions fully, except sin: he was swathed [in swaddling clothes] just like babies; fed with milk and nursed; carried in the arms and seated on the lap. He was circumcised according to the law and was cleansed by purifying sacrifices; [he himself was purified, who is] the new and only sacrifice of the world, the Lamb who takes away the sin of the world (John 1:29). He was worshipped by Simeon and called Saviour and Ruler simultaneously; he fled Herod with his mother and guardian, arrived in Egypt and returned again, feared *Archelaus*,[141] went to Nazareth, grew in stature and in wisdom. He was obedient to his parents, deeming worthy of full deference not only his mother but also her former betrothed, who later became his guardian and protector. He celebrated the feasts of the law, went to the temple regularly, put to shame the obtuseness of the Jews, and did this while only twelve years old. He was sought by acquaintances,[142] lost and reprehended by his mother; defended himself, and somehow slowly revealed his divinity. 'Did you not know, he said, that I must be in my Father's own [affairs]?' (Luke 2:49). Thus he showed that he is not only that which was visible, but also God hidden in the visible thing, the timeless and eternal one, who came forth from the Father. (*Yet about his divine–human life we are taught again from the Gospel.*)[143] To speak briefly: he went to John the Baptist, persuaded the reluctant [John] to baptise him, prefiguring our baptism in the Jordan. He fulfilled the law[144] and opened the gate of grace, being announced by the Father from the heavens, and was attested by the presence of the [Holy] Spirit, then led up by the Spirit into the wilderness as to a suitable wrestling-school.[145] He fasts, but not exceeding the measure of nature: he desires food, but dominates the hunger, does not serve the lusts. By fasting he challenges the opponent to battle, but defeats him with human wisdom and not with divine power; he fights, overcomes and wins, chases out [the devil], destroys his tyranny, shows his weakness, declares his defeat. He says, 'be of good cheer; I have overcome the world' (John 16:33). He directs everybody towards virtue, establishes the regulation of divine doctrines, gives the New Covenant pledged through the prophet, promises the kingdom of heaven and threatens the reckless with the flames of hell.

26 [25]. Concise exposition of the Ruler's miracles

He confirms his words by a miraculous work, giving for the wedding a wine that was not [a result of] viticulture,[146] making wine out of water without vine-branches, offering the guests at the wedding a wine, which was not [squeezed out of] a bunch of grapes. He changed the nature of water into wine without the intervention of a grapevine, thus extracting the juice of the earth. He honoured the wedding not only by his presence, but also with the miraculous work. Since he came forth of a virgin womb and extolled virginity with his way of living and his words, honouring celibacy with his works and sermons: in order to [prevent] anyone considering matrimony as intemperance and categorise marriage as unlawful, he honoured the wedding with his presence and augmented its esteem with the preciousness of his gift. He removed the distress of the bridegroom, surprised the guests with the good odour of the new beverage, proclaiming himself by the gift. Thus being untouched [himself], he furnished untouched wine.[147] Then he healed the ill, removed sicknesses by his word, relieved the pain of suffering by his command, delivered those possessed by demons from madness, showed the raving restored, healed the cripple, put the lame on their feet again. He showed the sun to those deprived of seeing, opened the gates of their bodies through which the vision of the soul diffuses upon the outer [realities]. He did this sometimes by [his] mere words, then cured blindness with clay, with the foe of the blind, turning the enemy [of the eyes] into medicine and proving the harmful [clay] to be protective. He gave back to the so-called organs of hearing the original ability they had been deprived of. He fed many thousands in the desert with a few loaves, putting the five loaves like seeds into the hands [of the apostles], bringing the blessing of his tongue [upon them] like a cloud, thus transforming the apostles' hands into a plentiful crop and a full granary. A granary, which needs neither a winnowing-shovel or sorting, a mill, a kneading-trough, fires and oven, but the loaves themselves rise and gush forth [from it]. To continue briefly: he stanched the [woman's] flow of blood, allowing her intentionally to [almost] steal the treatment [from him].[148] He gave back the still immature girl, stolen away by death and mourned by her relatives, to her parents. He brought another one back to life, a young man being carried out for burial, thus changing the mourning into joy, transforming the funeral lament into a wedding song. He led the already decomposing cadaver out of the tomb after four days, and commanded the one who was bound to walk. Death drew back immediately and the dead man ran released from putrefaction, being set free from the stench of decay, and escaping from the gates of death. He was not hindered in running by the bandages, and although the veil on his face obstructed his sight, he hurried unimpeded to the one who called him, recognising the Ruler's voice.

27 [26]. [Jesus Christ] voluntarily accepted the sufferings of salvation

By these and other miracles [Jesus] gave weight to his promises and trained the chorus of the apostles for virtue, willingly proceeding towards the predicted sufferings. He forecast these several times for the disciples, and even rebuked Peter for not receiving with delight the good news [euangelia] of the sufferings, and demonstrated that through these the salvation of the world would be effected. That is why, pointing to himself, he said to those who came [to arrest him]: 'I am the one you are looking for' (John 18:6). He did not gainsay when accused, and though able to hide, he did not do it, although he had often escaped before when he wanted. He rather mourned Jerusalem, which caused [its own] destruction by its unbelief, and sentenced the once famous temple to total devastation. He even endured to be smitten on the cheek, to be struck by a slave enduring a twofold slavery,[149] to be spat upon, vituperated, tortured, scourged and finally crucified. He accepted the robbers on both sides as fellows in punishment, and thus was numbered with murderers and malefactors (cf. Isa. 53:12), offered vinegar and gall from the evil vine-stock, crowned with thorns instead of vine-shoots and grape-bunches. [He endured] mockery with a scarlet [robe], smiting with a reed, being pierced in the side with a spear, and in the end was put in the tomb.

28 [27]. What was the cause of the Ruler's sufferings?

By enduring these things, he achieved our salvation. Because the servants of sin were liable to the punishment of sin, therefore he, who was immune from sin and pursued righteousness in all respects, accepted the punishment of sinners. By the cross he repealed the sentence of the ancient curse, for [Paul] says: 'Christ had redeemed us from the curse of the law, being made a curse for us: for it is written, "Cursed is every one that hangs on a tree"' (Gal. 3:13 and Deut. 21:23). By the thorns he put an end to Adam's punishments, because after the fall[150] it was heard: 'Cursed is the earth in your works, thorns and thistles shall it bring forth to you' (Gen. 3:17–18). With the gall (cf. Matt. 27:34) he took upon himself the bitterness and toil of mortal and passible human life, whereas with the vinegar he accepted for himself the changing of humankind for the worse, providing also the way of returning to the better. He signified his kingship by the scarlet and by the reed he alluded to the weakness and frailty of the devil's power. By the slaps [on his face] he proclaimed our deliverance, enduring our injuries, chastisements and lashings. His side was pierced like Adam's, yet showing not the woman coming forth from there, who by deceit begot death, but the fountainhead of life, which by [its] double stream vivifies the world. One of these renews us in the bath [i.e. the water of baptism] and clothes [us] with the garment of immortality, the other nourishes the (re)born at the divine table, as the milk nurtures the infants.

29 [28]. By the sufferings of Christ our salvation was accomplished

Our medication, therefore, is the suffering of our Saviour. While teaching this, the prophet exclaimed:

He carried our sins, and suffered for us: yet we did esteem him being in pain, smitten and afflicted. But he was wounded for our sins and bruised for our iniquities: the chastisement of our peace [was] upon him, and with his wounds we are healed. All we like sheep have gone astray, therefore he was brought as a sheep to the slaughter, and was mute as a lamb before its shearer.

(Isa. 53:4–7)

As the shepherd, when seeing his sheep dispersed, chooses one of them and brings it to the pasture he prefers, by that one attracting the rest towards himself; in the same fashion the God-Word, when he saw that the human race had gone astray, took on the form of a servant, conjoined it with himself and by that [form] he turned back towards himself the entire nature of humankind, leading the degraded who were threatened by wolves to the divine meadow. That is why our Saviour assumed our nature. That is why the Ruler Christ embraced the sufferings of salvation, was handed over to death and put in the tomb. Thus he removed that ancient and long-lasting tyranny and promised incorruptibility to those in the fetters of corruption. By rebuilding and resurrecting the destroyed temple he presented both for the dead, and those awaiting his resurrection, true and secure promises:

> In this way, he says, the nature assumed from you has obtained resurrection by the indwelling of, and union with, the Godhead, having put off the corruptible together with the passions, and entered into incorruptibility and immortality. In the same way you also shall be released from the burden of the slavery of death, and having cast off corruption together with the passions, you shall put on impassibility.

This is why he also sent the gift of baptism to all humankind through the apostles. He says, 'go and make disciples of all nations, baptising them into the name of the Father, and of the Son, and of the Holy Spirit' (Matt. 28:19). Baptism is a prefiguring and a model of the Ruler's death. Paul says, 'if we have been united in the likeness of his Son's death, we shall also be [united in the likeness] of his resurrection' (Rom. 6:5).

30 [29]. Demonstration of the perfect human nature from the writings of the Apostle

Thus was the Lord Christ born, thus was he nurtured, worked miracles, suffered, was crucified, died, sent out his holy disciples as messengers to all humankind and was taken up into heaven. The apostle taught us these things concisely in what he wrote to Timothy, saying:

> Without any doubt, the mystery of piety is great: God was revealed in flesh, justified in Spirit, seen by angels, proclaimed among Gentiles, believed in throughout the world, taken up in glory.
>
> (1 Tim. 3:16)

Thus, he coupled his appearance with the flesh; yet, according to the folly of the heretics, [he coupled his appearance] with his justi-fication, and was justified by the co-operation of the Spirit.[151] Is, then, the justifying Spirit greater than the justified Son? By no means! Our [nature] was justified by God, who manifested [himself] in it, was inseparably joined with it, instructed it in the highest virtue, and kept it from tasting the arrows of sin, intact and superior to the devil's deceit. Although allowing [the manhood] to taste death for a short while, he immediately delivered it from its tyranny and imparting his own life to it, took it up into heaven. He seated [the manhood] at the right hand side of majesty, granting it a name above every name, bestowing his own dignity upon it and taking the appellation of its nature.

31. The eternal Word of God was pleased to be called Son of Man[152]

For he says, 'no one has ascended into heaven, but he who descended from heaven, the Son of man, who is in heaven' (John 3:13 and Eph. 4:10). It was not that which was of David's seed[153] which descended from the heavens, but the Creator [of all],[154] the timeless Word of God, who is existent before the ages. Because of the union with the manhood he takes on the name of the Son of Man. Elsewhere [John] names him again thus: 'If you will see the Son of Man ascending where he was before' (John 6:62), [this being] not the form of the servant, but the form of God. And again he says:

> Because he is the Son of Man, do not marvel at this: for the hour is coming, in which [all] who are in the tombs will hear

his voice and come forth. Those who have done good, to the resurrection of life, and those who have done evil, to the resurrection of judgement.

(John 5:27–9)

This is not the property of the bare manhood, but of the inworking Godhead and indeed also of the visible humanity because of its conjunction and union with the Godhead.

32 [30]. The form of the servant can similarly be named 'Son' because of the conjunction

Thus the God-Word appropriates[155] the wretchedness of the form of the servant and [although] being God, he wants to be called man. And as he shared in the humility of the man, in the same fashion he confers on him exaltation. The infant of the Virgin is called Emmanuel; the one swathed in swaddling clothes, sucking the breast and being nurtured with milk is called Angel of great counsel, marvellous counsellor, mighty God, sovereign, prince of peace, Father of the coming age, Son of the Highest, Saviour, Lord and Creator of the universe (cf. Isa. 7:14 and Isa. 9:6). For he says, 'One Lord Jesus Christ, through whom all [things are]' (1 Cor. 8:6).[156] Truly the names 'Jesus' and 'Christ' are significant of the oikonomia. Yet the oikonomia happened neither before the creation, nor immediately after the creation, but in the last days. Therefore the name 'Christ' indicates not only the assumed one, but also the assuming Word together with the assumed (for it is significant for both God and the man). Paul also attributes the creation and arrangement of all to the visible, because of the union with that which was hidden. That is why elsewhere he calls Christ 'God above all', saying, 'and of them [i.e. the patriarchs], according to the flesh, is Christ, who is God above all' (Rom. 9:5). Not because the descendant of David is God by himself and God above all, but because he was the temple of God who is over all, having the divinity united and conjoined with himself.

33 [31]. There are two natures, but one person of Christ

That is why 'Jesus Christ is the same yesterday and today and forever' (Heb. 13:8). We neither divide the oikonomia into two persons [prosōpa duo], nor do we preach or teach two sons instead of the Only-begotten, but we have been taught and teach that there are two natures. Because different is the Godhead and different is the manhood. Different is that which exists, and different that which came into existence. The form of God is different from the form of man; the assuming is different from the assumed; the destroyed temple is different from the God who raised it up.

34 [32]. Pious [teaching] is to speak not about mixture, but about unity in Christ

Therefore we neither confound the natures, nor teach a mixture [*krasis*] of Creator and creature, nor do we introduce the [concept of] confusion [*synchusis*] by means of the word 'mixture', but we both recognise the nature of the God-Word and acknowledge the essence of the form of the servant; nevertheless, we worship either nature as one Son. For the one conjoined[157] with the other is named Christ, whereas the bare form of the servant, unclothed of the Godhead, was never thus called by the teachers of piety.[158] Those who speak about 'mixture', thereby introduce confusion, and with confusion, change [*trope*]. Once change has appeared, God would neither remain in his own nature, nor man in his own. For that necessitates each [of them] to leave the limits of their essence, and neither God would be recognised as God, nor man as man anymore. This cannot be accepted even for the structure of the human being by a sound-minded thinker. We do not say that the soul is mixed [*kekrasthai*] with the body, but rather that she is united [*henosthai*] and conjoined [*sunephthai*] [with it], dwells [*oikein*] and works inside [*energein*] it. Nobody would say that the soul is mortal or the body immortal without being entirely in foolish error. So while we separate [*diairoumen*][159] each [nature], we acknowledge one living being composed out of these. We name each nature with separate names: the former 'soul', the latter 'body', yet the living being composed out of both we call by a different name, for we label that 'man'. Therefore, taking this also as an image of the oikonomia, let us avoid that blasphemy [i.e. the confusion of natures], and abandoning 'mixture', let us apply consistently the terms of 'union' [*henosis*], 'conjunction' [*synapheia*] and 'togetherness' [*koinonia*], teaching the distinction [*diakrisis*][160] of nature, and the unity of the person. Thus we refute the blasphemy of Arius and Eunomius, applying on the one hand the humbly uttered and performed [words and deeds] of the Saviour Christ to the form of the servant, whereas the sublime, God-worthy and great ones we attribute to the sublime and great divinity, which surpasses every mind.[161]

35 [33]. The assumption of our nature into heaven granted us the gifts of the Spirit

It is time to pass on to the next [subject]. So, after being taken up into heaven and proffering himself to the Father as guarantor of the peace of humankind, the Ruler Christ sends to humankind the grace of the Spirit as a pledge of the promised goods, as an instructor, trainer and champion of the pious. [The Spirit is] like a vigilant protector of believers, an unquenched and never setting light for those going forward, a healer of psychic wounds, a doctor of injuries caused by sin, a leader who teaches [how] to fight courageously against the devil. [The Spirit] gives wings to those falling to the ground, educates the earthly for life in heaven, to disdain flesh and take care of the soul, to despise the present and long after the things to come, to behold those [things] they are waiting for in faith, to consider none of the things in [this] life illustrious, to laugh at fame, to look down on the flood of riches, to see bodily beauty as a fading flower, not to grieve [because of being] poor, not to suffer [when they are] ill, to rejoice when being wronged, to be happy when despoiled, to endure hardships bravely, to pray for their persecutors and bless those who curse them, and simply to follow close after wisdom. The grace of the Spirit taught these things, and thus instructed the earth and sea, this is the wisdom of the barbarians also, since the arrival of their Saviour, this [is the wisdom] of the inhabitants of the mainland, of the soldiers and of those who live at the edges of the world.[162]

36 [34]. Turning towards thanksgiving and turning away from excessive [curiosity][163]

Therefore let us exalt the donor of these innumerable goods, who led back our nature from the extreme of irrationality into its initial [state], who became poor for our sake, so that we might become rich by his poverty (2 Cor. 8:9). Together with him [let us praise] his true Father, who so loved the world, that he gave his only begotten Son for it, that whoever believes in him should not perish but have eternal life (John 3:16). And together with the Father and the Son [let us praise] the Holy Spirit, in whom, being baptised, we receive the pledge of the gift; through whom our souls will be enlightened, through whom we are taught about the oikonomia, through whom we are instructed in theology, through whom we are delivered from irrationality, through whom we have been liberated from straying and have perceived the truth. We should also cease meddling with the nature of the

Unbegotten [i.e. the Father], asking whether he is good and just, and whether someone could exist who is unborn and uncreated. Let us stop interfering with the birth of the Only-begotten, with the pursuit of [its] manner, with judging concerning the unborn and born, with measuring the immeasurable. Let us give up erroneously investigating the procession of the Holy Spirit and seeking to learn something which is known only to the Father, the Son and the Holy Spirit. Let us remain within the limits we inherited, not modifying the boundaries fixed by our fathers. Let us be content with the teaching provided by the Spirit. We should not want to surpass Paul's knowledge [*gnōsis*], who said that both his knowledge and prophecy were imperfect and that he saw the truth in a mirror dimly (1 Cor. 13:12). Let us wait for the enjoyment of the benefits hoped for. Then we shall be taught [to perceive] perfection, when we shall not be harmed by false pretension, nor fall into boasting, but shall live free from passions. Therefore at present let us stay within the teaching of the fathers, in order that by seeking for more we do not fall [even] from the less, as our forefather Adam suffered: he desired to become God and lost even to be the image of God.

37 {35}. It is appropriate to assert 'God-bearer' and 'man-bearer'

Therefore concerning theology nobody should be afflicted by unbelief, nobody should be lame [in faith] about the oikonomia,[164] but should confess the Christ born of Mary as God and man, *perfect*[165] in both respects. That is why the holy Virgin is labelled both God-bearer [*theotokos*] and man-bearer [*anthrōpotokos*] by the teachers of piety, the latter because she bore [someone] similar to her by nature, the former, inasmuch as the form of the servant has the form of God united [to it].[166]

Let us praise, then, through theology and oikonomia the one who made known to us the hidden mystery, and preparing ourselves [to be] temples for God by the purity of our life, let us accept him to dwell within us. Thus, being illuminated by his rays, let us walk with decency as in the day, awaiting the blessed hope and manifestation of the glory of our great God and Saviour Jesus Christ (Tit. 2:13), with whom to the Father together with the Holy Spirit [there shall be] glory and might forever and ever. Amen.

11

THEODORET'S *REFUTATION*
OF CYRIL'S TWELVE
ANATHEMAS

Introduction

The *Twelve Anathemas* or *Chapters* were Cyril's famous theological propositions appended to his *Third Letter to Nestorius*. The author made every effort to formulate these in the most extreme Alexandrian language to make sure that his opponent would not sign them, thus bringing ecclesiastical condemnation upon himself, a verdict which was absolutely necessary for the realisation of Cyril's further church-political plans.

As mentioned already, Theodoret's counter-statements were written at the end of the year 430, at John of Antioch's request. The Bishop of Cyrus could not interpret Cyril's ideas in any other way than as a disguised, or sometimes flagrant, Apollinarianism. One has to admit that the terminology of these chapters was indeed shockingly close to the phrases of the Laodicean heresiarch. The very introduction of the term *hypostasis* into Christology, its equation with *physis*, as well as the continuous *Logos–sarx* manner of speech, must have led Theodoret to believe that Cyril had simply revived one of the subtlest heresies concerning the Person of the Saviour. If in Trinitarian doctrine Arius was wrong in equating *hypostasis* with *ousia* (which led him to assert that three hypostases meant three essences, i.e. excluding the 'coessentiality' of Father and Son), then Apollinaris (and consequently Cyril) had to be corrected in his Christological equation of *hypostasis* with *physis*, a correction which was ultimately carried out by the *Chalcedonian Definition* itself.

It is also in this sense that the counter-statements of Theodoret represented an important contribution towards the clarification of Christological orthodoxy. The anathemas were not included in the list of orthodox documents at Chalcedon, although in 553 they became the measure of orthodoxy, and Theodoret's refutation was banned as part of the *Three Chapters* by Justinian's council. Cyril's zeal was to safe-guard the personal unity of Christ as a single subject of predication. Theodoret's statements often represent a complementary, rather than flatly opposing, view, i.e. the emphasis upon the difference between the two natures as well as the positive recognition of a human soul in Christ.

TEXT
ACO I, 1, 6, pp. 108–46

Cyril's First Anathema

If anyone does not acknowledge Emmanuel to be truly God and therefore the holy Virgin to be *Theotokos* (for she gave birth according to the flesh to the Word of God made flesh), let him be anathema.[1]

Theodoret's Reply to the First Anathema

We who follow the evangelic teachings proclaim that the God-Word was neither made flesh by nature, nor was turned into flesh: for the divine is immutable and invariable. This is why David the prophet also says, 'But you are the same, and your years shall not fail' (Ps. 102:27 in LXX). And this Paul, the great herald of truth, in his Epistle to the Hebrews, states to have been spoken of the Son (cf. Heb. 1:12). Yet elsewhere God proclaims through the prophet, 'I am, I am and I do not change' (cf. Mal. 3:6).[2] Therefore, if the divine is immutable and invariable, it is incapable of change or alteration. Yet if the immutable cannot be changed, then the God-Word did not become flesh by changing, but took on flesh and dwelt among us according to the word of the gospels (cf. John 1:14). The most divine Paul also makes this clear in his [Epistle] to the Philippians, saying:

> Let this mind be in you which was also in Christ Jesus: who, being in the form of God, thought it not robbery to be equal with God: but emptied himself and took on the form of a servant.
>
> (Phil. 2:5–7)

It is then clear from these words that the form of God did not change into the form of a servant, but remaining what it was, took on the form of a servant. Then, if the God-Word did not become flesh, but assumed living and reasonable flesh, then the One being before the ages, being God and with God, being together with the Father and known as well as worshipped together with the Father, was not himself by nature begotten of the Virgin after being conceived, fashioned and formed, not taking the beginning of [his] existence from there [i.e. from Mary], but rather he formed a temple for himself in the virgin womb and was together with that which was fashioned, conceived, formed and begotten. This is why we also label that holy Virgin 'God-bearer' [*theotokos*], because she gave birth naturally not to God, but to man united to the God who had fashioned him. If the one fashioned in the Virgin's womb was not man but the God-Word who is before the ages, then the God-Word is a creature of the Holy Spirit. For, as Gabriel says, that which was conceived in her [Mary] is of the Holy Spirit (Matt. 1:20, cf. Luke 1:35). Yet if the Only-begotten Word of God is uncreated and coessential as well as co-eternal with the Father, he is not something fashioned by, or a creature of the Spirit. If it was not the God-Word whom the Holy Spirit fashioned in the Virgin's womb, it remains to recognise that it was the form of the servant having been naturally fashioned, formed, conceived and begotten. Nevertheless, since the form [of the servant] was not disrobed of the form of God, but was a temple holding the indwelling God, according to Paul's words ('for in him', he says, 'all the fullness of the Godhead was pleased to dwell bodily' – cf. Col. 1:19 and 2:9), we label the Virgin not 'man-bearer' [*anthrōpotokos*] [only], but also 'God-bearer',[3] applying the former title to the fashioning, forming and conception, and the latter to the union. For this reason the child born is also called Emmanuel, neither God separated from human nature, nor man unclothed of Godhead. For 'Emmanuel' means 'God being with us' according to the words of the gospels. The phrase 'God with us' both shows the one who was taken of us for our sake and announces the God-Word who assumed. Therefore the child [is called] Emmanuel on account of the assuming God and the Virgin [is called] 'God-bearer' on account of the union of the form of God with the conceived form of the servant. The God-Word, then, was not turned into flesh, but the form of God took the form of the servant.

Cyril's Second Anathema

If anyone does not acknowledge the Word of God the Father to be united hypostatically with the flesh and to be one Christ together with his own flesh, that is, the same subject as at once both God and man, let him be anathema.

Theodoret's Reply to the Second Anathema

Having been persuaded by the divine teachings of the apostles, on the one hand we confess one Christ and we name the same one both God and man on account of the union. On the other hand, though, we are entirely ignorant of the union according to the hypostasis, as being alien and foreign to the divine Scriptures and to the fathers who have interpreted these.[4] And if the author of these [assertions] wants to say by the union according to hypostasis that it was a mixture of flesh and Godhead, we shall contradict him with all zeal and shall refute the blasphemy. For mixture is necessarily followed by confusion, and the admission of confusion destroys the property of each nature. Things which have been blended do not remain what they were before; to say this about the God-Word and the one out of the seed of David would be entirely absurd.[5] One has to obey the Lord who shows the two natures and says to the Jews, 'Destroy this temple and in three days I shall raise it up' (John 2:19). If a mixture had taken place, neither had God remained God nor was the temple recognised as a temple, but rather the temple was God by nature and God was the temple (for the notion of mixture involves this), and it was superfluous for the Lord to tell the Jews, 'Destroy this temple and in three days I shall raise it up'. He should have said, 'Destroy me and in three days I shall be raised' – if some mixture and confusion had truly taken place there. Yet in fact he shows the destroyed temple and God raising it up.[6] Therefore, the union according to hypostasis, which in my opinion is put before us instead of mixture, is superfluous. It is sufficient to talk about the union, which both shows the properties of the natures and teaches us to worship the one Christ.

Cyril's Third Anathema

If anyone, with regard to the one Christ, divides [*diairei*] the hypostases after the union, connecting them only by a conjunction in terms of rank or supreme authority, and not rather by a combination in terms of natural union, let him be anathema.

Theodoret's Reply to the Third Anathema

On the one hand, the meaning of the expressions is unclear and abstruse; on the other hand, their senselessness is clear for the pious. For whom is it not evident that the conjunction [*synapheia*] and concurrence [*synodos*] are not different in any respect? Concurrence is a concurrence of separated parts; and conjunction is a conjunction of the disconnected parts. The highly astute author of these phrases has made synonyms into opposites. One must not, he says, conjoin the hypostases by conjunction, but by concurrence [*synodos*], moreover, a natural concurrence [*synodos physichē*]. Either he is perhaps ignorant of what he is saying, or he blasphemes knowingly. For the nature is a matter of necessity, not will; for example, I say we are naturally hungry, [i.e.] we do not experience this intentionally but of necessity; for paupers would have surely ceased begging if the power not to hunger had lain in their will. We are naturally thirsty, we naturally sleep, naturally breathe the air: and as I have said, all these [belong to the category] of the involuntary. Hence, someone who experiences none of these by necessity is approaching the end of life. Therefore, if the union [*henōsis*] of the form of God and of the form of the servant was natural [*physichē*], then the God-Word was conjoined to the form of the servant under the constraint of some necessity rather than instructed by philanthropy, and the lawgiver of all is found to be a follower of the laws of necessity. This is not what the blessed Paul taught us; on the contrary, [Paul said] that 'he [Christ] emptied himself taking the form of a servant'. Nevertheless, the phrase 'emptied himself' shows the voluntary [act]. Thus, if he was united by intent and will to the nature assumed from us, the addition of the 'natural' is superfluous. For it suffices to confess the union [*henōsis*], yet the union is taken as referring to separated [things], for if there were no separation,[7] a union could never be perceived. Therefore, the perception of the union presupposes the separation. How then does he say that one should not separate the hypostases or natures? He knows that on one hand the hypostasis of the God-Word was perfect before the ages, and that on the other hand the form of the servant assumed by Him was perfect; this is in fact why he [Cyril] said 'hypostases' and not 'hypostasis'. Thus, if each nature is perfect, yet both came together [*synelthon*] into the same [one], the form of God obviously taking the form of the servant, it is pious on the one hand to confess similarly One Person [*prosōpon*] and One Son and Christ; on the other hand, to talk about the united hypostases or natures is not out of place, but is rather a very consequence.[8] For if in the case of a single human being we separate[9] the natures and call the mortal one 'body', and the immortal one 'soul', yet both 'man', it is much more reasonable to recognise the distinctive properties of the natures of the assuming God and of the assumed man. We find even the blessed Paul dividing the one man into two when in one instance he says, 'even though our outward man is wasted away, yet this inward man is renewed' (2 Cor. 4:16), and in another, 'I rejoice in the law of God according to the inward man' (Rom. 7:22); and again, 'that the Christ may dwell in the inner man' (Eph. 3:16–17). Hence, if the apostle divides the natural conjunction of the synchronous natures, how can the one who really teaches us mixture by other expressions[10] charge us with impiety when we separate the distinctiveness of the natures of the eternal God and of the man assumed at the end of days?

Cyril's Fourth Anathema

If anyone takes the terms used in the Gospels and apostolic writings, whether referred to Christ by the saints, or applied to himself by himself, and allocates them to two *prosōpa* or hypostases, attributing some to a man conceived of as separate from the Word of God and some, as more appropriate to God, only to the Word of God the Father, let him be anathema.

Theodoret's Reply to the Fourth Anathema

These statements also are similar to those already uttered. Having assumed that a mixture had taken place, he proposes that there is no distinction of terms in those uttered in the holy gospels or in the apostolic writings – and [whilst doing] this he even piously claims that he fights at once against Arius and Eunomius and the rest of the heresiarchs. Let then this exact teacher of the divine dogmas[11] explain how he would refute the blasphemy of heretics, while attributing to the God-Word what was uttered humbly and suitably by the form of the servant. Those who are doing this teach that the Son of God is inferior, a creature, made, a servant and 'out of non-existent things' [*ex ouk ontōn*]. To whom, then, should we who think the opposite of this and confess the Son to be coessential and co-eternal with God the Father, Maker of all, Creator, Beautifier, Sovereign, Ruler, All-wise, Almighty, or rather Himself the Power, Life and Wisdom, attribute the words 'my God, my God, why have you forsaken me?' (Matt. 27:46), or 'Father, if possible, let this cup pass from me' (Matt. 26:39), or 'Father, save me from this hour' (John 12:27), or 'no one knows that hour, not even the Son of Man' (Matt. 24:36), and all the other [passages] spoken humbly by him and written by the holy apostles about him? To whom should we attribute the hunger and the thirst? To whom the fatigue and the sleep? To whom the ignorance and the fear? Who was it who needed angelic aid? If these belong to the Word, how was Wisdom ignorant? How then could he be called Wisdom when afflicted by ignorance? How then could he speak the truth saying that he had all that belonged to the Father (cf. John 16:15) yet did not possess the knowledge of the Father? For, he says, 'only the Father knows that day' (Matt. 24:36). How then could he be the unchanged image of his Begetter if he does not have all that belongs to the Begetter? Thus, if on one hand he speaks the truth when saying that he is ignorant, anyone may accept this about him. On the other hand, though, if he knows the day, but wishing to hide it he says that he is ignorant, look into what a blasphemy the conclusion leads. Either the truth lies, or it cannot appropriately be called truth if it contains anything of its contrary. Yet if the truth does not lie, neither is the God-Word ignorant of the day which he himself made and he himself appointed, in which he intends to judge the world, but rather he has the knowledge of the Father, since he is [the Father's] unchanged image. Therefore the ignorance does not belong to the God-Word but to the form of the servant, which at that time knew as much as the indwelling Godhead had revealed. The same can be said also about the other similar [passages]. Otherwise, how would it be logical for the God-Word to say to the Father, 'Father, if possible, let this cup pass from me, nevertheless, not as I will but as you will'? Again many absurdities follow thence. First, that the Father and the Son are not of the same mind, and that the Father wishes one thing and the Son another, for he said, 'nevertheless, not as I will but as you will' (Matt. 26:39). Further, we shall have to observe great ignorance in the Son again, since he will be found ignorant whether the cup can or cannot pass [from him]: nevertheless, to say this of the God-Word is complete impiety and blasphemy. For the One who came for this very reason, who assumed our nature willingly, who emptied himself, knew exactly the end[12] of the mystery of the oikonomia, since for this reason he also foretold to the holy apostles, 'behold, we go up to Jerusalem and the Son of Man shall be handed over into the hands of the Gentiles to mock and to flog and to crucify him and on the third day he will rise again' (cf. Matt. 20:18–19). How then can the One who foretold these things and rebuked Peter – who wished that they might not happen – wish them away [himself], when he knows clearly all that is going to be? Is it not absurd for Abraham, many generations ago, to have seen his day and to have rejoiced, and for Isaiah in a similar fashion, and for Jeremiah, Daniel, Zechariah and for all the chorus of the prophets to have foretold his saving passion, and yet for him to be ignorant and to plead for release [from it], and to wish away what was intended to happen for the sake of the salvation of the world? Surely then these words are not of the God-Word but of the form of the servant, which fears death because death was not yet destroyed, which the God-Word permitted to utter these [thoughts], giving room for fear, so that the nature of that which had been received may be evident and for us not to consider that which [was] of Abraham and David as an appearance or phantasm. The company of the impious heretics has brought forth this blasphemy through entertaining these sentiments. Therefore, on the one hand we shall attribute those things which are God-worthily uttered and performed to the God-Word; on the other hand what is uttered and performed humbly we shall attach to the form of the servant, lest we be infected with the blasphemy of Arius and Eunomius.[13]

Cyril's Fifth Anathema

If anyone has the temerity to say that Christ is a divinely inspired man instead of saying that he is truly God, since he is by nature a single Son, in that the Word became flesh and shared in flesh and blood like us (cf. Heb. 2:14), let him be anathema.

Theodoret's Reply to the Fifth Anathema

On the one hand we declare that the God-Word partook, like ourselves, in flesh and blood, and in immortal soul through the union relating to these; on the other hand, however, that the God-Word was made flesh by any change [*tropē*] we not only refuse to say, but even charge with impiety those who do. Nevertheless, it can be observed that this is contrary to even the very terms laid down. For if the Word was changed into flesh, then he did not partake with us in flesh and blood; yet if he partook in flesh and blood, then he partook as [being] another besides these; hence, if the flesh is something different from him, then he was not himself changed into flesh. Therefore, whilst we apply the phrase 'partaking' [*koinōnia*] we worship both him who took [*ton labonta*] and that which was taken [*to lēphthen*] as one Son, nevertheless, we acknowledge the distinction [*diaphora*] of the natures. Nonetheless, we do not reject the term 'God-bearing man' [*theophoros anthrōpos*], as uttered by many of the holy fathers, one among whom is the great Basil, who uses this term in his work [addressed] to Amphilochius about the Holy Spirit, and in his explanation of Psalm fifty-nine.[14] But we call him man bearing God, not because he received some share of the divine grace, but as possessing all the Godhead of the Son united. For this is what the blessed Paul said in his interpretation, 'See to it that no one takes you captive through philosophy and empty deceit, according to human tradition, according to the elements of the universe, and not according to Christ, for in him dwells the whole fullness of the Godhead bodily' (Col. 2:8–9).

Cyril's Sixth Anathema

If anyone says that the Word of God the Father is Christ's God or Master, instead of acknowledging the same Christ as simultaneously God and man, since according to the Scriptures the Word became flesh (John 1:14), let him be anathema.

Theodoret's Reply to the Sixth Anathema

On the one hand the blessed Paul labels that which was assumed by the God-Word 'form of a servant' (Phil. 2:7); on the other hand, since the assumption preceded the union, and the blessed Paul was talking about the assumption when he labelled the assumed nature 'form of a servant', once the union has taken place, the name of 'servitude' no longer has place. Since, if when writing to those who believed in Him, the apostle said, 'so you are no longer a servant but a son' (Gal. 4:7); and the Lord [said] to his disciples, 'I shall no longer call you servants but friends' (John 15:15), how much more the first-fruits of our nature, by which we were also privileged with the benefit of adoption, would be freed from the title of 'servant'. Therefore we confess even the form of the servant 'God', because of God's form having been united with it, and we yield to the prophet who calls even the infant Emmanuel (Isa. 7:14) and the child which was born 'angel of great counsel, wonderful adviser, powerful God, mighty, prince of peace and Father of the coming age' (Isa. 9:6). Nevertheless, the very same prophet, even after the union, whilst proclaiming the nature of that which was taken, calls the one of the seed of Abraham 'servant' by saying, 'you are my servant, Israel, and in you I shall be glorified' (Isa. 49:3), and again, 'thus says the Lord who formed me from the womb [to be] his servant' (Isa. 49:5), and a little later, 'behold, I have given you for a covenant of nations, for a light to the Gentiles that you may be the salvation to the end of the earth' (Isa. 49:6). Hence, that which was formed in the womb was not the God-Word but the form of the servant. The God-Word was not made flesh by being changed, but rather assumed flesh which had a rational soul.

Cyril's Seventh Anathema

If anyone says that Jesus is a man controlled by the Word of God and that the glory of the Only-begotten is to be attributed to another existing apart from him, let him be anathema.

Theodoret's Reply to the Seventh Anathema

If the nature of the human being is mortal, yet the God-Word is life and life-giver, and raised up the temple which had been destroyed by the Jews (cf. John 2:19), and carried it into heaven, how is the form of the servant not glorified through the form of God? For if being mortal by nature it became immortal by its union with the God-Word, then it received what it did not have; hence, upon receiving what it had not and being glorified, it has been glorified by the One who has given. Wherefore the apostle also exclaims, 'according to the working of his mighty power which he accomplished in Christ when he raised him from the dead' (Eph. 1:19–20).

Cyril's Eighth Anathema

If anyone has the temerity to say that the assumed man should be worshipped along with God the Word and should be glorified and called God along with him as if they were two different entities (for the addition of the expression 'along with' will always necessarily imply this interpretation) instead of honouring Emmanuel with a single act of worship and ascribing to him a single act of praise in view of the Word having become flesh, let him be anathema.

Theodoret's Reply to the Eighth Anathema

On the one hand, as I have often said, the doxology which we bring forth to the Ruler Christ is one, and we confess the same One to be at once God and man, since this is what the term 'union' has taught us; on the other hand, we shall not decline from talking about the distinctive properties of the natures. For neither the God-Word accepted the change into flesh, nor yet again did the man lose what he had been and was transformed into the nature of God. Consequently, whilst upholding the properties of each nature, we worship the Ruler Christ.

Cyril's Ninth Anathema

If anyone says that the one Lord Jesus Christ has been glorified by the Spirit, in the sense that Christ used the power that came through the Spirit as something alien to himself and received from him the power to operate against unclean spirits and work miracles in human beings, instead of saying that the Spirit by which he also performed the miracles is his own, let him be anathema.

Theodoret's Reply to the Ninth Anathema

At this point he ventured to anathematise candidly not only those who at present are holding pious [opinions], but also those who in the old times were heralds of the truth, and even the very writers of the divine gospels, the chorus of the holy apostles and, above all these, Gabriel the archangel. For he was the first one indeed who, even before the conception, heralded the birth of the Christ according to the flesh from the Holy Spirit, and after the conception taught Joseph (cf. Matt. 1:20–2), and on one hand said to Mary when she asked, 'How shall this happen to me, since I do not know a man?' (Luke 1:34), 'The Holy Spirit will come upon you and the power of the Highest will overshadow you; therefore also the holy [thing] to be born will be called the Son of God' (Luke 1:35), and on the other hand, [he said] to Joseph, 'Do not fear to take Mary your wife, for that which is born in her is of the Holy Spirit' (Matt. 1:20). And the evangelist says, 'when his mother Mary had been betrothed to Joseph, she was found to be with child of the Holy Spirit' (Matt. 1:18). And the Lord himself, when he entered the synagogue of the Jews and took the prophet Isaiah, and upon reading the passage in which he says, 'the Spirit of the Lord is upon me, because he anointed me' (Luke 4:16–18) and so on, added, 'Today this scripture has been fulfilled in your ears' (Luke 4:21). Hence, this is what in his sermon the blessed Peter also said to the Jews, 'Jesus of Nazareth, whom God had anointed with the Holy Spirit' (Acts 10:38). Isaiah had also foretold these happenings many generations before:

> A rod will come forth out of the stem of Jesse, and a blossom will come up from his roots; and the Spirit of God will rest upon him, the spirit of wisdom and understanding, the spirit of counsel and strength, the spirit of knowledge and piety; the spirit of the fear of God will fill him.
>
> (Isa. 11:1–2)

And again, 'behold my servant [pais][15] whom I have chosen, my beloved one, in whom my soul has rejoiced, I shall put my spirit upon him: he will bring judgement to the Gentiles' (Isa. 42:1). Hence, the evangelist has also inserted this testimony into his own writings (cf. Matt. 3:17), and even the Lord himself declared to the Jews in the gospels, 'If I cast out the demons with the Spirit of God, then the kingdom of God has certainly come upon you' (Matt. 12:28). And John [the Baptist] says, 'He who sent me to baptise with water, he himself told me, 'Upon whom you see the Spirit descending and remaining upon Him, he is the one who baptises with the Holy Spirit' (John 1:33). Therefore, the accurate inspector of the divine dogmas has not only anathematised prophets and apostles or even the archangel Gabriel, but extended the blasphemy even to the Saviour of all himself. Since we have shown already that even the Lord himself on the one hand, after reading the [passage] 'the Spirit of the Lord is upon me, because he anointed me', said to the Jews, 'Today this scripture has been fulfilled in your ears'; yet on the other hand, to those who said that he was casting out demons with Beelzebub, he said that he was casting the demons out with the Spirit of God. Nevertheless, we declare that it was not God the Word, coessential and co-eternal with the Spirit, who was formed by the Holy Spirit and anointed, but the human nature which was assumed by him at the end of days. We shall confess together [with Cyril] that the Spirit of the Son was his own if he spoke of [the Spirit] as being of the same nature and proceeding from the Father, and shall receive the expression as pious. But if [he would speak of the Spirit] as being out of the Son, or as having [his] origin through the Son we shall reject this as blasphemous and impious.[16] For we believe the Lord when he says, 'The Spirit which proceeds from the Father' (John 15:26) and likewise the most divine Paul saying, 'We have received not the spirit of the world, but the Spirit which is of the Father' (1 Cor. 2:12).

Cyril's Tenth Anathema

Divine Scripture says that Christ became high priest and apostle of our confession (cf. Heb. 3:1) and gave himself up for us, a fragrant offering to God the Father (cf. Eph. 5:2). Therefore if anyone says that it was not the Word of God himself who became our high priest and apostle when he became incarnate and a man like ourselves, but someone different from him who was a separate man born of a woman, or if someone says that he made the offering for himself too instead of for us alone (for he who knew no sin had no need of an offering), let him be anathema.

Theodoret's Reply to the Tenth Anathema

The unchangeable nature was not changed into a nature of flesh, but rather assumed human nature and set this above the common [i.e. human] high priests, as the blessed Paul teaches, saying:

> Every high priest chosen from among men is put in charge of things pertaining to God on their behalf, to offer gifts and sacrifices for sins. He is able to deal gently with the ignorant and wayward, since he himself is subject to weakness; and because of this he must offer [sacrifice] for his own sins as well as for those of the people.
>
> (Heb. 5:1–3)

And a little further, whilst explaining this he says: 'As was Aaron, so also was the Christ' (Heb. 5:4–5). Then, showing the weakness of the assumed nature, he says:

> In the days of his flesh, Jesus offered up prayers and supplications, with loud cries and tears, to the one who was able to save him from death, and he was heard because of his reverence; although he was a Son, he learned obedience through what he suffered; and having been made perfect, he became the author of eternal salvation for all who obey him, having been nominated by God a high priest according to the order of Melchizedek.
>
> (Heb. 5:7–10)

Who then is the one made perfect by the labours of virtue, not being perfect by nature? Who is the one who learnt obedience by trial and before the trial was ignorant of this? Who is the one who lived with reverence and brought forward supplications with strong crying and tears, yet not being able to save himself, but entreating the one who is able to save him and begging for release from death? Not the God-Word, the immortal, the impassible, the bodiless, the remembrance of whom, according to the prophet, is good cheer and release from tears, 'For he has wiped away the tears from all faces' (Isa. 25:8), and again the prophet says, 'I remembered God and rejoiced' (Ps. 77:4; LXX: Ps. 76:4),[17] who crowns those who live in reverence, who knows all [things] before their genesis, who has all that belongs to the Father and is the unchanged image of his Begetter, who shows the Father within himself, but rather that which was taken by him of the seed of David, that which was mortal, passible, and afraid of death; yet after these even itself [i.e. human nature] destroyed the power of death by the union with the God who had assumed it; that which walked in all righteousness and said to John: 'Let it be so now, for thus it is befitting for us to fulfil all righteousness' (Matt. 3:15). This [manhood] took the appellation of the high priesthood according to the order of Melchizedek, since it was beset by the infirmity of nature, and was not the almighty God-Word. This is why a little earlier the blessed Paul also said:

> For we do not have a high priest who is unable to sympathise with our weaknesses, but one who in every respect has been tempted in the same fashion as [we are], yet without sin.
>
> (Heb. 4:15)

Hence, it was the nature taken from us for our sake which in the trial experienced our sufferings without sin, and not the one who for our salvation had taken it. And at the beginning of this chapter he teaches [us] in the same manner again, saying, 'consider the apostle and high priest of our confession, Jesus, who was faithful to the one who created [*poiēsanti*] him,[18] just as Moses also was faithful in all God's house' (Heb. 3:1–2). Yet no one maintaining the right doctrine would call the unmade and uncreated God-Word, who is co-eternal with the Father, a creature [*poiēma*], but rather the man assumed of us. Neither was the God-Word, from God himself, ordained to be our high priest, but rather the one of the seed of David, who being free from all sin became our high priest and victim, offering his very self for our sake to God, clearly having in himself the God-Word from God, united and inseparably conjoined to him.

Cyril's Eleventh Anathema

If anyone does not acknowledge that the Lord's flesh is life-giving and belongs to the Word of God the Father himself, but says it belongs to someone else who is joined to him on the basis of rank or simply possesses a divine indwelling, instead of saying it is life-giving, as we have said, because it became the personal property of the Word who is able to endow all things with life, let him be anathema.

Theodoret's Reply to the Eleventh Anathema

In my view he seems willing to cultivate obscurity in order that, by it veiling the erroneous opinion, he may not be noticed in teaching the same [doctrines] as the heretics. Nevertheless, nothing is stronger than the truth, which by its very own rays strips away the murkiness of falsehood. Enlightened by this we shall make his heterodox belief plain. First of all, he neither mentioned 'rational flesh' [i.e. flesh with a rational soul] anywhere, nor confessed that the assumed man was perfect, but rather says 'flesh' everywhere, following the doctrines of Apollinaris. Further, after introducing the notion of 'mixture' [krasis] by means of other terms, he disperses it in his statements. Since here he plainly proclaims the flesh of the Lord to be soulless [apsychon], for he says, 'if anyone does not acknowledge that the Lord's flesh belongs to the Word of God the Father himself, but that it belongs to someone else beside him, let him be anathema'. From these [statements] it is evident that he does not confess the God-Word to have assumed a soul, but merely flesh, [the Word] himself being in the place of the soul [in] the flesh.[19] Yet we proclaim the ensouled [empsychon] and rational [logikē] flesh of the Lord to be life-giving [zōopoion], through the life-giving Godhead united to it. Hence, even he himself unintentionally confesses the difference between the two natures, by talking about 'flesh' and 'God-Word' and labelling it 'his own flesh'. Therefore the God-Word was not changed into the nature of flesh, but rather has the assumed nature [as] his own flesh, and made it life-giving by the union.[20]

Cyril's Twelfth Anathema

If anyone does not acknowledge that the Word of God suffered in the flesh, and was crucified in the flesh, and experienced death in the flesh, and became the first-born from the dead, seeing that as God he is both life and life-giving, let him be anathema.

Theodoret's Reply to the Twelfth Anathema

Passions are proper to the passible, for the impassible is above passions. Thus, it was the form of the servant that suffered, the form of God of course being together with it, and permitting it to suffer on account of the salvation brought forth out of the sufferings, and making the sufferings its own through the union. Therefore it was not God who suffered, but the man taken of us by God. Wherefore also the blessed Isaiah exclaims by foretelling, 'Being a man in pain and acquainted with the bearing of sickness' (Isa. 53:3). Yet even the Ruler Christ himself told the Jews, 'Why do you seek to kill me, a man who had told you the truth?' (John 8:40). Nevertheless, it is not the very life [who] is killed, but rather the one who has the mortal nature. And teaching this in another place the Lord said to the Jews, 'Destroy this temple, and in three days I shall raise it up' (John 2:19). Therefore, on the one hand the one who was of David was destroyed; on the other hand, the Only-begotten God-Word, born impassibly of the Father before the ages, raised up the destroyed one.

12

THAT EVEN AFTER THE INHUMANATION OUR LORD JESUS CHRIST IS ONE SON

Introduction

This little tract was appended to Theodoret's *Letter* 151 *to the Eastern Monks* written in the winter of 431–2 (see PG 83, 1433–40). As Marcel Richard has conclusively proved, the tract was composed much later, after the *Eranistes*. According to Richard, Theodoret wrote this tract shortly before the *Latrocinium* (449), during the period when his orthodoxy was repeatedly questioned by the increasingly strong Monophysite party.[1] It is therefore possible that, after having been confined to his see by the imperial decision, Theodoret tries to summarise his answer to the main charge of teaching 'two sons', which Dioscorus and his band repeatedly brought against him.

The exposé is an apology for the 'two natures' Christology, supported by a liturgical defence of the 'adoration of a single person'. This line of argumentation is typical not only for Antiochene theologians, but was also used repeatedly by Basil of Seleucia at a home council in 448, retracted at the *Latrocinium* and then reiterated at Chalcedon, thus forming one of the key statements of the *Chalcedonian Definition*.[2] This idea, also termed as the Antiochene *cultic* or *liturgical prosōpon* was present in Theodoret's oeuvre long before Chalcedon.[3] As we have discussed already, the theological relevance of the 'one adoration of the one Person' in assessing the orthodoxy of Antiochene, as well as Alexandrian theologians, cannot and should not be underestimated.

TEXT
(PG 83, 1433–40)

Those who have compiled slanders against us claim that we are dividing our One Lord Jesus Christ into two sons. Yet we are so far from conceiving such things that we even charge with impiety all who venture to say so. For we have been taught by the divine Scripture to worship One Son, our Lord Jesus Christ, God's Only-begotten Son, the God-Word made man. We confess the same One [to be] both eternal God and made man in the last days for the sake of humankind's salvation. He was made man not by the change of the Godhead, but through the assumption of the manhood. For the nature of the Godhead is unchangeable and immutable, in the same fashion as that of the Father who begat him before the ages; and whatever one might perceive of the Father's essence he will also find it entirely in the [essence] of the Only-begotten, since he is begotten of that essence. This is what the Lord also taught when he said to Philip, 'He who has seen me has seen the Father' (John 14:9) and again in another place: 'all things that the Father has are mine' (John 16:15), and elsewhere: 'I and the Father are One' (John 10:30), and numberless other passages are to be found which signify the sameness of essence.

Therefore, on the one hand he did not *become* God, but he *was* [God], since 'in the beginning was the Word and the Word was with God, and God was the Word' (John 1:1). On the other hand, he *was* not man, but he *became* [man], and became [man] by assuming that which was ours. The blessed Paul says this, 'who being in the form of God, thought it not robbery to be equal with God, but emptied himself and took the form of a servant' (Phil. 2:6–7). And again: 'for truly he came to help not angels; but he came to help the seed of Abraham' (Heb. 2:16). And again: 'forasmuch then as the children are partakers of flesh and blood, he also likewise took part of the same himself' (Heb. 2:14). In this way he was both passible and impassible, both mortal and immortal. On the one hand passible and mortal as man; on the other hand impassible and immortal as God. As God he raised his own flesh which was dead, since these words are his: 'Destroy this temple, and in three days I shall raise it up' (John 2:19). As man he was passible and mortal until [the time of] the passion. After the resurrection he has impassibility, immortality and incorruptibility even as man;[4] and sends forth light-ings befitting to God, [yet] not by having been changed according to the flesh into the nature of the Godhead, but rather by preserving the properties of the manhood. Nor is his body uncircumscribed (for this is the property of the divine nature alone), but it remains in its earlier circumscription. This is what he also taught after the resurrection, when he said to the disciples, 'Look at my hands and my feet, that it is I myself. Handle me and see, for a spirit does not have flesh and bones as you see I have' (Luke 24:39). Thus being seen, he was taken up into heaven; thus he promised to come back again, and thus will believers as well as the crucifiers see him. For, as he says, 'they shall look on him whom they pierced' (John 19:37).

Therefore we worship one Son, but we behold in him each nature [in its] perfection, both that which took, and that which was taken; both the one from God and the [other] from David. That is why he is named both Son of the living God and Son of David, each nature attracting its suitable appellation. As a result, the divine Scripture names him both God and man, as the blessed Paul also exclaims, 'For there is one God, and one mediator between God and men, the man Christ Jesus, who gave himself as a ransom for all' (1 Tim. 2:5–6). But whilst here he calls him man, in another place he labels him God, for he says, 'awaiting the blessed hope and the manifestation of the glory of our great God and Saviour Jesus Christ' (Tit. 2:13). Elsewhere, however, he applies both names at once for he says, 'of whom according to the flesh is Christ, who is God over all forever. Amen' (Rom. 9:5). Hence he called the same One [to be] both of the Jews according to the flesh and God over all as God. In the same fashion the prophet Isaiah writes, 'a man being stricken and acquainted with sickness; this one bears our lawlessness and suffers for us' (cf. Isa. 53:3). A little further, 'who would set out his generation?' (Isa. 53:8). Yet this is not human, but divine. Thus says God through Micah:

> And you, Bethlehem, land of Judah, are by no means the least among the rulers of Judah, for from you shall come a ruler who will shepherd my people Israel, and his origins are from the beginning, from the days of eternity.
>
> (Mic. 5:2, cf. Matt. 2:6)

By saying 'from you shall come a ruler for me' he shows forth the oikonomia of the inhumanation, and by adding 'his origins are from the beginning, from the days of eternity' he announces the Godhead begotten of the Father before the ages.

Thus being taught by divine Scripture, and having found that the teachers who in different [times] were illustrious in the church thought the same, we strive to preserve the heritage we received inviolate. Hence, on the one hand, we worship One Son of God, as One God the Father, and One Holy Spirit; on the other hand, we acknowledge the difference between flesh and Godhead. Concerning those who divide our one Lord Jesus Christ into two sons we affirm that they have forsaken the path trodden by the holy apostles;[5] similarly, referring to those who claim that the Godhead and the manhood of the Only-begotten have become one nature, we assert that they have fallen into exactly the opposite ravine [i.e. the other extreme].[6] These things we think; these we proclaim; for these doctrines we wrestle.

The slanderers who assert that we venerate two sons [are refuted by] the blatant testimony of the facts. To all those who come to the all-holy baptism we teach the faith laid forth at Nicaea. And when we celebrate the mystery of rebirth we baptise those who believe into the name of the Father, and of the Son, and of the Holy Spirit, pronouncing each name by itself. And when we perform divine service regularly in the churches it is our custom to glorify the Father and the Son and the Holy Spirit: not sons, but Son. If then we proclaim two sons, which [of the two] is glorified by us and which one remains without honour? For we have not quite reached such a level of insanity as to assert two sons, yet not to honour one of them with any respect. From this, therefore, the slander becomes clear, since we worship one Only-begotten Son, the God-Word made man. We call the holy Virgin 'God-bearer', since she gave birth to Emmanuel, which means 'with us God'. Nevertheless, the prophet who foretold Emmanuel a little later on wrote of him again thus:

> A child is born to us, and a son is given to us, and the government will be upon his shoulders, and his name will be called Angel of great counsel, wonderful, adviser, mighty God, powerful, Prince of peace, Father of the coming age [*Patēr tou mellontos aiōnos*].
>
> (Isa. 9:6)

If the baby born of the Virgin is labelled 'mighty God', it is reasonable, then, that the one who gave birth is named 'God-bearer', since the birth-giver shares the honour of her progeny and the Virgin is both mother of the Ruler Christ as man, and again his servant as Ruler, Creator and God.

Because of this difference in designations he is called by the inspired Paul [to be] both without father, without mother, without genealogy, having neither beginning of days nor end of life. On one hand he is fatherless in respect of his humanity, for as a man he was born only of a mother. On the other hand, he is motherless as God, for he was begotten from eternity of the Father alone. And again he is without genealogy as God, whilst as man he has ancestry. For it says, 'the book of the generation of Jesus Christ, son of David, son of Abraham' (Matt. 1:1). The inspired Luke also gives his genealogy. Thus, again, as God, he does not have a beginning of days, for he was begotten before the ages; neither has he an end of life, for he has an immortal and impassible nature. Yet, as man he had both a beginning of days, for he was born in [the time of] the Emperor Augustus; and he also had an end of life, for he was crucified in [the time of] the Emperor Tiberius. But now, as I have said, even his human nature is immortal, and as he ascended so he will come again according to the words of the angels, for they said, 'this Jesus who was taken up from you into heaven will come in the same manner as you have seen him go into heaven' (Acts 1:11).

This is the teaching the divine prophets brought to us, this [is the doctrine] of the chorus of the holy apostles, this [is the doctrine] of the prominent saints of the East and of the West: of the widely famed Ignatius, who received his high-priesthood at the right hand of the great Peter, and for his confession of Christ became the food of wild beasts;[7] of the great Eustathius who was the chairman of the assembled synod and lived in exile because of his inflamed zeal for piety. Meletius proclaimed this amidst similar sufferings, for he too was driven from his flock three times for the apostolic doctrines; Flavian [taught] this, who adorned the throne of that place;[8] the wonderful Ephraem, the instrument of the divine grace [taught] this, who has left us the benefit of his [work] written in the Syriac language; Cyprian, the all-praiseworthy leader of Carthage and of all Libya [taught] this, who for the sake of Christ received death by fire;[9] and also Damasus, who directed great Rome, and Ambrose, who adorned the throne of Milan, having accomplished [the doctrine] by preaching and writing in Latin.

The same [doctrines were taught by] the great luminaries of Alexandria, the like-minded Alexander and Athanasius, who endured dangers and who are respected by all. The great teachers of the imperial city brought this herb for their flocks: Gregory [Nazianzen], the brilliant advocate of piety, John [Chrysostom], the teacher of the world, Atticus, the receiver of their see and teaching. Basil [the Great], the most shining light of piety, and Gregory [of Nyssa], who boasted the same parents as he, and Amphilochius [of Iconium], who received the gift of high-priesthood from him, not only brought forth the teaching for their contemporaries, but also left help behind for us by their writings. Nevertheless, the time fails me to enumerate Polycarp, and Irenaeus, and Methodius, and Hippolytus, and the other teachers of the church. In a word, therefore, we assert that we follow the divine oracles as well as all these saints. For through the grace of the Spirit, having plumbed the depths of the divinely inspired Scripture, they perceived its meaning themselves, and displayed it clearly for those willing to learn. For the difference of the languages did not produce a difference in doctrine, since they were channels of the grace of the divine Spirit, receiving the stream from one [and the same] fountainhead.

13

THEODORET'S *LETTER 16 TO BISHOP IRENAEUS*

Introduction

This letter was written in the spring or early summer of 449, during the months leading up to the *Latrocinium*. The addressee is Count Irenaeus (later Bishop of Tyre), a devoted friend of Nestorius, who in 431 unofficially accompanied the patriarch of Constantinople to Ephesus, and after the council obtained an audience with Theodosius, in an attempt to secure the emperor's support for the Eastern faction. The imperial decree which exiled Nestorius in August 435 pronounced the same verdict against Irenaeus and a presbyter named Photius. Irenaeus lost his position, had his property confiscated and was deported to Petra where he spent twelve years in Arabian exile. He reappears towards the end of 446 as the unanimous choice of the Phoenician bishops for the vacant see of Tyre, one of his chief supporters being Proclus of Constantinople himself. During these twelve years his doctrinal position may have undergone some changes, nevertheless, the main reason why his ordination as bishop of Tyre became possible seems to have been Cyril's death in 444. Irenaeus was consecrated by Domnus of Antioch, who thus exposed himself to harsh criticism from the Alexandrian party. The latter group successfully convinced the emperor to issue a new decree on 17 February 448, which not only renewed the previous edicts published against Nestorius' supporters, but also deposed Irenaeus from his bishopric, depriving him of the robe and title of priesthood, and compelling him to live as a layman in his own country and never enter Tyre again. Following Domnus' futile attempts to rehabilitate him (the Antiochene patriarch was strongly reluctant to consecrate a successor) on 9 September 448 Photius was made bishop of Tyre. After this event, Irenaeus disappears from church history: his deposition was confirmed by the *Latrocinium* in 449, which passed an anathema on him. The council of Chalcedon, however, does not mention his name, most probably because he was no longer alive.

During the second half of his life Irenaeus became one of Theodoret's most trusted and respected friends. The tone of Theodoret's *Letter* 16 bears witness that he clearly sees the danger which is about to befall the defenders of the 'two natures'. Having learned of the arrival of the letter of convocation (dispatched on 30 March 449) demanding that the bishops reunite in Ephesus on 1 August, the Bishop of Cyrus seeks to approach and warn all the opponents of Eutychian Monophysitism concerning the forthcoming condemnation which he believes inevitable (Irenaeus having already been deposed a year before by imperial edict). Unfortunately, his misgivings proved correct, the *Latrocinium* heralding both theological attack upon the 'two natures' and personal attack upon its supporters. By the conclusion of the proceedings, not only had the Lord Christ been 'deprived' of one of his natures, but the Eutychian Monophysite 'robbers' had usurped the offices and titles of highly honourable churchmen whilst driving others, including Flavian of Constantinople, to an early grave. The imperial decree restricting Theodoret to his diocese must have reached him at almost the same time as the news concerning the convocation of the second council of Ephesus: consequently, the prospect of deposition in his absence (and thus without a trial) was far from unlikely. The choice of the venue itself carried an unmistakable message.

In this context Theodoret attempted to dissipate all the apparent theological and/or terminological differences between him and all those who similarly resisted Monophysitism but who had criticised him for having abandoned the term 'man-bearer' (*anthrōpotokos*) in 431. The Bishop of Cyrus had also composed a defence for the 'two natures' party, in which he did not quote Diodore and Theodore (who had been ferociously criticised by Cyril a few years earlier), but only those – mainly Alexandrian – teachers, who were respected also by his opponents. This, however wise, decision to produce an unimpeachable defence for the orthodox viewpoint did not meet the approval of some members of his own group, who suspected that the Bishop of Cyrus had betrayed their cause by omitting these two illustrious Antiochene teachers. All these misunderstandings required clarification in this letter addressed to Irenaeus. As it is evident from the text itself, Theodoret was successful in answering all the questions and dispersing every false assumption.

Concerning the theological and terminological issues at stake, one may conclude both that the expression *anthrōpotokos* became one of Cyril's major instruments in his attempt to prove Nestorius' alleged

Arianism,[1] and that the term 'man-bearer' was not a key phrase within Theodoret's own theological thinking. Furthermore, as the Bishop of Cyrus clearly realised, adherence to a term so largely compromised by Cyril's harsh denigration would not have been a felicitous choice for the orthodox group at the peak of the Monophysite controversy. Similarly, his forensically impeccable answer to the charge of having abandoned his theological masters by not quoting them in the apology written in favour of the orthodox party, reveals the maturity of a great churchman who not only strove to achieve unity and peace among his companions, as well as within the whole church, but one who also knew and set forth the way in which this could be accomplished.

TEXT
(SC 98, 56–62)

It seems there is nothing beneficial to be expected, since the tempest of the church has not only not settled down, but rather as the saying goes, it increases day by day. The conveners of the synod have also arrived and handed over the letters of convocation to some of the metropolitans, including our own. I have sent the copy of the letter to your holiness for you to learn, my lord, how, according to the poet's words, 'woe has been welded by woe',[2] and we need only the Ruler's goodness to calm the wave.[3] Even this {would be} easy for Him, yet we are unworthy of the calm. The grace of perseverance is enough for us, so that we may thereby get the better of our opponents. This is what the divine apostle taught us to pray for, saying, 'for with the testing he will also provide the way out, so that you may be able to endure it' (1 Cor. 10:13). I entreat your Piety to stop the mouths of the critics and persuade them that, as the saying goes, it is not fitting for 'those out of the ranks'[4] {i.e. 'behind the lines'} to mock those fighting from within them, [who are already] both striking and struck. What does it matter whether a warrior uses one kind of weapon rather than another in defeating his enemy? Even the great David did not use full armour when he vanquished the champion of the Philistines (cf. 1 Sam. 17:38–9). Samson cut down thousands with one blow using the jawbone of an ass (cf. Judg. 15:15–17). Nobody complains about the victory or charges the conqueror with cowardice just because he overwhelmed his opponents without brandishing a spike, or holding a shield, or launching many spears, or stretching a bow. In the same way, therefore, those who fight for the sake of piety have to be examined, and {we} should not seek out expressions which arouse contention, but rather arguments which evidently proclaim the truth and fill with shame those who dare to resist it. What does it matter whether [we] name the holy Virgin as simultaneously man-bearer and God-bearer, or call her mother and handmaid [*doulē* = female slave] (cf. Luke 1:38) of her child, adding that she is mother of our Lord Jesus Christ as man, but his handmaid as God, thus on the one hand silencing the imminent pretext of the calumny, yet on the other presenting the same meaning by a different expression? In addition to these things, it must also be considered that the former [i.e. man-bearer] is a common name, whilst the latter [i.e. God-bearer] is the Virgin's very own, and that the entire controversy aroused around this latter [expression] in a way it should not have. The majority of the early fathers have also applied the more venerable title to the Virgin; moreover, your Piety has done the same in two or three treatises. I possess some of these sent to me by your holiness, and [in them] you have not joined the term 'man-bearer' with 'God-bearer', my lord, but have intimated its meaning by other names.

Nevertheless, since you blamed me for having omitted the holy and blessed fathers Diodore and Theodore from the list of [authoritative] teachers, I have deemed it necessary to touch briefly on this [question]. In the first place, my beloved superior, many others, both eminent and illustrious were left out. Further, one must take into account that the accused [i.e. the 'two natures' party] is bound to bring forward indisputable witnesses whom not one of the accusers is able to blame. Yet if the defendant were to call those charged by the prosecutors to testify,[5] not even the judge would agree to receive them. If I had left out these holy [doctors] while compiling a commendation of the fathers, I [would] have done wrong, I admit, and [would] have become ungrateful to [my] teachers. Nevertheless, if on being accused I have brought forward a defence [for the 'two natures' group] and presented impeccable witnesses, why do those unwilling to see any of these [testimonies] intend to cast blame [upon me] in vain? How I honour these men is testified by the book I have written in their defence, in which I have refuted the written [charges] laid against them,[6] without being afraid of the power of the accusers or of the plots made against us. Therefore, those who cleave to idle talk should find another, [more] subtle pretext. My goal is not to say and to do everything in favour of this or that [person], but rather to edify the church of God and to please her bridegroom and Ruler. My conscience bears witness that I do these things neither for the sake of material favours,[7] nor because I cling to the honour [i.e. of being a bishop] with all its worries, which I would shrink from calling a misfortune. I would long ago have resigned voluntarily had I not feared the divine judgement. And now, know well, my lord, that I await {my} fate. And I think it is coming near, for so the intrigues {against me} indicate.

14

A COMPENDIUM OF
HERETICAL MYTHIFICATION

Introduction

In the first four books of his last major literary work Theodoret presents an overview of Christian heresies from Simon Magus to Eutyches, whilst consecrating the fifth one to a systematic discussion of Christian theology. This five-volume work is generally referred to as the *Haereticarum fabularum compendium* (*HFC*), i.e. the *Compendium of Heretical Fables* or *History of Heresies* – to a certain extent against the original intent of the author, who gave this title only to the first four volumes of his treatise.[1]

On the basis of the first four books this work might be regarded as historical,[2] yet even in these, the theological issues come repeatedly to the forefront. Moreover, the fifth book (the longest, representing more than a half of the entire work) deals solely with doctrinal matters. It links Origen's masterpiece *On first principles*[3] to John of Damascus' *Fountain of Wisdom*, being one of the very few systematic summaries of Greek patristic theology and one of the best handbooks of early Christian heresiology, history of doctrine and systematics. The author himself defines the title of his work in the general *Preface*:

> On the one hand, the title [given] to the summary of the foul heresies is *A Compendium of Heretical Mythification*; on the other hand, [the title given] to the teaching of the truth is *A Compendium of Divine Doctrines*; yet the common [title] of both of these *The Discernment of Falsehood and Truth*.[4]

Therefore, as G. M. Cope has rightly observed, 'to place this last major work in the category of "history" is to miss what Theodoret was trying to do',[5] since the title by which the work is currently identified refers only to the first four volumes, the fifth one having a separate title, so that the entire work should be known as *The Discernment of Falsehood and Truth*. Although being highly acclaimed by reputable scholars,[6] the *Compendium* has been given very little attention, even in most recent times. Apart from Migne's edition (PG 83, 336–556), a modern critical text is still unavailable. G. M. Cope provided (to my knowledge) its first English translation.

Apparently, the work was written at the request of Sporacius, a military commander present at the Council of Chalcedon who wanted to learn more about the controversy. Sporacius became a consul in the East in 452 and remained Theodoret's supporter and correspondent.[7] The generally accepted date of composition is after Chalcedon, i.e. 452 or 453.[8]

The present text is a selection from the first four books, i.e. from the section entitled *Haereticarum fabularum compendium*. I have tried to choose the most famous heresies, save for the chapter on Nestorius and Nestorianism, the authenticity of which has been questioned.[9]

TEXT

Book I

Prologue (PG 83, 341)

The all-wise God of the universe handed over the cultivation of the infertile world to a few men, and these were fishermen, tax collectors and one tentmaker. Yet the utterly evil demon, the slayer of human-kind, upon seeing them pulling up the thorns of polytheism's deceit by the roots, and himself being stripped of followers, being a crafty worker and an artisan of evil, invented various plans of attack. After having selected men worthy of his own work and put the appella-tion of Christians as – so to speak – a mask [*prosōpeion*] on them, in the manner of one smearing the lip of the mug with some honey, he brought forth the mischievous medicine of falsehood to mankind. Thirsting for the ruin of humankind, he did not wait for the message of the apostles to be strengthened and then bring forth the deceit, but right after they had begun to cultivate and to disperse the seeds of piety, this [evil one] sowed tares among [them] (cf. Matt. 13:25).

Chapter 7: About Valentinus (PG 83, 353–7)

Valentinus, taking his start from all these heresies,[10] put together his endless myths. He brought his heresy together under Antoninus I. He established the first perfect Aeon [age, epoch], which he also calls Proarche [chief start/head], and Propater [first father], and Bythus [depth]; and a particular Ennoia [thought, notion, concept] who exists together with him, called Charis [grace] and Sige [silence]. He said that this [Aeon] embraced the Stillness for endless ages. At a later time Nous [mind, intellect] and Aletheia [truth] were born of both. Nous was named Monogenes [Only-begotten]. Now these two couples they named the Pythagorean quaternion and called them the root of all. From Nous and Aletheia, he says, the Logos [word] and Zoe [life] issued forth; from Logos and Zoe, however, Anthropos [human being, man] and Ecclesia [church] [came forth]. These four couples [were called] the first-begotten Ogdoad ['eightness' or 'octet'], both root and underlying support [*hypostasis*] of everything.

They said that Aeon was first, and after that [came] Logos and Zoe. Following the issuing forth [*probolē*] of Anthropos and Ecclesia, ten other Aeons were extrapolated: Bythion and Mixis [mixture], Ageratus [un-ageing] and Henōsis [union], Autophyes [self-grown] and Hedone [pleasure], Akinetus [unmoved] and Synkrisis [compounding], Monogenes [Only-begotten] and Makaria [happy, blessed]. From Anthropos and Ecclesia twelve other Aeons were emitted: Paracletos [counsellor] and Pistis [faith], Patricus [fatherly, paternal] and Elpis [hope], Metricus [motherly, maternal] and Agape [love], Aeinous [eternal mind] and Synesis [coming together, intelligence, conscience], Ecclesiasticus [ecclesiastical] and Makariotes [happiness, blessedness], Theletus [desired, willed] and Sophia [wisdom]. They [i.e. the Valentinians] said that these thirty Aeons were unknown to all the others, yet they were familiar to the Monads [*monois* = 'ones']. Then he [Valentinus] mythologised abundantly in order to show that the numbers 'eight', 'ten', 'twelve' and 'thirteen' are to be honoured; he said that Bythus was unattainable to all those who [were born] of him. Sige withheld the things born [of Bythus] from seeing him and prevented the[ir] attempt [to reach him]. Nevertheless, the last Aeon whom they call Sophia, having the same desire [to see Bythus], yet not being able to attain to the desired one, gave birth, he says, to a formless being [*ousia*]. Having been distressed because of such an offspring, she approached the Propater and described [her] suffering [*pathos*]; the rest of the Aeons also made supplication with her, so she received some pardon. They said that the formless offspring [*amorphon kuema*] was Hyle [matter], being brought forth of ignorance, distress, fear and blame.

Bythus, however, being cautious not to fall into a similar passion with the other Aeon, brought forth Horos [limit, rule, boundary] without a female mate; for each of the other Aeons was bound together with a female. This Horos they also name Stauros [stake, cross], nevertheless, they mythologise [about] other names. This is why, he says, even Sophia, being cleansed, was delivered from her passion. Horos, however, cast that Conception [*Enthymesis*] which they named 'Pathos' and 'formless offspring', as well as 'Hyle', far away from her.

After these, he says, Monogenes was emitted by the decision [*gnomē*] of the Father into the security and company of the Aeons, [as] Christ and Holy Spirit; for they claim that Christ taught the Aeons that the Father was incomprehensible: and the Holy Spirit bestowed better equality to the Aeons among themselves. The Aeons, however, having received these, sang praises to the Propater and each of them joined in common to bring the most beautiful [things] they had. By these they emitted Jesus, whom they also titled Saviour and Christ-Logos. They also brought forth other angels together with him to be his spear-bearers. All these they named as within the Pleroma [fullness]. These are the things spoken of as outside the Pleroma: the Conception of that Sophia, which they also titled as 'formless offspring', named Achamoth [unearthly]. Being begotten outside the Pleroma, [Achamoth] kept on living in shade and emptiness; yet, having received mercy, the one named Christ was extended through the one called Horos and Stauros and gave Achamoth form in respect of essence [*kat' ousian*], but left her bereft of knowledge. After this, he withdrew the power [*dynamis*] into himself. Nevertheless, upon having received that glimpse of light that she had obtained, she was running to investigate it, but was hindered from coming forth by Horos, saying 'Iao' [~healer]. Consequently, they say that this too became [Achamoth's] name. Then she suffered, having been hindered from coming forth and received pain and fear and troubles; afterwards, the desire of conversion[11] arose in her.

They say that this world was constituted from these passions; from the conversion the Demiurge and the souls of all, whilst from the other passions the rest [were made]; from her tears the fluid [or flabby] essence [*hygra ousia*], from her laughter the light and from the others the other things [were created]. I do not think that those who mythologise have no share in the blame in saying all these [things]. They say that she besought Christ, who already had pity on her, to give her a share of the light; and although he received the supplication, [Christ] did not attend to it, but sent Jesus, so that both the seen and unseen things, both thrones and dominions and divinities, as they say, were created in him.[12] Therefore, he reached [her] together with the emitted angels, and separated her from her earlier passions, and upon separating he condensed these [passions]. She, however, having been parted from her passions, received the desire of the angels and gave birth to a spiritual offspring [*pneumatikon kuēma*] similar to the angels, and this ran back upwards. They say that the living essence [*psychikē ousia*] was made out of the conversion [*ek tēs epistrophēs*] and from this God the Father and King of souls having the same nature with him [i.e. with the spiritual offspring] was formed, which they called Right, and the things of matter they named Left. They claim that he made all visible things separately and call him both Metropator ['Mother-Father'] and Father and Demiurge.

Still, why should one enumerate all the gibberish of mythification? The whole of their forgery is similar to what has been described so far. They say that the Saviour who appeared took that which was spiritual from Achamoth and from the Demiurge was clothed with the psychical Christ, and from the Oikonomia was invested with a body having a psychical essence, and having been created with ineffable wisdom, he became tangible, visible and passible. Nevertheless, they say, he did not assume anything material whatsoever, since nothing of what belongs to matter can receive salvation.

They say that they are saved solely by knowledge [*gnōsis*], but we by faith and good deeds. [They claim that] they do not need [good] works, for knowledge is adequate for salvation. Because of this the most perfect ones among them fearlessly practise all the things forbidden by divine laws. They celebrate the feasts of the Greeks, take part in meats offered to idols, are slaves of pleasure-craving, and they indiscriminately embark on every evil.

Chapter 20: About Tatian and Hydroparastatae or Encratitae (PG 83, 369–72)

Tatian the Syrian was a sophist first, and then became a pupil of the godly Justin the Martyr. After the passing away of his teacher, however, he yearned to become a protagonist of heresy. He gathered the basic resources of his forgery on the one hand from Valentinus, [that is] the emanation of the Aeons; on the other hand, from Saturnilus and Marcion, [that is] the despising of marriage and partaking in animal [meats] and in wine. Those called Hydroparastatae and Encratitae have him as their leader. They are named Hydroparastatae because they administer water instead of wine, and Encratitae, since they neither drink wine, nor partake of animal [meats]. They withhold themselves from these, being disgusted [by them] as by evil. They follow celibacy, labelling marriage as fornication and calling lawful intercourse diabolical.

This [Tatian] also composed a Gospel called the Diatessaron,[13] by cutting off both the genealogies and other [passages] which demonstrate that the Lord was born of the seed of David according to the flesh. Nevertheless, not only those belonging to that sect have used this [book], but also those who follow the apostolic doctrines, being unaware of the wickedness of this composition, but using it more simply as an abridged book. I also found more than two hundred such books kept in honour in the churches among us, and having collected and put all of them away, I introduced the Gospels of the four evangelists in their place.

Chapter 24: About Cerdon and Marcion (PG 83, 372–7)

Marcion and Cerdon, his teacher also took the basic resources of their blasphemy from the deceit of Simon [Magus], but they began a new impious pathway.

Cerdon lived under Antoninus I and claimed that God the Father of our Lord Jesus Christ, and unknown to the prophets, was different from the creator of all and giver of Moses' law. And that the one was righteous, whilst the other one good. He says that [the just one] ordered in the law the excision of an eye for an eye and a tooth for a tooth, yet the good one ordered in the Gospels turning the other cheek to anyone who hits the right cheek, and to someone who wants to take one's tunic giving the mantle also (cf. Matt. 5:38–40). Further, the [just one] also demanded in the law that one should love one's friend and hate one's enemy, yet the other one commanded love even of enemies (cf. Matt. 5:43–4). And the utterly crack-brained one did not realise that in the law [God] also commanded people to bring back the wandering ox of the enemy (cf. Exod. 23:4), and to help the [enemy's] fallen animal to stand up (cf. Exod. 23:5), and not to overlook the enemy in need of help (cf. Prov. 25:21). As the one called 'good' by him [declared that], whoever calls [his/her] brother a fool is threatened by Gehenna (cf. Matt. 5:22). And showing himself [as] just, he said, 'for with the measure that you use it will be measured back to you' (Luke 6:38). Nevertheless, confuting these [things] is not a task for the present, the more so since the blasphemy is very easily detectable by those who read the divine Scriptures.

Now Marcion of Pontus, being educated in these things by Cerdon, was not content with the teaching transmitted to him, but augmented the impiety. In [his] book he invented four unbegotten essences: one of them he called both 'good' and 'incomprehensible', whom he also named the Father of the Lord. [Another] he called both 'Demiurge' and 'righteous', whom he also named 'Evil'. In addition to these [he placed] matter, which is malign, and functions under another malign power. [He said that] the Demiurge prevailed over malice and by taking matter formed everything from it. From the purest [part] he created heaven, from the rest the four main elements [*ta stoicheia*], whilst from the sediment [he made] Hades and Tartaros {i.e. hell}. Again, he says, sifting the purest [stuff] of the earth, he built paradise, and by taking one clod of this, he moulded Adam, giving him the soul [*psychē*] from his own essence. Henceforth, he says, there is a fight [between] soul and body: the body struggles eagerly to drag down that [pure] matter, whilst the soul endeavours to draw the body up to the Demiurge. These people even venture to say that the serpent is better than the Demiurge. For [the Demiurge] prevented [man] from partaking of the tree of knowledge [*gnōsis*], yet [the serpent] exceedingly urged him {i.e. man} [to go] on. And these impious ones do not realise that the counsel of the serpent begot death. Therefore, some of them even honour the serpent. I even found among them a copper serpent in some chest stored there amidst their foul mysteries.

Further, they blaspheme not only against the Creator, but also label the patriarchs and prophets lawbreakers, in order to depict the Demiurge as a lover of evil. This one [Marcion] accepted only the Gospel according to Luke and cut out most of the genealogy; but he threw out the law and the prophets as well as the entire Old [Testament] as if it were given by an alien God. He said that our Lord Jesus Christ came down in order to deliver from the slavery of the Demiurge those who believed in him. Christ appeared to be human, though having nothing human, and appeared to suffer whilst not suffering at all. He threw out bodily resurrection as well, assuming that this was impossible. On one hand he asserted that Cain and all the Sodomites and all the other impious enjoyed the benefit of salvation, having come to the Saviour Christ while in Hades, and were taken up into the kingdom. On the other hand [he claimed that] Abel, Enoch, Noah and the patriarchs, as well as the rest of the prophets and the righteous, were not partakers in the deliverance given to those [i.e. to Cain and the Sodomites etc.], [because] they did not want to align themselves with him [i.e. Christ]. Indeed, this is why, he says, they were even condemned to dwell in hell.

Marcion hurled such ravings against the Creator, indeed even more grievous [ones] than these: for [the] more enormous blasphemies I have given over to silence. I know one of these: a certain 90 year-old man, after rising at early dawn, washed his face with plenty of spittle and when asked the reason, stated that he did not want to be indebted to the Demiurge and accept water from his creations. Those present asked [him]: 'then how do you eat and drink and dress and sleep and accomplish the usual mysteries?' Replying he said that he did so from necessity because it was impossible either to live or to accomplish the mysteries in any other manner. And the madman confessed involuntarily that the one called good by him [i.e. the 'good' God of Marcion] had nothing, but that he enjoyed [the benefit of] all good things from the creations of the Demiurge. I, however, omitting very many things, shall proceed to the next subject, for this group is again divided into many sections.

Chapter 26: About Mani (PG 83, 377–81)

Mani was, so they say, of Persian race, yet he bore the yoke of servitude for a very long time. While a slave, he was called Scythian. Having been made heir of his mistress, he was not content when he became wealthy beyond all hopes, nor did he praise the giver of [all] good things, but rather moved his tongue to blasphemy and impious mythology, becoming the most accomplished instrument of the enemy of truth. He asserted that there were two unbegotten and eternal [ones]: God and Matter, and he called God Light and Matter Darkness, whilst [calling] the Light Good and the Darkness Evil. He added other names also, for he named Light the good tree, filled with good fruits; yet Matter [he called] the bad tree, bearing fruits coming together at the root. He asserted that God had forsaken Matter, and that God was both entirely ignorant of Matter and Matter of him. [He claimed] that whilst God held the northern, the eastern and the western regions, the Matter [retained] the southern. After many ages Matter was divided against itself and its fruits likewise against each other. When war was joined, some pursuing and others pursued, they arrived at the borders of Light. Then, having observed the Light, they adored it and were amazed, and wanted to fight with all their strength against it and conquer it, and mix their own Darkness with Light. So Matter got going – so the confused, nonsensical and mindless myth tells – with the demons, the idols, the fire and the water against Light which had appeared. God, however, shrank from the sudden war, since, it says, he had neither fire in order to use thunder and thunderbolts, nor water to bring about a flood, nor iron or any other weapon; so, he devised the following plan. Taking a portion of Light, he sent it towards Matter like a bait [*delear*] and a hook [*agkistron*]: she [the Matter] pressing close, bent over it, swallowed the missile and was caught like something trapped in a snare [*pagē*].

Hereafter they said that God was forced to create the world. Nevertheless, they say that the parts of the world were not his, but rather Matter's creation. He created [this] wanting to put an end to division and to steer the conflicting [things] into peace, so as little by little to liberate the Light mixed in Matter. They also say that man was not formed by God, but rather by the ruler of Matter. They named this one Saklas, and likewise [said that] Eve came into existence through Saklas and Nebrod. [They said] that Adam was created in the form of an animal, while Eve was soulless [*apsychon* = lifeless] and motionless. The male virgin, whom they named the daughter of Light and called Joel, they claim to have imparted both life and light to Eve. [They say that] Eve delivered Adam from bestiality and then, in the end, she was bereft of the Light. Saklas, however, having had intercourse with her first, had a child from her with the form of an animal. Afterwards, they say, he had intercourse with her again.

Nevertheless, someone might perhaps blame me equally for enduring to write all this down. For this reason, then, whilst cutting out the other myths and gibberish, I shall briefly present the main points[14] of the impious heresy.

These [people] call the sun and the moon gods. Sometimes they call it [i.e. the sun] Christ. They provide evidence for this [in] the sun's eclipse during the time of the crucifixion. At other times they say that boats carry over the souls of the dead from Matter towards Light. In this manner, he [Mani] says, they are delivered from the mixture of evil by stages. They also assert that the moon becomes crescent-shaped and cut in half in order to be emptied. And the luminous souls, having been taken from Matter, are placed over into the Light; and in this manner little by little the Light is set free from the mixture of evil. Once the entire nature of the Light is set apart from Matter, then they say that God hands it over to the fire and creates one lump [of matter], and with this he [makes] the souls of those who do not believe in Mani. At times he calls the devil Matter, at other times the ruler of Matter. He also said that marriage was ordered by the devil. They [the Manicheans] rejected philanthropy towards the poor, saying that it was worship of Matter.

They asserted that the Lord assumed neither a soul nor a body, but appeared as a man, having nothing human; and [that] the cross, the passion and death were fantasy. They repudiate bodily resurrection as a myth, for they do not accept any particle of Matter as worthy of salvation. They say, however, that souls are reincarnated, being sent down into either birds or cattle or beasts or reptiles. They suppose that everything has a soul: fire, water, air, plants and seeds. This is why, of course, those who are called perfect by them neither break bread, nor cut a vegetable, yet they conspicuously denounce those who do these things as being defiled with blood. Nevertheless, they equally eat things cut and things broken.

They seek advice pre-eminently from enchanters when fulfilling their unholy mysteries; by this means their teaching is even fouler, and it is exceedingly difficult to release someone who has shared in their abominable orgies from the operation of the soul-corrupting demons, who bind fast people's souls by the incantations of the initiates [i.e. those performing the rites].

At the beginning this Mani had three pupils: Aldas, Thomas and Hermas. And he sent Aldas to be a herald to the Syrians and Thomas to the Indians. When they returned, reporting that they had been subjected to all kinds of dreadful experiences, with nobody content to receive Mani as teacher, the all-evil one ventured even to call himself Christ, and name himself the Holy Spirit, and asserted that he had been sent according to the promise of the Saviour, for the Lord had promised to send another Counsellor [*Parakletos*]. [Mani] made twelve disciples according to the example of the Lord and went into Mesopotamia, fleeing from the king of Persia. For having rashly promised to heal the son of the king who had been stricken with some illness, he threw him into even greater afflictions. Thereupon he was expelled, as an obvious anti-god, and having arrived in Persia, he was seized by the king and endured Persian punishment: being skinned alive, he was thrown to the dogs.

Such was the end of Mani, and this is the summary of his impious heresy. For if someone wished to go through all the nonsense of the myths, very many books would be needed. Such were the doctrines the all-evil demon introduced into the minds of the unholy, and such were the commanders and officers he used to go into battle against the truth. To speak according to the prophet, 'he has woven a spider's web' (cf. Isa. 59:5). The Ruler easily refuted the falsehood and dissolved the bands of its defenders.

Some excellent advocates of piety wrote against Mani's impiety, Titus and Diodore, the former the shepherd of the Bostrian church, the latter the leader of the metropolis of the Cilicians. George of Laodicea also wrote [against Mani], who on one hand was a champion of Arius's heresy, and on the other hand [he had been] nurtured in the teachings of the philosophers. In addition to all these, Eusebius the Phoenician also [wrote], whom we have mentioned before. Now I shall move onto another phalanx.

Book II

Chapter 1: About Ebion (PG 83, 388–9)

The leader of this phalanx was Ebion, which is the Hebrews' term for 'the poor one'. On the one hand he said, just as we do, that the One was unbegotten, and he showed that he was the demiurge of the world. On the other hand, he claimed that the Lord Jesus Christ was born of Joseph and Mary, being a man, yet superior to others in virtue and purity. They [the followers of Ebion] conduct their lives [*politeuontai*] according to the law of Moses. They receive only the *Gospel according to the Hebrews*[15] and call the apostle [Paul] an apostate. Symmachus, who translated the Old Testament from Hebrew into Greek, was one of them. Another group besides this one bears the same name, for they are also called 'Ebionites'. They agree in everything with the former ones, yet they say that the Saviour and Lord was born of a virgin. Nevertheless, they use only the Gospel according to Matthew, and both honour the Sabbath according to the law of the Jews, and celebrate the Lord's day very similarly to us.

Chapter 4: About Artemon (PG 83, 389–92)

A certain Artemon, whom some name Artemas, on the one hand held beliefs about the God of the universe very similar to ours, saying that he was the creator of everything. By contrast, he said that the Lord Jesus Christ was a mere man, born of a virgin, yet better than the prophets in virtue. He claimed that the apostles also proclaimed these things, misinterpreting the meaning of the divine Scriptures, [and] that it was those who [lived] after them [i.e. the apostles] who made Christ divine, although he was not God.

Chapter 8: About Paul of Samosata (PG 83, 393–6)

Paul of Samosata was bishop of Antioch. During that time Zenobia was the ruler (for the Persians, having defeated the Romans, handed authority over Syria and Phoenicia to her). [Paul] fell in with the heresy of Artemon, thinking that by this he would do service to that [teaching] which held Jewish beliefs. On being informed about this, the leaders of the church reckoned that it were not without danger to overlook such a quickly spreading plague, which even had the distinction of a very great city as an accomplice. And Dionysius, the bishop of Alexandria, a man famous for teaching, delayed his journey [to Antioch] because of the weakness of old age;[16] nevertheless, by letters he gave advice to him [i.e. Paul] concerning his duty and stirred up the assembled bishops to zeal for true religion. Gregory,[17] the great and celebrated bishop who accomplished wonders, lauded by all, through the Spirit's indwelling grace, presided over the assembled bishops, and also Athenodorus, his [Gregory's] brother, and Firmilian, the bishop of Caesarea in Cappadocia, a distinguished man, well versed in both secular and divine knowledge, and in addition to these Helenus, who was the church leader in the metropolis of Cilicia. These presided over the many who had assembled. At first they attempted to turn Paul away from his wicked views by explanations and consultations. As soon as he clearly denied having held such beliefs, and asserted that he followed the apostolic doctrines, they [i.e. the bishops assembled in Antioch], singing praises to the Ruler for their concord, returned to their own flocks.

After some time had passed, again the report ran everywhere, informing everyone of Paul's deviation. Even so the renowned men [i.e. the bishops] did not readily move forward to cut him off, but at first they attempted to cure the illness by letters. Nevertheless, when they realised that the affliction was incurable, they returned promptly to Antioch and again applied mild medicines, whilst exhorting and urging and reminding [Paul] of the agreement which had been reached. Then, on seeing that he remained in denial, yet his accusers persisted and promised to convict [him], they met together in a council [*synedrion*]. When a certain Malachion, who had previously been a sophist, and later by ordination became a respectable presbyter, disputed with Paul, the latter was found saying that Christ [was] a man, eminently privileged by divine grace. Therefore they then justly removed him from the holy lists with a unanimous vote.

Since he resisted, and clung to the control of the church, they notified Aurelian (who reigned at that time) of Paul's impudence, and persuaded [him] to drive him out of the church.[18] For [although] he [Aurelian] was enslaved in the adoration of idols, he considered it right that one who spoke against the decision of his fellow-believers should be separated from their company.

Chapter 9: About Sabellius (PG 83, 396)

Sabellius, the Libyan of Pentapolis, started the following heresy. He asserted that the Father and the Son and the Holy Spirit were one hypostasis and one three-named person [*hen triōnymon prosōpon*],[19] and he called the same One sometimes Father, sometimes Son, at other times Holy Spirit; and [said] that as Father he gave the law in the

Old [Testament], yet in the New [Testament] as Son he was made man, then as Holy Spirit he came to the apostles. Dionysius, the bishop of Alexandria, wrote against this heresy.

Chapter 10: About Marcellus (PG 83, 396–7)

Marcellus the Galatian, being much like Sabellius, denied the Trinity of the hypostases. He asserted that a certain extension of the Father's Godhead went into Christ and this he called God-Word. After the entire oikonomia, however, he was taken up again and withdrawn into God, from whom he had been extended. Marcellus said that the All-holy Spirit [was] a further extension of [this] extension [i.e. of Christ], and that this one had been given to the apostles. And in general he suggested that the Trinity was expanded and contracted according to the different dispensations.

Chapter 11: About Photinus (PG 83, 397)

Photinus claimed that there was a single operation [*mia energeia*] of the Father, Son and Holy Spirit, proclaiming the meaning of Sabellius' doctrines by different names. Against these four heretics the divine Diodore wrote, who governed the metropolitan [see] of Cilicia, demonstrating that Christ was eternal God, who was made man in the last days and achieved the salvation of humankind.

The scourge of humankind contrived all these heresies to overthrow the divinity of the Only-begotten; nevertheless, the One who rebukes and dries up the Abyss quenched them all, telling the Abyss, 'You shall be deserted and I shall dry up your rivers.' Not even a tiny trace of them remained, none of the Cerinthians, Ebionites, Theodotians, Elkesaites, Melchisedekians, Sabellians, Paulianists, Marcellians and Photinians, but all were given over once and for all to the gloom of oblivion, and not even their names are known to the majority [of people]. For the word of our Saviour is without falsehood: 'Every plant that my heavenly Father has not planted will be uprooted' (Matt. 15:13). The divine doctrines of the Gospels, however, have flourished, and the vine cuttings[20] planted by the apostles have extended as far as the sea, the offshoots have filled the world, and the entire earth is filled with the knowledge of the Lord as the water covers the seas (cf. Hab. 2:14). The testimony of the events has demonstrated the truthfulness of the prediction.

Book III

Chapter 2: About the Montanists (PG 83, 401–4)

Montanus started the heresy called 'Kataphrygian',[21] having come from a certain village which lay there called Ardabas. Obsessed by the lust of power, he called himself the Counsellor [*Parakletos*] and made two female prophets: Priscilla and Maximilla. The writings of these he called prophetic books, and the village of Pepuza he named Jerusalem. He commanded that even marriage should be dissolved, and introduced new fasts against the custom of the church. Nevertheless, he did not ruin the teaching about the divine Trinity and he taught like us about the creation of the world. Those who cling to this teaching are called Montanists after him, and Kataphrygians after his nationality, yet also Pepuzians after the village which he had called Jerusalem. The prophecies of Priscilla and Maximilla were, however, more honoured by them than the divine Gospel.

Concerning the mysteries, some of them criticised certain [things], nevertheless, they do not acknowledge [these charges], but call the accusation a calumny. Some of them denied the three hypostases of the divinity like Sabellius, saying that the Father and the Son and the Holy Spirit are the same one, similarly to the Asian Noetus. Against these Apollinaris wrote, the bishop of Hierapolis in Phrygia, a praiseworthy man, who, beside knowledge of theology also gained a secular education.[22] In the same manner Miltiades and Apollonius and others wrote against it. Yet against Proclus, who was a champion of that same heresy, Gaius wrote, whom we have mentioned before.[23]

Chapter 3: About Noetus of Smyrna (PG 83, 404–5)

Noetus was a Smyrnaean by race, who renewed the heresy which a certain man named Epigonus first conceived, but Kleomenes took over and strengthened it. Here is a summary of the heresy. They assert that God the Father, the creator of the universe, is one; he is unseen when he wills, yet he is seen whenever he wants to be. The same one is both visible and invisible, both begotten and unbegotten: unbegotten from the beginning, yet begotten when he wanted to be born of the Virgin. [God is] impassible and immortal, and again, on the contrary, passible and mortal. Though impassible, he says, [God] willingly endured the suffering of the cross. They name him both Son and Father, calling him by each name as needed. Those who accepted this heresy were called Noetians. Callistus defended it after Noetus, having added some things of his own contrivance to the impiety of this doctrine.

Chapter 5: About Novatus (PG 83, 405–8)

Novatus was a presbyter of the church of Rome. When a very fierce tempest fell upon the churches, it happened that some of those reared in piety, after many injuries, lost their resistance and used words of denial. Once calm returned, they asked to receive the medicines of repentance [*metanoia*].[24] To the excellent shepherds it appeared right indeed to fear the Ruler's indictment, which said, 'Oh shepherds, you have not bound up the bruised, and you have not brought back the errant, and you have not raised the fallen' (cf. Ezek. 34:4), and so to extend their hand towards the lapsed, and strengthen them according to the Ruler's commandment. For the Lord indeed said to the great Peter, 'Simon, Simon, Satan has demanded that you be sifted like wheat, and I have prayed for you that your faith may not fail' (Luke 22:31–2).

Novatus was displeased with these counsels, and spoke directly against them, saying that those who had denied should not receive salvation. He was acting like those who obstruct the sick from enjoying healing medicines. Yet those who asked to receive healing spoke against him, since [during the persecution] he had been called upon many times to run to them and strengthen at least with words those battered by the devices of the tyrant, but he went into hiding instead, and whilst trying to escape notice, even denied being a presbyter. Nevertheless, the bishops who had come together in Rome, even after hearing these words, still attempted to persuade him to agree with those of sound mind. But when they saw his madness and his legislating a cruelty hateful to God [i.e. to reject the lapsed], they separated him from the body of the church. At that time Cornelius was the leader in Rome.

This Novatus, having persuaded a few, easily countable [people] to join the heresy, went out to Italy and deceived three bishops of small towns whom he brought in to intercede on his behalf with the bishop of Rome. Arriving in a certain village with them, he compelled them to ordain him as bishop. They lamented this coercion upon reaching Rome, explaining what had happened. The despicable Novatus, having thus stolen ordination, became the founder of the heresy. He called those of his own company not only Novatians, but also 'Katharoi' ['the pure ones']. He did not fear at all the indictment of the Ruler God, which He made against some, saying, 'Those who say, "I am pure, do not touch me",' and added, 'This [is the] smoke of my wrath, the fire burns in it every day' (Isa. 65:5). For 'the Lord resists the proud' (Prov. 3:34; cf. 1 Pet. 5:5). His successors added other elements to his doctrine: they eliminate those who have entered second marriages from the holy mysteries, and totally exclude the word of repentance [*metanoia*] from their own gatherings. They do not apply the most holy anointing to those baptised by them. This is why the highly acclaimed fathers have ordered that those joining the body of the church from this heresy should be anointed.

Cornelius wrote many letters against this heresy. Dionysius, the bishop of Alexandria also [wrote] many, and many other bishops of the time as well, through which the harshness of Novatus was immediately made quite manifest to all.

Book IV

Prologue (PG 83, 412)

In the books already written it had been shown that the majority of the notorious heresies were handed over to the ancient gods of Valentinus, namely to Abyss and to Silence. The towns and villages liberated from them testify to this assertion. Nevertheless, the father of lies, whom the Lord suitably called a murderer (cf. John 8:44) – for he always attacks the souls of men – devised other schemes of assault. Having realised that what was said concerning the God of the universe by his pupils seemed totally abominable to all, and that their account of the oikonomia did not hold any credibility (for some declared that the bare Godhead appeared, yet others that only the manhood bereft of the Godhead fulfilled the oikonomia), he [Satan] concocted a [new] impiety free from each of these extremes.

Chapter 1: About Arius (PG 83, 412–16)

Having found Arius in quest of human glory, he [Satan] both inflamed in him the fever of haughtiness and injected into him the deceit of heresy. He was one of the list of the presbyters of the Alexandrian church, and seeing the great Alexander seated on the pontifical chair, he was struck by the goad. Seeking for a basis for conflict with him, he found impiety of doctrines as a pretext. While he [Alexander] provided apostolic nourishment to the flock and led the sheep to the springs of the gospel, this [Arius] spoke against him when the all-wise teacher [Alexander] called the Son of the Father coessential [*homoousios*]. He contradicted, calling [him] a creature, whom he also named a true son. When Alexander said that the God-Word was co-eternal with God the Father, existing in the beginning, the Word being both God and the reflection of the glory (Heb. 1:3), Arius said that the existing One came into being from the non-existent [things],[25] and asserted that he had a mutable nature. Moreover, he even mutilated the account of the inhumanation [*enanthrōpēsis*]. For he asserted that he [the Word] took a soulless body and that the divine being carried out [the functions] of the soul, so that to this [i.e. to the Godhead] he attached the experiences[26] arising from the body. Having abandoned the terms of doxology, which those who were from the beginning eyewitnesses and servants of the Word (cf. Luke 1:2) have handed down, he introduced a different type, teaching those deceived by him to glorify the Father through the Son in the Holy Spirit. He did not dare to modify the invocation [*epiklēsis*] included in divine baptism because of the obviousness of the transgression, but according to the Ruler's commandment he handed over [i.e. taught] baptism into the name of the Father and of the Son and of the Holy Spirit. Yet he banned the doxology according to the law of baptism, although our God and Saviour prescribed not simply baptism, but making disciples first. For he says, 'Go, make disciples of all nations, baptising them into the name of the Father and of the Son and of the Holy Spirit' (Matt. 28:19). According to this law, both the divine apostles and the teachers of the church after them, instructed those who came forward to believe in the name of the Father and of the Son and of the Holy Spirit and they baptised those who were made disciples into the name of the Father and of the Son and of the Holy Spirit. This is why indeed those who benefited from the gift in the sense that they were made disciples and baptised, glorify the Father and the Son and the Holy Spirit. It is abominable for those who were granted the gift of baptism from the Holy Trinity to offer doxology only to the Father and to leave the Son and the All-holy Spirit unhonoured.

We have spoken in detail concerning these issues in our writings against them; the purpose of the present composition, however, is to exhibit the character of each heresy. Therefore, the holy fathers who gathered in Nicaea openly renounced this Arius who held these opinions, as introducing doctrines entirely alien and foreign to divine oracles. Later, by simulating regret, he persuaded those who reigned together with[27] the great Emperor Constantine that he be given space for repentance. The emperor, having accepted the plea, ordered the bishop of the imperial city to extend his hand towards the one longing for salvation. The godly Alexander (for he held the rudder of that church) first attempted to persuade the emperor not to be carried away by the contrived words of Arius. Then, on seeing that he [the emperor] was annoyed, he withdrew in silence. It was agreed that Arius be admitted at dawn, for it was the Sabbath when these things were said. So the true man of God ran into the divine temple with two of his associates, besought the Ruler of the churches, and throwing himself on the ground before the holy altar and pouring forth tears, begged him not to allow the wolf to mingle with the sheep, even though [Arius], really wanting to behave like a wolf, veiled himself with the fleece of a sheep. They say that he [Alexander] also added these words to the prayer, 'If you permit one who devised such teachings to enter [the Church] through your ineffable oikonomia (for your judgements are unsearchable),[28] release me, your servant, from the present life.' With this prayer, he returned to his residence in tears.

Arius, however, thinking that the emperor's pledges would be confirmed, came forward at first dawn. Then his stomach urged excretion, and he went into the public toilet, leaving his escorting house-servant outside. Suddenly, his bowels having been loosened and having excreted, he died sitting inside. When those sitting nearby observing the incident cried out, the servant ran inside and on seeing him dead, disclosed what had happened to [Arius'] household. When the divinely struck blow was revealed to the whole of the populous city, everybody ran together into the divine temple. When they learned of the emperor's pledge and of the prayer of the priest, they sang praises to the Governor of the churches and cursed the impiety of the heresy. Yet despite these events, and the divine sentence having been demonstrated extraordinarily clearly, those who contracted the sickness carried on, sharpening their tongues against the Only-begotten and the All-holy Spirit.

Having written down these events in detail in the *Ecclesiastical History*,[29] I consider it superfluous to relate the same things [here]. Therefore, leaving aside Eusebius, Theognis, Theodotus the Perinthian, Menophantus the Ephesian and Patrophilus the Scythopolitan and the others, I shall mention only Eudoxius. The story of Aetius and Eunomius requires a mention of him.

Chapter 2: About Eudoxius (PG 83, 416–17)

This Eudoxius was bishop of the city of Germanicia which is near Taurus. Disdaining the small town, he rushed into Antioch on learning of the death of Leontius. Then he seized the throne against ecclesiastical ordinances. Driven out of there by imperial letters and commanded to go to the synod assembling in Seleucia in Isauria, he arrived as ordered, yet did not dare to enter into the council, instead he rushed into Constantinople, and flattering the imperial eunuchs, persuaded [them] to summon the synod there. In order to avoid being lengthy by telling everything (for I mentioned all these things in that writing [in *HE*]): he succeeded both in seizing the throne of that city and in denuding the churches of the heralds of truth.

Chapter 3: About Eunomius and Aetius (PG 83, 417–21)

Then, having driven out the all-praised Eleusius of Cyzicus, he ordained Eunomius in his place. Eunomius bragged about having as his teacher Aetius the Syrian, whose utterly wretched life and the pursuits he engaged in both Gregory of Nyssa and Theodore of Mopsuestia have accurately depicted in their books against Eunomius. He conspicuously expanded Arius' blasphemies. This is why Constantius expelled him to some distant [region] of Phrygia – and did so, having already been deflected from the straight path,[30] and turned aside onto another. For indeed after the death of his father, influenced by some [people] entrusted with the curing of his body, he instituted a law prohibiting anyone to dare to say that the Son of God [was] either coessential [*homoousios*] or of a different essence [*heteroousios*]. He said that it was unhallowed to enquire after the essence of God, but ordered that [the Son] should be said to be similar [*homoios*][31] to his Begetter in all respects.

Because of this, Aetius, the first one daring to say that the Son was dissimilar [*anomoios*] in all respects to the God who had begotten him, was also exiled into the aforementioned distant [region]. Knowing these things, Eudoxius persuaded Eunomius not to uncover their own opinion, but rather to keep it for a while in secret[32] and nurture [it] in darkness like a concealed pregnancy until they would gain advantage from [some] opportunity. Eunomius, conceding in these matters, brought forth a blurred teaching to the multitude in Cyzicus. Being in labour to give birth to impiety, he argued by hinting towards it and wounded the souls of the listeners. Then some of them, being inflamed by divine zeal [i.e. for orthodoxy], concealed this zeal and putting on the guise of heresy and going down to the home of Eunomius, besought him to teach clearly the truth of the doctrine. Taken in and assuming that [they] were of one mind with him, he spat out the poison, which he had concealed for a while. Again they pressed him more earnestly to present this teaching to all the people and honour his flock, eager to learn the truth, above compliance with the emperor. Thus, deceived again, Eunomius publicised his blasphemies. The zealous folk immediately took hold of many of the same faith, rushed to the [imperial] court and informed Eudoxius about his audacious impiety.

On learning that Eunomius had transgressed the articles of the common agreement, Eudoxius was worried. Nevertheless, he promised his accusers to take counsel, but he neglected it entirely, claiming lack of time [i.e. free time]. The accusers of Eunomius, however, perceived the aim of Eudoxius and notified the emperor about the blasphemies of Eunomius. The emperor first ordered Eudoxius to bring Eunomius in and to investigate the accusation which had been advanced. When he realised he [Eudoxius] was prevaricating (for the accusers came forward constantly), he threatened to send both into the distant [region] where Aetius was. Eudoxius, therefore, out of fear, brought Eunomius and first reminded him of the undertakings he had given. Then he condemned him as plainly proven guilty, although he too [Eudoxius] suffered from the same infection, for he feared the emperor's threats. Eunomius immediately announced himself as the leader of the heresy – and did so after being compelled to dwell in some far away [place] in Pamphylia. Hence arose a sect of the Eunomians.

He proclaimed theology as verbal sophistry [*technologia*] and conspicuously spewed out blasphemies against the Only-begotten and the All-holy Spirit. He said that the Son was the first and special creature of the Father. Further, that the All-holy Spirit was made by the Son before the other creatures. He overthrew even the ordinance of holy baptism, which had been handed down of old by the Lord and the apostles, and openly made contrary laws, saying that it was necessary neither to immerse the baptised three times, nor to perform the invocation of the Trinity, but rather to baptise once into the death of Christ. When baptising they drench with water as far as the chest, yet they forbid applying water to the other members of the body, [considering these] as accursed. This is why they baptise in a tub with the man standing outside of it, and lower his head down once as far as his chest into the water. Yet since it happened that someone was injured on the head as it struck the tub, they contrived another form of baptism: they stretch a person out head-first on a bench, raise his head from this, and pour water on it while not touching any other member [of the body]. Some of them, however, invented yet another mode of baptism. They prepare and consecrate a very long band [of cloth] and wind it around the man as far as his finger-tips, beginning from the chest, then they perform the pouring of water in this manner. Those who fled that impiety and joined the sheep of our Saviour and God recalled these things. They say that they also dare to practise something else, which I shall not dare to put down in writing, for the mere account of the uncleanness is enough to pollute the mind. Whether they dared to do such things or not, I for my part cannot confirm. I heard these things exactly in this manner from men who were well versed in their [practices].

Having thus raged against the truth, Eunomius was eager to aggravate the disease day by day. He ventured to say that he was ignorant of nothing concerning divinity, but knew the very essence of God itself and possessed the same knowledge about God, which God Himself possessed about Himself. Inebriated by him in this madness, those who shared in his plague dare to say openly that they know God as He [knows] Himself. He contrived other things in addition, in order to be thought the founder of new doctrines. Then the Arian sect was divided in two: and some were called Arians, and others Eunomians.

The Arians were also known as Eudoxians during the time of Eudoxius. Enslaved to empty glory, he eagerly imposed his own name upon the like-minded souls. These are also labelled Exakionians, receiving the name from the place in which they used to hold their meeting. The Eunomians are also called Aetians, since Eunomius named Aetius his teacher. They call themselves also Troglites or Troglodytes, holding assemblies in secret houses. Their numbers are very easily counted, since all avoid them like the plague for their shameless blasphemy. The majority of the world has been liberated from their outrage, nevertheless, a few easily numbered cities contain some of them and even these try to escape notice.

Chapter 5: About the Macedonians (PG 83, 424)

Apart from the aforementioned [heresies], another heresy issued from them, which was judged to be less impious. After the highly acclaimed Paul, the shepherd of the imperial city [i.e. Constantinople] had been driven away by those infected with the disease of Arius, and in his stead the rudders of that church were given into the hands of Macedonius. On the one hand, this Macedonius utterly and publicly renounced the Son's coessentiality with the Father. On the other hand, he ruled [that the Son was] similar [to the Father] in all respects,[33] and he invented the term 'of similar essence' [*homoiousios*] instead of 'coessential' [*homoousios*]. He persevered in blaspheming against the Holy Spirit, like Arius and Eunomius. So, those belonging to this sect were named Pneumatomachi.[34] The tares of the Macedonians were also disseminated from that source.

Chapter 8: About Apollinaris (PG 83, 425–8)

Apollinaris the Laodicean in some of his writings did not corrupt the teaching about the Trinity, but like us, proclaimed both the one essence of the divinity and the three hypostases. Nevertheless, in some [writings], he defined the degrees of dignity, ordaining himself as the distributor of divine distinction. He invented the 'Great', 'Greater' and 'Greatest': thus the Spirit being Great, the Son Greater, the Father Greatest. What could be more ridiculous than this? For if he says the essence of the Trinity is really one, how did he suppose the same essence [to be] both smaller and greater? In bodies quantity and size establish such measures; nature, however, is free from these, and does not allow measures of these kinds. For the present we have set out not to contradict,[35] but rather to demonstrate different opinions.

Moreover, in some of [his] writings he again mixed up the properties of the hypostases, and inflicted upon the Trinity the same as he ventured [to do] to the oikonomia. Hence he also received the accusation of Sabellianism, and asserted that the God-Word was made flesh [sarkōthēnai][36] by assuming a body and a soul, yet not a rational, but a non-rational one, which some call a vegetative or life-giving [soul]. Saying that the mind [nous] was something different from the soul [psychē], he asserted that [the mind] was not assumed, but that the divine nature sufficed to fulfil the function of the mind. Yet the wisest one[37] did not realise that he [i.e. the Word] neither needed a body unless he wanted it,[38] but would have appeared also without a body, just as [he appeared] earlier to the patriarchs.[39] We shall concentrate upon the teaching about the oikonomia in the book following this one.[40]

Chapter 13: About Eutyches (PG 83, 436–7)

Last of all, the slanderous demon introduced the notorious heresy of the Eutychians, by which he afflicted the churches all over the world. Finding an instrument receptive to his own wickedness in the wretched Eutyches, he made the long withered heresy of Valentinus to flourish again. Arius confessed only the assumption of the body; but Apollinaris confessed the assumption of the soul [psychē] also. Eutyches, however, denied even the assumption of the body. He asserted that the God-Word did not take anything human from the Virgin, was immutably changed and became flesh (I have used his own ridiculous language), merely passed through the Virgin, and that the uncircumscribed, unlimited and infinite Godhead of the Only-begotten was nailed and fastened to the cross and handed over to the tomb to attain resurrection.

Let us leave aside this exaggerated madness, observing that [according to it] nothing of any help to us emerged from the inhumanation, and we have no pledge of our resurrection. If it is God who was raised from the dead, then for certain man will not be raised: for there is a very great difference between the natures. Why, then, does the divine apostle strengthen the message of our resurrection with the resurrection of the Ruler, and writing to the Corinthians, exclaim, 'But if Christ is preached that he was raised from the dead, how can some among you say that there is no resurrection of the dead? Yet if there is no resurrection of the dead, then neither has Christ been raised' (1 Cor. 15:12–13)? For he has shown what was not believed through what was believed, and cast out that which was believed along with what was not. For if, he says, the resurrection of Christ is true, then our being resurrected is also true; hence, if this is false, then the resurrection of Christ is also false; for body is involved both for him and us.[41] After strengthening this by plenty of arguments, he explicitly concludes: 'But now Christ has been raised from the dead, the first-fruit of those fallen asleep' (1 Cor. 15:20). Through the first-fruit he clearly showed the main mass as well. For the first-fruit has the same nature as that of which it is a first-fruit. He also teaches the purpose of the oikonomia: 'For since death [came] through [a] man, the resurrection of the dead [comes] through [a] man also' (1 Cor. 15:21). Then he passes from the natures to the persons, 'For as in Adam all die, so also in Christ all will be made alive' (1 Cor. 15:22).

After having often written much about this, I reckon it superfluous to lengthen the present [discussion], the more so since in the fifth book, with God's help, I intend to enquire about these issues. Therefore, putting an end to this fourth book, I shall try to demonstrate to the best of my abilities the nobleness of evangelic teaching.

NOTES

1 THE YOUNG THEODORET

1 John Henry Newman, 'Trials of Theodoret' in *Historical Sketches* (London: Basil Montagu Pickering, 1873), 307–62; E. Venables, 'Theodoretus' in *DCB* IV, 904–19; Blomfield Jackson, *The Ecclesiastical History, Dialogues, and Letters of Theodoret*, NPNF III, 1–23; Johannes Quasten, *Patrology*, 4 vols (Utrecht: Spectrum, 1950–86), III, 536–54; Paul Bauchman Clayton, Jr, 'Theodoret, Bishop of Cyrus, and the Mystery of the Incarnation in Late Antiochene Christology' (unpublished doctoral dissertation, Union Theological Seminary, New York, 1985), 4–61 – hereafter: Clayton, 'Theodoret'; Theodoret of Cyrrhus, *A History of the Monks of Syria*, trans. by R. M. Price, Cistercian Studies, 88 (Oxford: Mowbray, 1985) – hereafter: Price, *HR*; Theresa Urbainczyk, *Theodoret of Cyrus: The Bishop and the Holy Man* (Ann Arbor: University of Michigan Press, 2002). Most of the material presented in this first part can be found in these and numerous other works (including encyclopaedias), so I quote them very sparingly.
2 See *HR* 9 in SC 234, 415–22 (Greek) and Price, *HR*, 83 (English).
3 *HR* 13 in SC 234, 503–9; Price, *HR*, 100–7.
4 A date accepted by most scholars based on Theodoret's own testimony in *HR* 9 (SC 234, 422). Cf. Price, *HR*, 84.
5 *HR* 13 in SC 234, 506–8.
6 Price, *HR*, 107.
7 The purity of his Attic is praised even by Photius. See Photius, *Bibliothèque*, ed. by René Henry, Collection Byzantine, 8 vols (Paris: Les Belles Lettres, 1959–77), III, 102–3.
8 Cf. Quasten, *Patrology*, III, 544. See also Y. Azéma, 'Citations d'auteurs et allusions profanes dans la *Correspondance* de Théodoret', *TU*, 125 (1981), 5–13.
9 For a more detailed discussion of the question of infant baptism in early Christian times see David F. Wright, 'At What Ages Were People Baptized in the Early Centuries?', *SP*, 30 (1997), 189–94.

10 SC 111, 156–8; NPNF III, 309. See also SC 429, 102; NPNF III, 326.
11 David Wright holds the same opinion over against Canivet's undocumented assumption. See D. F. Wright, 'Infant Dedication in the Early Church', in *Baptism, the New Testament and the Church: Historical and Contemporary Studies in Honour of R. E. O. White*, ed. by Stanley E. Porter and Anthony R. Cross, Journal for the Study of the New Testament Supplement Series, 171 (Sheffield: Sheffield Academic Press, 1999), 352–78 (p. 373). Cf. Pierre Canivet, *Le monachisme Syrien selon Théodoret de Cyr*, Théologie historique, 42 (Paris: Beauchesne, 1977), 44.
12 See *Letter* 113 *to Pope Leo* (SC 111, 66; NPNF III, 294).
13 See *Letter* 119 *to Anatolius the Patrician* (SC 111, 80; NPNF III, 297).
14 Cf. NPNF III, 276, note 1. Ibid., 277.
15 See *Letter* 138 *to Anatolius* (SC 111, 146; NPNF III, 307).
16 Newman, 'Trials of Theodoret', 321.
17 See e.g. Socrates Scholasticus, *Ecclesiastical History*, ed. by William Bright, 2nd edn (Oxford: Clarendon Press, 1893), VII, 13 and 29 – hereafter: Socrates, *HE*.
18 See *HFC* 1, 20 in PG 83, 372A – the chapter *About Tatian* is translated in this volume.
19 The Greek *obolos* was used both as a weight (= 0.57 grams) and as an Athenian coin (worth 1/6th part of a drachma).
20 SC 98, 196–7; NPNF III, 277.
21 For a detailed presentation, dating and other issues related to Theodoret's individual works, the reader is referred to the classic patrologies of Altaner, Cayrâe, Tixeront and Quasten, as well as to the CPG. See also Marcel Richard, 'L'activité littéraire de Théodoret avant le concile d'Éphèse', *RSPT*, 24 (1935), 83–106.
22 Théodoret de Cyr, *Thérapeutique des maladies helléniques*, ed. by Pierre Canivet, SC 57, 2 vols (Paris: Cerf, 1958), I, 31.
23 Here Theodoret says that he wrote a book 'against Jews and Greeks' – see PG 6, 1208A.
24 This is the opinion of Marcel Richard, 'L'activité littéraire de Théodoret', 103, and in essence, with some reservations, of Jean-Noël Guinot, 'L'*Expositio rectae fidei* et le traité *Sur la Trinité et l'Incarnation* de Théodoret de Cyr: deux types d'argumentation pour un même propos?', *Recherches Augustiniennes*, 32 (2001), 39–74 (pp. 69–74). Concerning the controversy around the dating of *Expositio* see R. V. Sellers, 'Pseudo-Justin's *Expositio rectae fidei*: A Work of Theodoret of Cyrus', *JTS*, 46 (1945), 145–60 and M. F. A. Brok, 'The Date of Theodoret's *Expositio Rectae Fidei*', *JTS*, 2 (1951), 178–83.

NOTES

2 THEODORET AND THE NESTORIAN
CONTROVERSY

1 We do not know for sure whether Theodoret and Nestorius were pupils in Theodore of Mopsuestia's school; nevertheless, the great Antiochenes, Diodore, Theodore and Chrysostom, visibly influenced their thinking.
2 Norman Russell, *Cyril of Alexandria*, The Early Church Fathers (London: Routledge, 2000) – hereafter: Russell, *Cyril*.
3 The dispute concerning original sin and human free will, between the Irish monk Pelagius and Augustine, at the beginning of the fifth century marked the entire Roman theology, and whilst the Pelagian argument was condemned in the West, its focus upon human responsibility and its claim to personal holiness appealed very much to Eastern theologians, including Nestorius, who – without being 'a Pelagian' (in the sense of denying the existence of original sin) – could see in this movement a confirmation of his own beliefs and gave shelter to some of these teachers.
4 See e.g. E. Amann, 'L'affaire Nestorius vue de Rome', *RevSR*, 23 (1949), 5–37, 207–44; 24 (1950), 28–52, 235–65.
5 See *DCB* IV, 908. The Greek text of the letter is in ACO I, 1, 1, pp. 93–6.
6 See e.g. Eduard Schwartz, 'Cyrill und der Mönch Viktor', *Sitzungsberichte der Akademie der Wissenschaften in Wien, Philosophisch-historische Klasse*, 208.4 (1928), 1–51.
7 Socrates, *HE* VII, 15.
8 Cyril of Alexandria, *Select Letters*, ed. and trans. by Lionel R. Wickham (Oxford: Clarendon Press, 1983), xvii.
9 The term *oikonomia* is frequently used by the Antiochenes in various contexts: it can express God's dispensation to save humankind; it can denote the act of incarnation itself or the theological discipline referring to the incarnation, its mode and purpose (i.e. Christology and soteriology together), or – occasionally – even refer to the person of the incarnate. This is the main reason why in most cases I have transliterated the term without translating it by 'dispensation', or other expressions, both in the introduction and in the translations.
10 See e.g. E. R. Hardy, 'The Further Education of Cyril of Alexandria', *SP*, 17 (1982), 116–22.
11 For a detailed discussion of the Apollinarian forgeries used by Cyril and other related issues see e.g. C. P. Caspari, *Alte und Neue Quellen zur Geschichte des Taufsymbols und der Glaubensregel*, 3 vols (Malling: Christiania, 1879). Cf. Newman, 'Trials of Theodoret', 351.
12 *DCB* IV, 908.
13 See Chapter 6, 'Terminology'.
14 See the introductory remarks preceding the translation of *De Trinitate* and *De incarnatione*.
15 As mentioned earlier, another pre-Ephesian work by Theodoret, *Expositio rectae fidei*, preserved under the name of Justin Martyr, was restored to

223

him by J. Lebon, 'Restitutions à Théodoret de Cyr', *RHE*, 26 (1930), 523–50 (pp. 536–50).

16 See István Pásztori-Kupán, 'Theodoret of Cyrus' Double Treatise *On the Trinity* and *On the Incarnation*, The Antiochene Pathway to Chalcedon' (unpublished doctoral dissertation, University of Edinburgh, New College, 2002) – hereafter: Pásztori-Kupán, 'Theodoret'.

17 For example, the standard charge against Theodoret for not applying *communicatio idiomatum* (i.e. the communication of properties between the two natures of Christ) is anachronistic indeed, since no validation of this principle took place in any ecumenical or local gathering of the Christian church before or after Theodoret's time.

18 The best example for this is the twofold evaluation of the closing passage from Ch. 34 [32] of *De incarnatione*, starting with 'taking this also as an image of the oikonomia' (PG 75, 1473B). The first who spoke against it – knowing that Theodoret was the author – was the Monophysite bishop Severus of Antioch (see J. Lebon, 'Restitutions', 531). Angelo Mai, who first published the treatise in 1833, believing that it was a genuine work of Cyril, takes the same paragraph of Ch. 34 [32] and praises 'the author' for clearly distinguishing the natures and removing Monophysitism (see Mai's footnotes No. 1–3 in PG 75, 1473). Recently, P. B. Clayton, whilst analysing the passage in his doctoral thesis, again condemns Theodoret – now proven to be the real author – for exactly the same thing (Clayton, 'Theodoret', 241–3). According to this unacceptable approach, the very same statement can be considered orthodox if coming from Cyril, and regarded as heretical if written by Theodoret.

19 See e.g. C. J. Hefele, *A History of the Councils of the Church*, ed. and trans. by William R. Clark, 5 vols (Edinburgh: T. & T. Clark, 1894–96), III, 46. Cf. Russell, *Cyril*, 46–8.

20 According to the ancient juridical axiom 'nemo esse iudex in sua causa potest' (nobody can be a judge of his/her own case). NB: the council was initially summoned upon Nestorius' request, after the former had read Cyril's *Anathemas* and considered them Apollinarian, and certainly not *against* him.

21 See F. Loofs, *Leitfaden zum Studium der Dogmengeschichte* (Halle: Max Niemeyer, 1906), 295 (my translation from German). Cf. Martin Parmentier, 'A Letter from Theodoret of Cyrus to the Exiled Nestorius (CPG 6270) in a Syriac Version', *Bijdragen*, 51 (1990), 234–45 (p. 234).

22 For further details see Chapter 3, 'From Ephesus to Chalcedon and Beyond'.

23 There is plenty of evidence to prove Cyril's rather unconventional manner of dealing with the crisis. The highly confidential letter from his archdeacon (Epiphanius) to Maximian of Constantinople (Nestorius' successor) bears witness to the extent to which the Alexandrian patriarch was prepared to go in gaining imperial support by an impressive variety of gifts including carpets, furniture, as well as gold (see ACO I, 4, pp. 222–5). Cf. P. Batiffol, 'Les Présents de Saint Cyrille à la cour de

Constantinople', *Études de liturgie et d'archéologie chrétienne* (Paris: J. Gabalda, 1919); see also Russell, *Cyril*, 52.

24 SC 429, 82–4; cf. *Letter* 169 in NPNF III, 341.

25 See SC 429, 96.

3 FROM EPHESUS TO CHALCEDON AND BEYOND

1 See e.g. William Bright, *The Age of the Fathers* (London: Longmans, Green and Co., 1903), II, 338. Cf. *DCB* IV, 910 and also Marijan Mandac, 'L'union christologique dans les oeuvres de Théodoret antérieures au Concile d' Éphèse', *ETL*, 47 (1971), 64–96.

2 The term *homoousios* means 'of the same essence'. Although most translations render *ousia* with 'substance', the ambiguity of this usage, because of the term *hypostasis*, would cause unfortunate misunderstandings. I therefore translate *ousia* always with 'essence'. See also Chapter 6.

3 ACO I, 1, 4, p. 17, lines 9–20.

4 See Chapter 6, 'Terminology'.

5 Russell, *Cyril*, 181; cf. NPNF III, 25.

6 The letter is extant in three Latin translations and in one Syriac version. See SC 429, 250–9 and Parmentier, 'A Letter from Theodoret'.

7 These famous lines written to Nestorius are quoted by Pope Pelagius II in his *Letter 3 to the bishops of Histria* in ACO IV, 2, p. 129, lines 16–17; Cf. SC 429, 252, 256 and 258.

8 See NPNF III, 345.

9 See Nestorius' reply in ACO I, 4, pp. 150–3 and Parmentier, 'A Letter from Theodoret', 239.

10 See ACO I, 4, p. 189 and Parmentier, 'A Letter from Theodoret', 241. The letter is in SC 429, 318–21.

11 Alexander did not fully agree to the wording of the *Antiochene Formula* in September 431 either.

12 SC 98, 218. See also Marcel Richard, 'Théodoret, Jean d'Antioche et les moines d'Orient', *MSR*, 3 (1946), 147–56 (pp. 153–4).

13 See SC 98, 216. Cf. Richard, 'Théodoret, Jean d'Antioche et les moines', 154–5.

14 Cyril died in 444.

15 I.e. the Monophysite 'robber synod' of Ephesus (449) – as Pope Leo labelled it – which deposed Theodoret also. See below.

16 CPG 5369. The Latin version of this passage is in ACO I, 4, p. 227. Cf. ACO IV, 1, p. 108 and PG 77, 340C.

17 See Luise Abramowski, 'Reste von Theodorets Apologie für Diodor und Theodor bei Facundus', *SP*, 1 (1957), 61–9.

18 See Theodoret of Cyrus, *On Divine Providence*, trans. by Thomas P. Halton, Ancient Christian Writers, 49 (New York: Newman Press, 1988) – hereafter: Halton, *Providence*.

19 See P. M. Parvis, 'Theodoret's Commentary on the Epistles of St. Paul: Historical Setting and Exegetical Practice' (unpublished doctoral dissertation, University of Oxford, 1975); concerning the editions and translations see the Bibliography.

20 Theodoret, *Kirchengeschichte*, ed. by L. Parmentier and F. Schweidler, GCS 44, 2nd edn (Berlin: Akademie Verlag, 1954). See also NPNF III, 33–159. It is a very subtle solution on Theodoret's part to conclude his *Ecclesiastical History* with Theodore's death, thus avoiding the discussion of the events around Nestorius (which began practically in the same year), and in which he himself was involved. He finished the composition of the work during his exile in Apamea in 449–50 (see Quasten, *Patrology*, III, 551).

21 See *DCB* IV, 911. Cyril's letter to John is No. 63 in PG 77, 328BD.

22 John of Antioch died in 442, Cyril in 444, and Proclus (who was the patriarch of Constantinople from 434) in 446.

23 Domnus became bishop of Antioch, Dioscorus was made patriarch of Alexandria, whilst Flavian was invested as patriarch of Constantinople.

24 See e.g. Grillmeier's valid affirmation: 'Right up to the Council of Chalcedon, none of the strictly orthodox theologians succeeded in laying the foundations for such a vindication in the form of a speculative analysis [i.e. that *communicatio idiomatum* was, in fact, a valid standard].' Aloys Grillmeier, *Christ in Christian Tradition, From the Apostolic Age to Chalcedon (451)*, trans. by J. S. Bowden, 2nd rev. edn (London/Oxford: A. R. Mowbray, 1975), 436.

25 SC 111, 62–5; NPNF III, 294.

26 *Letter* 80 *to the prefect Eutrechius* in SC 98, 190 and in NPNF III, 276.

27 ACO II, 1, 2, pp. 129–30.

28 See Leo's *Letter* 119 *to Maximus, Bishop of Antioch* in NPNF XII, 86.

29 Leo's letter is also in ACO II, 4, pp. 78–81.

30 See ACO II, 1, 2, p. 124.

31 Marcel Richard, 'La Lettre de Théodoret à Jean d'Égées', *SPT*, 2 (1941–2), 415–23.

32 Kevin McNamara, 'Theodoret of Cyrus and the Unity of Person in Christ', *ITQ*, 22 (1955), 313–28; Patrick T. R. Gray, 'Theodoret on the *One Hypostasis*, An Antiochene Reading of Chalcedon', *SP*, 15 (1984), 301–4; Clayton, 'Theodoret', 501–6.

33 See Glenn Melvin Cope, 'An Analysis of the Heresiological Method of Theodoret of Cyrus in the *Haereticarum fabularum compendium*' (unpublished doctoral dissertation, Catholic University of America, Washington DC, 1990), 53.

34 Canivet, Pierre, 'Theodoret of Cyr', *New Catholic Encyclopedia*, 18 vols (New York: McGraw Hill, 1967–88), XIV, 20.

35 Ernest Honigmann, 'Theodoret of Cyrrhus and Basil of Seleucia (the Time of Their Deaths)', in his *Patristic Studies*, Studi e testi, 173 (Rome: Biblioteca Apostolica Vaticana, 1953), 174–84 (p. 180). Cf. Y. Azéma, 'Sur la date de la mort de Théodoret', *Pallas*, 31 (1984), 137–55.

36 Canivet, 'Theodoret of Cyr', 20.
37 Theodoret's condemned works in 553 were the following: the *Refutation of Cyril's Anathemas*, the now lost *Pentalogos* (i.e. his five books against Cyril's Ephesian council), his *Defence for Diodore and Theodore* (of which only fragments survived), some letters and speeches. See ACO IV, 1, 130–6. Cf. Pásztori-Kupán, 'Theodoret', 37–9.
38 See NPNF III, 13.

4 THEODORET'S TRINITARIAN DOCTRINE

1 See e.g. Silke-Petra Bergjan, *Theodoret von Cyrus und der Neunizänismus, Aspekte der altkirchlichen Trinitätslehre*, Arbeiten zur Kirchengeschichte, 60 (Berlin: Walter de Gruyter, 1994); cf. Pásztori-Kupán, 'Theodoret', 57–132.
2 See *De Trinitate* 4 in PG 75, 1152A.
3 Ibid.
4 Concerning the procession of the Spirit as it appears in Theodoret and Cyril see André de Halleux, 'Cyrille, Théodoret et le *Filioque*', *RHE*, 74 (1979), 597–625; George C. Berthold, 'Cyril of Alexandria and the *Filioque*', *SP*, 19 (1989), 143–7; cf. Pásztori-Kupán, 'Theodoret', 115–21.

5 THEODORET'S CHRISTOLOGY

1 See e.g. Clayton, 'Theodoret', p. vi.
2 The idea of divine impassibility as a result of philosophical borrowing is to some extent accepted by M. Slusser, 'The Scope of Patripassianism', *SP*, 17 (1982), 169–75 (p. 174). See also John J. O'Keefe, 'Kenosis or Impassibility: Cyril of Alexandria and Theodoret of Cyrus on the Problem of Divine Pathos', *SP*, 32 (1997), 358–65, esp. pp. 359, 364–5.
3 H. Chadwick, 'Eucharist and Christology in the Nestorian Controversy', *JTS*, 2 (1951), 145–64 (p. 158).
4 See e.g. the descriptive titles of the *Eranistes*: 'The immutable', 'The unconfused', 'The impassible'. The fact that the idea of God's impassibility was not a peculiar characteristic of Antiochene theology, but a common feature of patristic thought, could be documented at some length. To save space I give only two representative examples. See Pope Leo's *Tomus ad Flavianum* 4 in ACO II, 2, 1, p. 28, as well as Cyril's *Epistola dogmatica to Nestorius* in ACO I, 1, 1, p. 27; cf. ACO II, 1, 1, p. 105.
5 *Theopaschism*: a theological trend emphasising God's suffering in Christ. Its extreme version was that in Christ even 'the Father suffered' on the

cross – hence the label 'Patripassianism' (from the Latin 'Pater passus est').

6 See also Theodoret's reply to Cyril's first anathema.

7 Grillmeier, *Christ in Christian Tradition*, 325. See also Thomas Böhm, *Die Christologie des Arius, Dogmengeschichtliche Überlegungen unter besonderer Berücksichtigung der Hellenisierungsfrage*, Studien zur Theologie und Geschichte, 7 (St Ottilien: EOS, 1991), 65.

8 See J. Burnet, ed., *Platonis opera*, 5 vols (Oxford: Clarendon Press, 1900–7), II, 246ff.

9 See Price, *HR*, 6.

10 PG 83, 645–8. Unfortunately, Halton's English translation does not retain this Platonic connection. See Halton, *Providence*, 75.

11 See *De incarnatione*, 18 [17].

12 Grillmeier traces their origin back to Paul of Samosata: 'If we can accept the tradition about Paul of Samosata as genuine, it would be possible that we had here the common root of Arianism, Apollinarianism and some aspects of the Christology of the Alexandrian church.' See Grillmeier, *Christ in Christian Tradition*, 165.

13 '*Mia physis, mia hypostasis, mia energeia, hen prosōpon*'. See Apollinaris, *De fide et incarnatione* 6 in Hans Lietzmann, *Apollinaris von Laodicea und seine Schule* (Tübingen: Mohr, 1904), 199 – hereafter: Lietzmann, *Apollinaris*.

14 See *De incarnatione*, 14–17 [16].

15 See e.g. *De incarnatione*, 10.

16 The statement '*en apatheia biōsometha*' is not 'apathy'. Among Christ's benefactions is our deliverance from the tyranny of sin and suffering. Therefore, in God's kingdom, we shall also be 'impassible' [i.e. free from torment] as our Lord himself. Clayton seems to miss the point behind Theodoret's use of the term (Clayton, 'Theodoret', 244).

17 Clayton, 'Theodoret', vi; ibid., 232–42 etc. My opinion concerning the so-called 'Arian syllogism' as it appears in Clayton's thesis (who borrowed it from Sullivan), and its applicability in Theodoret's Christological thinking, can be found in Pásztori-Kupán, 'Theodoret', 87–93 and 196–200. See also F. A. Sullivan, *The Christology of Theodore of Mopsuestia*, Annalecta Gregoriana No. 82 (Rome: Annalecta Gregoriana, 1956); cf. Clayton, 'Theodoret', 201.

18 See M. J. Rouet de Journel, *Enchiridion Patristicum* (Freiburg: Herder, 1922), 407.

19 An interesting parallelism is notable between this passage of the *Chalcedonense* and Cyril's *Epistola dogmatica to Nestorius*. His text does not allow (at least verbally) a *communicatio idiomatum* either. Although the second part of the passage in his letter differs from the *Definition*, yet even there we do not find a clear statement of an exchange of properties. See ACO I, 1, 1, p. 27, lines 1–5. Cf. G. Ludwig Hahn, *Bibliothek der Symbole und Glaubensregeln der Alten Kirche*, 3rd edn (Breslau: E. Morgenstern, 1897), 311 – hereafter: Hahn, *Bibliothek*.

20 'Salva igitur proprietate utriusque naturae et substantiae'. As shown by Luise Abramowski, the idea derives from Tertullian, *Adversus Praxean* c. 27, 11 (CSEL 47, 281–2): 'et adeo salva est utriusque proprietas substantiae'. See L. Abramowski, '*Synapheia* und asynchutos *henōsis* als Bezeichnung für trinitarische und christologische Einheit' in *Drei christologische Untersuchungen* (Berlin: Walter de Gruyter, 1981), 63–109 (p. 68) – hereafter: Abramowski, '*Synapheia*'.

21 NB: Cyril's *Epistola synodica*, which contained the *Twelve Anathemas* (see ACO I, 1, 1, pp. 33–42) was not formally recognised by Chalcedon, only his *Epistola dogmatica*, i.e. the *Second letter to Nestorius* (ACO I, 1, 1, pp. 25–8) and his *Epistola ad Orientales*, i.e. the one written to John of Antioch, which began with 'Let the heavens rejoice . . . ' and contained the *Formula of Reunion* (ACO I, 1, 4, pp. 15–20). Loofs, who himself gave up his former opinion that the *synodica* was implicitly acknowledged by Chalcedon, presents his conclusive evidence in F. Loofs, *Nestorius and His Place in the History of Christian Doctrine* (Cambridge: Cambridge University Press, 1914), 98. This is the reason why I do not quote the anathemas concerning the issue of *communicatio idiomatum*, since although they were composed in the same period, their theological validity was first attested only in 553.

22 It is this reading of the 'union' which the *Chalcedonense* seeks to avoid in the quoted passage.

23 Because of lack of space I cannot elaborate here on the differences between e.g. Luther's and Calvin's Christology, yet the former was undoubtedly closer to the Alexandrian, the latter to the Antiochene position.

24 *De incarnatione* 23 [22] in PG 75, 1460A.

25 Theodoret refers here to Diodore and Theodore. See e.g. H. B. Swete, ed., *Theodori Episcopi Mopsuesteni in Epistolas B. Pauli Commentarii*, 2 vols (Cambridge: Cambridge University Press, 1880–2), II, 310.

26 See e.g. Cyril's *Letter* 50 *to Valerianus* in PG 70, 276.

27 For a fuller account of this and related issues see Pásztori-Kupán, 'Theodoret', 188–209.

28 See D. F. Winslow, 'Soteriological "Orthodoxy" in the Fathers', *SP*, 15 (1984), 393–5 (p. 394).

29 Milton V. Anastos, 'The Immutability of Christ and Justinian's Condemnation of Theodore of Mopsuestia', *DOP*, 6 (1951), 125–60 (p. 126).

30 Diepen, 'Théodoret et le dogme d' Éphèse', *RSR*, 44 (1956), 243–7; Parvis, 'Theodoret' s *Commentary* on Paul', 305; Clayton, 'Theodoret', 219–26.

31 Günter Koch, *Strukturen und Geschichte des Heils in der Theologie des Theodoret von Kyros, Eine dogmen- und theologiegeschichtliche Untersuchung*, Frankfurter Theologische Studien, 17 (Frankfurt am Main: Josef Knecht, 1974), 141.

32 Diepen, 'Théodoret et le dogme d' Éphèse' (followed by Daniélou's answer on 247–8).

33 See *De incarnatione*, 11.

34 This solution would harm God's justice in Theodoret's view. That is why he speaks thus to Apollinaris: 'the God-Word would not need the body either, for he was not in want! He could have accomplished our salvation [simply] by his mere command! But he wanted us to be partakers in [his] success: *that is why* he took on the sinful nature' (ibid., Ch. 18, PG 75, 1448C).

35 Marcel Richard, 'Notes sur l' évolution doctrinale de Théodoret', *RSPT*, 25 (1936), 459–81 (p. 481). See e.g. the *Confession of Athanasius* written perhaps before the Nicene Creed in Hahn, *Bibliothek*, 265; cf. *The Formula of Sardica* of 342 in Hahn, *Bibliothek*, 189; see also the longer version of the *Palestinian Symbol* in Hahn, *Bibliothek*, 136, as well as the explanation of the Nicene Creed initially ascribed to Basil the Great, yet which was composed between 428 and 450, thus already after the outbreak of the Nestorian controversy by an Alexandrian (!) author in Hahn, *Bibliothek*, 310 etc. If such concrete terms could be used even during the time of Cyril's ferocious clash with Nestorius, it would appear that the validity of such language was not seriously questioned or suspect in those years and indeed during the preceding century.

36 For further examples and a more detailed analysis see Pásztori-Kupán, 'Theodoret', 200–9.

37 See the translation in this volume.

38 Since Theodoret uses at least two main expressions – *lambanō* and *analambanō* – to express the Word's action of 'assuming' or 'taking on' the human nature, I chose to translate *analambanō* with 'assume' and *lambanō* with 'take on'.

39 See the translation of Theodoret's *Refutation* in this volume.

40 See PG 6, 1229D–1232A.

41 Apart from the reply to Anathema 8, the idea of the single worship returns in the answers to the first, second and fifth anathemas.

42 See e.g. Athanasius' *Confession* in Hahn, *Bibliothek*, 265. Cf. Gregory Nazianzen's *Oratio* 41 *on Pentecost* (PG 36, 441C).

43 Cf. Gregory of Nyssa's following statement: 'thus also from our part one worship and glorification [is offered] to the three as to One God.' See his *First Sermon on the Creation of Man* in Gregory of Nyssa, *Opera*, 9 vols + Suppl., ed. by F. Müller, W. Jaeger *et al.* (Leiden: Brill, 1952–96), Suppl., 8a.

44 Theodoret's answer to the first anathema contains the very same idea (see ACO I, 1, 6, p. 109).

45 Cf. his *Letter* 126 to *Aphtonius* etc. in SC 111, 98.

46 See also the introduction to the translation of this tract.

47 The same liturgical defence of Theodoret's orthodoxy returns almost word by word in his *Letter* 146 *to the monks of Constantinople* written in the first half of 451. See SC 111, 178.

48 See also the following letters of Theodoret: *Letter* 151 written in 431–2 in SC 429, 114–16 and 122; *Letter 99 to Claudianus* written in Nov. 448 in SC 111, 16; *Letter 104 to Flavian* written in Dec. 448 in SC 111, 24–6 and 28; *Letter 131 to Bishop Timotheus* written in mid-450 in SC 111, 116–18; *Letter 146 to the monks of Constantinople* written in the first half of 451 in SC 111, 178; *Letter 147 to John the Oeconomus* written in 451 in SC 111, 201–20.

49 See e.g. Theodoret's *Commentary on the Pauline Epistles*, especially on Rom. 8:29 (PG 82, 141B); on Eph. 1:20–2 (PG 82, 517A); on Heb. 1:6 (PG 82, 685BC) etc. See also Theodoret of Cyrus, *Commentary on the Letters of St. Paul*, trans. by Robert C. Hill, 2 vols (Brookline: Holy Cross Orthodox Press, 2002), I, 95; II, 37; II, 142–3.

50 See Athanasius, *Commentary on* Ps. 99:5 (LXX: Ps. 98:5) in PG 27, 421C. Cf. also the *Confession* of the Apollinarian Bishop Jobius (Hahn, *Bibliothek*, 285).

51 For the *Confession* of Apollinaris in his *On the incarnation of the God-Word* see Hahn, *Bibliothek*, 267–8. As mentioned above, Caspari proved the authorship of Apollinaris in Caspari, *Alte und Neue Quellen*, I, 119. In his *Address to the Most Pious Ladies* (of the imperial court) Cyril quotes almost the entire text of Apollinaris' *Confession* introducing it with the following formula: 'the truly thrice-blessed and famously pious Athanasius asserted' etc. (ACO I, 1, 5, p. 65). For *The detailed confession of faith* [*hē kata meros pistis*] see Lietzmann, *Apollinaris*, 177–9.

52 See Hahn, *Bibliothek*, 303.

53 See ACO I, 1, 4, p. 10, lines 27–9.

54 See ACO I, 1, 1, p. 28.

55 The Greek particle *syn* generally means 'with, together', e.g. like the Latin and English 'con'.

56 See ACO I, 1, 6, p. 131.

57 Concerning the importance of the unity of worship for both parties as a sign of teaching 'one Son' during the Nestorian controversy see ACO I, 1, 1, pp. 18, 23, 35, 37, 41, 53, 62–3; ACO I, 1, 2, pp. 44, 48–9, 71, 92, 95, 101; ACO I, 1, 4, pp. 25, 27; ACO I, 1, 5, pp. 21–3, 31, 49, 64, 65; ACO I, 1, 6, pp. 8, 20, 32, 46–54, 132; ACO I, 1, 7, pp. 39, 48–50, 83, 93, 98–9, 108–9, 139; ACO I, 5, 1, pp. 225, 230.

58 Concerning 'the Basilian formula' see André de Halleux, 'La définition christologique à Chalcédoine', in *Patrologie et œcuménisme*, Bibliotheca Ephemeridum Theologicarum Lovaniensinum, 93 (Leuven: Leuven University Press, 1990), 445–80 (pp. 467–70).

59 See R. V. Sellers, *The Council of Chalcedon, A Historical and Doctrinal Survey* (London: SPCK, 1961), 58, note 6; cf. p. 67, note 4; p. 122; pp. 215–16.

60 Concerning the issue of worship not belonging to 'two sons' see also Emperor Marcian's letters sent to Macarius (ACO II, 1, 3, pp. 131–2) and to the synod of Palestine (ACO II, 1, 3, pp. 133–5).

61 Note again the resemblance with the Apollinarian line of thought: 'one worship' => 'one nature'.
62 See ACO II, 1, 1, p. 179: 'during the reading of the minutes Basil, the bishop of Seleucia of Isauria said, "I agree with the faith of the holy Fathers [. . .] I worship the one nature of the Godhead of the Only-begotten made man as well as made flesh".'

6 TERMINOLOGY

1 E.g. the term *ousia* occurs 14 times in *De Trinitate* and 16 times in *De incarnatione*, whilst *physis* appears 36 times in *De Trinitate* and 84 times in *De incarnatione*.
2 Although a total identification of the two terms should not be inferred, they are practically equivalent in Theodoret's Trinitarian doctrine and Christology.
3 J. H. Newman, *The Arians of the Fourth Century* (London: Longman, 1908), 432–44; Marcel Richard, 'L'introduction du mot *hypostase* dans la théologie de l'Incarnation', *MSR*, 2 (1945), 5–32, 243–70; G. L. Prestige, *God in Patristic Thought* (London: SPCK, 1952), 157–78. See also the note in NPNF III, 36.
4 Prestige, *God in Patristic Thought*, 174.
5 Ibid., 176–7.
6 Ibid., 177–8.
7 See Abramowski, '*Synapheia*', 89.
8 We find e.g. Marius Mercator translating *hypostasis* with *substantia*. By the time the Cappadocians' more refined Neo-Nicene terminology emerged, it was not possible to revert to a translation of *homoousios* with *coessentialis*. There was indeed no reason to do it, since in the West the meanings of these terms were hardly under question compared to the intensity of Eastern terminological disputes. Moreover, most Latin writers had already found another comfortable equivalent for *hypostasis* by translating it with *subsistentia*, i.e. subsistence (although not all of them were consistent in doing this). The issue arose again in the fifth-century Eastern terminological debates, until the two Greek terms (*ousia* and *hypostasis*) were adequately distinguished by the *Chalcedonense*, which confesses Christ as being two *physeis*, but one *hypostasis*. By this time it was indeed too late for the West to address the question again and to replace a term (i.e. *consubstantialis*) for no urgent reason, a term which by then had been used for more than 120 years. This revision of Latin Trinitarian and Christological termi-nology did not take place in the West for understandable reasons. Its effect can be traced through the history of Western theological scholarship: e.g. even the nineteenth-century editor of Theodoret's two treatises *De Trinitate* and *De incarnatione*, Angelo Mai, still continued to translate both *ousia* and *hypostasis* with *substantia*,

although from a theological viewpoint – also for Theodoret – the two terms denote different concepts.

9 See Socrates, *HE*, III, 7.
10 Socrates argues in the same place that Irenaeus the grammarian even labelled the term 'barbarian'.
11 See e.g. ACO I, 1, 1, p. 35, lines 9–11.
12 See e.g. Theodoret, *HE*, II, 8; cf. Hahn, *Bibliothek*, 188.
13 Cf. Newman, *The Arians*, 435.
14 Cf. Newman, *The Arians*, 436–7.
15 Rowan Williams, *Arius, Heresy and Tradition*, 2nd edn (London: SCM Press, 2001), 234.
16 See *In illud: Omnia mihi tradita sunt* in PG 25, 220A.
17 Lietzmann, *Apollinaris*, 194.
18 Lietzmann, *Apollinaris*, 198–9. It is hard not to observe the obvious Theopaschite 'confusion of natures' bound together with Apollinaris' *mia physis, mia hypostasis* formula.
19 Lietzmann, *Apollinaris*, 201. As M. Richard points out, the fourth occurrence of 'one hypostasis' in Apollinaris' *Detailed confession of faith* (which Cyril held and quoted as written by Athanasius) was contested. Nevertheless, based on further evidence, Richard corrected Lietzmann's critical text. The genuine version therefore is, 'one *hypostasis* and one *prosōpon* and one worship of the Word and of [his] flesh'. See M. Richard, 'L'introduction du mot *hypostase*', 7. Cf. Lietzmann, *Apollinaris*, 177.
20 This latter conclusion was corrected by Luise Abramowski. See below.
21 M. Richard, 'L'introduction du mot *hypostase*', 21–9.
22 L. Abramowski, 'Über die Fragmente des Theodor von Mopsuestia in Brit. Libr. add 12.516 und das doppelt überlieferte christologische Fragment', *Oriens Christianus*, 79 (1995), 1–8. The *Supplement* of CPG published in 1998 contains this correction under No. 3856.
23 M. Richard, 'L'introduction du mot *hypostase*', 32 (my translation from French).
24 Hahn, *Bibliothek*, 212.
25 Although the Trinitarian and Christological language of some post-Nicene fathers – like Athanasius and Basil – cannot be kept neatly apart, nonetheless, the term *hypostasis* as referring to the *union* of Godhead and manhood in Christ, and especially the key phrases like 'hypostatic union' or 'the union according to hypostasis' were entirely lacking from their vocabulary.
26 The interaction between the Trinitarian and Christological vocabulary of earlier fathers cannot be ignored. Nevertheless, the term *hypostasis* was primarily used in *theologia* and seldom referred to the *oikonomia*. Although the complete lack of *hypostasis* from the Christological terminology of earlier theologians may not be inferred, nevertheless, most emphatically, the phrase 'union according to hypostasis' was beyond doubt absent from their writings. It is peculiarly this usage which Theodoret targets in his counter-statement, the more so since

Cyril made it the equivalent of his 'union according to nature'. See below.

27 Marcel Richard gives an adequate explanation concerning the lack of *hypostasis* from Theodoret's Christological vocabulary. See M. Richard, 'L'introduction du mot *hypostase*', 253. Cf. ACO I, 1, 6, p. 117 and PG 76, 404B. In the light of L. Abramowski's correction, one may add that in 430 *hypostasis* was missing not only from Theodoret's, but everyone else's, Christological vocabulary – save for Cyril of Alexandria.

28 I.e. being included in a solemn anathema to be subscribed by Nestorius as proof of his orthodoxy.

29 Apollinaris, the only champion of *hypostasis*, died in 392, having been in open war with the orthodox since 376.

30 Strictly speaking, the juxtaposition would logically describe Christ as very God and very man. Mary is 'God-bearer' since the Word was born into human life through her, yet also 'man-bearer' since who is born of her is very man also. The doctrinally motivated Cyrilline refusal of the latter term paradoxically denies Mary a quality which is by nature due to every human mother.

31 I cannot enter into the discussion whether Cyril might have used *hypostasis* in its old Nicene sense (as Athanasius sometimes did), whilst Theodoret interpreted it in the Neo-Nicene manner of the Cappadocians. I would rather apply Newman's valid conclusion as vindicating both Cyril and Theodoret concerning their attitude towards the term: 'The outcome of this investigation is this: – that we need not by an officious piety arbitrarily force the language of separate Fathers into a sense which it cannot bear; nor by an unjust and narrow criticism accuse them of error; nor impose upon an early age a distinction of terms belonging to a later' (*The Arians*, 444).

32 See Marcel Richard, 'La lettre de Théodoret à Jean d'Égées', *SPT*, 2 (1941–2), 415–23.

33 The occurrences in the *Expositio* will be analysed in connection with *prosōpon*. See below.

34 Cf. the explanation of Socrates Scholasticus mentioned above.

35 I could not establish whether Theodoret was dependent on Socrates or whether both of them were using a common source.

36 Following Prestige's analysis Theodoret seems to interpret *hypostasis* here in the sense of 'giving support' – at least according to the active form *to hyphestos* (Act. Part. Perf. Neut. Nom. Sg).

37 I am aware that Cyril used *physis* both in the sense of 'nature' and 'person'. Nevertheless, apart from the fact that this does not constitute the subject of my investigation, I intend to explain why Theodoret might have been puzzled by this ambivalent usage.

38 See e.g. *Expositio*, 3 (PG 6, 1212B).

39 I do not intend to suggest that *hypostasis* is merely a synonym for *prosōpon* in the *Chalcedonense*. Its function is also to evince Cyril's positive contribution to strengthen the concept of union. What I wanted to

NOTES

emphasise was that Chalcedon accepted Cyril's input (i.e. the union according to hypostasis) in a manner which excluded the (by then) ambiguous formula 'union according to nature'. This was most effectively achieved by ranking *hypostasis* with *prosōpon* and not with *physis* or with *ousia*. That is also why the Monophysites could never accept Chalcedon, since it implicitly rejected the famous 'one incarnate nature of God the Word', to the letter of which the Eutychian party was still clinging.

40 Prestige, *God in Patristic Thought*, 157.
41 Ibid., 162.
42 See P. Joseph Montalverne, *Theodoreti Cyrensis doctrina antiquior de verbo 'inhumanato' (a circiter 423–435)*, Studia Antoniana, 1 (Rome: Pontificium Athenaeum Antonianum, 1948), 78.
43 See Mandac, 'L'union christologique', 69–70 and 72. See also SC 57, 156: 'in order to show the difference between the *prosōpa*'. Cf. SC 57, 386.
44 See *De Trinitate* Ch. 12 in PG 75, 1164D; Ch. 16 in PG 75, 1173A; and Ch. 22 in PG 75, 1180C.
45 See PG 6, 1212AB; cf. PG 6, 1216B, 1216C, 1217B.
46 See e.g. Grillmeier, *Christ in Christian Tradition*, 491–2: 'For Theodoret, prosopon still has much of its original significance of "countenance". His view can be seen in his comments on Ezek. 11:22–3.'
47 See PG 81, 1161AB; cf. PG 81,1248B (*on Ezekiel*). Cf. 'these are uttered by the *prosōpon* of the Ruler Christ, who is the seed of Abraham according to flesh' (*Commentary on Isaiah* in SC 315, 72; cf. SC 315, 76 etc.).
48 See PG 6, 1216C.
49 See *Hē kata meros pistis* in Lietzmann, *Apollinaris*, 179.
50 See PG 75, 1436CD (three times), 1456A, 1456D, 1460A, 1460B (twice), 1472A, 1472D.
51 It appears twice in connection with 1 Cor. 3:16–17 (PG 75, 1181C).
52 PG 75, 1433A, 1457A: followed by *synēpse* and *henōsis*; PG 75, 1468D and 1473A.
53 It is once ascribed to Apollinaris in PG 75, 1444A, whilst on its own in 1452AB and 1457D.
54 See *Fragment* 2 in C. Datema, ed., *Amphilochii Iconiensis Opera* (Turnhout: Brepols, 1978), 228. Athanasius uses the term on several occasions in his *De incarnatione Verbi*. See Athanasius, *Contra Gentes and De incarnatione*, ed. and trans. by Robert W. Thomson (Oxford: Clarendon Press, 1971), 152; cf. Ch. 9 (154), Ch. 20 (184), Ch. 26 (198). See also *Orationes tres contra Arianos* (PG 26, 265C). Cf. Chrysostom on the story of *Transfiguration* (Matt. 17:2) in PG 52, 404D.
55 PG 75, 1456A (title of Ch. 22 [21]), 1456B, 1460A, 1469C, 1472B, 1472C (title of Ch. 34 [32]), 1473B, 1477A.
56 PG 75, 1433A, 1457A, 1450D, 1469D, 1472B, 1473A (union of soul and body), 1473B.
57 See e.g. Mandac, 'L'union christologique', 85–6.
58 See ACO I, 1, 6, p. 116.

59 Tertullian applies 'coniungere' and 'cohaerere' as equivalents for *synaptein*, referring both to Trinitarian and Christological union. He seems to be the earliest theologian for whom *synaptō* is a synonym for *henoō*. See Abramowski, '*Synapheia*', 80–1. For Ambrose see ibid., 89–93; for Augustine and Novatian see ibid., 95–8.

60 See Abramowski, '*Synapheia*', 71. The conclusions of this study necessarily correct the assumptions concerning *synapheia* in the article of P. T. R. Gray, 'Theodoret on the *One Hypostasis*' (written in 1975, i.e. six years before Abramowski's study, yet published only in 1984) as well as of Kevin McNamara, 'Theodoret of Cyrus and the Unity of Person in Christ' (written in 1955). Significantly, however, Clayton does not seem to have been acquainted with it either (he does not list it in his bibliography), although it had been published four years before the submission of his thesis (1985).

61 In order to assess the legitimacy of this conclusion, one ought to read through the study of Prof. Abramowski, which dispels quite a few false assumptions.

62 ACO I, 1, 6, p. 131. Cf. his *Epistola dogmatica*: 'in order to avoid any appearance of division by using the word "along with" [*syn*]' (ACO I, 1, 1, p. 28).

63 The article of E. R. Hardy, 'The Further Education of Cyril of Alexandria'. does not provide any substantial evidence concerning the extent of Cyril's secular education. I have not yet encountered any modern analysis proving satisfactorily his familiarity with the philosophical tradition of crucial terms employed in Christian systematic theology.

64 See Abramowski, '*Synapheia*', 95.

65 *Homily* on Ps. 46:5 (LXX: 45:5) in PG 29, 424B.

66 See e.g. Gregory of Nyssa, *Opera*, 9 vols + Suppl., ed. by F. Müller, W. Jaeger *et al.* (Leiden: Brill, 1952–96), VIII/1, 204–5.

67 See PG 26, 296B; cf. PG 28, 464B.

68 'But when Cyril criticises the use of the term "conjunction", as implying a conjunction like that of the Lord and the believer who are "joined together" in one Spirit (cf. 1 Cor. 6:17), or like that of the curtains of the Tabernacle in the Wilderness (Exod. 26:6), which were "coupled together" with clasps (*Apol. adv. Theod.* X; *Adv. Nestor.* II, 6), he does not take into account that it had its place in the common stock of theological words and phrases. Apollinaris himself had used "conjunction" when referring to the union of God and flesh in Jesus Christ.' See Sellers, *The Council of Chalcedon*, 169.

69 See *Fragm.* 162 from a *Letter to Terentius* in Lietzmann, *Apollinaris*, 254. Cf. ibid., pp. 187, 240, 242, 246.

70 A typical example of *synapheia* qualifying the manner of *henōsis* as 'unmixed' is in *Letter* 146 in SC 111, 196. See also the *Confession* against Paul of Samosata in Hahn, *Bibliothek*, 183.

71 Cf. the third Antiochene Synod of 345 in Hahn, *Bibliothek*, 195.

72 The term *synapheia*, however, remains the synonym for *asynchutos henōsis*, i.e. 'unmingled union' in Theodoret's thinking.

73 *Synapheia* reappears in Theodoret's *Commentaries*, in the *Eranistes* and *HFC* also.

74 Cf. the *Second formula* of the Antiochene synod of 341 (Hahn, *Bibliothek*, 185). Even Apollinaris anathematised those who taught 'the change of the Godhead into flesh, or its confusion and alteration, as well as the suffering of the Son's Godhead' (Hahn, *Bibliothek*, 268).

7 THEODORET'S LEGACY

1 *De incarnatione*, 36 [34] in PG 75, 1476C–1477A.

2 This issue is outside the focus of this book. Nevertheless, for example, Anselm of Canterbury's doctrine of 'satisfactio' and his Christological model in *Cur Deus homo* show a striking resemblance to Antiochene Christology. The same goes for the Helvetic Reformers, especially Calvin and Bullinger, for the *Confessio Helvetica Posterior* (1566) and for the *Catechism of Heidelberg* (1563).

3 Karl Barth, *Church Dogmatics*, ed. by G. W. Bromiley and T. F. Torrance, trans. by G. T. Thomson and others, 4 vols (Edinburgh: T. & T. Clark, 1936–58), I/2, 24.

9 A CURE OF GREEK MALADIES

1 Thomas Gaisford, ed., *Theodoreti episcopi Cyrensis Graecarum affectionum curatio* (Oxford: Oxford Academic Press, 1839).

2 SC 57 (2 vols).

3 See e.g. Ludwig Kösters, 'Zur Datierung von Theodorets *Hellēnikōn therapeutikē pathēmatōn*', *ZKTh*, 30 (1906), 349–56.

4 SC 57, 28–31.

5 Or 'beginning' (*archē*).

6 The term *skytotomos* refers to the apostle Paul, the tentmaker.

7 The 'Pythian' and the 'Dodonian' are nicknames of Apollo of Delphi and Zeus of Dodona respectively.

8 The title can be interpreted either as 'from Greek philosophy', or, in a certain sense, 'apart from Greek philosophy'.

9 Greek *ēranismenoi* – two decades later Theodoret uses the same term, i.e. 'beggar' (*Eranistēs*) to depict the main character representing the Monophysite heresy.

10 Theodoret's sources are Plutarch and Porphyry, *The Life of Pythagoras*, 11. See SC 57, 107, note 1.

11 Cf. Clement of Alexandria, *Stromata* I, 15, 66.

12 See Gen. 17:10ff. and Exod. 2:5–6, and also Theodoret's *Quaestiones in Exodum* (PG 80, 228B).

13 See Diodorus Siculus, *Bibliotheca historica* I, 96, 4–5.

14 See Demosthenes, *Orationes* XXV, 11 (*In Aristogitonem* 1).

15 Theodoret suggests that there are plenty of names which refer to nothing real.

16 It should not be inferred that Theodoret considers Pherecydes a Syrian. The Greek word *Syrios* can denote both a Syrian and someone from the Greek island Syros (see the beginning of this chapter, where he refers to Pherecydes as *Syrios*). Nevertheless, since Theodoret's argument here is to show that not only those who were born in the so-called heartland of Greece (like Athens, Sparta, Corinth etc.) were great philosophers, but those from the peripheries as well, the island of Syros can also be considered as lower in rank in comparison to these illustrious places. I therefore do not necessarily share Canivet's opinion in SC 57, 109, note 4.

17 I.e. from Stageiros, a city in Macedonia.

18 Porphyry, *History of Philosophy*, fragment 11.

19 Ibid.

20 Plato, *Apology*, 17 b–c.

21 Plato, *Apology*, 18 a.

22 Plato, *Politics*, 261 e.

23 Cf. Plato, *Republic*, V, 475 d–e. Cf. Clement of Alexandria, *Stromata* I, 19, 93. See also SC 57, 112, note 2.

24 Perhaps the above also means 'to the improvement of life'.

25 Cf. Plato, *Laws*, III, 689 c–d. Theodoret's text diverges from Plato's at some points. See SC 57, 113, note 2.

26 Plato, *Theaetetus*, 174 a. In Theodoret's quotation we find 'behind him' instead of Plato's original 'before him'. Theodoret's present text is thus near to 'behind and before'.

27 Ibid., 174 d–e.

28 Ibid., 176 c.

29 Porphyry, *On the Philosophy of the Oracles*, 147.

30 Cf. Eusebius, *Praeparatio evangelica*, 14, 10, 3.

31 Porphyry, *Epistula ad Anebonem*, 29.

32 Ibid., 45.

33 Plato, *Timaeus*, 22 b.

34 Plato, *Timaeus*, 40 d–e.

35 Plato, *Gorgias*, 524 a–b.

36 Plato, *Laws*, I, 634 d.

37 The Greek text says: *ton trophimon tēs pisteōs*. Theodoret uses the same expression in *De Trinitate*, 3 (PG 75, 1149D), in his *Letter 92 to Anatolius* (SC 98, 244), in the *Commentary on the Psalms* (PG 80, 860), *on Galatians* (PG 82, 477), as well as in *HFC* (PG 83, 525 and 537).

38 Or 'the trustworthy/faithful man'.

39 Theognis, *Elegiae*, 1, 77–8.

40 Heraclitus, *Fragment* 34.

41 Empedocles, *Fragment* 5, 1–2.
42 Parmenides, *Fragment* 4, 7.
43 Theodoret's argument is based on the classical opposition between visible (*horatos*) and perceptible or intelligible (*noētos*) realities. While the former mostly requires eyesight, the latter also needs the abilities of the mind or intellect.
44 Solon, *Fragment* 16.
45 Empedocles, *Fragment* 133.
46 Antisthenes, *Fragment* 24.
47 Xenophon, *Memorabilia* IV, 3, 13.
48 Cf. Bacchylides, *Fragment* 5. See also SC 57, 124, note 2.
49 *Epopteia* means in fact the highest degree of initiation in divine mysteries (e.g. of Eleusis). See also SC 57, 124, note 3.
50 Or 'their firm opinion', depending on how one interprets *doxa* in this context.
51 The Greek *geneseis* can also mean 'the sources', 'beginnings', or even 'the becoming things', i.e. the future.
52 Plato, *Theaetetus*, 155 e.
53 Epicharmus, *Fragment* 246. Cf. *Fragment* 10. The above verse contains a barely translatable wordplay between the *physeis* (natures) of men and men themselves being *pephysēmenoi* (puffed up, i.e. drunk or stuffed like a leather bag).
54 This is the stoic *prolēpsis*. See also SC 57, 125, note 2.
55 Plato, *Crito*, 46 b.
56 Plato, *Alcibiades*, 109 e.
57 Plato, *Phaedo*, 67 b.
58 Orpheus, *Fragment* 245, 1. The two quotations (from *Phaedo* and from *Orpheus*) contain the same term *themis* and *themitos* respectively, which means something 'laid down', 'customary' or in a stronger sense, something 'permitted by the laws of God and men'.
59 Euripides, *Bacchae*, 472.
60 Euripides, *Phoenicians*, 471–2.
61 Euripides, *Fragment* 432.
62 Pseudo-Epicharmus, *Fragment* 249. Cf. SC 57, 127, note 3.
63 Heraclitus, *Fragment* 18.
64 Heraclitus, *Fragment* 22.
65 Aristotle, *Topica*, V, 3, 131 a, 23–6.
66 Or 'presumption'. See Epicurus, *Fragment* 255.
67 The Greek *ormē* in Stoic philosophy means 'appetition' including both the reasoned choice and the irrational impulse.
68 The length of a *stadion* was 177.60 meters.
69 The hierophant's duty was to teach the rites. In Eleusis, he also initiated into the mysteries. See SC 57, 132, note 2.
70 Pindar, *Fragment* 180.
71 Plato, *Letter* 2, 314 a.
72 Orpheus, *Fragment* 245, 1.

73 Plato, *Laws*, V, 730.

74 Plato, *Phaedo*, 69 c.

10 ON THE HOLY AND VIVIFYING TRINITY AND ON THE INHUMANATION OF THE LORD

1 The most likely time of composition was between 429 and the middle of 431. See Pásztori-Kupán, 'Theodoret', 34.

2 See PG 75, 1147–90 and 1419–78. Mai's editions are listed below.

3 Albert Ehrhard, 'Die Cyrill von Alexandrien zugeschriebene Schrift *Peri tēs tou Kyriou enanthrōpēseōs* ein Werk Theodorets von Cyrus', *ThQ*, 70 (1888), 179–243, 406–50, 623–53.

4 Eduard Schwartz, 'Zur Schriftstellerei Theodorets', *Sitzungsberichte der Bayerischen Akademie der Wissenschaften, Philosophisch-philologische und historische Klasse*, 1 (1922), 30–40; Joseph Lebon, 'Restitutions à Théodoret de Cyr', *RHE*, 26 (1930), 523–50; Robert Devreesse, 'Orient, antiquité', *RSPT*, 20 (1931), 559–71; Marcel Richard, 'Les citations de Théodoret conservées dans la chaîne de Nicétas sur l'Évangile selon Saint Luc', *RB*, 43 (1934), 88–96.

5 For a detailed discussion of dating, textual tradition etc. see Pásztori-Kupán, 'Theodoret', 23–56 and 279–88.

6 The letter survived only in a Latin translation. See SC 429, 150.

7 SC 111, 64. Cf. NPNF III, 296.

8 See *Marii Mercatoris S. Augustino aequalis Opera quaecumque extant*, Prodeunt nunc primum studio Joannis Garnerii Societatis Jesu presbyteri (Paris: 1673); the relevant excerpts are reprinted in PL 48, 1075–6.

9 See *Beati Theodoreti Episcopi Cyri Operum Tomus V*, Nunc primum in lucem editus, Cura et studio Joannis Garnerii, presbyteri e Societate Jesu, opus posthumum (Paris: 1684) – see also PG 84, 82. These are preserved together with a few others coming from a (now lost) work of Theodoret entitled *Pentalogos* (rendered as *Pentalogium* by Garnier), written against Cyril's Ephesian council.

10 Lebon, 'Restitutions', 524–36.

11 See Joseph Lebon, ed., trans., *Severi Antiocheni Liber Contra Impium Grammaticum, Orationis Tertiae Pars Prior*, CSCO, Scriptores Syri, Series 4 (Louvain: Marcel Istas, 1929), V. Until recently one sentence of *De Trinitate* quoted by Severus has been the only known excerpt of the work apart from Vat. gr. 841 itself. See below, in connection with Euthymius Zigabenus.

12 Lebon, 'Restitutions', 534–5.

13 According to Lebon, the pseudepigraphy was motivated by the desire to save Theodoret's two treatises from destruction after 553 by ascribing them to Cyril. Cf. Jean-Noël Guinot, 'L'*Expositio rectae fidei* et le traité

Sur la Trinité et l'Incarnation de Théodoret de Cyr: deux types d'argumentation pour un même propos?', *Recherches Augustiniennes*, 32 (2001), 39–74 (p. 59, note 64).

14 Schwartz, 'Zur Schriftstellerei Theodorets', 31; Pásztori-Kupán, 'An unnoticed title', 106–9. In the translation the PG chapter numbers are put in square brackets.

15 See Pásztori-Kupán, 'Theodoret', 37–9.

16 Several manuscripts survive of Nicetas' *Catena*, which were described and classified by Joseph Sickenberger, 'Die Lukaskatene des Niketas von Herakleia', *TU*, 22.4 (1902), 1–118. Following his description, I located, and used for my translation, four manuscripts representing the main branches of the textual tradition: Biblioteca Apostolica Vaticana, Vaticanus gr. 1611; Bibliothèque Nationale de France, Parisinus gr. 208; Österreichische Nationalbibliothek, Vindobonensis theol. gr. 71; Bayerische Staatsbibliothek, Monacensis gr. 473.

17 See Ehrhard, 'Die Schrift', 199.

18 See István Pásztori-Kupán, 'Quotations of Theodoret's *De sancta et vivifica Trinitate* in Euthymius Zigabenus' *Panoplia Dogmatica*', *Augustinianum*, 42 (2002), 481–7.

19 The fact that the two works were neglected as belonging to Cyril is also evinced by Jean Aubert's first edition of Cyril's works: the six large volumes comprising Cyril's oeuvre do not contain either of them, although based on the single testimony of Vat. gr. 841, at that time they should have belonged there. See Johannes Aubertus, ed., *S. P. N. Cyrilli Alexandriae Archiepiscopi Opera in VI. Tomos Tributa* (Paris: 1636–8).

20 Jacobus Sirmondus, ed., *Beati Theodoreti Episcopi Cyri Opera Omnia in Quatuor Tomos Distributa*, 4 vols (Paris: 1642).

21 Garnerius, Johannes, ed., *Beati Theodoreti Episcopi Cyri Operum Tomus V*, Nunc primum in lucem editus, Cura et studio Joannis Garnerii, presbyteri e Societate Jesu, opus posthumum (Paris: 1684), 256. Cf. PG 84, 363A–364B.

22 Cf. PG 84, 65–88.

23 Combefis' *Bibliotheca Patrum Concionatoria* (Paris: 1662) was reprinted in Venice in 1749. Schwartz quotes from this second edition (II, 525–6). See Schwartz, 'Zur Schriftstellerei Theodorets', 32. Cf. M. Richard, 'Les citations de Théodoret', 94, note 4. For M. Richard's valid argument concerning the two different codices used by Combefis and Garnier, see Pásztori-Kupán, 'Theodoret', 287.

24 Andreas Gallandius, ed., *Bibliotheca Veterum Patrum Antiquorumque Scriptorum Ecclesiasticorum Graeco-Latina*, 14 vols (Venice: 1788), IX, 418–21.

25 Angelo Mai, ed., *Scriptorum Veterum Nova Collectio* (Rome: 1833), VIII, 27–58 (*De Trinitate*) and VIII, 59–103 (*De incarnatione*); Angelo Mai, ed., *Nova Patrum Bibliotheca* (Rome: 1844–71), II (1844), 1–31 (*De Trinitate*) and II, 32–74 (*De incarnatione*).

26 See Mai's introduction to the two works in *Nova Patrum Bibliotheca* II, p. vi, as well as his comments reprinted in PG 75, cols 1456, 1472–4, 1477.

27 Cf. e.g. PG 75, 1460–1 with PG 84, 65B–68C etc. References to these identical texts published in PG once under the name of Cyril and of Theodoret respectively can be found in Pásztori-Kupán, 'Theodoret', 279–88.

28 This first sentence of Theodoret's *Prooemium*, the common introduction of both treatises, was not preserved in Greek. It survived only in Syriac, in Severus of Antioch's *Contra Grammaticum*, written around 520. See Lebon, *Severi Antiocheni Liber Contra Impium Grammaticum*, V, 46.

29 To the heavenly Jerusalem, i.e. to the city of God.

30 The expression 'death-bringing passages with many splits' is a reference to the miscellaneous heresies, which in Theodoret's view represent not only one diversion from the straight path of orthodox faith, but rather a variety of sidetracks leading to perdition, which are again 'split' as the followers of one heresy suddenly begin to follow separate ways.

31 The author refers here to those believers who were deceived by heretic doctrines.

32 Or 'until they inherit the royal city', i.e. they attain the kingdom of heaven by following the road of piety.

33 Cf. the first discourse of the *Cure of Greek Maladies* (see SC 57, 105).

34 Theodoret refers here to his works written before Ephesus. See p. 6.

35 A hardly translatable wordplay: *kērukes megalophōnoi te kai megalophrones*.

36 In this very condensed chapter Theodoret defends God's *eternal* fatherhood over against that of pagan gods and of human begetting. The latter two are not eternal, but evolutionary: a human being is somebody else's son before becoming a father. The timeless begetting of the Son is thus well founded in the chapter concerning God the Father already. The author knows that human language is inadequate to express timeless truths: thus, whilst using the word 'since', a time expression referring to realities beyond time within the last sentence, he also adds: 'yet he is eternally' – thus to show that the expression 'since' should not be taken as a chronological point. God the Father was, is and shall be eternally a Father. The same phrase ('yet he is eternally') returns in the next chapter.

37 This was the main Nicene argument against Arianism.

38 This sentence is connected with the previous one by the word *hen* (= one). Theodoret argues that according to John 'nothing was made' (*egeneto oude hen*) without the Word, yet time itself is *one* element of the whole creation (*hen de tōn pantōn*).

39 In the above verses we find the verbs: *ēn, ōn, hyparchōn*.

40 It is a common feature of Theodoret's writing style to put a longer explanatory sentence or even a short discourse in Jesus' mouth after a

biblical quotation. In the present case the antitheses of the Sermon on the Mount are summarised in this manner.

41 The term *pais* (= son, servant) was one of Jesus' typical messianic titles in early Christian times.

42 The original text contains *ho ōn* (= the one who is/exists) in both places, i.e. the participle used in the LXX version of Exod. 3:14.

43 *Ho theologos Iōannēs* = 'John, who speaks God's words', i.e. a *theologian* in a literal sense.

44 As explained in the Introduction, p. 9, the term *theologia* means the doctrine concerning God's divinity, and *oikonomia* is the technical term for the doctrine concerning the incarnation (i.e. both soteriology and Christology). In the above sentence Theodoret argues that the terms 'was made', 'assumed' and their synonyms are used by the biblical writers not referring to *theologia* (i.e. to God's unchangeable divinity), but to *oikonomia* (i.e. to the incarnation) and thus to the human nature of Christ, which can be said to have been made or assumed).

45 This is a recurrent allusion to the anathema following the Nicene Creed, which condemns those who assert that the Son is *ex ouk ontōn*, i.e. 'of the non-existent things'. See also Chapter 15 of this tract, Theodoret's *Reply to Cyril's Fourth Anathema* (p. 177), and *Chapter 1: About Arius* of *HFC*.

46 Vat. 841 has: *odynēn* (= pain, sorrow). Mai recommends *ōdina* (= labour-pain), since it reappears in Ch. 10.

47 The Greek word *organa* can mean both 'organs' as well as 'instruments' even in the sense of surgical tools. The phrase *hylē proypokeimenē* means 'the already underlying or given matter', by which the author emphasises the matter-dependent human birth as opposed to the divine, which is free from it. Finally, the word *apotuchia*, which generally means 'failure', in the present context of human birth may also have the meaning of 'miscarriage'.

48 In the Hebrew OT: Ps. 22:23; in the LXX and Vulgate: Ps. 21:23.

49 Or 'superior and inferior'. As well as Arian subordination, Theodoret repeatedly attacks the Trinitarian doctrine of Apollinaris, to whom he ascribes the invention of 'Great' (the Holy Spirit), 'Greater' (the Son) and 'Greatest' (the Father). See also *HFC* IV, 8: *About Apollinaris*.

50 Or 'who makes his angels spirits and the flaming fire his servants'. Ps. 104:4 (LXX: Ps. 103:4).

51 Theodoret uses *prosōpon* and *hypostasis* as synonyms in his Trinitarian teaching.

52 Mai's addition.

53 Or 'they are of equal dignity' (Greek *to isotimon*).

54 Zigabenus has *horos* (= definition, standard, measure) instead of *logos*.

55 The LXX translates the Hebrew *shalach* (= to send, to let go) with *apostellō*. Theodoret uses this expression throughout.

56 This is a good example of Theodoret's ontological 'communication of names'.

57 PG has: *allos*, Vat. 841 reads: *allēs*.

58 A recurrent allusion to the Nicene anathema. See also Chapter 8 of this tract.

59 Greek *despoteia*.

60 Mai and PG omit here a sentence preserved both in Vat. 841 and by Euthymius: *oude hetera men ta autō prosēkonta*. See PG 130, 657B.

61 Euthymius has *tēs exousias* (= of the power) instead of *tēs despoteias* (= of the dominion). See PG 130, 657C.

62 Cf. *De incarnatione*, Ch. 36 [34].

63 Theodoret speaks of the Spirit as of a divine person. To avoid any confusion of 'who' and 'what' I translate his references to the Spirit with the masculine, although in the Greek text we encounter the appropriate neuter form.

64 Although most English Bible translations (including the King James and the New Revised Standard Version) translate this passage with 'in the name', I have chosen to follow closely the original *eis to onoma*, which literally means 'baptise [i.e. immerse] them *into* the name' etc., thus excluding the interpretation by which the priest or minister of the church could be regarded as acting 'in the name' of God, i.e. on His behalf, whilst distributing the sacrament. He/she is rather following the commandment, that is to immerse this person, his/her life *into* the name of the Triune God.

65 Theodoret interprets the first person plural from Gen. 1:26 as referring to the Trinity. This is not an innovation, since the confession drawn up at an Antiochene council against Paul of Samosata, as well as the fourteenth anathema of the first council of Sirmium in 351, practically compelled him to do this. The latter even anathematises those who would not interpret the above biblical verse as the Father's address to his Son. See Hahn, *Bibliothek*, 179 and 198.

66 Vat. 841 reads: *ou dēmiourgikōs oude gennētikōs*.

67 Textual correction based on Vat. 841.

68 The above quotation corresponds better to Eph. 4:11–12 than to 1 Cor. 12:28.

69 Theodoret here quotes a version preserved in a lot of manuscripts. It is hard to determine whether he deliberately avoids a 'verbal Theopaschism' (i.e. the expression 'God's own blood') or simply the text was known to him in this form.

70 Literally: 'observe *the theology* of the Spirit'. Here *theologia* means again the discipline concerning God's existence.

71 Here we find two notable textual differences. Instead of 'to the purifying of the flesh' Theodoret says 'to perfection', and instead of '*through the eternal Spirit*' (*dia pneumatos aiōniou*) he quotes 'through the Holy Spirit' (*dia pneumatos hagiou*). The second alteration is probably a copying error, since the reason why Theodoret in fact quoted this text was to prove the eternity of the Spirit (cf. the title of the chapter as well as the following sentence).

72 Greek: *mian ousian en trisin idiotēsin gnōrizomenēn*.

73 Or 'threeness'.

74 For an explanation of 'hypostasis' see pp. 57–65 in the Introduction.

75 LXX: Ps. 118:105.

76 Since *De incarnatione* is the continuation of *De Trinitate*, *theologia* refers to the teaching on the being of God (i.e. the Trinity), whereas *oikonomia* denotes the doctrine concerning the dispensation.

77 *Psychē* can also mean 'life'.

78 I.e. by creating man in his own image.

79 Cf. Isa. 14:12; Luke 10:18.

80 This chapter title was introduced by A. Mai. It does not appear in Vat. 841.

81 Literally: 'to preserve the spark *for the* [human] nature'.

82 Vat. 841 and Nicetas have: *hypo tou iou tēs ponērias* (= by the rust/poison of evil) and not *tou huiou tēs ponērias* (= the son of evil).

83 I.e. the nature of Adam.

84 The word *saphōs* in Vat. gr. 841 is missing from PG.

85 The word *haploun* in Vat. gr. 841 is missing from PG.

86 Theodoret refers here to a mainly Gnostic theological trend, called Docetism (the Greek word *dokeō* means 'to suppose', 'to seem' or even 'to doubt'). The followers of this idea claimed that the divine Word became human in a manner which did not involve the taking on of anything material (the matter itself being evil for most Gnostics). Thus, in their view, every human aspect of Christ's earthly existence (including his own body) could not be anything else than appearance, a mere phantasm. The opposite extreme of this heresy was Adoptionism (a view held by Paul of Samosata and most Arians), according to which Jesus Christ was in fact a human being, his divine sonship being a result of his adoption by the Father on the occasion of his baptism in the Jordan.

87 Vat. 841 has: *saphē tēn dianoian* and not *tēs dianoias*.

88 Theodoret is perhaps referring to Melito of Sardis (apologist of the second century), who was charged by Origen (see his *Selecta in Gen.* in PG 12, 93 and *De principiis* I, 1, 1), and by Gennadius (*De eccl. dogm.* 4) of suspecting God as having flesh. The very few surviving works of Melito show that his Christology was based on the *Logos–sarx* model, but he was not necessarily an 'Anthropomorphite'.

89 Vat. 841 reads: *all' hapasēs ēn hamartias eleutheros* ('*ēn hamartias*' omitted by Mai and PG).

90 Greek *mē kata sarka tou nomou* – this version is absent from Nestle's critical apparatus and from Theodoret's *Commentary on the Pauline Epistles*.

91 This sentence may be interpreted either as a positive, affirmative statement or as a rhetorical question. Mindful of Theodoret's frequently rhetorical style I chose the latter option.

92 Vat. 841 reads: *oude eidēlon* (omitted by Mai and in PG).

93 Greek *empsychon*, which literally means 'in-souled', i.e. containing the soul within itself.

94 *Logos* might be understood both as the living Word of God and/or Scripture itself. Mai interprets it as 'sermo noster', i.e. the author's own line of thought.

95 The text literally means that once the injustice of sin was proven, 'it is thrown out of [God's] power'.

96 Vat. 841 has: *tēn hēmeteran aparchēn anelabeto* (PG 75, 1437A), whereas Nicetas had: *tēn ex hēmōn anelaben aparchēn* (see also PG 84, 77A).

97 Vat. 841 reads: *dio kai auton katekrine* (omitted by Mai and in PG).

98 Nicetas preserves a sentence here, which in Vat. 841 appears only in Ch. 24 (PG 75, 1464A): *kai nēsteuei men ou pera de tōn metrōn tēs physeōs* (cf. PG 84, 77B).

99 I.e. to show the weakness of the starving human nature so that Satan may dare to tempt him.

100 Theodoret's text – as in most cases – is closer to the LXX.

101 Vat. 841 has: *hōs eide* (PG 75, 1440C), Nicetas had: *hōs heuren* (= 'as he found' – PG 84, 77D).

102 Nicetas had: 'that this stone' (PG 84, 80A).

103 So Vat. 841. Nicetas had: *ho hagios tou theou* (the Holy One of God) – PG 84, 80A.

104 So Nicetas in PG 84, 80B.

105 I.e. named you the Son of God.

106 Here I followed Nicetas (see PG 84, 80B) instead of Vat. 841 (see PG 75, 1441A), because it better agrees with Theodoret's argument.

107 The text *akousas goun tōn tou Ponērou hrēmatōn ho Kyrios* was preserved only by Nicetas (see PG 84, 80B).

108 Nicetas adds: *hapax* (he also has *ho ponēros* instead of *diabolos*) – see PG 84, 81A.

109 The text in italics was preserved only by Nicetas (see PG 84, 81A).

110 Or 'by vainglory'. The text in italics was preserved only by Nicetas (PG 84, 81A).

111 Later, in his *Discourse on Divine Providence* Theodoret says that Satan 'approached Christ as Adam, but he found the Creator of Adam wrapped around with Adam's nature' (PG 83, 752C).

112 Greek *erastai* – the same term is used in *De Trinitate*, 3 (PG 75, 1152A). The expression returns in Theodoret's *HR*, correspondence and commentaries in a positive sense, e.g. like 'the lovers of wisdom' [*philosophias erastai*] (Letter 12 *to Palladius* in SC 40, 83), 'the lovers of God' [*tou theou erastai*] (*Letter 36 to Theodotus* in SC 40, 101) etc.

113 This sentence was probably the title of a new chapter. The scribe who copied it into Vat. 841 overlooked the expression *hoti* (= that) introducing the new section. See Schwartz, 'Zur Schriftstellerei Theodorets', 31. From now on, PG chapter numbers are given in square brackets. See also Ch. 30 [29] with the second copying error.

114 Literally: 'even if suffering from apostasy [or rebelliousness]'.

115 This sentence was preserved only by Nicetas (see PG 84, 81D).

116 Vat. 841 says: *en autō*, i.e. 'in it' or 'in him'. Euthymius had: *en tō*

NOTES

proslēmmati, i.e. 'in that which was assumed'. Cf. PG 75, 1444C with PG 130, 925B.

117 The text in italics was preserved by Euthymius (PG 130, 925B).

118 Euthymius has *atonia* (= lack of vigour) instead of *adunamia* (Cf. PG 75, 1444D with PG 130, 925C).

119 Vat. 841 reads: *eiper ho theos logos alēthōs anoun anelaben anthrōpon* (cf. PG 75, 1445B), whereas Euthymius had: *eiper alēthōs ho theos logos anoun elaben anthrōpon* (PG 130, 925D). Mai's and Migne's text is the result of a faulty reading of the manuscript.

120 The term *hēniochos* is an unmistakable reference to Plato's *Phaedrus*, 246a–247e.

121 The text of this verse both in Vat. 841 as well as by Euthymius differs from the LXX by the use of *chous* (= dust) instead of *chortos* (= grass, hay, straw). See PG 75, 1449A and PG 130, 908C.

122 This fragment (Ps. 77:39) exists only in the LXX and in the Vulgate.

123 Euthymius permits the restoration of this text. Thus, instead of Mai's addition (*legei hē graphē* = says Scripture), one ought to have *heurois kaloumenous sarka* (= found to be called flesh). I am indebted to Prof. Jean-Noël Guinot for this correction. See PG 75, 1449B; cf. PG 130, 908C.

124 In the Nestle–Aland edition of the New Testament we find *oude* (= neither), whereas Vat. 841 contains *alla* (= but, instead). In his *Commentary on Galatians* Theodoret also uses '*oude*' (PG 82, 468B). One conclusion might be that '*alla*' in Vat. 841 is a copying error. This, however, is not provable, since Euthymius quotes the same passage from *De incarnatione* (PG 130, 908C) exactly as it is in Vat. 841. The only common link between Euthymius and Vat. 841 is that both ascribe the treatise to Cyril, which is perhaps not a sufficient ground to assume that they belong to the same manuscript tradition, thus continuing a previous copying error. Therefore, one might even suppose that the insertion of '*alla*' instead of '*oude*' in the text of *De incarnatione* was the author's own error, who quoted the passage from memory. When commenting on the Pauline Epistles a few years later, he surely checked the biblical text.

125 Greek *teleion anthrōpon*.

126 I.e. to make the mortal, corruptible and passible human nature immortal, incorruptible and impassible. Concerning labour-pain as belonging to the passible human nature see e.g. Chapter 9 of *De Trinitate*. 'Relieving the labour-pains of corruption' therefore means that Christ, the firstborn from the dead, forecasts through his appearance our new, redeemed condition, in which no room is left for further corruption or suffering. This is a painless new birth indeed.

127 Greek *psychē noera*.

128 This passage is the only one where Theodoret can be claimed to refer to his opponents. Quasten drew a major conclusion concerning its significance: 'The author explicitly denies any polemical purpose and

247

pretends [*sic*!] only to be defending the orthodox faith against the Apollinarists. But the "Apollinarists" turn out to be, of all people, Cyril and the Fathers of Ephesus!' (*Patrology*, III, 547). Theodoret does not 'pretend' to be defending the orthodox faith: according to his own words, the purpose of this treatise is to *present* the divine teaching to those nurtured in piety. Further, within the context of the treatise the reference to 'the heirs of Apollinaris' is not merely a clever label placed on Cyril's party, but in the same measure it emphasises that the denial of Arianism is not yet a guarantee of orthodoxy, since Apollinarian thought – which was undoubtedly lurking in some Alexandrian circles of the time – is no less dangerous. The Monophysite heresy, based largely on Apollinarian ideas, proved just how right Theodoret already was in 431. That is why both the Arian and Apollinarian heresies are 'ranked together', the emphasis falling precisely upon the equal gravity of these two heterodoxies. Returning to Quasten's comment: Cyril and those present at his council cannot 'turn out to be' the Apollinarists of *De incarnatione* if the work itself preceded the council of 431, save for the case of their being Apollinarians indeed, which I would certainly disprove. Quasten's comment therefore is an overstatement. See also my note attached to Chapter 37 [35] of this treatise.

129   I have translated this title as it appears in Severus: 'Demonstrating the distinction of natures and the unity of the *person*'. His text contains *parsopa*, the Syriac equivalent of *prosōpon*. Mai's reading of Vat. 841 is faulty: the last line of fol. 196ᵛ contains three letters similar to a sequence of *a*, *s* and *ō*, which may be a corruption of *prosōpon*, but certainly not *Logos*, as Mai edited it. See Pásztori-Kupán, 'An unnoticed title', 108, note 16.

130   The text in italics was preserved only by Severus. See CSCO, V, 67 (Syriac) and V, 47 (Latin).

131   The entire passage is repeated almost literally in Theodoret's reply to Cyril's tenth anathema.

132   The word 'Christ' (present in Vat. 841) is omitted by Mai and PG.

133   Ps. 94:4 in the LXX.

134   The Greek sentence '*tēn asparton kai anēroton skēnēn diaplattei*' speaks of the Lord's 'unploughed' and 'untilled' human nature. These images receive an interesting connotation when Theodoret speaks about the formation of man out of the dust of the earth. The idea that the 'tent' or the 'temple' of the God-Word is 'unploughed' means that this temple is truly chaste and pure, as God originally formed it. It was not altered by human 'ploughing' such as original sin (see Ch. 14 also).

135   Garnier's *Auctarium* contains *anthrōpos* also (PG 84, 65A).

136   The Greek word *ageōrgētos* means 'uncultivated' in the sense of 'unploughed' (just like a few lines above) – therefore 'pure', 'untouched'. We encounter Theodoret using the term '*geōrgia*' (= tillage, husbandry) elsewhere in a negative sense also. In his letter written to the Eastern monks (431–2), interpreting Cyril's attitude towards the Spirit's

procession (vis-à-vis the ninth anathema), our author writes: 'He [i.e. Cyril] blasphemes even against the Holy Spirit, saying that he does not proceed from the Father according to the Lord's words, but as having his beginning from the Son. Yet this is also the fruit of the seeds of Apollinaris: he comes near even to the evil tillage/husbandry [*ponēra geōrgia*] of Macedonius.' See SC 429, 102; cf. NPNF III, 326.

137 Vat. 841 reads: *anermēneuton* ('inexplicable' – see PG 75, 1461A); Nicetas had: *akatalēpton* ('incomprehensible' – see PG 84, 68A).

138 The text in italics was preserved only by Nicetas (see PG 84, 68A).

139 In translating this passage I followed Nicetas' longer version instead of Vat. 841 (see PG 75, 1461B and PG 84, 68B).

140 The text in italics was preserved only by Nicetas (see PG 84, 72C).

141 Vat. 841 reads: *agōnia* (= feared). Nicetas quotes: *agōnia ton Archelaon* (cf. Matt. 2:22). See PG 84, 72D.

142 According to Luke 2:44 Jesus was sought among his parents' kinsfolk and not *by* them. See PG 75, 1461–2.

143 The text in italics was preserved by Nicetas (PG 84, 73A). The sentence is at the end of a passage quoted from this chapter, so it might be a redactor's remark to summarise the remaining part of the chapter. This is likely also because the term *theandrikē* (= 'godly–manly') appears neither in the treatise, nor – at least to my knowledge – in the rest of Theodoret's extant works.

144 The Greek sentence '*didōsi telos tō nomō*' can also be interpreted as: 'he gave aim/purpose to the law' or even 'he put an end to the law' i.e. in the sense of renewing it by the New Covenant. For the latter version see the last sentence of this chapter. Further, in Ch. 28 [27] of this treatise, Theodoret uses exactly the same formula to say that by his suffering Christ 'put an end to Adam's punishments' (*telos didous tais Adam timōriais*).

145 The Greek *palaistra* was a place devoted to the public teaching and practice of wrestling and athletics.

146 We re-encounter the expression 'unploughed' (*ageōrgētos*). See below.

147 Theodoret uses *ageōrgētos* both for Christ as coming from an untouched virgin womb and for the wine that was made without grapes. See also Jean-Noël Guinot, 'Les lectures patristiques grecques (IIIᵉ–Vᵉ s.) du miracle de Cana (Jn 2:1–11). Constantes et développements christologiques', *SP*, 30 (1997), 28–41.

148 I.e. by letting the woman touch him from behind and be cured. Cf. Luke 8:43–8.

149 The servant who struck Jesus on the face (see John 18:22) was under a double slavery according to Theodoret: as a human being he was the slave of sin and death, and in addition, he was also the slave of another man.

150 Instead of *hamartian* (= the sin, i.e. 'the fall'), Vat. 841 contains *timōrian* (= punishment). See PG 77, 1468.

151 This sentence is a little puzzling, yet it can be elucidated with the help

of Theodoret's *Commentary* on Tim. 3:16, where the author says: '*God was revealed in the flesh*: being God and Son of God, and being by nature invisible, he became manifest to everyone by becoming man. Now, he clearly brought out the two natures, saying the divine nature was revealed in the flesh. *Justified in Spirit*: having taken on the human nature, he kept it free from sins.' See Theodoret of Cyrus, *Commentary on the Letters of St Paul*, trans. by Robert C. Hill, 2 vols (Brookline: Holy Cross Orthodox Press, 2001), II, 220.

152 This sentence must have been another title of a new chapter. As Lebon pointed out, Severus had quoted a text from Ch. 32, whilst considering it as being from Ch. 34. Thus, the copying error mentioned by Schwartz regarding Ch. 15 must have happened once again before Ch. 32. One may observe that the next title (of Ch. 32 [31]) is logically connected with this one: the two chapters are balancing each other. The first speaks of the Word being called the Son of Man, the second deals with the form of the servant named Son. For more details see Pásztori-Kupán, 'An unnoticed title'.

153 In opposition to Mai's edition and PG, Vat. 841 reads: '*ou to ek spermatos David*', i.e. not 'who', but 'what' was of David's seed.

154 Mai's suggestion: 'of the heavens'. See PG 75, 1469C.

155 Here the term *oikeioō* (= to appropriate) reappears with practically the same meaning as in Ch. 19 [18], showing the author's zeal to evince how the sufferings and wretchedness of the human nature can be ascribed to the Word.

156 Cf. Rom. 11:36 and Col. 1:16.

157 According to Severus' text, the expression *synaphthen* (= conjoined) should be inserted after '*thateron gar thaterō*' of Vat. 841. I am indebted to Dr Paul Parvis for this correction based on CSCO, V, 257, line 19.

158 Here we have first-hand evidence concerning the concrete designations of the manhood as understood by the Antiochenes: these occasional references to the assumed humanity as to a 'who' (instead of a 'what') are allowed only after its union with the Word – in just the same manner as the name 'Christ' is due to it only after the union.

159 The more accurate term *diakrinō* (= to distinguish) will replace this expression in Theodoret's later writings. See below.

160 As mentioned above, this term will replace *diairesis* in Theodoret's later works, yet in this treatise – as well as in his early Christology, including the *Refutation of Cyril's Anathemas* – the two are mostly synonyms.

161 Theodoret expresses the same idea of distinguished attribution in his refutation of the fourth Cyrilline anathema. Cf. with the closing remark of the *Formula of Reunion*.

162 Although the term *philosophia* (= wisdom) in the fifth century had also a meaning which connected it to the Christian monastic ideal, the author of the *Cure of Greek Maladies* has a more universal and receptive approach, showing that all wisdom comes from the Holy Spirit, and whatever is good and positive among the people of the world derives somehow from

the Counsellor. This statement could also be regarded as his guiding principle concerning Christian mission, especially if one considers Theodoret's firm rejection of using military force to facilitate the expansion of the Christian church.

163 Here I tried to somehow render the wordplay of *protropē* and *apotropē*. This chapter is in fact the closure of *De Trinitate* (that is why the Spirit's procession and other Trinitarian issues reappear), whilst the next one is the conclusion of *De incarnatione* and as such, the ending of both tracts.

164 Since this chapter is the finale of both works, therefore the two terms, *theologia* and *oikonomia* represent the two treatises and the theological disciplines they are dealing with. See also Ch. 1 of this treatise.

165 Mai and PG omit here the word *teleion* present in Vat. 841.

166 Concerning this last chapter, Quasten wrote: 'At the end the term *anthrōpotokos* is defended as being at least as exact [*sic*!] as *theotokos*' (*Patrology*, III, 547). Although the text speaks for itself, a short clarification is perhaps needed. *Anthrōpotokos* is asserted here as a proper balancing expression of *theotokos*, the author insisting upon the simultaneous use of both. Based on the text itself one cannot conclude that '*anthrōpotokos* is at least as exact as *theotokos*', as if e.g. one could play off one against the other. On the contrary: the two expressions are presented here as being two sides of the same coin, one being valid only together with the other, which is a perfectly legitimate Christological point. Moreover, as the later development of Theodoret's terminological evolution evinces, this may well have been the last occasion when he defended this (otherwise completely justifiable) juxtaposition. The *Antiochene Formula* drawn up by him in Ephesus already does not contain *anthrōpotokos* at all, the author defending his abandonment of the term in his *Letter 16 to Irenaeus*. Although inherited prejudices may often lead us to read a text with the wrong spectacles, clarifications must be made in order to remove unfounded assumptions.

11 THEODORET'S *REFUTATION OF CYRIL'S TWELVE ANATHEMAS*

1 Cyril's *Anathemas* and their *Apology* can be found in a modern English translation in Russell, *Cyril*, 176–89, from which I have quoted the texts of the anathemas with the kind permission of Routledge Publishers.

2 Theodoret seems to have paraphrased Mal. 3:6, since according to the LXX, the text should say 'I am the Lord your God and I do not change'. By the repetition of 'I am' he might also hint at Exod. 3:14.

3 I have followed the version in the critical apparatus of the ACO in translating this passage, which includes the word *monon* ('only'), since it construes best with Theodoret's line of thought.

NOTES

4 See pp. 61–4 in the Introduction. Cf. Pásztori-Kupán, 'Theodoret', 234–9.

5 Greek: '*tōn atopōtatōn an eiē*' (= would be entirely out of place, strange). This is a very rare grammatical construction; in fact only Demosthenes can be shown to have used it once in his *Olynthiaca* 1 (26, 4). See S. H. Butcher, ed., *Demosthenis orationes* (Oxford: Clarendon Press, 1903), I, 9–17. The expression appears as a *hapax legomenon* by Libanius, Nemesius of Emesa, Eusebius, Athanasius and John Chrysostom in his *Third Homily* uttered in Antioch (PG 49, 53). Apart from Demosthenes, John is Theodoret's most likely source of inspiration.

6 The same argument is to be found in *De incarnatione*, 19 [18].

7 The term *diairesis* and the verb *diaireō* (division, separation; to divide, to separate) are used here by Theodoret to express a clear distinction between the two natures of Christ *in reaction* to what he considered at the time as being a total confusion and mixture on Cyril's part (in his anathema, Cyril used and condemned the same verb: 'if anyone divides [*diairei*] the hypostases' etc.). Theodoret will replace this term later with a much more appropriate one, i.e. *diakrinō* and *diakrisis* (to distinguish, distinction). The most likely reason for using *diairesis* here is precisely the need to answer Cyril's criticism in a terminological sense. For how the two terms (*diairesis* and *diakrisis*) can be considered as synonyms in the works of the young Theodoret, see e.g. *De incarnatione*, 34 [32], written in the same period as the *Refutation of the Anathemas*.

8 It is important to note that the only occasion where Theodoret could be claimed to admit two hypostases in Christ in his entire theological career is his answer to the third Cyrilline anathema. He never challenges the term again, although in the light of the available evidence he was right in claiming that the term was alien to the Christology of the fathers.

9 This is an instance where it can be observed that *diairesis* has a lesser meaning for Theodoret than 'division' or 'separation' and is closer to the idea of 'distinction', since it would be absurd to separate or divide the body and soul of a human person. See also *De incarnatione*, 34 [32]. One may even be entitled to say that Theodoret only 'separates' or 'divides' the two natures of Christ to the same extent as the soul of a living human being can, or may, be 'separated' from his/her body.

10 Or 'who describes the mixture to us by means of other terms'.

11 This is obviously an ironical formula addressed to Cyril.

12 Or 'the purpose'.

13 The closing remark of the *Formula of Reunion* expresses exactly the above idea. Even the use of the same terms, like 'God-worthy' [*theoprepōs*], 'humbly' [*tapeinēs*] etc. betrays that Theodoret is the author of both. See also *De incarnatione*, 34 [32].

14 See Basil, *De Spiritu Sancto* 5, 12 in SC 17, where he uses the term 'God-bearing flesh' (*theophoros sarx*). This expression returns in his *Homilies on the Psalms* (PG 29, 424B; cf. PG 29, 468A), yet I have not encountered the term 'God-bearing man' here. Theodoret is either

quoting these from memory or perhaps the versions in his possession contained 'man' instead of 'flesh'.

15 As mentioned earlier, *paīs* in the LXX was largely used as a translation of the Hebrew *ebed* (= servant) in the relevant passages of Isaiah, nevertheless, in the early centuries it became an honorific title to denote Christ as the Son of God [*paīs theou*]. Therefore, when the LXX says, 'behold my *paīs*', the early Christian reader could automatically regard this as a direct reference to Christ, the Son of God.

16 For a detailed discussion of what was involved on both sides concerning the Spirit's procession, over against an alleged 'creation' by the Son, as Theodoret interprets Cyril's statement see de Halleux, 'Cyrille, Théodoret et le *Filioque*'.

17 Only the LXX version of the passage quoted can be interpreted as 'rejoicing' and not 'moaning'.

18 Most English translations render *to poiēsanti auton* with '[God] who appointed him [i.e. Jesus]'; nevertheless, Theodoret's subsequent argument is based precisely upon the primary meaning of *poieō*, which is 'to make, create'. He intends to show that whilst the manhood can rightly be regarded as a creation of God, the Word himself evidently does not belong to this category.

19 See also *De incarnatione*, 19 [18] and 20 [19].

20 Theodoret clearly omits any reference to the Eucharist in his reply, although from Cyril's subsequent *Apology* the Eucharistic line of thought comes to the forefront.

12 THAT EVEN AFTER THE INHUMANATION OUR LORD JESUS CHRIST IS ONE SON

1 Marcel Richard, 'Un écrit de Théodoret sur l'unité du Christ après l'Incarnation', *RSPT*, 24 (1935), 34–61. See especially p. 52, where Richard argues for a composition in 448 or at the beginning of 449.

2 See pp. 55–6 of the Introduction.

3 See e.g. *De incarnatione* 22 [21] in PG 75, 1456D.

4 In Theodoret's Christology there is hardly any evidence of a real *communicatio idiomatum* (save perhaps for the use of *oikeiōsis* in *De incarnatione* 19 [18] and 32 [30]). Nevertheless, after the resurrection Theodoret repeatedly states that the manhood received the properties of the divine nature, such as immortality, incorruptibility and impassibility. In this sense he follows 1 Cor. 15:40–54 faithfully.

5 In the *Foreword* of *De Trinitate* the author also speaks of 'the royal path trodden by the pious' (PG 75, 1148B).

6 Theodoret emphasises that both the division of the two natures (i.e. 'Nestorianism') and their mingling (i.e. Eutychian Monophysitism) are equally erroneous Christological ideas.

7 Reference to Ignatius of Antioch's *Epistle to the Romans* 4:1.

8 Theodoret refers here to Flavian of Antioch who was consecrated as Meletius' successor in 381, ordained John Chrysostom as a presbyter and defended the people of Antioch against Theodosius I when the emperor wanted to avenge the destruction of his statues. Flavian died in 404. Blomfield Jackson, however, interpreted the above sentence as referring to Flavian of Constantinople, one of the last champions of orthodoxy against Monophysitism, who undoubtedly suffered a martyr's death (see NPNF III, 332) a few days after the *Latrocinium* in August 449. Nevertheless, 'the throne of *that* place' in the above text refers to the see of Antioch, previously occupied by Meletius, not to Constantinople. Moreover, if this statement were indeed to be taken as referring to Flavian of Constantinople, then the dating of the tract would have to be placed after the *Latrocinium*. The other similar list where these names appear in this order – as indicated by Marcel Richard – can be found in *Letter* 146 (145 in PG) in SC 111, 190 where they appear as 'the luminaries of the East'. It is also notable that all the personalities listed by Theodoret died at least forty years before the *Latrocinium*.

9 Cyprian of Carthage (*c.* 200–58), who was not burnt but beheaded at Carthage, on 13 August 258, was confused with another martyr of the same name, a Christian of Antioch who suffered martyrdom together with St Justina during the persecution of Diocletian at Nicomedia in 304. Both Gregory Nazianzen and Prudentius confounded this Cyprian with Cyprian of Carthage, and their mistake was often repeated in later times. Nevertheless, this second Cyprian of Antioch was also beheaded together with Justina on the bank of the river Gallus. We cannot exclude the possibility that the story of a third Cyprian might also have influenced Theodoret's reference above to the fire. We know of a Christian martyr called Cyprian, contemporary to Cyprian of Carthage, who was executed under the emperor Decius. Alphaios, Philadelphos and Cyprian were sons of a governor in Italy, named Vitalius. After their conversion they suffered in Sicily, in the city of Mesopolis Leontii, where they had been sent from Rome in the year 251. The tongue of St Alphaios was cut out and he bled to death, Philadelphos was burnt over an iron lattice, and Cyprian was burnt on a hot pan. It is almost impossible to ascertain the manner in which these stories became conflated.

13 THEODORET'S *LETTER 16 TO BISHOP IRENAEUS*

1 This was obviously unjust, since Nestorius clung to a juxtaposition of *theotokos* and *anthrōpotokos* in opposition to a one-sided emphasis upon either of them.

2 Reference to Homer, *Iliad* 16: 111. Theodoret's vast secular education

comes often to the forefront in his correspondence. See e.g. Azéma, 'Citations d'auteurs et allusions profanes', 5–13.

3 The text is somewhat ambiguous, since the word 'only' could be interpreted either as 'the merest form' or as 'the only possible form' of help. The following sentence seems to support the former interpretation, whilst the next again appears to validate the latter.

4 Reference to Zenobius III, 62 and 89. For details see SC 98, 57, note 6.

5 Diodore and Theodore were already 'charged' by Cyril, the former 'prosecutor'. Although Cyril was not alive at the time of the composition of this letter (he died in 444), his reputation and authority before and after the *Latrocinium* were stronger than ever.

6 Theodoret is obviously referring here to his *Apology for Diodore and Theodore*, written in response to Cyril's attack upon the two Antiochene theologians.

7 The text literally says *somatike therapeia*, which would literally mean 'bodily favours' or 'corporeal cures', which in the above context means material and financial advantages including perhaps bribery, which was typically Cyril's way of dealing with ecclesiastical issues. Theodoret consciously isolates himself from such practices.

14 A COMPENDIUM OF HERETICAL MYTHIFICATION

1 The Greek title is: *Hairetikēs kakomythias epitomē*. *Kakomythia* could be rendered as 'evil mythification' or 'wicked myth-making' rather than merely 'fables'.

2 This is how Quasten treats it in his *Patrology* III, 551–2.

3 I.e. *Peri archōn* (Greek), or *De principiis* (Latin).

4 The three Greek titles are: *Hairetikēs kakomythias epitomē*, *Theiōn dogmatōn epitomē* and *Pseudous kai alētheias diagnōsis*. See PG 83, 340.

5 See Cope, 'An Analysis of the Heresiological Method of Theodoret', 42.

6 Concerning the fifth book (i.e. the *Compendium of Divine Doctrines*) Quasten affirms that it 'is unique in Greek patristic literature and very valuable for the history of dogma'. Quasten, *Patrology* III, 551.

7 See Theodoret's *Letter* 97 *to Sporacius* in SC 111, 12–14. Concerning Sporacius see e.g. SC 40, 53.

8 See Quasten, *Patrology* III, 552; cf. Cope, 'An Analysis of the Heresiological Method of Theodoret', 45–53.

9 One of the reasons to doubt the authenticity of the chapter on Nestorius is the spurious *Letter against Nestorius to Sporacius* (PG 83, 1153–64), which repeats this chapter word by word, and mounts a new attack upon Nestorius.

10 The heretics presented in *HFC* before Valentinus were: Simon Magus, Menander, Saturnilus, Basilides, Isidore, Carpocrates, Epiphanes and Prodicus.

NOTES

11 Or 'turning about', also in the sense of 'changing'.
12 Or 'by him'.
13 *Dia tessaron* = 'out of/through the four', i.e. of the four Gospels. Concerning Tatian's *Diatessaron* see e.g. Quasten, *Patrology* I, 224.
14 Theodoret uses the term *ta kephalaia* (= the main points, the summary) whilst encapsulating the teaching of Mani, whose main work was also entitled *Kephalaia*.
15 Concerning the clarification of the misunderstandings around the *Gospel according to the Hebrews* see Cope, 'An Analysis of the Heresiological Method of Theodoret', 141, note 25.
16 Against Paul of Samosata three synods were probably held between 264 and 266. Dionysius could not attend the first one because of his infirmities. Although being condemned by an Antiochene council in 268, Paul could not be driven away from his see until Emperor Aurelian occupied Antioch in 272.
17 I.e. Gregory Thaumatourgos (the Wonderworker).
18 This happened in 272.
19 Cf. with *De Trinitate*, 28.
20 The expression *ta klēmata* ('the branches') is a clear allusion to John 15:1–6.
21 I.e. 'of the territory of Phrygia'.
22 Greek *tēn exōthen paideian* (= the 'outer' education). Just as above in Firmilian's case (in the chapter about Paul of Samosata), Theodoret clearly refers here to secular education, which he always respected in Christian theologians.
23 In Book II, in the chapter *About Cerinthus*, not translated in this volume.
24 *Metanoia* (= changing one's mind or thinking) is the term for both 'repentance' and 'conversion'.
25 Theodoret's recurrent allusion to the Nicene anathema. See e.g. *De Trinitate*, 8 and 15.
26 Greek *sympatheia* (= 'suffering together').
27 The term *paradynasteuontas* can mean 'those who reigned together with' or 'those who had great influence/authority with' the emperor.
28 Cf. Rom. 11:33.
29 See *HE*, I, 1–13.
30 Cf. Isa. 40:3, Isa. 45:13, Matt. 3:3, Mark 1:3, Luke 3:4–5, John 1:23 etc.
31 I.e. not 'the same', only 'similar' to the Father, with the complete omission of *ousia* (essence).
32 Literally: 'in a corner'.
33 I.e. 'similar' in the sense of being 'like him', but not being 'the same'.
34 The literal meaning of *pneumatomachoi* is: 'those who fight against the Spirit', i.e. against the Spirit's divinity.
35 I.e. 'for the very sake of speaking against something'.
36 Apollinaris' key term concerning the incarnation was *sarkōsis* (= 'becoming flesh') instead of *(en)anthrōpēsis* (= 'becoming human',

'inhumanation'). The Laodicean heresiarch applied it consistently in order to be able to claim that the Word indeed did not assume flesh together with a rational soul. Concerning Theodoret's rejection of this practice see e.g. *De incarnatione* 9–10 and 15–20 [19].

37 Ironic title addressed to Apollinaris.

38 Cf. with *De incarnatione* 19 [18].

39 For Theodoret it goes without saying that it was the divine Word of God who appeared (at that time without a body) and spoke to the chosen people in the Old Testament. Concerning the calling of Moses, for example, see *De Trinitate* 7.

40 I.e. in the fifth book of this work, entitled *A Compendium of Divine Doctrines*.

41 Literally: 'for both that and these [is] body'.

BIBLIOGRAPHY

Texts of Theodoret

Theodoret's works were first edited by Jacques Sirmond in four volumes, to which Jean Garnier's posthumous work was added. Another good collection of material (reprinted in PG 80–84) was furnished by J. L. Schulze and J. A. Noesselt in five volumes. They are the following:

Theodoret of Cyrus, *Beati Theodoreti Episcopi Cyri Opera Omnia in Quatuor Tomos Distributa*, ed. by Jacobus Sirmondus, 4 vols (Paris: 1642).

Theodoret of Cyrus, *Beati Theodoreti Episcopi Cyri Operum Tomus V*, Nunc primum in lucem editus, Cura et studio Joannis Garnerii, presbyteri e Societate Jesu, opus posthumum (Paris: 1684).

Theodoretus, *Opera Omnia*, ed. by J. L. Schulze and J. A. Noesselt, 5 vols (Halle: 1769–74).

Angelo Mai edited two of Theodoret's works under Cyril's name:

Mai, Angelo, ed., *Nova Patrum Bibliotheca*, 8 vols + Appendix (Rome: Sacr. Conc. Prop. Chr. Nom., 1844–71), II, 1–31 (*De Trinitate*) and II, 32–74 (*De incarnatione*).

—— *Scriptorum Veterum Nova Collectio* (Rome: Sacr. Conc. Prop. Chr. Nom., 1833) VIII, 27–58 (*De Trinitate*) and VIII, 59–103 (*De incarnatione*).

In the nineteenth century, Thomas Gaisford edited Theodoret's *A Cure of Greek Maladies*, which was reprinted in PG 83, 783–1152. Following the edition of J. Raeder, the list culminates with Canivet's two-volume publication in SC:

Theodoreti episcopi Cyrensis Graecarum affectionum curatio, ed. by Thomas Gaisford (Oxford: 1839).

Theodoreti Graecarum affectionum curatio, ed. by J. Raeder (Leipzig: Bibliotheca Teubneriana, 1904).

Théodoret de Cyr, *Thérapeutique des maladies helléniques*, ed. by Pierre Canivet, 2 vols, SC 57/I–II (Paris: Cerf, 1958).

Gaisford also edited Theodoret's *Church History*:

Theodoreti Episcopi Cyri Ecclesiasticae Historiae Libri Quinque, ed. by Thomas Gaisford (Oxford: 1854).

Some of Theodoret's works are still not published in a critical edition. Apart from the PG reprints, a selected list of modern editions is provided here:

Iustini Philosophi et Martyris Opera Quae Feruntur Omnia, ed. by I. C. Th. de Otto, Corpus Apologetarum Christianorum Saeculi Secundi, 4, 3rd edn (Iena: Gust. Fischer, 1880) – it contains Theodoret's *Expositio rectae fidei* under the name of Justin Martyr.

Theodoret, *Kirchengeschichte*, ed. by L. Parmentier and F. Schweidler, GCS 44, 2nd edn (Berlin: Akademie Verlag, 1954).

Théodoret de Cyr, *Correspondance*, ed. by Yvan Azéma, 4 vols, SC 40, 98, 111, 429 (Paris: Cerf, 1964–98).

Theodoret of Cyrus, *Eranistes*, ed. by Gerard H. Ettlinger (Oxford: Clarendon Press, 1975).

Théodoret de Cyr, *Histoire des moines de Syrie*, ed. by P. Canivet and A. Leroy-Molinghen, 2 vols, SC 234, 257 (Paris: Cerf, 1977–9).

—— *Commentaire sur Isaïe*, ed. by Jean-Noël Guinot, 3 vols, SC 276, 295, 315 (Paris: Cerf, 1980–4).

Theodoreti Cyrensis Quaestiones in Reges et Paralipomena. Editio critica, ed. by Natalio Fernandez Marcos and Jose Ramon Busto Saiz, Textos y estudios Cardenal Cisneros, 32 (Madrid: Instituto Arias Montano, 1984).

English translations

The English translations are very few in number. The only nineteenth-century translation is the following:

Jackson, Blomfield, trans., *The Ecclesiastical History, Dialogues, and Letters of Theodoret*, ed. by Henry Wace and Philip Schaff, NPNF, III (Oxford: James Parker, 1892) – it contains the English translation of Theodoret's *Church History*, *Eranistes* and his *Correspondence* based on the PG edition.

A few modern translations have been made in the twentieth century. Currently Robert Charles Hill is providing translations of Theodoret's *Commentaries*, while G. H. Ettlinger has provided a fresh translation of *Eranistes*. This is one of the reasons why I have omitted translations from

Theodoret's exegetical oeuvre and from *Eranistes* in the present volume. The modern English translations of Theodoret's works are the following:

Theodoret of Cyrrhus, *A History of the Monks of Syria*, trans. by R. M. Price, Cistercian Studies, 88 (Oxford: Mowbray, 1985).

Theodoret of Cyrus, *On Divine Providence*, trans. by Thomas P. Halton, Ancient Christian Writers, 49 (New York: Newman Press, 1988).

—— *Commentary on the Psalms*, trans. by Robert C. Hill, Fathers of the Church, 101–2 (Washington, DC: Catholic University of America Press, 2000–1).

—— *Commentary on the Song of Songs*, trans. by Robert C. Hill, Early Christian Studies, 2 (Brisbane: Centre for Early Christian Studies, Australian Catholic University, 2001).

—— *Commentary on the Letters of St Paul*, trans. by Robert C. Hill, 2 vols (Brookline: Holy Cross Orthodox Press, 2001) (Indispensable).

—— *Eranistes*, trans. by Gerard H. Ettlinger, Fathers of the Church, 106 (Washington, DC: Catholic University of America Press, 2003) (Indispensable).

Other texts and translations

Athanasius, *Contra Gentes and De incarnatione*, ed. and trans. by Robert W. Thomson (Oxford: Clarendon Press, 1971).

Burnet, J., ed., *Platonis opera*, 5 vols (Oxford: Clarendon Press, 1900–7).

Butcher, S. H., ed., *Demosthenis orationes* (Oxford: Clarendon Press, 1903).

Combefis, François, *Bibliotheca Patrum Concionatoria* (Paris: 1662).

Cyril of Alexandria, *S. P. N. Cyrilli Alexandriae Archiepiscopi Opera in VI. Tomos Tributa*, ed. by Johannes Aubertus (Paris: 1636–8).

—— *Select Letters*, ed. and trans. by Lionel R. Wickham (Oxford: Clarendon Press, 1983).

Datema, C., ed., *Amphilochii Iconiensis Opera* (Turnhout: Brepols, 1978).

Gallandius, Andreas, ed., *Bibliotheca Veterum Patrum Antiquorumque Scriptorum Ecclesiasticorum Graeco-Latina*, 14 vols (Venice: 1788)

Gregory of Nyssa, *Opera*, 9 vols + Suppl., ed. by F. Müller, W. Jaeger *et alii* (Leiden: Brill, 1952–96).

Hahn, G. Ludwig, *Bibliothek der Symbole und Glaubensregeln der Alten Kirche*, 3rd edn (Breslau: E. Morgenstern, 1897).

Lietzmann, Hans, *Apollinaris von Laodicea und seine Schule* (Tübingen: Mohr, 1904).

Marius Mercator, *Marii Mercatoris S. Augustino aequalis Opera quaecumque extant*, Prodeunt nunc primum studio Joannis Garnerii Societatis Jesu presbyteri (Paris: 1673).

Photius, *Bibliothèque*, ed. by René Henry, Collection Byzantine, 8 vols (Paris: Les Belles Lettres, 1959–77).

Rouet de Journel, M. J., *Enchiridion Patristicum* (Freiburg: Herder, 1922).

Russell, Norman, *Cyril of Alexandria*, The Early Church Fathers (London: Routledge, 2000) (Indispensable).

Severus of Antioch, *Liber Contra Impium Grammaticum, Orationis Tertiae Pars Prior*, ed. by Joseph Lebon, CSCO, Scriptores Syri, Series 4, V – Syriac text (Paris: Reipublicae, 1929).

—— *Liber Contra Impium Grammaticum, Orationis Tertiae Pars Prior*, ed. and trans. by Joseph Lebon, CSCO, Scriptores Syri, Series 4, V – Latin translation (Louvain: Marcel Istas, 1929).

Socrates Scholasticus, *Ecclesiastical History*, ed. by William Bright, 2nd edn (Oxford: Clarendon Press, 1893) (Important).

Theodore of Mopsuestia, *Theodori Episcopi Mopsuesteni in Epistolas B. Pauli Commentarii*, ed. by H. B. Swete, 2 vols (Cambridge: Cambridge University Press, 1880–2).

Wace, Henry, and Philip Schaff, eds, *A Select Library of Nicene and Post Nicene Fathers of The Christian Church*, 14 vols (Oxford: James Parker, 1886–1900).

Referred secondary literature

Abramowski, Luise, 'Reste von Theodorets Apologie für Diodor und Theodor bei Facundus', *SP*, 1 (1957), 61–9.

—— 'Synapheia und asynchutos henōsis als Bezeichnung für trinitarische und christologische Einheit' in *Drei christologische Untersuchungen* (Berlin: Walter de Gruyter, 1981), 63–109 (Indispensable).

—— 'Über die Fragmente des Theodor von Mopsuestia in Brit. Libr. add 12.516 und das doppelt überlieferte christologische Fragment', *Oriens Christianus*, 79 (1995), 1–8 (Important).

Altaner, Berthold, *Patrology* (Freiburg: Herder, 1960).

Amann, E., 'L'affaire Nestorius vue de Rome', *RevSR*, 23 (1949), 5–37, 207–44; 24 (1950), 28–52, 235–65.

Anastos, Milton V., 'The Immutability of Christ and Justinian's Condemnation of Theodore of Mopsuestia', *DOP*, 6 (1951), 125–60.

Azéma, Y., 'Citations d'auteurs et allusions profanes dans la *Correspondance* de Théodoret', *TU*, 125 (1981), 5–13.

—— 'Sur la date de la mort de Théodoret', *Pallas*, 31 (1984), 137–55.

Barth, Karl, *Church Dogmatics*, ed. by G. W. Bromiley and T. F. Torrance, trans. by G. T. Thomson and others, 4 vols (Edinburgh: T. & T. Clark, 1936–58).

Batiffol, P., 'Les Présents de Saint Cyrille à la cour de Constantinople', in *Études de liturgie et d'archéologie chrétienne* (Paris: J. Gabalda, 1919).

Bergjan, Silke-Petra, *Theodoret von Cyrus und der Neunizänismus, Aspekte der altkirchlichen Trinitätslehre*, Arbeiten zur Kirchengeschichte, 60 (Berlin: Walter de Gruyter, 1994).

Berthold, George C., 'Cyril of Alexandria and the *Filioque*', *SP*, 19 (1989), 143–7.

Böhm, Thomas, *Die Christologie des Arius, Dogmengeschichtliche Überlegungen unter besonderer Berücksichtigung der Hellenisierungsfrage*, Studien zur Theologie und Geschichte, 7 (St Ottilien: EOS, 1991).

Bright, William, *The Age of the Fathers, Chapters in the History of the Church During the Fourth and Fifth Centuries*, 2 vols (London: Longmans, Green and Co., 1903).

Brok, M. F. A., 'The Date of Theodoret's *Expositio Rectae Fidei*', *JTS*, 2 (1951), 178–83.

Canivet, Pierre, 'Theodoret of Cyr', *New Catholic Encyclopedia*, ed. by the editorial staff of the Catholic University of America, Washington, 18 vols (New York: McGraw-Hill, 1967–88), XIV (1967), 20–2.

—— *Le monachisme Syrien selon Théodoret de Cyr*, Théologie Historique, 42 (Paris: Beauchesne, 1977).

Caspari, C. P., *Alte und Neue Quellen zur Geschichte des Taufsymbols und der Glaubensregel*, 3 vols (Malling: Christiania, 1879).

Cayré, Fulbert, *Manual of Patrology and History of Theology* (Paris: Society of St John the Evangelist, Desclée, 1936–46).

Chadwick, H., 'Eucharist and Christology in the Nestorian Controversy', *JTS*, 2 (1951), 145–64 (Important).

Clayton, Paul Bauchman, Jr, 'Theodoret, Bishop of Cyrus, and the Mystery of the Incarnation in Late Antiochene Christology' (unpublished doctoral dissertation, Union Theological Seminary, New York, 1985).

Cope, Glenn Melvin, 'An Analysis of the Heresiological Method of Theodoret of Cyrus in the *Haereticarum fabularum compendium*' (unpublished doctoral dissertation, Catholic University of America, Washington DC, 1990).

Devreesse, Robert, 'Orient, antiquité', *RSPT*, 20 (1931), 559–71.

Diepen, H. M., 'Théodoret et le dogme d' Éphèse', *RSR*, 44 (1956), 243–7.

Ehrhard, Albert, 'Die Cyrill von Alexandrien zugeschriebene Schrift *Peri tēs tou Kyriou enanthrōpēseōs* ein Werk Theodorets von Cyrus', *ThQ*, 70 (1888), 179–243, 406–50, 623–53.

Gray, Patrick T. R., 'Theodoret on the *One Hypostasis*, An Antiochene Reading of Chalcedon', *SP*, 15 (1984), 301–4.

Grillmeier, Aloys, *Christ in Christian Tradition, From the Apostolic Age to*

Chalcedon (451), trans. by J. S. Bowden, 2nd rev. edn (London and Oxford: A. R. Mowbray, 1975) (Indispensable).

—— *Fragmente zur Christologie, Studien zum altkirchlichen Christusbild*, ed. by Theresia Hainthaler (Freiburg: Herder, 1997).

Guinot, Jean-Noël, *L'exégèse de Théodoret de Cyr*, Théologie historique, 100 (Paris: Beauchesne, 1995) (Indispensable).

—— 'Les lectures patristiques grecques (IIIe–Ve s.) du miracle de Cana (Jn 2, 1–11). Constantes et développements christologiques', *SP*, 30 (1997), 28–41.

—— 'L'*Expositio rectae fidei* et le traité *Sur la Trinité et l'Incarnation* de Théodoret de Cyr: deux types d'argumentation pour un même propos?', *Recherches Augustiniennes*, 32 (2001), 39–74.

Halleux, André de, 'Cyrille, Théodoret et le *Filioque*', *RHE*, 74 (1979), 597–625.

—— 'La définition christologique à Chalcédoine', in *Patrologie et oecuménisme*, Bibliotheca Ephemeridum Theologicarum Lovaniensinum, 93 (Leuven: Leuven University Press, 1990), 445–80.

Hardy, E. R., 'The Further Education of Cyril of Alexandria', *SP*, 17 (1982), 116–22.

Hefele, Carl Joseph, *A History of the Councils of the Church*, ed. and trans. by W. R. Clark, 5 vols (Edinburgh: T. & T. Clark, 1894–96) (Important).

Honigmann, Ernest, 'Theodoret of Cyrrhus and Basil of Seleucia (the Time of Their Deaths)', in Ernest Honigmann, *Patristic Studies*, Studi e testi, 173 (Rome: Biblioteca Apostolica Vaticana, 1953), 174–84.

Kelly, J. N. D., *Early Christian Creeds*, 3rd edn (London: Longman, 1972).

—— *Early Christian Doctrines*, 5th rev. edn (London: A. & C. Black, 1977).

Koch, Günter, *Strukturen und Geschichte des Heils in der Theologie des Theodoret von Kyros, Eine dogmen- und theologiegeschichtliche Untersuchung*, Frankfurter Theologische Studien, 17 (Frankfurt am Main: Josef Knecht, 1974).

Kösters, Ludwig, 'Zur Datierung von Theodorets *Hellēnikōn therapeutikē pathēmatōn*', *ZKTh*, 30 (1906), 349–56.

Lebon, Joseph, 'Restitutions à Théodoret de Cyr', *RHE*, 26 (1930), 523–50.

Loofs, Friedrich, *Leitfaden zum Studium der Dogmengeschichte* (Halle: Max Niemeyer, 1906).

—— *Nestorius and His Place in the History of Christian Doctrine* (Cambridge: Cambridge University Press, 1914).

McNamara, Kevin, 'Theodoret of Cyrus and the Unity of Person in Christ', *ITQ*, 22 (1955), 313–28.

Mandac, Marijan, 'L'union christologique dans les œuvres de Théodoret antérieures au Concile d' Éphèse', *ETL*, 47 (1971), 64–96.

Montalverne, P. Joseph, *Theodoreti Cyrensis doctrina antiquior de verbo* 'inhumanato' (a circiter 423–435), Studia Antoniana, 1 (Rome: Pontificium Athenaeum Antonianum, 1948).

Newman, John Henry, 'Trials of Theodoret' in *Historical Sketches* (London: Basil Montagu Pickering, 1873), 307–62.

—— *The Arians of the Fourth Century* (London: Longman, 1908).

O'Keefe, John J., 'Kenosis or Impassibility: Cyril of Alexandria and Theodoret of Cyrus on the Problem of Divine Pathos', *SP*, 32 (1997), 358–65.

Parmentier, Martin, 'A Letter from Theodoret of Cyrus to the Exiled Nestorius (CPG 6270) in a Syriac Version', *Bijdragen. Tijdschrift Voor Filosofie en Theologie. International Journal in Philosophy and Theology*, 51 (1990), 234–45.

Parvis, Paul M., 'Theodoret's Commentary on the Epistles of St Paul: Historical Setting and Exegetical Practice' (unpublished doctoral dissertation, University of Oxford, 1975).

Pásztori-Kupán, István, 'An Unnoticed Title in Theodoret of Cyrus' *Peri tēs tou Kyriou enanthrōpēseōs*', *JTS*, 53 (2002), 102–11.

—— 'Quotations of Theodoret's *De sancta et vivifica Trinitate* in Euthymius Zigabenus' *Panoplia Dogmatica*', *Augustinianum*, 42 (2002), 481–7.

—— 'Theodoret of Cyrus' Double Treatise *On the Trinity* and *On the Incarnation*, The Antiochene Pathway to Chalcedon' (unpublished doctoral dissertation, University of Edinburgh, New College, 2002).

Prestige, G. L., *God in Patristic Thought* (London: SPCK, 1952).

Quasten, Johannes, *Patrology*, 4 vols (Utrecht: Spectrum, 1950–86) (Important).

Richard, Marcel, 'Les citations de Théodoret conservées dans la chaîne de Nicétas sur l'Évangile selon Saint Luc', *RB*, 43 (1934), 88–96.

—— 'Un écrit de Théodoret sur l'unité du Christ après l'Incarnation', *RSPT*, 24 (1935), 34–61.

—— 'L'activité littéraire de Théodoret avant le concile d'Éphèse', *RSPT*, 24 (1935), 83–106.

—— 'Notes sur l'évolution doctrinale de Théodoret', *RSPT*, 25 (1936), 459–81.

—— 'La lettre de Théodoret à Jean d'Égées', *SPT*, 2 (1941–2), 415–23.

—— 'L'introduction du mot *hypostase* dans la théologie de l'Incarnation', *MSR*, 2 (1945), 5–32, 243–70 (Important).

—— 'Théodoret, Jean d'Antioche et les moines d'Orient', *MSR*, 3 (1946), 147–56.

Schwartz, Eduard, 'Zur Schriftstellerei Theodorets', *Sitzungsberichte der Bayerischen Akademie der Wissenschaften, Philosophisch-philologische und historische Klasse*, 1 (1922), 30–40.

—— 'Cyrill und der Mönch Viktor', *Sitzungsberichte der Akademie der*

Wissenschaften in Wien, Philosophisch-historische Klasse, 208.4 (1928), 1–51.

Scipioni, Luigi I., *Nestorio e il Concilio di Efeso*, Studia Patristica Mediolanensia, 1 (Milan: Università Cattolica del Sacro Cuore, 1974).

Sellers, R. V., 'Pseudo-Justin's *Expositio rectae fidei*: A Work of Theodoret of Cyrus', *JTS*, 46 (1945), 145–60.

—— *The Council of Chalcedon, A Historical and Doctrinal Survey* (London: SPCK, 1961).

Sickenberger, Joseph, 'Die Lukaskatene des Niketas von Herakleia', *TU*, 22.4 (1902), 1–118.

Slusser, M., 'The Scope of Patripassianism', *SP*, 17 (1982), 169–75.

Smith, William, and Henry Wace, eds, *A Dictionary of Christian Biography*, 4 vols (London: John Murray, 1877–87) (Important).

Sullivan, F. A., *The Christology of Theodore of Mopsuestia*, Analecta Gregoriana No. 82 (Rome: Analecta Gregoriana, 1956).

Swete, H. B., ed., *Theodori Episcopi Mopsuesteni in Epistolas B. Pauli Commentarii*, 2 vols (Cambridge: Cambridge University Press, 1880–2), II, 310.

Tixeront, J., *A Handbook of Patrology* (St Louis: Herder, 1947).

Urbainczyk, Theresa, *Theodoret of Cyrus: The Bishop and the Holy Man* (Ann Arbor: University of Michigan Press, 2002).

Williams, Rowan, *Arius, Heresy and Tradition*, 2nd edn (London: SCM Press, 2001).

Winslow, D. F., 'Soteriological "Orthodoxy" in the Fathers', *SP*, 15 (1984), 393–5.

Wright, David F., 'At What Ages Were People Baptized in the Early Centuries?', *SP*, 30 (1997), 189–94.

—— 'Infant Dedication in the Early Church', in *Baptism, the New Testament and the Church: Historical and Contemporary Studies in Honour of R. E. O. White*, ed. by Stanley E. Porter and Anthony R. Cross, Journal for the Study of the New Testament Supplement Series, 171 (Sheffield: Sheffield Academic Press, 1999), 352–78 (Important).

INDEX OF SCRIPTURAL
CITATIONS

Old Testament

Genesis: 1:26 129, 244; 1:26–7
66; 2:7 36, 162; 3:17–18 165;
6:3 155; 17:10 237; 32:26
125; 46:26–7 155
Exodus: 1:1–5 155; 2:5–6 237;
3:14 90, 116, 243, 251;
23:4 203; 23:5 203; 26:6
236
Deuteronomy: 10:22 155; 21:23
165
Judges: 15:15–7 195
1 Samuel: 17:38–9 195
Job: 32:8 131
Psalms: 22:22 119; 22:23 (in the
LXX and Vulgate: Ps. 21:23)
243; 46:5 (LXX: Ps. 45:5) 236;
76:4 (LXX, KJV Ps. 77:4) 184;
77:39 (LXX and Vulgate only)
247; 95:4 (LXX: Ps. 94:4) 123,
161, 248; 99:5 (LXX: Ps. 98:5)
231; 102:25–7 (LXX: Ps.
101:26–8) 120; 102:27 173;
104:4 (LXX: Ps. 103:4) 243;
119:105 (LXX: Ps. 118:105)
137, 245; 137:6 (LXX: Ps.
136:6) 126
Proverbs: 3:34 212; 25:21 203
Isaiah: 7:14 158, 168, 180; 7:16
149; 9:6 168, 180, 191;
11:1–2 182; 14:12 245; 25:8
184; 30:1 131; 40:3 256; 40:6

155; 40:12 123, 161; 40:22
123; 42:1 183; 45:13 256;
45:14 66; 45:23 67; 48:16
131; 49:3 180; 49:5 180; 49:6
180; 53:3 186, 190; 53:4–7
166; 53:8 190; 53:9 143;
53:12 165; 59:5 207; 65:5
212; 66:1 161
Jeremiah: 31:31 116
Ezekiel: 11:22–3 235; 18:4 155;
34:4 212
Joel: 2:28 131
Micah: 5:2 190
Habbakuk: 2:14 210
Haggai: 2:4–5 131
Malachi: 3:6 156, 173, 251

Old Testament Apocrypha

Baruch: 3:36–8 117

New Testament

Matthew: 1:1 191; 1:18 182;
1:20 174, 182; 1:20–2 182;
1:21 44; 2:6 190; 2:22 249;
3:3 256; 3:15 185; 3:17 149,
183; 4:3 150; 4:4 150; 4:6
151; 4:10 151; 5:21–33 116;
5:22 203; 5:38–40 203;
5:43–4 203; 8:29 150;
10:19–20 131; 10:28 36;
11:27 120; 12:28 135, 183;

12:29 148; 13:25 199; 15:13
210; 17:2 235; 20:18–9 178;
24:36 177, 178; 25:26–7 113;
26:38 157; 26:39 177, 178;
27:34 165; 27:46 177; 28:19
130, 166, 214
Mark: 1:3 256; 1:24 150
Luke: 1:2 115, 214; 1:34 182;
1:35 174, 182; 1:38 196; 2:40
158; 2:44 249; 2:49 163; 2:52
158; 3:4–5 256; 4:16–8 182;
4:21 182; 4:34 150; 6:38 203;
8:43–8 249; 10:18 148; 10:19
149; 22:31–2 212; 24:39 189
John: 1:1 115, 189; 1:1–2 114;
1:3 114; 1:4 115; 1:9 115;
1:14 33, 155, 173, 179; 1:18
115; 1:23 256; 1:29 143, 149,
156, 162; 1:33 183; 2:1–11
249; 2:19 39, 156, 175, 181,
187, 189; 3:13 167; 3:16 170;
3:36 126; 5:17 123; 5:21 123;
5:27–9 168; 6:44 123; 6:62
167; 8:14–9 124; 8:16 125;
8:17 125; 8:18 125; 8:19 126;
8:29 125; 8:40 186; 8:44 213;
10:9 123; 10:15 121; 10:18
157; 10:27–30 122; 10:30 67,
189; 10:37–8 123; 12:26 126;
12:27 177; 12:31–2 148;
12:44–6 127; 13:31–2 128;
14:5 127; 14:6 123;
14:6–11 127; 14:9 189; 14:10
67, 125; 14:30 148; 15:1–6
256; 15:15 180; 15:26 183;
16:11 148; 16:15 178, 189;
16:33 148, 163; 17:1 128;
17:5 129; 17:6 129; 17:10
129; 18:6 164; 18:22 249;
19:37 190
Acts: 1:11 192; 2:27 157; 5:3–4
134; 7:14 155; 10:38 182;
13:2 134; 14:16–7 107;
14:26–7 134; 15:12 135;
15:40 135; 20:28 135
Romans: 5:15 147; 5:18–19 147;

6:5 166; 7:22 177; 8:2 130;
8:3–4 143, 147; 8:4 144; 8:9
131; 8:14 131; 8:15 130; 8:17
148; 8:27 132; 8:29 119, 231;
8:29–30 148; 9:5 42, 168,
190; 11:33 256; 11:36 250;
14:10 67
1 Corinthians: 2:10–11 132; 2:12
183; 2:12–16 132; 3:16–17
69, 133, 235; 6:11 133; 6:17
236; 6:19–20 133; 8:6 161,
168; 10:13 195; 12:4–6 130;
12:8–9 135; 12:11 130; 12:28
244; 13:12 ix, 77, 120, 171;
14:24–5 136; 15:12–3 220;
15:20 220; 15:21 220; 15:22
147–8, 220; 15:47 162;
15:40–54 253
2 Corinthians: 3:13–16 127; 3:17
131; 4:16 176; 5:7–10; 5:17
119; 5:21 156; 8:9 170; 9:4
58; 11:17 58; 13:13 130
Galatians: 1:15–17 155;
3:13 155, 165; 3:16 161;
4:7 180
Ephesians: 1:19–20 181; 1:20–2
231; 3:16–17 177; 4:10 167;
4:11–12 135, 244; 5:2 183
Philippians: 2:5–7 37, 142, 173;
2:6–7 142, 189; 2:7 180; 2:8
145
Colossians: 1:15 115, 119; 1:16
160, 250; 1:18 119, 157;
1:19 174; 2:8–9 180; 2:9 158,
174
1 Timothy: 2:5 161; 2:5–6 190;
3:16 167, 250
2 Timothy: 2:12 148
Titus: 2:13 171, 190
Philemon: 2:6 115; 3:21 119
Hebrews: 1:1–2 115; 1:3 58, 115,
141, 158, 214; 1:3–4 158; 1:6
231; 1:8–9 159; 1:12 173;
2:6–7 159; 2:9 159; 2:14 179,
189; 2:16 189; 2:16–17 160;
3:1 183; 3:1–2 185; 3:14 58;

4:15 160, 185; 5:1–3 184;
5:4–5 184; 5:7–9 160; 5:7–10
184; 9:13–14 136; 11:1 58;
11:6 105; 13:8 32, 161, 168

1 Peter: 3:18 157; 4:14 136; 5:5
212
1 John: 1:1 115; 4:13 136
Revelation: 1:5 119

INDEX OF NAMES AND SUBJECTS

Abramowski, Luise 7, 10, 51, 61–3, 70, 229n20, 233n20, 234n27, 236n59–61
Acacius of Melitene 18
Adoptionism 69, 245n86
Aetius, Aetians 215–18
agenētos or 'unmade' 29, 185
agennētos or 'unbegotten' 28–9, 113, 144, 171, 203, 205, 208, 211
Alcibiades 101
Alcmeon 92
Alexander of Hierapolis 11–12, 15, 17
Alexander of Alexandria 192, 213–15
Alexandria: city of 7–8, 17, 19, 54, 192, 208, 210, 213, 226n23; Alexandrian school/theology/tradition 9–12, 14, 17–18, 20, 23–4, 34, 46, 53–4, 74, 78–80, 172, 188, 192–4, 228n12, 229n23, 230n35, 247–8n128; council of Alexandria (362) 60
Ambrose 59, 70, 192
Amphilochius of Iconium 39, 69, 179, 192
Anacharsis the Scythian 92
anarchos ('unbegun' or without beginning) 28, 60, 113, 144
Anastos, Milton V. 46
Anatolius of Constantinople 25

Anaxagoras 103
Anaximander 103
Anaximenes 103
Anselm of Canterbury 237n2
Antioch: city of 3–5, 7, 13, 17–18, 134–5, 193, 208–9, 215, 244n65, 252n5, 254n8, n9, 256n16; Antiochene school/theology/tradition, Antiochenes 7, 9, 11–12, 15, 18–20, 23–4, 27–8, 31–3, 37, 43, 45, 49, 51, 63, 66, 70, 74–5, 78–80, 84, 109, 188, 194, 223n1, 223n9, 226n23, 227n4, 229n23, 237n2, 250n158, 255n6; council of (268) 256n16; synod of (341) 237n74; synod of (345) 236n71; synod of (431) 13
Antiochene Formula (431), later known as the *Formula of Reunion* (signed 433) 11, 14, 18, 19, 24, 42, 55, 65, 71, 225n11, 229n21, 250n161, 251n166, 252n13
Antisthenes 100
anthrōpotokos or 'man-bearer' 8, 41, 42, 171, 174, 194–6, 234n30, 251n166, 254n1
Apamea 4, 226n20
apatheia (impassibility) 20, 29, 31–3, 36, 38, 48–9, 76, 117–18, 160, 166, 184, 186–7,

189, 191, 211, 227n2, 227n4, 228n16, 247n126, 253n4
Apollinarian(ism) 10–11, 18, 33, 35–7, 47, 62–3, 73, 172, 223n11, 224n20, 228n12, 231n50, 232n61, 247–8n128
Apollinaris of Hierapolis 211
Apollinaris of Laodicea 9–10, 33–7, 49, 53–4, 56, 61, 63, 68, 71, 142, 144, 151, 152, 154–5, 157, 172, 186, 211, 219, 228n13, 230n34, 231n51, 233n17, n18, n19, 234n29, 235n49, n53, 236n68, n69, 237n74, 243n49, 247–8n128, 248–9n136, 256n36, 257n37
appropriation see *oikeiōsis*
Arians, Arianism 6, 8, 29, 33, 35, 37, 43, 47, 58, 60, 71, 195, 218, 228n12, 228n17, 232n3, 233n13–14, 234n31, 235n54, 242n37, 243n49, 245n86, 247–8n128
Arian syllogism 228n17
Aristarchus 92
Ariston 90, 93
Aristoxenus 92
Aristotle 86–7, 92, 97, 102, 239n65
Arius 29, 33, 35, 37, 59–60, 67, 124, 132, 137, 142, 144, 157, 169, 172, 177, 179, 207, 213–16, 218–19, 228n6, 233n15, 143n45, 262, 265
Artemon 208
asynchutos henōsis 'unmingled union' or 'union without confusion' 10, 14, 23–4, 39, 49–50, 53, 65, 70–1, 76, 78, 229n20, 237n72
Athanasius, Athanasian 10, 34, 36, 38, 49, 53, 58, 60, 62, 69, 71, 192, 230n35, 230n42, 231n50–51, 233n19, 233n25, 234n31, 235n54, 252n5

Aubert, Jean 241n19
Augustine (Aurelius Augustinus) 70, 223n3, 236n59
Azéma, Yvan 26, 221n8

Bacchylides 100
Barth, Karl 79, 251n3
Basil the Great 30, 49, 58, 70–1, 179, 192, 230n35, 233n25, 252n14
Basil of Seleucia 55–6, 188, 226n35, 232n62
Brok, M. F. A. 222n24

Canivet, Pierre 26, 85–6, 222n11, 238n16
Caspari, C. P. 223n11, 231n51
Celestine, Pope of Rome 7, 12
Cerdon 203
Chalcedon: city of 12, 22, 24; council of 17–18, 21–7, 31, 40, 53, 55, 63–5, 71, 73–4, 76, 78–9, 83, 172, 188, 193, 199, 226n24, 229n21, 234–5n39, 236n68
Chalcedonian Christology 11, 24, 31, 63, 73, 80
Chalcedonian Definition or (*Definitio*) *Chalcedonense* 14, 20, 23–4, 26, 31, 39, 55–6, 61, 65, 78, 172, 188, 228n19, 229n22, 232n8, 234n39
change see *tropē*
Christotokos 'Christ-bearer' 8
Chrysaphius, imperial eunuch 19–20
Clayton, Paul Bauchman 38, 47, 224n18, 228n16–17, 236n60
Clement of Alexandria 58, 65, 85, 237n11, 238n23
coessential or consubstantial see *homoousios*
Combefis, François 111, 241n23
communicatio idiomatum or 'communication of properties' 20, 24, 30, 38–45, 74, 77,

224n17, 226n24, 228n19, 229n21, 253n4
communicatio onomaton or 'communication of names' 38–45, 53, 243n56
Constantinople: city of 7–8, 19, 74, 78, 109, 215, 218, 224n23, 230n47, 254n8; council of (381) *see* Second Ecumenical Council; local council of (448) 19, 55; council of (553) *see* Fifth Ecumenical Council; council of (680–1) *see* Sixth Ecumenical Council
consubstantial *see homoousios*
Cope, Glenn Melvin 198, 199, 256n15
cultic (or liturgical) *prosōpon* 50–6, 188
Cynics 100
Cyprian of Carthage 192, 254n9
Cyril of Alexandria 7, 18–19, 21, 27, 31, 54, 80, 109–11, 193–5, 224n23, 236n63, 240n13, 241n19, 242n27, 247n124, 247–8n128, 255n5; and Apollinaris (as well as Apollinarian forgeries) 10, 36, 53, 56, 61–3, 223n11, 231n51, 233n19, 247–8n128, 248–9n136; doctrine and terminology 9–10, 15–17, 19, 23–4, 36, 42, 49, 51, 54, 61–5, 70–1, 78, 172, 224n18, 228n19, 229n21, 233–4n26, 233n30–31, 233n37, 233n39, 236n68, 252n7, 253n16, 253n20; and John of Antioch 14–15, 18; and the Nestorian controversy (including the Council of Ephesus) 5, 7–8, 12–14, 22, 25, 227n37, 229n21, 230n35; and Pope Leo 25–6; and Theodoret 11, 17–18, 47, 80, 224n18, 227n37, 255n6

Cyril of Alexandria, works cited: *Against Diodore and Theodore* 18; *Letter 69 to Acacius of Melitene* 18; *Twelve Anathemas* or *Chapters* 10–11, 15–16, 24, 51–2, 54, 62–3, 65, 69–70, 78, 83, 172–87, 224n20, 243n45, 250n160–1, 252n8, 253n16

Damasus, Pope of Rome 60, 192
Daniélou, Jean 47
Demosthenes 92, 252n5
Devreesse, Robert 109
Diagoras 87
diakrinō, diakrisis see distinction (of natures)
diaphora, diaphoron (difference) *see* distinction (of natures)
Diepen, H. M. 47, 229n30, 230n32
difference (of natures) *see* distinction (of natures)
Diodore of Sicily (Diodorus Siculus) 92
Diodore of Tarsus 9, 18, 28, 34, 37, 64, 194, 196, 207, 210, 223n1, 227n37, 229n25, 255n5–6
Diogenes 92, 97
Dionysius of Alexandria 208, 210, 213, 256n16
Dioscorus of Alexandria 17–22, 25, 188, 226n23
distinction (of natures) 20, 23, 31, 37, 39–40, 43, 50, 52–4, 67, 72–4, 117, 126, 156–8, 160, 169, 173, 176–7, 179, 181, 183, 186, 190, 220, 224n18, 248n129, 250n159, 252n7, 252n9
Docetism 245n86
Domnus of Antioch 20, 193, 226n23

Ebion, Ebionites 208, 210

Ehrhard, Albert 109, 240n3, 241n17

Empedocles of Agrigentum 92, 100

enoikēsis or 'indwelling' of the Word in the manhood 10, 37–8, 57, 68–9, 72, 75–6, 133, 145, 151, 156, 158–60, 166, 169, 174, 177–8, 180, 185

Ephesus: city of 100, 103, 194, 215, 251n166; council of (431) ix, 6, 7, 10–15, 18–22, 24–5, 37, 40, 42, 45, 49, 53, 61, 63–5, 71, 109, 111, 193, 223–4n15, 227n37, 240n9, 247–8n128, 251n166; council (*Robber Synod*) of (449) see *Latrocinium*

Ephraem 192

Epicharmus, comical poet 101, 239n53

Epicharmus, Pythagorean philosopher 102

Epicurus 87, 102

Epiphanius of Salamis 58

Epiphanius (Cyril's archdeacon) 224n23

Ettlinger, Gerard H. 83

Eudoxius 215–18

Eunomius, Eunomians 6, 35, 37, 67, 71, 124, 132, 142, 144, 157, 169, 177, 179, 215, 216–18

Euripides 102

Eusebius, church historian 85

Eustathius of Antioch 192

Eutyches, Eutychians, Eutychianism 19–21, 23, 25–6, 79–80, 83, 194, 198, 219, 234–5n39, 253n6

Fifth Ecumenical Council (Constantinople, 553) 13, 24, 27, 78–80

finitum non capax infiniti (the finite cannot contain the infinite) 44, 123

Firmilian of Caesarea 209, 256n22

First Ecumenical Council see Nicaea

Flavian of Antioch 192, 254n8

Flavian of Constantinople 12, 19–21, 25, 194, 226n23, 254n8

'form of God' (Godhead of Christ) 37, 40, 42, 115, 118, 142–5, 167, 169, 171, 173–4, 176, 181, 186, 189

'form of the servant' (manhood of Christ) 37–8, 40, 42–3, 50–1, 63, 72, 117–18, 142–5, 166–9, 171, 173–4, 176–81, 186, 189, 250n152

Formula of Reunion (signed 433) see *Antiochene Formula*

Fourth Ecumenical Council see Chalcedon

Gaisford, Thomas 85

Gallandi, Andrea 111

Garnier, Jean 47, 109, 111, 241n23, 248n135, 258

Gennadius 26, 245n88

gennētos 'begotten' 29

Gnostics, Gnosticism 245n86

God-bearer see *Theotokos*

Gray, P. T. R. 236n60

Gregory Nazianzen 28, 30, 70, 192, 230n42, 254n9

Gregory of Nyssa 30, 71, 192, 216, 230n43

Gregory Thaumatourgos (the Wonderworker) 209, 256n17

Grillmeier, Aloys 7, 34, 226n24, 228n12, 235n46

Guinot, Jean-Noël 7, 109–10, 222n24, 240n13, 247n123, 249n147

Hainthaler, Theresia 7

Halleux, André de 55, 227n4,
231n58, 253n16
Hardy, E. R. 236n63
Hefele, Carl Joseph 7
henōsis (Christological) union 8–10,
14–15, 19, 23–4, 36, 37–9,
42–5, 48–52, 53–7, 62, 64–5,
67–74, 76, 145, 159, 169,
166–9, 174–6, 179–81, 185–6,
200, 229n22, 233n25,
234–5n39, 235n52, 236n59,
236n68, 236n70, 237n72,
250n158; and *synapheia* 9–10,
68–73, 76, 169, 236n70
Henoticon (482) 27, 78
Heraclitus of Ephesus 100,
102–3
Herodotus 92
Hesiod 98
Hill, Robert Charles 83,
249–50n151
Hippolytus 192
Homer 98, 254–5n2
homoousios or 'coessential'
(commonly translated as
'consubstantial') 14, 23, 29, 42,
59–60, 65, 84, 126, 133, 172,
174, 177, 183, 213, 216, 218,
225n2, 232–3n8
Honigmann, Ernest 26
Hypatia, Alexandrian female
philosopher 8
hypostasis 9, 15, 23, 36, 57–65, 70,
72, 84, 119, 122, 128, 137,
176, 200, 225n2, 228n13,
232n8, 233n26, 234n27,
234n31, 234n36, 245n74,
252n7–8; introduction into
Christology 60–5, 172,
234n29; and *ousia* 59–60,
64–6, 172, 232n8;
philosophical background
57–9; and *physis* 10, 24, 36, 62,
64–5, 172, 176, 228n13,
233n18; and *prosōpon* 23–4, 26,
28–30, 56, 61–2, 64–5, 177,

209, 233n19, 234–5n39,
243n51; and *substantia* 59,
232n8; as Trinitarian term
28–30, 51, 59, 144, 209–11,
219
hypostatic union 10, 47, 51, 62–3,
77, 175, 233n25, n26,
234–5n39

Ibas of Edessa 20
idiotēs or 'property', 'attribute' 9,
20, 23–4, 28–31, 34, 37,
39–40, 43, 45, 48, 51, 54–5,
57, 62, 69, 73–4, 76, 128, 136,
144, 160–1, 168, 175–6, 181,
185, 189, 219, 244n72
Ignatius of Antioch 192
image of the *oikonomia see oikonomia*
immortal, immortality 37–8, 72,
74, 99, 137–8, 154, 156–7,
160, 165–6, 169, 176, 179,
181, 184, 189, 191–2, 211,
247n126, 253n4
immutable, immutability 20, 23,
29, 32–3, 38, 118, 137, 141,
173, 189, 219, 227n4,
impassible, impassibility
see apatheia
incorruptible, incorruptibility
37–8, 76, 137, 154, 156, 166,
189, 247n126, 253n4
indwelling *see enoikēsis*
intellect *see nous*
Irenaeus of Lyons 192
Irenaeus of Tyre 42, 193–4,
251n166

Jackson, Blomfield 254n8
John of Aegea 26
John of Antioch 7–8, 10, 12,
14–15, 17–18, 172, 226n21,
n22, 229n21
John Cassian 7
John Chrysostom 4, 19, 54, 69,
192, 252n5, 254n8
John of Damascus 39, 40, 198

Justin Martyr 6, 202, 222n22, 223n15
Justinian, emperor 27, 78, 173
Juvenal of Jerusalem 22, 25–6

Kelly, J. N. D. 7
Koch, Günter 47
koinōnia or 'community', 'togetherness' (Antiochene Christological term) 10, 52, 57, 65, 69, 73, 169, 179

Latrocinium (Ephesinum), or the *Robber Synod of Ephesus* (449) 18, 20–2, 25, 55–6, 109, 188, 193–4, 225n15, 254n8, 255n5
Leander 92
Lebon, Joseph 109–10, 223–4n15, 224n18, 240n13, 250n152
Leo (I) the Great, Pope of Rome 12, 20–1, 24–6, 40, 109, 225n15, 227n4
Libanius 252n5
Logos–anthrōpos or 'Word–man' (Antiochene Christological model) 9, 23
Logos–sarx or 'Word–flesh' (Alexandrian Christological model) 9, 23, 33, 35, 172, 245n88
Loofs, Friedrich 7, 12, 229n21

Macedonius (heretic), Macedonians 6, 218, 248–9n136
Macedonius, hermit 3
Mai, Angelo 109, 111, 224n18, 232–3n8, 242n26, 243n46, 243n52, 244n60, 245n80, 245n89, 245n92, 246n94, 246n97, 247n119, 247n123, 248n129, 248n132, 250n153–4, 251n165
man-bearer *see anthrōpotokos*
Mandac, Marijan 47, 66, 225n1
Mani, Manichaeism 142, 145, 205–7, 256n14

Marcellus of Ancyra 84, 137, 144, 210
Marcian, emperor 21–2, 231n60
Marcion, Marcionites 6, 142, 145, 202–5
Marius Mercator 7, 47, 109–10, 232–3n8
McNamara, Kevin 226n32, 236n60
Meletius 192, 254n8
Melito of Sardis 245n88
mia physis or 'one nature' 15, 19, 36, 56, 62, 190, 228n13, 232n61, n62, 233n18
mia physis tou Theou Logou sesarkōmenē or 'one incarnate nature of the God-Word' 10, 36, 234–5n39
Migne, Jacques-Paul 109, 111, 199, 247n119
mind *see nous*
misleading (Christological) terms 72–3
Monophysite controversy 19–20, 195, 225n15, 254n8
Monophysites, Monophysitism 16, 20–1, 25, 27, 49, 78, 110–11, 188, 194, 224n18, 234–5n39, 237n9, 247–8n128, 253n6, 254n8
Montalverne, P. Joseph 66
Montanus, Montanists 211

naos or 'temple' as the human nature 14, 41–3, 50, 65, 68–9, 75–6, 133, 149, 156–7, 159, 161–2, 165–6, 168–9, 171, 174–5, 181, 187, 189, 248n134
nature *see physis*
Neanthes 92
Nemesius of Emesa 252n5
Nestorius of Constantinople, Nestorianism 5, 7–8, 10, 12, 15–19, 21–4, 26, 42, 47, 54–5, 63, 68, 79–80, 109, 172,

193–4, 199, 223n1, 223n3, 224n20, 224n23, 225n7, 225n9, 226n20, 227n4, 228n19, 229n21, 230n35, 234n28, 254n1, 255n9

Nestorian controversy 5–13, 56, 62, 64, 70, 72, 83, 230n35, 231n57, 253n6

Newman, John Henry 58, 234n31

Nicaea: city of 21–2; council of (325) 44, 52, 59–60, 191, 214; Nicene Creed (Nicaeanum) and (Neo-)Nicene terminology 14, 22, 29, 59–60, 65–6, 75, 230n35, 232–3n8, 233n25, 234n31, 242n37, 243n45, 244n58, 256n25

Nicetas of Heracleia 110–11, 241n16, 245n82, 246n96, 246n98, 246n101–4, 246n106–10, 246n115, 249n137–41, 249n143

Noetus of Smyrna 211

Novatian 70, 236n59

Novatus 212–13

nous as 'mind', 'intellect' or 'rational soul' 34–6, 46, 49, 84, 100–2, 112, 117–8, 121, 142, 151–4, 200, 217, 219, 239n43

Numenius, Pythagorean philosopher 91

oikeiōsis or 'appropriation' 38–9, 76, 147, 168, 250n155, 253n4

oikonomia 9, 32, 42–3, 57, 63–4, 68, 72–3, 84, 109, 117–9, 138, 141–2, 148, 153–4, 168–71, 178, 190, 202, 210, 213, 215, 219–20, 223n9, 224n18, 233–4n26, 243n44, 245n76, 251n164; image of 72–4

one nature *see mia physis*

Origen, Origenian 58–60, 198, 245n88

Orpheus 92, 102, 105–6

ousia or 'essence' (commonly translated as 'substance') 9, 15, 28–9, 57–60, 64–6, 72, 84, 121, 142–5, 153, 155, 172, 200–4, 218–19, 225n2, 232n1, 232n8, 234–5n39, 256n31

Parmenides of Elea 100

Parmentier, Martin 16, 224n21

Parvis, Paul M. 47, 250n157

Patripassianism *see* Theopaschism

Paul the Apostle 18, 37, 41–3, 45, 67, 74, 78, 113, 115, 117–19, 130–6, 142–8, 155, 158-62, 165–6, 168, 171, 173–4, 176, 179–80, 183–5, 189–91, 208

Paul of Emesa 54

Paul of Samosata 69, 144, 208–10, 228n12, 236n70, 237n6, 244n65, 245n86, 256n16, 256n22

Peirithos 92

Pelagius, Pelagians, Pelagianism 7, 223n3

Pherecydes of Syros 90, 92, 98, 238n16

Photinus 137, 144, 210

Photius of Constantinople 221n7

physis or 'nature' 9–10, 14–15, 19–20, 23–4, 28–45, 47–58, 60–9, 71–6, 78, 106–7, 112, 117–22, 124–6, 128, 130–4, 137–51, 153–6, 158–63, 166–81, 183–90, 194, 196, 219, 220, 224n18, 232n61, 233–4n26, 234n37, 234–5n39, 239n53, 243n44, 245n81, 246n111, 247n126, 248n129, 248n134, 249–50n151, 250n155, 252n7, 252n9, 253n4, 253n6

Pindar 105

Plato 34, 86–7, 90, 93–4, 97–9, 101–2, 105–6, 228n10, 238n25–6, 247n120

Plotinus 87

Plutarch 91–2, 237n10

Polycarp 192
Porphyry 86, 91, 93, 96–7,
   237n10
Prestige, G. L. 58–9, 65–6,
   234n36
Proclus of Constantinople 18, 193,
   226n22
property 'attribute' see idiotēs
prosōpon 9–10, 15, 23–4, 26,
   28–30, 39, 41, 43–4, 49–51,
   53–4, 56–8, 61–2, 64–9, 71,
   73, 76, 84, 122, 128, 132, 158,
   168, 176–7, 188, 209, 228n13,
   233n19, 234n33, 234–5n39,
   235n43, 235n46–7, 235n51,
   248n129
Prudentius 254n9
psychē and psychē logikē or
   'rational soul' 14, 33–6, 84,
   142, 186, 202, 204, 206, 219,
   245n77, 245n93
Pulcheria, empress 5, 21–2
Pythagoras, Pythagoreans 90–2,
   97–8, 102, 108, 200, 237n10,

Quasten, Johannes 222n21,
   226n20, 247–8n128, 251n166,
   255n2, 255n6

resurrect, resurrection 37–8, 44,
   68, 75–6, 137, 156–7, 166,
   168, 189, 204, 206, 219–20,
   253n4
Richard, Marcel 47, 49, 58, 61–3,
   109, 188, 222n21, 222n24,
   225n12, 233n19, 234n27,
   241n23, 253n1, 254n8
Robber Synod of Ephesus see
   Latrocinium
Russell, Norman 7, 224n19,
   224–5n23, 251n1

Sabellius, Sabellianism 58–9, 65,
   137, 144, 209–11, 219
Schwartz, Eduard 109, 223n6,
   241n23, 250n152

Scipioni, Luigi I. 7
Second Ecumenical Council
   (Constantinople, 381) 18, 64
Sellers, R. V. 7, 55, 71, 222n24,
   236n68
Severus of Antioch 49, 110,
   224n18, 240n11, 242n28,
   248n129–30, 250n152,
   250n157
Sickenberger, Joseph 241n16
Sirmium, council of (351) 244n65
Sirmond, Jacques 111
Sixth Ecumenical Council
   (Constantinople, 680–1) 78–9
Socrates, philosopher 90–4, 97,
   99–101
Socrates Scholasticus, church
   historian 59, 64, 233n10,
   234n34, n35
Solon of Athens 90, 97, 100
Sophroniscus 91–2
subject of predication 45–50
subordination (in Trinitarian
   doctrine) 29, 60, 243n49
Sullivan, F. A. 228n17
synapheia or 'conjunction' 10, 57,
   68–73, 76, 169, 175, 236n60,
   236n70, 237n72–3; see also
   asynchutos henōsis
symplokē 'combination' or
   'connection' 10, 68, 71

Tarsus, synod of (431) 13
Tatian 5, 202–3, 222n18, 256n13;
   Diatessaron 5, 203
temple see naos
Temptation of Christ 32, 36,
   45–6, 48, 79, 149–52, 160–1,
   185, 249n99
tertium quid 43–4, 73
Thales of Miletus 90, 92, 95
theodicy 48
Theodore of Mopsuestia 9, 18, 28,
   37, 46, 54, 61, 68, 194, 196,
   216, 223n1, 226n20, 227n37,
   228n17, 229n25, 255n5–6

Theodoret of Cyrus: accession to episcopate 5–6; anthropology 33–8; and Apollinaris 33–7, 47, 54, 63, 68, 73, 142, 144, 151, 230n34; and Arius 6, 29, 33, 35, 37, 43, 47, 67, 71; baptism 4; birth and infancy 3–4; and *communicatio idiomatum* 36, 38–44, 74, 77, 224n17, 253n4; and the Council of Chalcedon 21–4; and Cyril of Alexandria 11, 17–18, 47, 63, 80, 172–73, 224n18, 227n37, 255n6; death and posthumous condemnation 26–7; and Dioscorus 17–18, 20–1, 188; early writings 6; and the *Formula of Reunion* 14–16; deposition by the *Latrocinium* 20–1; and Pope Leo 21, 24–6; monastic life 4–5; and the Monophysite controversy 19–20, 193–5; and 'naming' 39–45, 243n56; involvement in the Nestorian controversy 7–8, 10–13; and Nestorius 16–17, 80, 223n1; and *theotokos* 8, 14, 42, 171, 174, 194, 196, 251n166; Trinitarian doctrine 28–30

Theodoret of Cyrus, works cited: *A Cure of Greek Maladies* or *Curatio* 4, 6, 31–2, 66, 83, 242n33, 250–1n162; *Apology for Diodore and Theodore* 18, 255n6; *Church History* 18, 79, 215, 226n20; *A Compendium of Heretical Mythification* 26; *De incarnatione* or *On the Inhumanation of the Lord* 11, 32–3, 35, 38, 41–6, 50, 55-6, 65, 67–9, 72–4, 83–4, 224n18, 232–3n8, 245n46, 247n124, 247–8n128, 251n163, 252n9, 256–7n36; *De Trinitate* or *On the Holy and Vivifying Trinity*

11, 28, 40, 51–2, 66, 68–9, 83, 240n11, 446n112, 251n163, 253n5; *Eranistes* 20, 53, 64, 83, 188, 227n4, 237n73; *Expositio rectae fidei* or *Exposition of the Right Faith* 6, 28, 51, 66–7, 73–4, 86, 222n24, 223–4n15, 234n33; *Historia religiosa* or *History of the Monks* (*HR*) 3, 34, 246n112; *On Divine Providence* 18, 34, 228n10, 246n111; *Pentalogos* or *Five Books against Cyril's Ephesian Council* 13, 227n37, 240n9; *Refutation of Cyril's Twelve Anathemas* 10–11, 83, 227n37, 250n160, 252n7

Theodosius II, emperor 8, 12–4, 18, 20–2, 25, 193, 256n27

Theognis, poet of Sicily 99

theologia (the doctrine concerning God's being) 9, 57, 109, 116, 233–4n26, 243n44, 244n70, 245n76, 251n164

Theopaschism and Patripassianism 33, 227–8n5, 233n18, 244n69

Theopompus 92

theotokos or 'God-bearer' 7–8, 14, 23, 42, 63, 71, 171, 173–4, 191, 196, 234n30, 251n166, 254n1

Third Ecumenical Council *see* Ephesus

Thomas Aquinas 39–40

Three Chapters controversy 27, 78, 110, 173

Tomus ad Flavianum or *Leo's Tome* 12, 20–1, 24–6, 40, 227n4

tropē or 'change', 'alteration' 23, 29, 32–3, 37–8, 57, 72–3, 142, 144, 146, 169, 173, 178–81, 184, 186, 189, 202, 219, 237n74

unbegotten *see agennētos*
unbegun *see anarchos*

unconfused 20, 23, 30, 39, 43, 71, 76, 227n4
union (of natures) *see henōsis*
union of worship 50–6
unmade *see agenētos*
unmingled union *see asynchutos henōsis*

Valentinus, Valentinians 199–200, 202, 213, 219

Venables, E. 10

Williams, Rowan 60
Wright, David F. 84, 221n9, 222n11

Xenophanes of Colophon 100
Xenophon of Athens 100
Zamolxis the Thracian 92

Related titles from Routledge

Early Christianity
Mark Humphries

Examining sources and case studies, this accessible book explores early Christianity, how it was studied, how it is studied now, and how Judaeo-Christian values came to form the ideological bedrock of modern western culture.

Looking at the diverse source materials available, from the earliest New Testament texts and the complex treatises of early Christian authors such as Lactantius and Eusebius, to archaeology, epigraphy, and papyrology, the book examines what is needed to study the subject, what materials are available, how useful they are, and how the study of the subject may be approached.

Case study chapters focus on important problems in the study of early Christianity including:

- the book of Acts as a text revelatory of the social dynamics of cities and as a text about the inherent tensions in Hellenistic Judaism
- orthodoxy and Organization in early Christianity
- early Christianity and the Roman Empire.

Also including a comprehensive guide for students that lists major collections of literary and non-literary sources, the chief journals and series, and important textbooks, *Early Christianity* is an excellent aid to the study of Christianity in history.

Hb: 0-415-20538-7
Pb: 0-415-20539-5

Available at all good bookshops
For ordering and further information please visit:
www.routledge.com

Related titles from Routledge

Gregory the Great
John Moorhead

Gregory's life culminated in his holding the office of pope (590–604). He is generally regarded as one of the outstanding figures in the long line of popes, and by the late ninth century had come to be known as 'the Great'. He played a critical role in the history of his time, and is regarded as one of the four great fathers of the Western Church, alongside Ambrose, Jerome and Augustine.

This volume provides an introduction to Gregory the Great's life and works and to the most fascinating areas of his thinking. It includes English translations of his influential writings on such topics as the interpretation of the Bible and human personality types. These works show Gregory communicating what seem to be abstruse ideas to ordinary people, and they remain highly current today.

Hb: 0-415-23389-5
Pb: 0-415-23390-9

Available at all good bookshops
For ordering and further information please visit:
www.routledge.com

Related titles from Routledge

Evagrius Ponticus
A. M. Casiday

Evagrius Ponticus (c. 345–99) was a seminal figure for Eastern monasticism and had a strong influence on Western monasticism as well. He left more writings than any other father from the Egyptian desert. However, many of his writings were lost after he was condemned as an Origenist in the sixth century. During the twentieth century, numerous works were recovered (especially in ancient oriental translations from the original Greek) but very few of these works are available in English translation; many of them are not readily available at all.

This collection presents complete works drawn from the full range of his writings, many of which have not previously appeared in English, offering translations of some of Evagrius' letters, his notes on various books of the Bible, his treatises and his 'chapters' (a genre popularised by Evagrius that consists of condensed, interconnected sentences). All of the works included here are translated in full.

The translations aim to present the material accurately and accessibly. The volume is prefaced by a substantial introductory essay that presents Evagrius, his works and influence, and modern scholarship about him in a way that is of great use to students and also comprehensible to beginners.

Hb: 0-415-32446-7
Pb: 0-415-32447-5

Available at all good bookshops
For ordering and further information please visit:
www.routledge.com